What People Are Saying About This Book

An indispensable tool for anyone settling an estate...For skilled professionals, it will help them better organize and implement estate administration duties, establish time lines and mutual expectations with clients as to the process. For others with less experience, it will give them a practical sense of what estate settlement involves and what should be expected, whether they are tackling the job themselves or relying on the expertise of others.

—MARK W. JANNOTT, CTFA
Managing Director, Talmer Bank and Trust

...A cogent guide for the layman faced with assuming the task of being a Trustee or Personal Representative. Virtually every twist and turn of the estate settlement procedure is explained. Recommended best practices and cautionary tales are provided as well.

—JOHN A. SCOTT, Attorney at Law, Traverse City, Michigan
Fellow, American College of Trust and Estate Counsel
Former Chairperson, State Bar of Michigan Probate and Estate Planning Council

The Executor's Companion is truly a user-friendly legal guide for non-lawyers. It remains remarkably easy to read throughout, yet it does so without scrimping on details or "dumbing-down" the subject matter. As a result, this exceptional book will help non-lawyers understand the administration process, identify potential practical problems and legal issues, and interview and engage attorneys and other specialists when needed. The Executor's Companion genuinely lives up to its name.

—TRACY SONNEBORN
Former Assistant Attorney General (retired)
Charitable Trust Section
Michigan Attorney General's Office

The Executor's Companion will be an invaluable resource for anyone trying to navigate the complex world of estate settlement. The authors explain legal concepts in straightforward language that non-lawyers like myself can not only understand, but also find interesting. This book will greatly help anyone faced with settling an estate.

—KIMBERLY PALMER, Washington, D.C.
Personal Finance Columnist for U.S. News & World Report
Author of "*Generation Earn*"

There are only two reasons you need to read this book. (1) You work in the complicated world of wills, trusts and estate settlement. (2) You don't. This book navigates the subject in a way that allows professionals and lay people alike to be on the same page in planning and executing a plan.

—David Techner, Funeral Director
Owner, The Ira Kaufman Chapel
Southfield, Michigan

The Executor's Companion is a modern, complete guide to the clean-up after death process, useful for the living to make advance preparation for the inevitable, and offers timely, practical guidance for any Personal Representative or family member.

—Lorraine F. New, Attorney
George W. Gregory, PLLC, Troy, Michigan
Former IRS Estate Tax Manager/Michigan (retired)

A wonderful tool for professionals! Our firm prides itself on process and execution, and this guide provides and illuminates why that is so critical, and does it in a way that makes sense. This should be required reading for professionals who practice in this very complicated and often overwhelming area.

—Robert V. Schechter,[z"l] MBA, CLU, ChFC
President, Schechter Wealth Strategies
Birmingham, Michigan

People today are bombarded with information everywhere they go about estate administration. Based on years of professional experience, this thorough and up-to-date guide will take you confidently through anything you may face in this complicated process.

—Suzanne Simpson, Vice President
International Genealogical Search, Inc
Seattle, Washington / Vancouver, British Columbia

In over three decades of settling estates, as a legal assistant and then a trust officer, this is the most comprehensive, yet readable resource I have seen on the broad range of topics involved in estate administration. A real treasure trove of useful information!

—Carol Cerwin, President
Cerwin Consulting, LLC
Grosse Pointe Farms, Michigan

THE EXECUTOR'S COMPANION

A PRACTICAL GUIDE TO ESTATE ADMINISTRATION

ROBERT E. KASS, JD, LLM
ROBERT H. DOWNIE, MBA
YUH SUHN KIM, JD, EDITOR

Carob Tree Press, LLC
Detroit

Published by Carob Tree Press, LLC.

Permissions Department
Carob Tree Press, LLC
211 West Fort Street, Suite 1500
Detroit, Michigan 48226-3281
Telephone: 1-877-537-4178 (toll-free)
Fax: 313-983-3325
E-mail: inquiries@carobtreepress.com

This book is available at special quantity discounts when purchased in bulk by corporations, organizations, or groups. For more information, please contact the publisher at the above address or see our website, www.carobtreepress.com.

Also available in e-book format.

Cover design and interior layout: www.authorsupport.com

Printed in the United States of America

ISBN 978-0-9856814-0-1

CONTENTS

Warning and Disclaimer

This book is intended to provide general information regarding the probate, tax, and other laws applicable to administration of a decedent's estate, and to provide suggestions regarding appropriate action which might be taken in various situations. It is not intended as a substitute for legal, tax, accounting, financial, or other professional advice, and you must therefore not consider this book as your professional advisor in book form.

While every effort has been made to provide accurate, comprehensive, current information on the subject matter, we cannot predict the ways in which the laws will change – and they will change – and court decisions, regulations, and administrative rulings will also be issued which may change the outcome in a particular case. In addition, the facts of a particular situation are crucial to the outcome, and the conclusions described in this book might be different with even slight variations of the facts. Please carefully read the preface, "About this Book," for further discussion of these issues.

The estate which you are handling may be very simple, and you may be able to handle it on your own. However, by reading this book you may become aware of areas which challenge your personal skills, and you will acquire the background to know when to call for help, and what kinds of professionals are available to serve on your team.

From time to time we mention third party service providers, who may be helpful you to in administering an estate. The fact that we mention them should not be taken as a recommendation or endorsement. We leave you to make you own independent evaluation and decision as to whether you wish to use these firms or others who provide similar services.

Neither the authors or editor, nor the law firm with which they are affiliated, nor the publisher shall have any liability or responsibility to any person or entity with respect to any loss or damage caused, or alleged to be caused, directly or indirectly by the information contained in this book, which is intended as educational material and does not constitute legal advice.

If you do not wish to be bound by the above, you may return this book, together with your original receipt, to the publisher for a full refund.

Acknowledgments

The first edition of this book would not have been possible without close collaboration with my co-author, Rob Downie, a consummate professional, dedicated to the task in every way. This new edition benefitted greatly from the support of Rob's successor, Yuh Suhn Kim, whose knowledge of the probate process is astounding.

Thanks also to Judy Meshefski, a key member of our Estate Planning and Administration Team at Barris, Sott, Denn & Driker, PLLC, whose keen eye and dedication helped this book through the final stages.

I also wish to express my thanks to my fellow members at BSD&D, for their continued support of our estate planning and administration practice over the years. Their wisdom, creativity, and enthusiasm for the practice of the law have been contagious.

Thanks also go to those who encouraged the preparation of this new edition by taking the time to review the draft and offer comments. Special thanks to John A. Scott, a dear colleague and Fellow of the American College of Trust and Estate Counsel, and our Michigan Chair, who offered detailed, chapter by chapter comments and suggestions.

Thanks also to Carol Cerwin, President of Cerwin Consulting, LLC; Mark W. Jannott, Managing Director, Talmer Bank and Trust; Lorraine F. New, retired IRS Estate Tax Manager / Michigan; Kimberly Palmer, Personal Finance Columnist for U.S. News & World Report; Robert V. Schechter,z"l President of Schechter Wealth Strategies; Suzanne Simpson, Vice President of International Genealogical Search, Inc.; Tracy Sonneborn, retired Assistant Attorney General, Charitable Trust Section, Michigan Attorney General's Office; and David Techner, of The Ira Kaufman Chapel. Each of them has great familiarity with the estate administration process, from different vantage points, and their input and encouragement was most helpful.

I am most grateful to Nancy Little and Mary Schrauben, for their excellent article on handling insolvent estates, which inspired our own checklist on that topic.

I would also like to acknowledge the tremendous contribution of those attorneys and judges who respond to questions with thoughtful answers on the "EPIC Q&A," available to members of the State Bar of Michigan Probate & Estate Planning Section on the website of the Institute of Continuing Legal Education. Their analysis has been invaluable in preparing this book, as well as in our practice. I am also most thankful to ICLE for hosting that service.

The responsibility for any errors obviously remains with the authors.

Thanks also to the many clients who have entrusted their family's estate planning and administration to our firm over the more than three decades since I joined BSD&D in 1979, who have permitted us to learn from their experiences, and who have allowed us to share those lessons with the public at large.

Finally, my deepest gratitude to my wife, Sonja, whose patience and support for this project – and all my projects – over the years is worthy of a Medal of Valor.

R.E.K.

About the Authors and Editor

ROBERT E. KASS is a tax attorney whose practice is heavily concentrated in the areas of estate planning and administration. An honors graduate of the University of Michigan Law School, he is a recipient of a Fulbright-Swiss University Fellowship to the Graduate Institute of International Studies in Geneva, Switzerland, and earned his Master's Degree in Taxation from New York University. Bob is a member of the Detroit law firm of Barris, Sott, Denn & Driker, PLLC, where he serves as Chairman of the Tax, Estate Planning and Probate Group, and is a member of its Executive Committee.

His practice is also heavily involved in charitable and planned giving techniques. He is an active advisor and member of the Planned Giving Professional Advisory Committees of the Community Foundation for Southeast Michigan, Barbara Ann Karmanos Cancer Institute, Henry Ford Health System, Detroit Institute of Arts, the Jewish Federation of Metropolitan Detroit, and the Holocaust Memorial Center.

He is a Fellow of the American College of Trust and Estate Counsel, and is listed in Michigan Super Lawyers and in Best Lawyers in America in the fields of Trusts and Estates.

A frequent and lively speaker on tax topics, Bob has delivered numerous lectures for the Institute for Continuing Legal Education and the Michigan Association of Certified Public Accountants, and to many civic, professional, and religious groups on subjects related to estate planning and wealth preservation. He has also appeared on the CNN and CNN/Financial television networks, on radio throughout the United States, as well as on cable television.

Along with Robert H. Downie, he co-authored an earlier edition of this book, published under the title WHAT DO WE DO NOW? A PRACTICAL GUIDE TO ESTATE ADMINISTRATION FOR WIDOWS, WIDOWERS AND HEIRS. He also co-authored Kass and Carrie, WHO WILL CARE WHEN YOU'RE NOT THERE? ESTATE PLANNING FOR PET OWNERS.

YUH SUHN KIM serves as the Estate Administrator of the law firm of Barris, Sott, Denn & Driker. She is an attorney who dedicates her practice to settling probate and trust estates and other probate matters. Her practice also includes guardianships and conservatorships of minors and adults, the preparation of gift and estate tax returns, and trust funding, administration, and termination. She also handles hearings in Probate Courts involving proceedings to modify irrevocable trusts, contested matters involving the validity of estate planning documents, capacity issues, objections to inventories and accountings, and breaches of fiduciary duty.

Yuh Suhn joined BSD&D in 2005, and was formerly an attorney for UAW-GM Legal Services, where she handled several hundred estates over a period of seven years.

She is a graduate of the Detroit College of Law at Michigan State University, cum laude, and is a member of the State Bar of Michigan, the Women Lawyers Association of Michigan, Oakland County Bar Association, Macomb County Probate Bar Association, and the Wayne County Probate Bar Association.

Yuh Suhn served as Editor of the current edition of this book, bringing it up to date and helping expand it with timely new topics.

ROBERT H. DOWNIE co-authored the first edition of this book. He was previously the Estate Administrator of Barris, Sott, Denn & Driker. Prior to joining the firm he served as a Vice President in the Trust Tax Department of NBD Bank (now JP Morgan Chase), handling the tax administration of more than 200 decedents' estates and trusts.

Rob's extensive background in estate administration helped make this book the practical guide that it is. He taught federal estate and gift tax in the Master of Science in Taxation program at Wayne State University in Detroit, and was on the faculty of the Midwest Trust School. He holds a BA from the University of Michigan and an MBA from Michigan State University. He was also designated an Enrolled Agent by the Internal Revenue Service and was admitted to practice before the IRS.

Although Rob has retired to Oregon (where we understand he is as busy as ever), we remain ever grateful for his friendship, dedication, energy and solid contributions to the first edition of this book, over a decade ago.

PREFACE

About This Book

The material contained in this book is intended as a general guide to issues which must be addressed in settling an estate. It is also intended to provide other valuable information for survivors. It is not intended to be a substitute for a qualified estate planning or probate attorney, a competent accountant, knowledgeable tax or investment counsel, or a trained grief support counselor. While this book will certainly make you more aware of the issues, you should not rely on it in place of professional guidance.

Having this book as a companion can make it easier to understand when and why to seek counsel and support. It should also facilitate dialogue with your professionals, make the process go more smoothly, and help you develop reasonable expectations of what has to be done, by whom, and when. This is probably the first step in avoiding the frustration that often comes with administering an estate.

Why shouldn't you simply rely on the general rules and conclusions contained in this book?

First, general rules may be helpful as a starting point, but they cannot be relied upon for the specific answer in a given situation. Other circumstances may exist which could yield a dramatically different result. An attorney will help uncover the facts and will know their significance. This book is therefore intended to serve an educational purpose, not as specific legal advice in your situation.

Second, many aspects of estate administration are subject to local law. Federal law also comes into play in some cases, particularly with regard to the federal gift tax and estate tax, and rights under qualified retirement plans (and sometimes even under life insurance provided by governmental employers), but wills, trusts, and probate are largely governed by the laws of the various states. It would be very difficult if not impossible for any book of this size to address the laws of all fifty states with regard to these topics, and we have not even attempted to do so. For example, some states have community property law, which we have not considered at all in our discussion.

Therefore, where particular state law is relevant we have based our discussion on the law in effect at the time of this writing in the State of Michigan, where we practice. In some cases we specifically indicate that the conclusion is based on Michigan law, but if the applicable law is not stated then you should assume that Michigan law is the basis for our conclusion.

Also, the law is constantly changing. Michigan re-wrote its probate law several years ago, in a comprehensive statute, the Estates and Protected Individuals Code, or EPIC, and more recently enacted the Michigan Trust Code. Court decisions, regulations, and administrative rulings are issued which can change the outcome in a particular case. You should not assume that the law is static.

Even if the estate you are dealing with is being administered in another state, this book will make you sensitive to the issues. For example, must a will or trust be in writing, and must a person sign his or her own will or can someone else sign it on the person's behalf? What circumstances may cause a person who is named in a will or trust not to be entitled to receive the amount left for him? Once you are aware of the issues, you can ask your attorney how the situation should be addressed in your case, wherever you are.

However, most of this book deals with areas which are not specific to the law of any state, and the checklists, tips, resources and insights should be helpful to anyone attempting to handle administration of an estate or deal with issues faced by survivors.

INTRODUCTION

If you are reading this book, you probably have been named Executor, Personal Representative, or Successor Trustee of the estate of someone who has recently passed away. Or perhaps you are nervously anticipating that painful moment.

Traditional wisdom has it that the person charged with administering a decedent's estate has three duties: Gather all the assets of the deceased; pay the debts, expenses, and taxes; and then distribute whatever is left to the beneficiaries.

If life – and death – were that simple, you would have to read no further.

Unfortunately, even a relatively small estate can involve a fair amount of work to settle. In many cases issues arise which can test the patience of even the most dedicated person who is simply trying to carry out the decedent's wishes.

The purpose of this book is to level the playing field – to give you an even chance to succeed in an area which is probably new to you and which can challenge even the most experienced attorney. We will provide you a detailed road map based on decades of collective experience in planning and administering estates and advising Personal Representatives and Trustees, accountants, bank trust officers, and attorneys who handle estate administration.

Our goal is not to make a lawyer or professional estate administrator out of you. Rather, we believe that nonprofessionals charged with this responsibility must be able to identify the issues in administering an estate. Our main objective is therefore to provide you extensive checklists of issues to consider.

Along the way, we will alert you to the strict time limits for addressing some of these issues. If you fail to act within the time limit – which can be as short as a few days or as long as several months – there can be disastrous consequences.

For example, you could be liable to the IRS for penalties and interest on the decedent's income taxes, or on the estate's income taxes or estate taxes if not paid when due. You could be removed by the Probate Court for failure to fulfill your legal obligations. Or you could be liable to the beneficiaries – yes, even your own family members – for market losses suffered on the estate's stock portfolio.

This book is also for the survivors, those who are left behind to deal with the loss from an emotional point of view. While traditional estate administration focuses on distribution of the property of the decedent, we have started earlier in the process with thoughts concerning preparation for the funeral, whom to notify, how to notify them, and how not to notify them. We also touch upon the need for grief support and provide numerous resources for the survivors, and how to preserve and pass on digital assets.

In this age of the Internet, we are constantly discovering sources of information on the web which relate to estate administration, which we also want to share with you. You will be amazed how many Internet resources can lead you to valuable information, shorten your wait, and provide you contact with governmental agencies, organizations, and people who can be of assistance.

We will also share insights into other areas of particular interest to those administering an estate: When should you call for help, whom should you put on your team, how should you locate and select those people, and how should they be compensated?

And how do you keep peace in the family? The expectation of receiving something from an estate not infrequently brings out the worst in people. We cannot counter years of jealousy, sibling rivalries, and greed. However, we can provide you tips on how to anticipate some of the typical problems which arise, how to keep your head and your balance, and how to avoid losing your own assets in a challenge by beneficiaries who allege that you have acted improperly.

To bring the subject full circle, we end with considerations for the financial and estate planning of the survivors. As you work your way through the administration of the estate of the decedent, you will probably realize that your own planning needs some attention. You will appreciate this even more after you have experienced estate administration first hand.

Ultimately our goal is to help you through the estate administration process as quickly as possible. You have suffered the loss of a loved one or dear friend. You need closure, not years of work and anxiety. We offer you this guide to help you through your journey, without necessarily taking short cuts, but at least avoiding the proverbial quicksand and the very real minefields which the system has laid for those who are not properly advised.

This book is a fully updated and expanded version of our earlier work, WHAT DO WE DO NOW? A PRACTICAL GUIDE TO ESTATE ADMINISTRATION FOR WIDOWS, WIDOWERS AND HEIRS. That book had readers from Guam to the United Kingdom, and not only in Michigan but throughout the United States. It was widely used as course material for legal assistants learning about estate administration. Attorneys used it for in-house staff training, as a resource for themselves, and gave copies to clients to help them understand the process of settling an estate. We have preserved what we felt was timeless advice, added many new topics, and after many years of uncertainty have fully updated the estate and gift tax discussion based on 2012 federal tax legislation.

We hope that you find this new edition useful, and welcome any comments. Either call us directly at 313-965-9725, or toll-free at 1-877-537-4178, or email inquiries@carobtreepress.com.

CHAPTER 1

Getting Started

You are embarking on a journey through what may be new territory. This book is your road map, and will get you to the end with as few bumps in the road and detours as possible.

This book is a guide, not a treatise. Like a map, you can use it to find your way through uncharted territory. It's not necessary to read it cover to cover, word for word. If there is an area which you know is of interest in the estate you're handling, you can flip through the chapters and find the material which interests you, or locate your topic through the Table of Contents or Index.

Although this is not an estate planning book, many purchasers of the first edition bought copies for their entire family.

One reader said, "If my children are going to have to deal with this some day, and they don't have the necessary information, this book is a great way to start the conversation."

If Death Is Expected

Even though this book can be very useful in pre-planning, it is not an estate planning book. For the most part, we assume that death has already occurred and that the person either did or did not do proper estate planning.

However, if death has not yet occurred, and if the person involved is able to assist you, it would be extremely worthwhile to review the checklists with that person, who may have information you will soon need. If you don't take this opportunity it could take you days or months to find what that person could direct you to in a moment.

You will have to be the judge of how to approach this subject. Many people, knowing that the end is near, will be greatly relieved to know that they have helped you "put everything in order." It may give them a sense of satisfaction to help you in this task, particularly if there are facts which only they know and can share with you.

Consider Chapter 2, "Keys to Achieving Peace and Harmony When Settling an Estate." While you are still in "planning mode" there may be ways to avoid friction among family members in the future.

Also see Chapter 3, "Passing on Digital Assets," which could provide you the ability to locate and access accounts which today are so important in the lives of many people.

You may also have an opportunity to discuss the issues discussed in Chapter 4, "Organ Donation; Funeral Arrangements."

If Death Was Unexpected

If death has occurred unexpectedly, you may be overwhelmed with grief, confused, and not sure where to start. You should use this book to organize your thoughts and as a guide to the process upon which you are about to embark.

With this book at your side, you should feel confident that you can deal with whatever challenges the administration of this estate will bring. You will know what to expect, where to go, whom to call, and when.

You're Not Alone

Although the topic "Where to Turn for Help" is addressed in Chapter 12, you should feel free to consider the issues dealt with in that chapter at any time.

In many books of this sort the authors recommend that you seek help from an attorney immediately after the death or funeral, and some people do that. However, we wanted to give you an idea of some of the issues with which you will be dealing before suggesting that you bring in third parties.

You will certainly be a more educated client if you gather the important documents and consider a number of issues before your first meeting with the attorney.

The Case Studies and Special Resources

Throughout this book we share case studies which are generally based either on our experience in practice, or on court cases. The names used in those descriptions are fictional, to protect the confidences of those involved. Some are hypothetical cases which commonly occur. However, the basic fact situations have actually occurred and could certainly happen again. We hope that you find them helpful in understanding how the legal concepts relate to real life situations.

We also have found some interesting resources – websites, phone numbers, reference books and third party service providers – which we felt you may find helpful. We make no representations about them, but offer them for your consideration. Many of these are highlighted in special boxes with a magnifying glass in the upper left corner.

Take A Deep Breath

Finally, we urge you to resist the temptation to rush through the administration of the estate, helter skelter, without proper consideration of the issues and options.

The refrain "I just want to get it all done" is not uncommon in these situations. By reading through these chapters you should gain an appreciation of the tasks which have to be done, and the time it takes to do them.

If you have realistic expectations, of yourself and of those on your team, you will reach your goal in due time, and avoid the anxiety, frustration, and disappointment that comes with failed or unrealistic expectations.

It may seem like some things which ought to be very simple take an inordinate amount of time to accomplish. You may submit documents and they may become lost and have to be resubmitted – not once but possibly twice or more. You may leave voice mail at a company or government agency and never receive a return call.

Always consider your "Plan B" and, when the first method doesn't work, be persistent and try another. The business world is not a perfect place, and you should consider yourself very fortunate if everything you do in the estate goes like clock work.

Murphy's Law ("Whatever can go wrong, will") seems to prevail. Yet, with proper precautions you can guard against the worst. Consider these measures in self-defense:

- Keep copies of whatever you send, whether that be correspondence or important documents such as stocks or bonds.
- Send important letters via certified mail, return receipt requested, or use a private overnight courier service.
- Buy yourself a daily agenda and use it. Keep notes of important telephone conversations in it. Include what was said and by whom, and that person's direct dial telephone number, if available. You may start out calling one number in a large organization and be transferred through several people to the one who can finally handle your problem. You'll be thankful you kept the name and number when you have to contact that person again.
- If you are contemplating taking a fee for your services, use your agenda to keep track of what you do and the time you spend. You may need this detail to justify your fee to the Probate Court or to defend against a challenge by disgruntled beneficiaries. (See Chapter 22, "Should You Take Fiduciary Fees?")
- If someone promises to do something for you, politely ask them when they expect to have it done, and keep a tickler file to follow up a few days after the promised date. Consider writing short letters to confirm what is to be done and by when. Be tactful, but be clear.

With these tips in mind, and this book in hand, you're on your way to successful administration of the estate. ■

Notes

*"If you're going to do something,
you might as well do it cheerfully
and enthusiastically."*

— Lucille Babcock

CHAPTER 2

Keys to Achieving Peace and Harmony When Settling an Estate

Settling an estate often brings out the worst behavior. Knowing the causes of friction and how to avoid them can help you achieve peace and harmony going forward.

Settling an estate too often brings out the worst in people. While some poor relationships may never be healed, in our experience there are a number of issues which repeatedly give rise to problems when settling an estate. Proper handling of these issues may help reduce points of contention.

If there is still time to change the estate plan (i.e., the person is alive and competent) – what we call "planning" mode – steps can be taken to address them in the estate plan. If you are settling an estate, it's not too late to deal with these issues. At the end of this chapter we offer pointers which will hopefully help you to keep peace in the family when you are in what we call "clean-up" mode.

Major Causes of Friction

Every family situation is unique, and there are probably causes for friction that we haven't seen. Here are the most common reasons families fall apart when settling an estate:

Some family members aren't happy with whoever has been selected to settle the estate. That person could have the role of Personal Representative under the will, if we're dealing with a probate estate, or Trustee if under a trust. In this discussion we will generally refer to that person as the "fiduciary."

Some of those who haven't been designated as fiduciary feel slighted – even though they may not want the job themselves. This may stem from personalities, sibling relationships, or other factors affecting family members that have absolutely nothing to do with the task of settling the estate.

Someone may be having marital problems, be unemployed, or may have just had his 401(k) account disappear before his eyes. For whatever reason, he is an unhappy person, and he isn't satisfied with whomever has been nominated to get him his share of Mom or Dad's estate.

Sometimes family members don't get what they want or expect. Whatever this person gets was the decedent's decision, but he may not have known about it and is surprised – and miffed.

This dissatisfaction with their share of the estate translates into unhappiness with whatever is being done to settle the estate, including sale of assets, for example, which can't happen fast enough, and the price will certainly not be high enough. Heaven forbid the fiduciary decides that now is not the right time to sell and that everyone should wait a couple of years for the market to improve!

Having someone else handle the estate is enough of a reason for a "control" person to grumble. Those who aren't directly involved in settling the estate may feel things aren't going fast enough. (Can things ever go fast enough for anyone who is just waiting for money?)

Family members are suspicious of those who are handling the estate. They are concerned that some property will be taken, or bought at a low price, or fiduciary fees taken which they feel are unjustified. Sometimes they feel that any fee at all is too much.

Family members harbor bad feelings from decades of poor relationships that have nothing to do with settling the estate. Parents may have kept a lid on it, but now they are gone and the children can act out their jealousies and anger.

Some family members may have been treated better than others over the years – larger gifts, loans, big wedding, college expenses, houses, and so on. Others may feel that now's the time to whine about how they have been treated unfairly, and perhaps put a guilt trip on those who were favored and get a larger share of the estate to even things up.

It is also possible that there is friction due to valid grounds for dissatisfaction with whomever is charged with handling the estate:

They may be acting too quickly, without following the documents, disregarding their legal obligations, or not obtaining valuations. They may even be abusing their authority.

They may not be acting quickly enough because they don't have a sense of urgency and there is no mutual expectation of how long it should take to get things done.

They may be acting without proper legal, tax and accounting advice, just bumbling along as if they were just organizing a garage sale when, in fact, much more may be involved.

They may be totally unaware of the strict standards which apply to them in their new job and the fact that they may be held liable for doing the wrong thing, or for not doing whatever they should have done in a timely manner. For example, they may sit on a stock portfolio without getting independent investment advice, while the stocks slide in value.

Finally, we are seeing an increase in probate litigation due to various factors, which are not necessarily avoidable: (a) multiple marriage situations with half-siblings who don't particularly like each other; (b) our society's increased focus on material wealth; and (c) a depressed economy and unemployment, resulting in heirs looking wherever they can to improve their own economic situations.

If You Are Still in Planning Mode

If there is still time to address some of these issues within the estate plan, you may have a better chance to avoid or minimize friction and unhappiness in settling the estate. At least you can try to get it right.

The All Important Choice of Fiduciary

The fiduciary is the quarterback – the person who will be given the responsibility of settling the estate. This may be the Personal Representative if under a will, or Successor Trustee if you are going to be dealing with a revocable living trust.

If the person whose estate you are going to be dealing with doesn't have a will or trust, then now is perhaps the time to put something in place. That way the fiduciary can be specifically designated. If there is no will or trust, the law provides an order of priority as to who should be named Personal Representative. Is that person satisfactory? If not, since you are still in planning mode, you can do something about it.

While some people might consider it an honor to be named a fiduciary and handle an estate, it's a real job which can be quite time consuming and frustrating, and can also involve legal and financial liability. Who should you saddle with that job, and what are the implications of choosing one person or group over another? Let's assume we are dealing with a family with children and no surviving spouse, so the children would be the prime candidates.

Should You Name One Child?

What if you pick one child out of several? One advantage would be that this person would have the legal authority to get the job done without having the others vote on every decision. That could also be a negative.

Why are you picking one over another? Is it just because this person is the oldest or perhaps lives closest to you? Is he or she more qualified than the others?

Ideally a fiduciary should be well organized, trustworthy, and make decisions in a thoughtful way. A smooth personality would help. Ideally this would be someone who realizes that everyone's opinion has value, but who can make a decision to get the right outcome even if it is not in his or her own interest. Someone who can reach out to others who have more experience in a given area would be a better choice than a know-it-all.

What If You Name All the Children?

Some parents feel it is offensive to the other children if one child is appointed Personal Representative or Successor Trustee. So they simply appoint all of the children, to serve together. That way, they feel, no one is offended.

Whether this is a better decision depends on the number of children and the personalities. Also, if you provide that they must act by unanimous decision, any one of them will be able to veto decisions of the others. This could result in a stalemate and absolutely nothing getting done

Some parents rationalize that this situation will force the children to agree on something, because without "working things out" nothing will happen and no one will get anything. That may be true, but it may also empower the bully or the one with more staying power. If some of them are more needy or have weaker personalities, they may just concede on major issues because they want the estate settled so they can receive their share and/or so they can avoid conflict.

This is merely an adult variation of schoolyard politics. If the children have had problems getting along their entire lives, why assume that they will be able to cooperate in settling an estate when the senior generation is no longer there to act as referee?

Most parents will either pick one child or a group of children to act as fiduciaries, or even all the children. In some cases if a group is involved, they will allow them to decide by majority rule, rather than requiring a unanimous decision. They feel that one should not be allowed to veto a decision on which the majority has come to an agreement. However, if there are existing alliances, some parents feel that majority rule will allow one group to govern. The "odd man out" will always be outvoted and this will be a source of frustration.

What About a Third Party?

In some cases, faced with the disadvantages of either selecting one person or a group, a decision is made to select a third party. That could be another family member, who is not a beneficiary, or perhaps a professional such as a bank or trust company, attorney or accountant.

In some cases the Personal Representative role is given to the third party alone; the children are not named at all. In other cases, the third party is named as one of the group, or perhaps just given special powers with regard to certain decisions only. For example, the third party may be appointed Special Trustee or Trust Protector, with the right to veto certain important decisions such as sale of property or a business.

Numerous Factors Come Into Play

The decision on choice of fiduciary should not be taken lightly, and should consider the realities, not just simple concepts like "she's the oldest" or "she lives close by and it will be easier to handle things."

What is the history of this person in handling difficult, sensitive tasks? Will he or she be mindful of the rules, or just charge ahead and get the job done without thinking about the implications of his or her decisions? If naming several people to serve as a team, will they be able to work together?

Even if you feel that your nominees will be able to work together, consider the possible influence of their spouses. Though they may not have a legal role, they may have influence as a practical matter and get things off track.

Do your nominees have different situations such that some may need money sooner than others, which could make group decisions difficult with regard to sale of property? (Some may be willing to wait to get a better price, others may feel that things should be sold as soon as possible, regardless of price.) Do they owe money to the person whose estate they may be asked to settle? A debtor is generally a poor choice for a fiduciary.

What About Fiduciary Fees?

A Probate Judge once said, in a private conference with one of the authors in her chambers, that people consider the letters of authority of a Personal Representative a license to steal. What she was saying was that once a person is appointed Personal Representative, and receives the document from the Probate Court evidencing that official appointment (letters of authority), that person often feels that with the estate's checkbook comes the right to write checks for Personal Representative's fees in whatever amount he or she feels is reasonable. We have even seen Personal Representatives write themselves checks for $50,000 the day after their appointment, for services they had clearly not rendered yet.

It is true that a fiduciary is entitled to reasonable compensation for services rendered on behalf of the estate. The problem is that there may be very different views of what is "reasonable," and some beneficiaries may be incensed that a family member is taking any fee at all. The entire subject of fees should therefore be approached with great caution. This is an area which can definitely tear the family apart.

Do You Expect the Fiduciary to be Paid?

In most cases, a family member does not expect to be paid for services in settling an estate, and will not accept a fee. This doesn't mean that you should never consider compensating a fiduciary. Depending on the size and complexity of the estate, a fee may be in order. People often underestimate how much time it takes to settle an estate, and in fact it may amount to a second job which could last from several months to several years.

However, for those who are not administering the estate, seeing a family member paid a fee for settling the estate may be hard to accept. They may consider it a boondoggle.

Whatever the feelings on the subject, it is best that you spell out intentions in the documents. If family members are not to receive compensation, then this should be said. If the person whose estate you are going to be handling doesn't mind if the fiduciary receives compensation, then either make it subject to a written agreement with the beneficiaries, which they can then negotiate between themselves, or specify the basis on which compensation will be determined.

For example, you could specify a flat dollar amount, a percentage based on the total value of the estate, or an hourly rate based on time spent. (Check with a local attorney to make sure that whatever method you choose is legal.)

If compensation will be based on time spent, specify that the fiduciary must keep contemporaneous written time records so that the beneficiaries (and possibly the Court) can see what was done and how long each task took. If a fiduciary merely submits a bill for a number of hours at a certain hourly rate, that will not go over well with the beneficiaries. It is also unlikely to be approved if the Probate Court is asked to review the fees for reasonableness.

What is a Reasonable Rate?

If nothing is said in the will or trust about how the fiduciary will be compensated, then you are leaving it up to the fiduciary, at least in the first instance. Under Michigan law, a Personal Representative has the right to pay himself or herself compensation without prior Probate Court approval. However, the Court has the right to review compensation to determine whether it is reasonable based on all the facts and circumstances. If the Court later determines that it was excessive, then the excess will have to be paid back.

Absent clear instructions in the will or trust, the Probate Court will probably allow only a very low hourly rate for someone who is not a professional fiduciary. This means, for example, that even though the person appointed earns $200 per hour in his or her normal job, that will probably not be a reasonable rate for a person whose profession is not settling estates.

Make it clear that whatever can be done by lower paid people should be done by them, and not by the fiduciary, e.g., lawn cutting, or arranging for an estate sale. The fact that the fiduciary is giving up time that he or she could spend on his or her main job does not justify paying at the same rate as the main job.

If a person isn't happy working without compensation, or on the basis which is set forth in the will or trust, that person should consider declining. Better yet, since you are still in planning mode, talk to the person in advance and see if he or she will agree to do the job for the compensation intended, or for no compensation, if that's the intent. If the proposed fiduciary has a different view on this and if the two positions can't be resolved, consider appointing someone else.

In the past, it made sense to pay fiduciary fees even to family members, where the estate was subject to estate tax, the fees were deductible in computing that tax, and the estate tax rate was higher than the income tax payable on the fee. Today, however, with an extremely high estate tax exemption, most estates are not subject to estate tax. Therefore, the fiduciary should also consider that whatever is received as a fee will be subject to income tax, while if received as an inheritance it would be received free from income tax.

Non-family fiduciaries may be paid based on their normal hourly rates, such as generally apply for accountants and attorneys, or based on their normal fee schedules, as would be the case for a bank or trust company.

The topic of fiduciary fees is discussed further in Chapter 22, "Should You Take Fiduciary Fees?"

Leaving Personal Property

How is personal property going to be allocated? Personal property generally refers to everything except real estate, cash and marketable securities. Furniture, furnishings, clothing, jewelry, collectibles, art work, cars, boats, planes, fishing and hunting gear, and even family memorabilia are personal property. According to one Probate Judge, this is the "stuff" that gives rise to most disputes. Consider making lifetime gifts of sensitive items to avoid people squabbling about them when you are gone.

Alternatively, make a detailed list, signed at the end, specifying who should get what. (This is legal in Michigan, and doesn't have to be contained in a will but should be referred to in the will. In other states, check with a local lawyer to make sure it will be binding and if there are other formalities required.) There will be less to gripe about if the beneficiaries don't have to decide among themselves. Make sure your lawyer has the latest list.

Consider soliciting preferences from the beneficiaries. Relative value of the items may not be the source of a dispute. It may be that someone is emotionally attached to an item, and you may be totally unaware of that when you leave it to someone else or put your beneficiaries in the position of having to fight over it.

Do not rely on yellow sticky tags on the back of items. They are not legally binding, can fall off, get switched, etc.

Bad attitudes among beneficiaries can translate into heated disputes over who gets the gun collection, golf clubs, oriental rugs, jewelry, etc.

If there are items of particular value, consider establishing a procedure to allocate them fairly, including appraisal and a way of deciding who gets to choose first. Consider putting this procedure in the hands of a third party such as your attorney.

Leaving the Family Business or Farm

Be careful how you leave major assets.

Should the child who is active in the business or farm get it, while the other gets cash or marketable securities? How is the business or farm to be valued? Are you assuming that a thriving business or farm will always be profitable?

How will the one getting cash or marketable securities feel? What if the securities plummet in value?

If the estate will be subject to estate tax, how are the taxes being allocated? Sometimes the business or farm is left as a specific bequest (for example, "I leave my interest in ABC Company to my son, John..."), with the other child getting the balance or "residue" of the estate. If the taxes come out of the residue, then it is possible that the residue will be wiped out by the taxes.

Should you consider life insurance as an equalizer?

You may have to decide what is really important: Value, or keeping someone in the business, family farm, family compound, or horse farm that they have been running.

Planning for Pets

If there are pets to be considered, now may be the time to discuss who will take care of them, what care instructions should be provided, and how their care will be funded. In many cases, family members simply step up and take over the responsibility for the pets. In other cases, however, depending on the family situation, the number and type of pets, and their own special needs, it may be important to address their future care and welfare in a more formal way.

Planning for a Pet's Future Welfare

For insights into the process of planning for the future care, welfare and happiness of a pet, and helpful checklists, see **WHO WILL CARE WHEN YOU'RE NOT THERE? ESTATE PLANNING FOR PET OWNERS**, by Robert E. Kass and Elizabeth A. Carrie (www.carobtreepress.com).

Need to Coordinate the Plan

Many people do not realize that an estate plan needs to be coordinated to work properly.

Often a will or trust will say one thing (for example, "I leave my estate equally to my three children…"), and the assets are titled jointly with one child. Or a beneficiary designation on life insurance or retirement plans may be inconsistent with the overall plan.

Joint ownership and beneficiary designations will usually be given effect, or "trump," whatever you have in your will or trust. There are certain exceptions, but if you are still in planning mode you should realize that who will get which assets does not depend solely on the will or trust. You must also check any joint ownership and beneficiary designations, and make sure they are consistent with the person's intent and the overall plan. Even if the person is disabled – but still alive – it may be possible to "fix" joint ownership and beneficiary designations to conform to the overall plan if someone has authority to act under a durable power of attorney.

If joint ownership and beneficiary designations are not consistent with the overall plan, that could lead to disputes, and maybe even the wrong people getting the money or other property, depending on the intent.

Forfeiture Clauses

Consider a forfeiture or "no-contest" clause in the will or trust if you anticipate that some of the beneficiaries may be unhappy with what is being left to them and may challenge the plan. This type of clause provides that if a person challenges the estate plan, they will lose whatever has been provided for them. The intent is to discourage frivolous challenges.

These clauses are frowned upon by the law and the courts, and will not always be enforceable. The rules vary from state to state, and change over time. However, discuss your situation with your attorney and determine how best to implement your objectives.

Legacy Statements

Consider some type of "legacy" statement, outlining your hopes and dreams for your family, and the values which are important to you. These are sometimes also referred to as ethical wills, and are not the same as living wills, which deal with end-of-life care.

A legacy statement could elevate the discussion and get them to think about more lofty objectives. If they are involved in its creation, they may feel some obligation to avoid clawing.

Should You Discuss the Plan While You Are Alive?

Many of our clients ask whether they should discuss their estate plan with their beneficiaries while they are alive. There is no right answer to this question, only issues to consider, which will vary in each situation.

If you discuss the plan it will let them know what's coming and avoid surprises. You may be able to change the plan if it seems advisable to do so. On the other hand, you may hear about it the rest of your life, and you may, in fact, be pressured to change your plan.

Also, consider that you are free to change your plan at any time, so long as you are competent. So why get them involved in your plan when it might change anyhow?

If an estate is being divided evenly and there is no reason to suspect unhappiness on the part of anyone, then perhaps there will be no problems if you share the plan with your beneficiaries. But if you are allocating the estate unequally, or cutting someone out, you may find it better to keep your planning private, and it is certainly your right to do so.

If You Are In Clean-Up Mode

If the person has already died, and you are now faced with settling the estate, you are in what we refer to as "clean-up mode." It may be too late to change the documents, but there may be some ways to avoid or minimize friction and unhappiness, even if the documents are already in place.

Communication is Key

Communication is an important part of avoiding suspicion and dissatisfaction.

The best defense may be a good offense: Provide beneficiaries as much information as you can, as often as reasonable (even more often than the documents or the law may require).

Make sure they get copies of the relevant estate planning documents, as soon as possible, unless there are reasons to provide them only the relevant portions. Give them information about assets and liabilities, unless they are to receive specific items or dollar amounts. Discuss with your attorney exactly how much financial information they should receive.

It is important to establish mutual expectations, so they won't be constantly nagging you. Identify the relevant issues relating to the administration of the estate so they know why things may take some time. Establish a written time line so you all have the same expectations as to what has to be done, by whom, and when.

Decide if some of this should come through your attorney to keep the focus on the task and off the personalities. It may be important to have the attorney do most of the initial communication to set the tone, keep it business like, and steer clear of personal issues you may have with the beneficiaries or they may have with you. (You may want to have subsequent communication on important issues come from the attorney as well.)

After an initial meeting on the estate, and a comprehensive letter outlining what there is and what has to be done, let them know how often you expect to be able to provide updates.

This topic is discussed further in Chapter 16, "Keep the Beneficiaries Informed."

Strive for Consensus

Solicit input and attempt to obtain buy-in on important decisions. It is harder for someone to second guess a decision where they were allowed to have input into the decision-making process.

If they just will not agree, then you can rely on your authority as fiduciary to do certain things.

In certain cases you may want to seek Probate Court approval to make sure you are not second guessed. This will give everyone an opportunity to express their views and allow a third party (the judge) to make a binding decision. In case of sale of an asset, for example, a third party appraisal may be required.

Try to limit meetings to direct beneficiaries, not spouses of beneficiaries (i.e., in-laws), and not grandchildren (unless the grandchildren are the beneficiaries). Keeping the discussion to the true "interested parties" will avoid people with no direct interest fomenting discord. Let the interested parties deal with their own family members.

Use Third Parties

Consider using third parties for certain types of decisions, as appropriate, and if possible solicit input on the process and the selection of these types of professionals: Investment advisors (interview several if the assets warrant it, and consider having the beneficiaries attend the meetings); appraisers; specialty dealers in certain items (e.g., collectibles); attorneys as to legal options and ways of resolving issues; and accountants for tax return work and to help lay out a proper accounting system.

In each case, seek someone with expertise who is independent, who will have the respect of all parties, and has no axe to grind.

Protect Yourself

In agreeing to settle an estate, you are taking on an assignment that can result in legal liability. You should become familiar with the rules you must follow in exercising your fiduciary duties. Have your attorney explain the guidelines you must follow as a fiduciary. For further discussion on fiduciary duties, see Chapter 8, "Who Should Administer the Estate?"

No one will thank you if you handle things well and everything turns out fine, but if you stub your toe they will not hesitate to let you know, and you may be personally liable.

Consider getting a release and indemnification agreement from the beneficiaries when you make a distribution or when you take a certain course of action that you have discussed and with which they agree. Alternatively, consider having the Probate Court approve your actions.

If you are distributing assets before being absolutely sure that all liabilities (including back taxes) of the estate have been covered, get a refunding agreement from each beneficiary. Otherwise, you could be personally liable.

Settling an estate requires skill, tact, and a willingness to deal with beneficiaries who often don't realize the effort required. Before you accept this responsibility, make sure you are aware of the challenges. It can be done, and without getting you in trouble, but you should not naively assume that all will go well. Don't hesitate to get professional advice. Sometimes that's the least expensive way to handle the situation. ■

"You can't have a family fuss without the whole town knowing about it."

— Proverb

CHAPTER 3

Passing on Digital Assets

Digital assets can be a significant part of an estate. We show you how to plan to pass down digital assets, if planning is still possible. If death has already occurred, we offer tips on how to find them.

In this chapter we deal with what has become an increasingly important issue: How can you make sure you have access to the decedent's "digital assets." And if there is still time to work with the person before death, what steps can you take to facilitate this process?

What Are "Digital Assets"?

When we refer to "digital assets," we are talking about data of any type in which a person has some right or proprietary interest. Immediately we think about information in a person's email accounts and accounts with financial institutions. But digital assets also include information in a person's smartphone, on computers and other devices, CD's, DVD's, USB keys, backup drives, and backup systems "in the cloud."

There could be picture and video files, music files, social networking accounts, blogs, websites, word processing documents, spreadsheets and even medical information. There may also be subscriptions and purchases which are on a monthly or even weekly "auto-ship" basis, charged to a credit card.

Backups of tax returns, family histories, photo albums, and online photo archiving and sharing sites may also exist, and in fact some people will have made photo books with the basic files residing on the system of the printing or publishing company so additional copies can be made in the future.

Digital assets can have significant value. The value may be monetary, such as websites or blogs that generate revenue, or intellectual property rights such as domain names, or financial accounting records. They may also have purely emotional or sentimental value, such as family photos, family archives, or video files. From a purely monetary perspective, it may be necessary to access a person's online services to learn about a business or investments, or pay bills.

If a business is conducted on a computer, on the web, or primarily by email, access will be required to continue or close down the business. Without access, orders won't be taken, deliveries won't be made, suppliers' inquiries won't be answered, and contracts may be breached, resulting in claims against the business and/or the estate.

What will happen with all of the digital assets if the person dies without listing them and providing access? Will they be lost? Will the survivors spend months looking for them and, in some cases, seeking permission from online service providers to access, manage and possibly close these accounts? Will they have to go to court to access these accounts? Will business opportunities be lost or liabilities created?

Today, digital media has evolved to the point where it makes sense to ask questions about it to someone whose financial affairs are going to be your responsibility. Further, if you don't already have the necessary information and you have the task of pulling everything together, you need a road map to help you on that journey.

Planning Ahead

If there is time to plan ahead, the person must determine who is to have access to his or her important documents and online accounts. The process is much like dealing with regular assets: Identify the digital assets, select a trusted person to manage them in case of incapacity or death, and provide locations, usernames and passwords.

Without this information, the Personal Representative or Trustee may be unable to gain timely access to email accounts, online financial accounts, online retailers and service providers. In addition, the Personal Representative or Trustee will probably not have timely access to email accounts, online financial accounts, and online retailers and service providers that hold credit card information. Assets such as digital photos, Facebook pages, and other information stored online or on the computer may never be retrieved.

No Paper Check Register

Fifteen years ago John died and a friend came to his wife claiming that John owed him $10,000. The wife was certain that John had paid off the debt, but didn't have John's check register because he kept that on his computer and she didn't have access to it. He had not left her the password.

At their attorney's suggestion, they hired a 13-year old who was able to hack into the computer. They located the digital check register, found the date of the payment, and requested a copy of the canceled check from the bank to prove that the payment had been made.

At that time, the thought that someone might have something of importance on a computer and not leave a password was a new idea.

Identifying Digital Assets

The first step is to make a list of hardware, including computers, backup hard drives, thumb drives or compact disks used to store important information. Some people have multiple computers at home, and some have computers at home and at work or in a vacation residence. Others back up their computer data to an online service or to "cloud" storage.

The list should indicate what is of importance on each of these systems. Physically label them with a summary of the contents, if that is feasible, or prepare a separate list. Determine if the person uses a financial management program such as Quicken or Quickbooks to keep the books for the family or the person's business on a computer.

List all online accounts, such as bank and brokerage accounts, retail accounts, loyalty accounts (such as frequent flier accounts), as well as personal accounts such as email addresses, YouTube, and social networking pages. If the person maintains a blog or website, or does online backup, gather information on those accounts as well.

For all of these online accounts, prepare or make sure that there exists a current list of the usernames, passwords and other information needed to log on. This could well become a point of contention because you are asking someone who may have security concerns to lay out in written form everything that could jeopardize the security of the accounts. The reality is that this information is going to be essential in the event of the person's disability or death.

The major decision is whether this information will be stored in a master document which is on a password protected computer, with the password given to a trusted person but which could be hacked and the information misused, or in paper format, either in a hard copy notebook or perhaps in a 3 x 5 card file.

We acknowledge that this could be a sensitive issue. But not having the information when it is needed will create real problems. A decision has to be made as to how it will be recorded, where it will be stored, and who will have access.

Online Alternatives

It should come as no surprise that companies have sprouted up which now offer online services to protect and pass on digital assets to loved ones. These types of services typically establish procedures to release passwords and other information to a designated beneficiary in the event of the death or incapacity of the person who owns the digital assets. Some require a death certificate or other confirmation before releasing the information. Others send periodic emails to the client and will release information to a designated representative if the client fails to respond.

Selecting the Digital Assets Agent

Whether it's a secure online service which will hold the account information and passwords, a family member, trust officer, accountant or attorney, someone must be identified as the right organization or person to be trusted as the "digital assets agent."

That person or organization must be highly trustworthy. It might be the same person as is designated as Personal Representative or Successor Trustee. However, consider whether the person selected for that role has sufficient knowledge to deal with digital assets. If not, some people have considered a different, more "tech savvy" person – a separate "Digital Asset Trustee/ Personal Representative" or "Digital Asset Agent" – to deal only with digital assets.

The skill level will have to be accompanied by a high level of trustworthiness, since that person may well have access to accounts which are ripe for abuse – not only by the Digital Asset Agent, but by third parties. For example, if the person uses a wireless network that is not secure, others may easily get access to this information.

But once that road map has been created and the person or organization identified, and once the triggering event has occurred (e.g., death or disability), that person should have the information and the authority to take control over the digital assets.

Online Digital Asset Vaults

There are many companies which will store your passwords and other digital information. Some of these are **AssetLock (www.assetlock.net)**, **DataInherit (www.datainherit.com)**, **Deathswitch (www.deathswitch.com)**, **Legacy Locker (www.legacylocker.com)**, **SecureSafe (www.securesafe.com)**, and **VitalLock (www.vitallock.com)**.

There are even more services which are referred to as "password managers." Do a Google search for "best password managers." See an article in Wikipedia about advantages and vulnerabilities of these systems. http://en.wikipedia.org/wiki/Password_manager

Many individuals would be concerned with their information being online, even if it is password protected and the system purports to be hacker-proof. Do your own evaluation and decide which, if any, is best for your situation, or if you prefer another method.

We have not investigated any of these services, are not recommending any of them, and expressly disclaim any liability for your use of such a system.

Supplementary Instructions

It may be useful to have supplementary instructions, in addition to locations, usernames and passwords. These instructions might fall into the following categories:

Notifications

In the event of death, how should people be notified? In the old days, perhaps a family phone squad was set up and friends received a phone call with funeral information. Or maybe the family relied on a death notice in the local newspaper.

Today many of us have Facebook friends, connections on LinkedIn, followers on Twitter, or others with whom we regularly communicate on a blog or website. If those people are to be notified, someone has to provide access and instructions as to how that should be done. In some cases survivors continue to post memories online after someone dies, which can be important to the sharing community and the healing process. If notification is to be made via email, perhaps an email group should be established to facilitate that process.

Keep in mind, however, that while posting information on Facebook or Twitter provides instant notification, it may also inform those who want to steal an identity, or target the decedent's home, and other assets in the absence of the decedent. Therefore, you must carefully balance sharing information about the status of the decedent with the need to protect the decedent's personal information.

Continuing or Closing Sites

A Personal Representative or Trustee, named to settle an estate, may reasonably conclude that all websites and blogs of the decedent should be closed. If there are no contrary instructions, that may well happen. Is this what is intended? In some cases these websites and blogs contain information gathered and posts made over many years, which can continue to be a valuable resource for decades to come, and can easily be carried on by someone else.

Therefore, it's best that the issue be addressed, and if the person wants a site to be continued, instructions should be provided as to how that should be done. Should it be left intact and remain static? Should it be continued by someone and, if so, how should that person be identified or is there already a decision? Should the person have to pay for the site and, if so, how much?

If a site or account is to be closed, should copies of the relevant files be kept, along with pictures, audio and video?

Realizing Value

Imagine a domain name, website and/or blog that lead to the generation of substantial income each year, which could easily be taken over by someone else. It would be wasting a valuable estate asset to simply shut that down. Some websites are also used to sell e-books, hard copy books or other items. If the blog has photography or online videos, there could be the potential to generate revenue from licensing, making and selling art prints "on demand," creating books or having the files used in books created by others, or other ways of "monetizing" the files on the website.

Who knows better what the possibilities may be than the person who has maintained the site? That person may already have started to develop these projects, or may have ideas that have not yet been brought to fruition.

"Do Not Destroy"

The tendency of a Personal Representative or Trustee may be to have a hard drive "cleaned" and then donate the computer to charity, unless some other provision is made for it. The tendency to want to preserve privacy and confidentiality comes instinctively, but should be balanced against the need to keep some items for future reference. Who knows better than the owner of the digital data what should be done with it?

These days people routinely digitize things that are important to them: Important documents, tax returns, appraisals, receipts for collectibles, recipe collections, inventories of personal property, photos and videos. One family has gathered family photos from 150 descendants of a great-grandmother, including some which date back to the 1800's, and scanned them along with immigration papers and other family documents. This represents an archive which is of tremendous sentimental value and cannot easily be reproduced. Others will have family videos spanning decades of family history. Yet others will have research notes and partial text for novels or screenplays they have been working on for many years.

These should be identified as "Do Not Delete" or they will end up in "trash" and be gone forever, as the computer makes it way to a new owner or to high-tech recycling.

"Bequeathed" Information

Some of this information should perhaps be given to a specific person, whether that be one of the beneficiaries of the estate, the family genealogist who is not even among the beneficiaries, someone who will continue the business, or even a historical or ethnic society, a university, museum, or other archive.

100% Paperless and No Clues

Larry died suddenly of a heart attack and his family found his apartment barren of paper files. No paper bills, no paper bank or brokerage account statements. He had gone "paperless." Everything was done online and he had not left anyone a clue as to his accounts.

They knew about one email account and suspected he would have had bill paying notices and statements sent to that account, but after spending months to gain access they found no clues in that email box.

It turned out he had a second email account with another provider that he used solely for financial transactions. They located this email account only because by mistake he had sent one email message to his attorney using that account, and the attorney found the email in his inbox.

It took months to figure this out, and the family was extremely frustrated. Moreover, late charges had been incurred on accounts where payments had not been made on a timely basis.

How to Convince Someone to Address Digital Assets

What do you do if a person who is very ill is not inclined to spend time thinking about the details of preserving digital assets? To graphically make the point of how important it is to plan for digital assets, simply ask if they know, from memory, where all their valuable documents and files are on their computers, all the digital accounts they have, their usernames and passwords. If there is any hesitation, ask them to imagine how hard it will be for someone else to find everything they need, especially if it's a struggle for them now.

In those cases where the person uses a thumbprint scanner or other biometric device to access their computer, ask how you should access the computer if they die. The answer should lead to the immediate realization that some other solution is required to enable successors to access digital assets.

What If the Person Did Not Create a Digital Asset Estate Plan?

The discussion thus far addresses action items which apply when there is still time to obtain digital asset information from a person whose estate you are ultimately going to administer.

Next, let's assume we are no longer in "planning" mode, but in "cleanup mode." You weren't able to get the information during the person's lifetime, they are unable to help you, and now you have to deal with the lack of information. This discussion might more properly be included later in the book when we discuss how to find assets, but for the sake of preserving continuity, we'll address this topic here.

Do not be overwhelmed. As one person has said, "Life is 10% what happens to you, and 90% how you deal with it." Dealing with digital assets in the absence of a road map – accounts, usernames and passwords – can be a nightmare, but here are some suggestions if you find yourself in that position:

Preserve the Digital Data

Your first step should be to immediately secure the decedent's computers, backup drives, and hand-held devices. Put them someplace safe. The worst thing to do is leave them where intruders – or even household help – could get access to them.

We are aware of a case where the decedent's will left his entire estate worth several hundred thousand dollars to charity, and it took the Personal Representative a few months to get involved. By that time there had been a burglary in the decedent's house, and the bank account passwords (which had been left a in binder next to the computer) had been used to empty the accounts.

If you do not act quickly enough to secure the digital assets, not only might abuses occur, but some accounts deactivate if not used, and all data in the account could be permanently deleted.

Buy an external hard drive and make a copy of all hard drives, flash drives and other data and keep the backups in a safe, secure place. Hard drives fail, and you don't want to lose the data on the primary drive without having made a backup.

Attempt to Locate and Access Other Digital Assets

Consider the following methods of locating and gaining access to the decedent's digital assets:

Do some "detective" work yourself

Search the computer for a file named "passwords.doc" or which has "password" in the file name.

If you have access to the decedent's primary email account, look for notification emails from other digital assets accounts. These can permit you to prepare a digital asset inventory. The primary email account may also reveal personal emails with other information of interest. If you get access to email and social media accounts, review email lists and contacts and decide who is to be notified of the death.

You may be able to use the "forgotten password" feature to reset the password and thereby gain access to the accounts. See if you can reset the password. You may be able to answer the challenge questions. Try pet names, elementary school, favorite colors, first city of residence, mother's maiden name, first child's name. If you bring in a computer person he or she may know some tricks.

Check the history settings on the web browser for recently visited sites. Look for banks and other financial institutions. Then have the Personal Representative contact the institution.

Put Google Desktop on the computer, let it index the computer, then do searches of Internet bank names, regular banks and other financial institutions. It should pull up any file or email with the name.

Although you may be able to change passwords, do not close the accounts, shut down website hosting, or email services until you figure out exactly what you are going to do. Remove credit card information from online shopping accounts.

Get your arms around the person's online presence. You may want to identify some of the people the decedent has interacted with in social media, as they may be of assistance to you. Don't immediately close down sites or you could lose data which you may ultimately decide you want. If the digital data includes financial information of the decedent or third parties, such as clients, isolate all of that material and make sure it is secure. Ask your lawyer how to handle client information.

When you finally decide you are going to delete data or dispose of computers or hard drives or other memory devices, do it right. Make sure to follow forensic standards so data cannot be retrieved by others. In some cases there will be severe financial liability if you do not handle this correctly. For example, if the decedent retained client Social Security numbers in his or her business and "dumpster divers" retrieve that information from discarded computers which have not been properly wiped, there could be significant liability.

Hire a data forensics expert

Using a data forensic expert may be costly and time-consuming, and maybe even the expert will not be able to locate and access all the digital assets, but at least consider it if you have no leads.

Conclusion

The same concepts apply to handling digital assets as other types of assets. The problem, however, is multiplied by the fact that there can be so many types of digital assets, and they can be difficult to access without usernames and passwords, which are likely to vary, account by account.

As you can see, in most cases it will be far better to get a road map from the decedent than to have to start the job in a virtual vacuum, without any clues. Having the decedent discuss the matter in advance, and address the issues discussed in the first part of this chapter, will surely save countless hours of time and frustration in most 21st century estates. ■

Notes

"If no instructions are left, or preparations made, a deceased person's digital assets may be in limbo or, worse yet, may be lost forever."

— Anonymous

CHAPTER 4
Organ Donation; Funeral Arrangements

If organ donation is an issue, you should address it with urgency. We also show you why planning for the funeral involves much more than making a call to the funeral director.

Organ Donation

The first job of the survivors – even before the death occurs – is to determine whether any organs are to be donated, i.e., whether any anatomical gifts are to be made.

Who Can Decide on Anatomical Gifts?

Under the Michigan Anatomical Gift Act, an anatomical gift of all or any physical part of an individual's body for any purpose as specified in the law may be made by an individual of sound mind and 18 years of age.

In Michigan, the gift may be made on a driver's license, or state identification card, in a will or other acceptable gift document or registry, subject to certain execution requirements. The statute does not refer to gifts made in a trust, and so it would seem that a trust will not govern this issue. Query, however, whether a trust falls within the category of another acceptable gift document.

Generally, the gift document must be signed by the donor in the presence of two adult witnesses, at least one of whom must be a disinterested witness.

During a terminal illness or injury of the donor, an anatomical gift may be made by any form of communication addressed to at least two adults, at least one of whom is a disinterested witness. However, the physician who attends the donor during the terminal illness or injury may not act as a recipient of the communication.

Check the Will Without Delay

It is important to check the will, back of driver's license or state I.D., and other personal papers of the deceased as soon as possible, to determine whether there are any special wishes concerning anatomical gifts, funeral, burial, or cremation. Family members may also have this information.

If the donor cannot sign, the document of gift may be signed for the donor at his or her direction and in his or her presence. It must also be signed in the presence of two witnesses, who must sign the document in the donor's presence.

Delivery of the document of gift during the donor's lifetime is not necessary to make the gift valid.

An anatomical gift may be made to a specified donee or without specifying a donee.

What If the Anatomical Gift Is By Will and the Will Is Not Probated?

If the gift is made by will, then the gift becomes effective upon the death of the testator without waiting for probate. If the will is not probated, or even if it is declared invalid for testamentary purposes, to the extent that it has been acted upon in good faith the gift is nevertheless valid and effective.

How Can An Anatomical Gift Be Revoked?

If the will, card, or other document or copy has been delivered to a specified donee, the donor may amend or revoke the gift by any of the following methods:

- The execution and delivery to the donee of a signed statement.
- An oral statement made in the presence of two persons and communicated to the donee.
- A statement during a terminal illness or injury addressed to an attending physician and communicated to the donee.
- A signed card or document found on the donor's person or in the donor's effects.

Any document of gift which has not been delivered to the donee may be revoked by the donor as set forth above or by destruction, cancellation, or mutilation of the document of gift and all executed copies of the document of gift.

Any gift made by a will may also be amended or revoked in the manner as a will may be amended or revoked.

What If the Family Is Not In Agreement with the Anatomical Gift?

In the absence of an express, contrary indication by the donor, a person other than the donor cannot amend or revoke an anatomical gift of a donor's body or body part.

However, if a donor who is an unemancipated minor dies, a parent of the minor may revoke or amend an anatomical gift of the donor's body or body part. If an unemancipated minor who signed a refusal dies, a parent of the minor may revoke the minor's refusal.

Anatomical gifts are sensitive issues, and time is of the essence. If an anatomical gift is contemplated, make sure that the proper authorization has been given.

Making Anatomical Gifts

The demand for healthy organs vastly outpaces those available for transplantation today. In Michigan, about 3,000 people are waiting for a transplant and new hope for life.

Michigan shattered a record as 524,418 people joined the Michigan Organ Donor Registry in 2012. That was 31 percent higher than the nearly 400,000 who did so in 2011, and it brings the state's total to nearly 3 million registered donors

For more information on anatomical gifts, see the website of **Gift of Life**, the Michigan Organ Donation Program, **www.giftoflifemichigan.org.**

Funeral Arrangements

After addressing the possibility of organ donation, make all the necessary arrangements for the funeral, which can involve a myriad of details which should be addressed as soon as possible. If you are working closely with a funeral director, he or she will guide you through this process.

Who Has the Right to Make Funeral Arrangements?

Prior to the most recent amendments to Michigan law, there were long-standing problems concerning who can make funeral decisions and the appropriate jurisdiction when a dispute arose.

Now Michigan law places jurisdiction with the Probate Court, establishes who has priority to make funeral decisions concerning the disposal of a decedent's body, and establishes a procedure to resolve disputes.

The following is the order of priority to make decisions about funeral arrangements, including disposition of the decedent's body:

1. Surviving spouse;
2. Decedent's children 18 years or older;
3. Surviving parents;
4. Surviving brothers and sisters;
5. Next closest blood relative;
6. Personal Representative;
7. Guardian (if the decedent was under a guardianship at the time of death);
8. A county public administrator, if willing;
9. Medical examiner where the decedent was domiciled at the time of his or her death.

Note that the designated Personal Representative under the will does not have priority over family members. Also, the Successor Trustee under the trust does not have priority. Thus, for example, even though the children may be designated Personal Co-Representatives, the surviving spouse will have higher priority to make these decisions.

If two or more people share the rights because they have the same level of priority, then the majority rules. If the individuals are unable to come to a decision, or cannot be located, then a petition may be filed with the Probate Court in the county in which the decedent was domiciled at the time of death to determine who has authority to make these decisions. The petition may be filed by someone who has the right to make funeral arrangements, or the funeral establishment with custody of the decedent's body.

If you know the decedent's intent (for example, the decedent left written instructions for cremation), and the person with priority is not going to carry them out, consult your attorney. It may be possible to file a court action to rebut the statutory presumption of priority.

If you are dealing with a decedent in a state other than Michigan, consult a local attorney as the rules may differ substantially.

Making the Arrangements

While each family situation will differ, and religion and custom will dictate practice in some cases, you may find the following checklist helpful.

- Determine if funeral and/or burial prearrangements or prepayments have been made by the deceased. Determine if the decedent had a safe deposit box or used an online storage service which could contain this type of information.
- If there are differences of opinion within the family with regard to funeral arrangements, determine who has the legal right to make these decisions, as discussed above.
- Select the funeral home or funeral director.
- Arrange for the release of the body to the funeral home.
- If death occurred in another state or country, coordinate transport of the body with your funeral director, who can provide support and invaluable assistance in this process.
- Check the will or other papers of the deceased, and check with other family members, regarding special wishes (for example, possible desire for cremation, location for burial, nature of memorial service, and who will be pall bearers).

- Determine if there are family burial plots. If so, determine which space should be opened for the deceased.
- If there are no available family burial plots, determine where burial should take place.
- Decide the type of casket and burial vault or crypt, if any. Have a frank discussion about how much the estate can afford to spend. Guilt and grief often result in enormous funeral bills, compromising the estate's ability to pay other necessary expenses.
- Decide what clothing should be used for the deceased. (In some traditions only a burial shroud is used.)

Planning the Service

- Determine when and where the funeral or memorial service should take place.
- Determine whether to publish notice of the funeral in the local papers or online.
- Decide on the type of service (for example, religious, military, or fraternal).
- Determine who should speak.
- Decide on special readings, if any.
- Decide which clergy should officiate.
- Decide on honoraria to be paid to clergy and musicians, if any.
- Provide information for the eulogy.
- If possible, arrange a meeting with the clergy and the family, so that the family can share memories which may be incorporated into the eulogy.
- Ask the funeral director if a tape recording of the eulogy can be made available.
- Decide who will be pall bearers. Discuss this with them and make sure they are agreeable.
- Decide which charitable organizations or fund should be suggested to receive memorial contributions.
- Decide on flowers. If no flowers are desired, then provide a charitable organization or fund for memorial contributions in lieu of flowers.
- Decide on music, if any, for the funeral or memorial service.

Attending to Family

- Decide what items, if any, should be brought to the funeral home for the visitation period, or to the family home if there will be a visitation period after the funeral (for example, family photos, videos, and other memorabilia).
- Decide if therapy or grief counseling is needed immediately for any of the members of the family.
- Decide on clothing for yourself and children for the funeral.
- Make arrangements for young children during the funeral period.
- Decide on transportation for family and guests, including airport transportation if needed, and plan funeral car list.
- Consider having out-of-town relatives and guests met at the airport.
- Arrange lodging for out-of-town relatives and guests.

- Make preparations for the funeral luncheon or other meal, and food and refreshments at home for family and guests.
- If necessary, make arrangements for help at home, and extra chairs.
- Secure the residences of close family members during the visitation and funeral, particularly if notice is to be published in the local newspaper.
- Discuss whether transportation expenses of immediate family members will be reimbursed.

Post-Funeral

- Obtain the register of those persons who visited or attended the funeral from the funeral home, and send acknowledgment cards, if appropriate.
- Make a list of callers, floral tributes, those who provided meals and moral support, and charitable contributions, and send thank you cards.
- Ask the funeral director to order multiple copies of the death certificate.
- Obtain copies of the tape of the eulogy, if desired.
- Consider whether funeral expenses, if paid personally by family members, can be reimbursed by the estate or trust, and keep records of those expenses. ■

Correcting a Death Certificate

Certified copies of the death certificate will be needed for many purposes, including transferring joint property to the surviving joint owner, claiming insurance and other benefits, and filing with the federal estate tax return.

If a mistake has been made on the death certificate, you may have it corrected by filing an application, together with the incorrect death record, supporting documentation, and the required fee. You may download the application at **www.michigan.gov/documents/deathcorrpublic_6733_7.pdf.** The application may be filed by a funeral service licensee or next of kin.

CHAPTER 5

Notify Key People

Time is of the essence in notifying key people of the death. We offer checklists to make sure you don't forget anyone, tips on how to notify them, and how to avoid theft of the decedent's identity.

Prompt notification of key people is critical. It is important that everyone who should know about the death be provided timely information, so they can attend the funeral or visitation. Late notice or none at all can also come back to haunt you when people are miffed and interpret it as a sign of how you or the decedent felt about them.

If there is no listing available of all the people who should be contacted, you will have to develop one quickly. Enlist the assistance of family members, friends, and the decedent's associates from work if the deceased was working. Divide the list between several people, if necessary, to reduce the burden on any one person.

Check the decedent's computer or cell phone for a contact list, and Facebook or other social networking website for others who should be notified. Determine if a notice should be posted with details of arrangements.

Don't forget people who live out of town or abroad. They may not be able to come for the funeral, but in some cases they will, and in any event they will appreciate being notified.

Do keep track of your long distance telephone charges. They should be reimbursed by the estate, and if the estate is subject to estate taxes these expenses will be deductible, so Uncle Sam will pay part of the bill. Keep copies of your phone bills and highlight the charges. Also keep track of your time throughout the entire process. (See Chapter 22, "Should You Take Fiduciary Fees?")

Proper notification is also the first step in avoiding family conflicts. If someone who thinks they should have been notified is not, you may hear about it for years. Consider, also, if there are sensitivities in deciding who will contact certain people. "She couldn't take the time to call me herself" may be a refrain you wish to avoid.

In large families, delegate to certain people the responsibility of notifying others within their family. Impress upon your "team" the importance of following up if a person is not reached with the first call. Assure each of your helpers that their calls can be kept brief if they simply provide the necessary information.

Wherever possible, avoid using e-mail or leaving voice mail or messages on an answering machine. Even where the death is expected because of advanced age or a long illness, it can be very shocking to learn of a death in these ways.

In addition, when you leave a message on voice mail or an answering machine you do not know who will pick up the message or if it is received by the right person. It may be accidentally deleted, or may be heard or seen by someone who is ill equipped to deal with the sad news. If accidentally left at a wrong number the message could have devastating consequences.

Whom to Notify

The following is a checklist of various categories of people who should be contacted in appropriate cases (and not necessarily in this order):

- Relatives
- Friends
- Neighbors
- Clergy
- Employer
- Employees
- Household help
- Business partners
- Employers of relatives taking off work due to the death
- Pall bearers
- Religious, fraternal, and veterans' organizations
- Members of clubs, social, religious, hobby, and study groups
- Unions to which the decedent belonged
- Funeral director
- Newspapers regarding death notices or possibly an obituary
- Cemetery or memorial park
- Doctors
- Attorney
- Accountant
- Banker
- Stockbroker and/or investment advisor
- Life insurance agent
- The person who will care for the decedent's pets, or the pets of family members who may be busy with the funeral
- The Post Office, to temporarily stop delivery or forward mail, as necessary.

Consider Public Interest

If the deceased had an interesting life, for whatever reason, the local newspaper may want to run a feature-type obituary. You may wish to contact the paper to provide them the necessary background.

This type of story can provide an emotional boost to the family, and also act to transmit the values of the deceased to the broader community, via comments of family and friends included in the article.

Avoiding Identity Theft and Securing the Property

Identity theft occurs when someone obtains personal identity information of another person, such as official identification, name, date of birth and Social Security number, with the intent to unlawfully use that information to commit an illegal act.

Identity theft is often part of a larger criminal enterprise, and the theft of personal information is the fastest growing crime. If the decedent was a victim of identity theft before death, then he or she may have already contacted the appropriate agencies. If so, the appropriate person should notify them of the death.

Otherwise, the following is a suggested list of things to do so personal identity information doesn't fall into the wrong hands:

- Limit the personal information contained in any published death and/or funeral notices. For example, state only a town rather than an exact address, and list only the month and year of birth rather than the full date of birth. This will prevent identity thieves from gaining information to apply for credit cards, replacement driver's licenses and other forms of identity or credit.
- Hire an off-duty police officer or ask a trusted friend or family member to watch the home while the family is at the funeral. Identity thieves don't only steal personal information online; sometimes they take information in a breaking-and-entering.
- Notify all credit card companies and charge account issuers of the death. Follow up in writing, submitting the requested support documentation. Cancel or close accounts, as appropriate. (In some cases, the accounts will not be canceled because there is a surviving spouse.)
- Notify the following four major credit reporting agencies of the death to flag the account, so new credit cards will not be issued (a sample letter is provided at the end of this chapter):

  Transunion
  Fraud Victim Assistance Division
  P.O. Box 6790
  Fullerton, CA 92834-6790

  Experian
  P.O. Box 9532
  Allen, TX 75013

Equifax
P.O. Box 740241
Atlanta, GA 30374-0241

Innovis
P.O. Box 1358
Columbus, OH 43216-1358

- Stop pre-approved credit card offers from being sent by permanently opting out from these mailings. This can be done by calling **1-888-5OPTOUT (888-567-8688)** or online at **www.optoutprescreen.com**. Once a request for permanent removal is made by telephone or online, a form will be provided for completion and must be mailed in. The form is not available until personal information is first provided online.
- You may also contact the **Direct Marketing Association** to register a deceased person's name to be removed from commercial marketing lists, including pre-approved credit card offers. The registration may be done online or in writing, and all DMA members are required to eliminate the registered names from their marketing lists. The registration form can be accessed at **www.dmachoice.org**.

Other Considerations

- There are services, such as the **LifeLock Identity Alert**™ system, **www.lifelock.com**, which monitor many forms of credit applications for the misuse of the decedent's information. For a monthly fee, they will monitor for individual pieces of the decedent's identity in applications for credit cards, wireless services, retail credit, utilities, check reorders, mortgage loans, auto loans, and payday loans. They alert you by email, postal mail and, in some cases, by phone, of potential identity threats.
- Decide whether a notice of the funeral should be published in the newspaper. Some people are concerned that this could let potential burglars know that the decedent's residence, and the residences of close family members, will be unoccupied at a given time.
- Contact the state motor vehicle department to request cancellation of the decedent's driver's license, and to refuse any requests for replacements.
- Notify the appointed fiduciary to secure the home, and change the locks, if necessary.
- Prepare an inventory of the assets located in the home, or other property of the decedent (e.g., a vacation residence). This can be done by video or other photographic record, and may be crucial to preserve the ability to make an insurance claim, if something is stolen or damaged before distribution, or to protect the fiduciary against claims by beneficiaries. You may need to be able to prove that something was there, or that it was not there.
- Remove valuable tangible property and store it in a safe location.
- Advise relatives not to remove property from the decedent's residence.
- Advise anyone with signature authority over the decedent's personal bank accounts, or safe deposit box, that their authority has expired, and that they should no longer sign on those accounts or access the safe deposit box. Surviving joint owners of accounts with the decedent, and joint owners of a safe deposit box with the decedent, may continue to

use those accounts and access the safe deposit box (subject to consideration of whether true joint ownership was intended, a topic which is considered later in this book).

- Notify the homeowner's insurance agent of the death and occupancy status of the decedent's home. If a residence is left unoccupied, that could affect homeowners insurance coverage.
- Promptly remove mail from the mailbox. Thieves will steal mail and other important documents from the mailbox in an attempt to gather personal information. Depending on the circumstances, request a hold delivery of mail, or permanent or temporary change of address/mail forwarding card. Forms for both services, discussed below, may be completed online at **www.usps.com**.

The above list is not a comprehensive list of actions which must be taken, but is merely a guideline of some steps which may be taken to limit the risk of misuse or theft of the decedent's property or identity.

Dealing with the Mail

Sometimes it is necessary to either have the mail held or forwarded to another address, for various reasons. If no one is residing at the decedent's residence, it may be prudent to keep mail from piling up, as bills may not be paid, checks could be lost or stolen, or bank statements and credit card bills may provide information useful to identity thieves.

Accumulated mail may also be a signal to potential burglars that the house is unoccupied and thus an easy target. Even if the home is occupied, it could be that the person who is living there is not the one who should be dealing with the mail.

In any of these circumstances, consider either putting a temporary "hold" on the mail, or filing a change of address to have it forwarded to another address.

Filing a Request to Hold Mail

A request to hold mail can be submitted to the **U.S. Post Office** in several ways:

- File online at **www.usps.com**. You will need to enter your 5-digit ZIP code to verify that your post office works with the online system. If it does not, you will need to submit a request to hold mail using one of the other options available.
- Submit a completed PS Form 8076, ***Authorization to Hold Mail,*** at your local post office.
- Call **1-800-ASK-USPS (1-800-275-8777)**, where a representative can assist you.

A request to hold mail is not necessary for a post office box, as mail will be allowed to accumulate for up to 30 days.

Filing a Change of Address

If there will be no one living at the decedent's address, or if the mail should be forwarded to another address even if someone is still living there, consider filing a change of address with the post office.

PS Form 3575 , ***Change of Address***, is available for this purpose. It can be filed at the post office, but you will need to establish your authority to do so.

A change of address may also be filed online (you will need a valid credit card and valid email address), or by telephone **(1-800-ASK-USPS (1-800-275-8777)**, and in each of those cases a $1.00 verification fee is required. If you file online you need to make a representation about your authority, but you do not need to prove it. ■

Sample Letter to Credit Reporting Agencies

Re: <DECEDENT'S NAME>, Deceased
Social Security Number: XXX-XX- ____
Date of Birth: ____________________

Dear Sir or Madam:

Please be advised that <DECEDENT'S NAME>, the last four digits of whose Social Security number are indicated above, died on <DATE OF DEATH>. A copy of the death certificate is attached. <If there was a will or trust:> Also enclosed is <a copy of the letters of authority of the Personal Representative> OR <pages from the decedent's trust showing my authority as Successor Trustee>>. Please note the death in your records so that no new credit cards will be issued or other credit granted in the decedent's name.

Should you have any questions or require additional information, please do not hesitate to contact me.

Sincerely,
<Next of Kin/Personal Representative/Trustee, as appropriate>
<Address>

CHAPTER 6

Grief Support

Grief after a death is normal, but sometimes requires grief support. Knowing how to identify the need for grief support is the first step in dealing with it.

Why Grief Support?

The loss of a loved one will affect different people differently, and the ways of dealing with grief will vary from case to case, from person to person. You, the reader, may be the one who is grieving, or you may see that others around you are suffering. In this chapter we will make you aware of the possible need for grief support, and provide some sources of grief support services.

Why should a book on estate administration even touch upon the topic of grief support? This book is not only for Personal Representatives and Trustees, but also for the survivors. Our goal is to provide useful advice and tools to help you through the loss, whether on a financial level or on a personal level.

At the same time, a grieving Personal Representative or Trustee may become frozen, virtually immobilized. Comments may be made such as "It's too much to deal with," but the real problem will not be the enormity of the administrative task, but the inability to cope with the loss.

Tremendous prejudice may result to the estate, to the survivors, and to other beneficiaries if those responsible for administration of the estate are unable to function. Assets may not be gathered, tax returns may not be timely filed, decisions may not be made, and investments may be allowed to languish. The situation can go on for years.

The first step, therefore, is to realize that there may be a need for grief support.

Recognizing the Need

Each of us will react differently to a loss, depending on our relationship with the person who has died, our relationships with others, the depth of the loss, and our own physical and emotional makeup.

The effects can range from physical and mental, to emotional and spiritual. For some, grieving can bring with it symptoms not unlike those of depression, which can make it difficult if not impossible to care for oneself.

The person who is grieving may or may not be able to see changes taking place within himself or herself. However, you may see those changes within yourself or in others, and should be sensitive to any of the following:

- Changes in appearance.
- Changes in attitude.
- Changes in habits or patterns of behavior.
- Changes in belief systems.

First Steps

One of the first steps in grief support is probably to find someone with whom to talk about the loss. For some, verbalizing your feelings may be very helpful in moving through the grieving process.

Learning about the grieving process itself can also be helpful. Knowing that there are stages in grieving and that there is "light at the end of the tunnel," can attenuate the overwhelming feelings that accompany a loss. Truly believing the adage, "This, too, will pass," can provide a needed sense of optimism that eventually things will settle down.

Sharing one's feelings often helps the process. Communicating with others who have suffered a similar loss leads to the recognition that your situation is not unique and can be overcome. As you learn about grief – including what grief is – you will also learn answers to the following:

- Is there a time frame for my grieving?
- Are there common stages of grief that everyone passes through?
- When should I be really concerned about my grief, or the grief that someone else is experiencing?
- What help can I get, or give to someone else who is grieving?

Grief Support Sources

Grief support groups and services exist within every community. Each of the following will either offer grief support services or be able to provide referrals to other organizations:

- Churches, synagogues, and temples.
- Hospice organizations.
- Funeral homes.
- Hospitals.
- Community mental health centers.

In the appropriate case, a psychologist or other therapist can assist those suffering from grief.

The Internet has become a resource for grief support. To get an idea of the huge number of sites dedicated to grief support, you need only use your Internet search engine to search for the words "grief support." A recent search turned up over 400,000 sites which refer to this expression.

Many of the support groups you will find by doing such a search focus on the needs of those who have suffered certain kinds of losses. For example, they may deal with deaths of children, an infant, a twin, death in an airline crash, or from a certain cause. However, many of them provide general educational literature on the grieving process.

Many Internet sites also offer the opportunity to exchange views and feelings with others who have suffered a loss, either via email or in chat groups. Grief support professionals recommend these sites be approached with caution, however, as the person leading the online session may or may not be a qualified grief counselor or have mental health care training, and you may not be able to determine that person's background and training in these areas. ■

The Need to Heal

John and Maxine had been married 40 years when John suddenly passed away.

Maxine was first in denial, then became totally confused by all of the financial matters that required her attention. She refused to open mail, pay bills, or deal with the details of administering John's estate.

It was not so much the difficulty of the task as the grief she was suffering. With caring grief support, Maxine eventually adjusted to her situation and was able to go on with her life and attend to all those details which initially seemed so difficult.

Notes

"He that conceals his grief
finds no remedy for it."
— Proverb

CHAPTER 7
Gather Important Documents

The first step in estate settlement is to identify all the decedent's assets and liabilities. We offer helpful checklists, and places to look for assets which may never have occurred to you.

The Documents Tell the Story

In the great majority of cases, existing documents will be the starting point in administering the estate. While people may say what the decedent "intended," intentions which are not expressed in a written document are generally not sufficient to be legally binding. For example, under Michigan law, a will must be in writing and witnessed by two persons, unless the material portions are in the decedent's own handwriting, and it is signed and dated by the decedent. Such a will does not need to be witnessed. However, unlike a will, an oral trust may exist under Michigan law. A written document will generally override what someone says that the decedent wanted.

There are many documents which should be located to properly administer an estate. Family members can help locate these documents. The decedent's attorney or accountant, or business partners, may also be helpful to you in this search. Also, do not overlook the important information which may be contained on the decedent's computer, cell phone or in a virtual safe. See Chapter 3, "Passing On Digital Assets."

The following is a checklist of some of the documents which may exist. However, most of these documents will not exist in every case, so do not be overly concerned if you do not locate many of them unless you have reason to believe they do exist.

We recommend you make copies and preserve the originals in a safe place until it is determined what to do with the originals. Do not unstaple any documents for copying. A question could be raised about the authenticity of some of the pages. If it is not possible to copy a document without removing the staples or having the document come apart, then do not copy it. You may wish to scan the documents to make it easier to provide them to interested persons or professionals in the future.

We suggest that these documents be organized in manila folders, labeled to indicate the contents of each folder, one type of document in each folder, which are then stored in banker's boxes available at any office supply store. This will make it easier to store and transport the documents, and to retrieve them for future reference.

If you will be handling the administration of the estate on your own, the documents will form the cornerstone of your work. If you retain an attorney to assist you, the attorney will need to carefully review them.

If there is a safe deposit box, a surviving *joint owner* can access it. But if the box was rented by the decedent and there were only additional persons named on a card with permission to access to it, the box can now only be accessed with a Probate Court order, and only to determine if there is a will or burial deed. ***Petition and Order to Open Safe Deposit Box to Locate Will or Burial Deed,*** PC 551, is filed for this purpose. If the box contains these documents, the bank must forward them to the Probate Court. Nothing else may be removed from the box. A probate proceeding will be required to appoint a Personal Representative of the estate to gain entry to remove anything else.

Wills and Trusts

- Last will and testament and any codicils (amendments). This includes any document which is not labeled as a will but is intended as such. A handwritten note may, in certain circumstances, constitute a valid will.
- Prior wills, even though they may have been superseded. (They may be necessary in the event of a contest over the terms or validity of the current will.)
- Side letters with regard to disposition of personal property or other aspects of the estate.
- Trust instruments (for example, revocable trusts and any amendments, irrevocable trusts, qualified personal residence trusts, and irrevocable life insurance trusts). These trusts may have been created by the decedent, or by someone else and the decedent may have been merely a beneficiary or Trustee under these trusts. In some cases amendments may not be

Filing the Will

Under Michigan law, anyone who is holding an original will of a decedent is required to file it with the appropriate Probate Court with reasonable promptness after the death, by personal delivery or registered mail, or may be liable for damages, unless there is reasonable cause for not filing it.

The will should be filed with the Probate Court where the decedent was domiciled at death, even if there is no probate estate and no probate proceedings will be started.

labeled as such, so be sure to retain any documents which look like they are intended to amend or modify another document.

- Prenuptial and post-nuptial agreements and amendments.
- Durable powers of attorney. (Even though the power of attorney is not effective after death, it may still be important to show that certain actions by the attorney-in-fact or agent were authorized.)

Insurance

- Insurance policies and certificates of insurance for all types of insurance. This would include life, health, long-term care, accident, disability, homeowners (including lists of scheduled property), and any other insurance as to which the decedent was either the owner, beneficiary, or premium payor. See Chapter 11, "Life Insurance," for resources to help locate life insurance.
- Assignments of insurance policies or rights under policies.
- Split-dollar agreements.
- Life insurance beneficiary designations.
- Correspondence with insurance companies or insurance agents concerning changes in beneficiaries, policy loans, policy provisions, or other matters.
- Credit cards and some club and association memberships may provide life insurance coverage in certain cases. For example, they may provide life insurance benefits to cover the outstanding credit card balance. They may also pay death benefits in case of accidental death or in other cases. There may also be credit life insurance to pay off mortgage or auto loan balances.

Bank Accounts and Securities

- Bank account statements, certificates of deposit, and savings account passbooks.
- Check books and check registers.
- Canceled checks for the past six years. (Hold these for safekeeping; do not copy. See the comment later in this chapter regarding the importance of canceled checks.)
- Brokerage firm statements and mutual fund statements.
- Annuity statements.
- Shares of stock in certificate form and information on dividend reinvestment programs.
- U.S. government bonds (for example, savings bonds, and Series HH and I bonds).
- Statements with regard to bonds held in the U.S. Treasury Direct program.
- Foreign government bonds.

Why Keep Canceled Checks?

Canceled checks can be important for many reasons. For example:

- They could be requested by the IRS in case of an income tax audit.
- They may be needed to prove that the decedent paid off a debt.
- They may indicate that gifts were made which should have been reported on a federal gift tax return.
- They may also show that monies were considered loans and not gifts, or gifts and not loans, if so indicated on the check.
- They may also prove that taxes were paid, even though erroneously credited to the wrong account.

Real Estate

- Deeds to real estate.
- Shares in cooperative housing associations.
- Real estate tax bills.
- Mortgages of real estate.
- Title insurance policies; title searches; abstracts of title; title opinions.
- Closing papers with regard to purchases and sales of real estate or cooperative housing association shares.
- Land contracts.
- Real estate leases (business or residential).
- Documents with regard to purchase and ownership of vacation time share units, and obligations for payment of ongoing maintenance fees.
- Condominium association or cooperative housing association bylaws.
- Cemetery or memorial park certificates of ownership.

Vehicles, Boats, and Aircraft

- Vehicle and boat titles; aircraft registration papers.
- Logs of usage of business-related vehicles, boats, and aircraft, which may be needed in the event of an IRS audit.
- Vehicle, boat, or aircraft leases, and financing documents with regard to vehicles, boats, or aircraft.
- Insurance polices with regard to vehicles, boats, or aircraft.

Contracts and Obligations

- Leases with regard to personal property (for example, automobiles, equipment, machinery, computers, and telephones).
- Cellular phone service contracts and satellite radio contracts.
- Internet service provider agreements.
- Terms and conditions relating to credit cards, auto club, buying club, and other club and association memberships.
- Other contracts.

Tracking Down Frequent Flyer Points and Rules

There are companies which keep track of frequent flyer and other loyalty points. One of those companies, which offers this as a free service, is **Traxo, www.traxo.com**. If the decedent used this service, contact Andres Fabris, email andres.fabris@traxo.com, and mention you are a reader of this book. He will provide you a report of the decedent's loyalty points accounts, after receiving evidence of your authority on behalf of the decedent's estate or trust.

For a helpful table summarizing the rules of some of the major airlines, see **www.airfarewatchdog.com/blog/3802304/transferring-miles-from-deceased-person-frequent-flyer-account-to-an-inheritor-it-can-be-done-but-rules-vary-by-airline.html.** However, check with the airlines directly, as rules can change. For example, as this book goes to press Delta Airlines announced that it will no longer allow transfer of Delta Skymiles after death.

- Promissory notes, either made by the decedent or by someone else in favor of the decedent.
- Bank loan documents; guarantees made by the decedent or someone else in his favor.
- Warranty information.
- Frequent flyer and other loyalty account information. Points may be transferable in the event of death. Check with each airline and/or loyalty program administrator, as the rules differ from program to program and change over time.

Employee and Retirement Benefits

- Employment agreements.
- Independent contractor or consulting agreements.

- Employee benefits statements, summaries of benefits, and employee benefit plan documents. (These may relate to plans other than retirement plans, such as nonqualified deferred compensation, stock bonus plans, and phantom stock plans.)
- Pension, profit sharing, IRA, and 403(b) account statements.
- Beneficiary designations.
- Work papers and/or schedules with regard to computation of required minimum distributions from qualified retirement plans and IRAs (where the decedent was over age 70-1/2).
- Extended benefit payment elections made with regard to qualified retirement plans (the so-called "TEFRA Section 242(b)(2) election"). (This may have been made prior to 1984, to allow the decedent to take distributions from qualified retirement plans under rules then in effect, rather than be subject to the general rules which are now effective which prescribe that required minimum distributions must start in the year after attaining age 70-1/2.)

Tax Returns and Social Security

- Income tax returns of the decedent (federal, state, and local).
- Federal gift tax returns (Form 709).
- Foreign tax returns.
- Tax returns of any entity (closely held corporation, general or limited partnership, limited liability company, or trust) in which the decedent had an interest.
- Social Security earnings statements.
- W-2 statements and Forms 1099. (These are particularly important for the year of death, for income tax return preparation. They may also lead to other assets.)

Closely Held Companies

- Agreements with regard to entities in which the decedent was an owner (for example, shareholder agreements and buy-sell agreements, partnership agreements, limited partnership agreements, and limited liability company operating agreements or governing agreements).
- Stock registers and minute books with regard to closely held corporations.
- Documents with regard to any private foundation which the decedent operated. For example, the corporate minute book, IRS exemption letter, Forms 990-PF filed with the Internal Revenue Service, and filings with state authorities. In Michigan, filings would be made with the Michigan Attorney General, Charitable Trust Division.

Personal Property

- Appraisals of real estate, jewelry, art work, or other personal property which may be found in the files of the decedent. You may need new appraisals for various purposes, but old ones may be helpful, and may also cause you to look for the appraised property.

- Lists of valuable personal property, such as jewelry, art work and antiques, which may be attached as schedules to homeowner's insurance policies.
- Photos or videos of personal property which the decedent may have retained for purposes of insurance or identification of various items.
- Safe deposit box keys, and safe deposit box rental billing information. Take note of the location of any safe deposit box and box number. The safe deposit may be sealed upon death, unless there was a joint owner.
- List of any guns owned by the decedent, including serial numbers, and gun permits. (Guns should be held under lock and key for safekeeping.)
- Information with regard to people or companies interested in the decedent's collections, who may be helpful for purposes of appraisal or sale.

Vital Information

- Full name and any other names used; religious name, if any.
- Current address and previous addresses used over the last five years.
- Birth certificate, or date and place of birth.
- Father's name and birth place.
- Mother's maiden name and birth place.
- Driver's license or other state identification cards
- Social Security card or Social Security number.
- Medicare card.
- Health insurance card.
- Credit cards.
- Marriage certificate.
- Divorce judgments and divorce property settlement agreements.
- Military service discharge papers.
- Naturalization papers.
- Recent financial statements.
- Family tree or other genealogical information; a list of names, addresses, and relationship of closest living relatives (for example, spouse, parents, children, grandchildren, and siblings).

Finding the Assets

Some assets will be easy to locate, and some will be hidden, but others may be simply difficult to find.

As recently as a decade ago, a person's possessions – photo albums, bank account information, and important correspondence – were tangible and readily identifiable, and passed on to loved ones at death. However, as times have changed, so has the manner in which we store our personal information. Today, in many cases those assets and the information leading to them will be stored somewhere in digital format, on a computer, a backup drive, or on someone else's computer (in "the cloud").

The decedent may have shared user names and passwords with a trusted friend or family member. They may be in a desktop folder on his or her personal or work computer, or even in a 3 x 5 card box in the decedent's residence or at work.

The decedent may have even subscribed to a growing number of Internet services which store this information. Those websites generally make information available to the family after death, with various levels of security. If anyone in the family believes this type of service has been used, you should try to determine which service, and contact that service. See Chapter 3, "Passing on Digital Assets," for further discussion. ■

Hiding Places

While most people will keep their valuables in the bank or brokerage firm, in a safe deposit box, or home safe, some have been known to hide them in rather unusual places.

Attorneys, bank trust officers and Probate Court judges around the country have provided the following information about where Personal Representatives have found assets of decedents who didn't trust the usual places:

In kitchen cabinets; under the stairs; in electric wall outlets; in dryer vents; in cold air returns; tucked above heating ducts or rafters in the basement; taped under the bottom of desk drawers; taped on the sides of and behind dresser drawers; inside mattresses; inside upholstered furniture; wrapped in freezer paper and kept in the freezer; inside a drop ceiling; under loose wall-to-wall carpeting; under carpeting covering an interior stairway; inside bags, boxes, and books; inside stacks of papers and magazines; between towels and sheets in the linen closet; behind mirrors and paintings; under loose floorboards inside the main area of the house and in the attic; in secret compartments behind closets; behind a panel in a wall in a secret room; in a stack of plastic wash basins; in pickle jars in the basement; inside the hems of drapes; in clothing pockets; inside cabinets with false backs, or in boxes tucked away out of sight in the upper part of a base cabinet; inside reams of blank copier paper, or inside what appear to be books, in which a storage compartment has been made (filled with loose diamonds).

One attorney has even recommended that you mark off the backyard with kite string in one foot grids, then hammer a thin steel rod at least two feet down the center of each grid. You may be surprised to find metal boxes of treasure!

If the decedent was a hunter or outdoorsman, check nearby fields and forests for cash boxes hidden in tree trunks and rock crevices.

While the proverbial cookie jar has always been a place to stash cash, don't forget what appears to be a mayonnaise jar, which has been emptied of the original contents and painted white inside, then filled with cash, jewelry or other valuables. It may be sitting at the rear of a pantry shelf, or in the refrigerator, and the expiration date may be many years in the past.

CHAPTER 8

Who Should Administer the Estate?

Who settles the estate is determined by the will or trust, or state law. However, the documents may be challenged, or the person named may not want the job. Anyone who does serve must be aware of the risks and obligations.

A Word About Terminology

The term *estate* means different things in different contexts. There is the *probate* estate, which includes only those assets, if any, which were owned in the decedent's *sole name,* or which are specifically *payable to the estate* as a beneficiary, or which are distributed to the estate because there is no named beneficiary or the beneficiary is deceased (the estate is a default beneficiary). There may also be the *trust estate,* which includes any assets which are titled in the name of the decedent's trust. Then there is the *taxable* estate, which includes all assets which are included for purposes of possible estate tax.

Unless otherwise indicated, however, we will use *estate* in a general, non-technical sense to encompass all of the legal and financial affairs of a decedent. We will employ the term *estate administration* to refer to the process by which these affairs are wound up and brought to a proper close.

The estate is administered by one or more *fiduciaries*. A fiduciary may be an individual or an institution such as a bank or trust company. A fiduciary who is responsible for the probate estate is known variously as a *Personal Representative, Executor, Executrix, Administrator,* or *Administratrix,* under the laws of the various states. A fiduciary who is responsible for a trust of the decedent or a trust created by another person is called a *Trustee*.

Although we may be skipping ahead a bit, once you determine who will administer the estate, that person must establish his or her authority to do so, in order to be recognized by third parties. For Michigan probate estates, this is generally done by presenting *letters of authority* (issued by the Probate Court for a Personal Representative of the probate estate), or a *certificate of trust existence and authority* (for a revocable trust which became irrevocable on the decedent's death.) Ask your attorney about these documents.

The Michigan Trust Code ("MTC") was the first major change in Michigan probate law since the Estates and Protected Individuals Code ("EPIC") in 2000. The MTC was effective April 1, 2010, and applies to all trusts in Michigan, regardless of whether they were created before or after the MTC took effect.

However, the MTC is basically a set of "default" rules. A person setting up a trust (the *settlor*) has the ability to craft a trust that best reflects his or her wishes and avoid the application of much, but not all, of the MTC. Therefore, you must read the trust carefully to determine which provisions apply instead of the default provisions of the MTC. However, there are certain mandatory provisions which apply, for example, the duty of a Trustee to administer a trust, the powers of the Probate Court to modify or terminate a trust, require or dispense with or modify or terminate a bond, and to adjust a Trustee's compensation.

Consult an attorney knowledgeable in this area of the law to make certain you are administering the estate or trust correctly in accordance with current law.

As you will see below, an individual has no legal authority to act in estate matters solely by virtue of being the surviving spouse, child, next of kin or other close relative of the decedent.

It May Not Be Necessary to Admit the Will to Probate

Before becoming too concerned about potential issues regarding a will, determine if there is a reason to admit the will to probate. Is there property owned in the decedent's sole name, or payable to the estate? Is there a power of appointment under someone else's trust which must be exercised in a will admitted to probate?

If none of these circumstances exist, it may not be necessary to admit the will to probate. An anatomical gift contained in a will can be effective on death, without admitting the will to probate.

For example, if all property is owned by the decedent and someone else as "joint tenants with rights of survivorship," it will generally pass to the surviving joint owner, not under the will. Likewise, any property which passes from a funded revocable trust, or by beneficiary designation, such as life insurance or retirement plan benefits, will generally pass to the named beneficiary, not to the estate, unless the estate is the named beneficiary, or there is no living beneficiary and the policy or retirement plan provides that the benefits are then payable to the estate.

In the vast majority of estates being administered today in the United States, the decedent's property will pass under joint ownership or beneficiary designation, or from a trust, and there will be no reason to admit the will to probate. The contents of the will are not relevant, as nothing will pass under the will.

Is There a Valid Will or Trust?

Since the person who will administer the estate is usually named in the will or trust instrument, if these documents have been located you should first determine if they are valid.

Normally, the most recent will and any codicils are valid if they have been executed in accordance with the formalities required by state law in the state where the decedent lived when they were executed. The same is true of the most recent trust instrument and any amendments.

Generally, the decedent's attorney should be able to identify the most recent will and trust and account for all codicils and amendments which may have been executed. This is not always foolproof, however, as the decedent may have used more than one attorney. Other professional advisors such as the decedent's trust officer, accountant, or insurance agent may be able to provide clues. Family members may have recollections which might prove helpful. The decedent may also have drafted his or her own documents.

Check with the Probate Court in the county in which the decedent was domiciled during his or lifetime and at death, to make certain there are no other wills or codicils filed for safekeeping. Some courts may provide you with this information over the phone, but others will require you to personally visit and present a certified death certificate before confirming the deposit of the original will or providing you with a copy.

If a copy of a will is found but the original will cannot be located, you should proceed with caution and with the assistance of a competent estate planning or estate administration attorney. It is possible that the original was simply lost. But it is also possible that the decedent destroyed it with the intention of revoking it. Depending on which scenario is assumed, there could be different fiduciaries, different beneficiaries, and different property rights.

If you have found documents which you believe to be valid, bear in mind that your determination is not conclusive. The documents are subject to challenge by any person who has an interest in the decedent's estate.

Requirements for a Valid Will

Under Michigan law, a person must be 18 years or older and have sufficient mental capacity to make a will. In Michigan, an individual has sufficient mental capacity to make a will if all of the following requirements are met:

- The individual must have the ability to understand that he or she is providing for the disposition of his or her property after death.
- The individual must have the ability to know the nature and extent of his or her property.
- The individual must know the natural objects of his or her bounty.
- The individual must have the ability to understand in a reasonable manner the general nature and effect of his or her act in signing the will.

The will must either be signed by that person, called the *testator*, or by someone else in the testator's conscious presence and at the testator's direction. In other words, the testator himself does not have to sign it.

In addition, it must be signed by at least two individuals, each of whom signed within a reasonable time after witnessing either (a) the actual signing of the will by the testator, or (b) the testator's acknowledgment of his signature or acknowledgment of the will.

If the will contains certain acknowledgment language specified in the statute, it is considered *self-proved*, which will create a presumption that it is legally valid as to signature requirements, but still may be contested for other reasons, such as duress or fraud.

The mere fact that one or more of the witnesses are also beneficiaries of the will does not invalidate the will, nor does it automatically invalidate bequests made to the witness under the will.

In some cases, a document other that does not meet the general requirements for a will may be valid as a will. In Michigan, a writing in which the material portions are in the decedent's handwriting and which is signed and dated by the decedent is valid. It is known as a *holographic* will. Other writings may also be valid if it can be established, by clear and convincing evidence, that the decedent intended the writing to constitute his will.

Requirements for a Valid Trust

Under current Michigan law, the capacity to make a revocable trust is the same as to make a will. The trust used to require a different, higher standard, but the Michigan Trust Code made the will standard apply to trusts. If you are dealing with a document signed in another state, or if it was signed before April 10, 2010 (the effective date of the Michigan Trust Code), consult your attorney. There could be a different standard.

However, there are fewer formalities required for a trust than a will. No particular number of witnesses is required for a trust to be valid. Also, although most often a trust is notarized, that is not a requirement for validity.

Under Michigan law a trust does not have to be in writing; an oral trust may exist. However, the burden of proving the contents of the oral trust agreement will be on the person who is trying to enforce it. Even an unsigned trust amendment has been held valid in the appropriate circumstances.

Issues Applicable to Both Wills and Trusts

The following issues can apply to both wills and trusts. If you feel any of them apply to your situation, review the matter with your attorney:

- Do you have any reason to believe that the document may be a forgery? The fact that the document leaves the estate to people whom you did not expect to receive it may surprise you, or offend you, but is certainly not conclusive. In appropriate cases, your attorney will recommend that a handwriting expert be retained to determine the authenticity of the document.
- Examine the will and all codicils and any trust instrument and all amendments for possible irregularities, such as removal of staples, different kinds of paper, different type styles, words stricken out, or words inserted.

- What was the decedent's state of mind at the time the instrument was executed? Was the decedent legally competent? Was the decedent influenced by alcohol or drugs? Evidence of competency or lack thereof may be obtained from interviews with those who knew the decedent, including friends and family members, doctors, and nurses, as well as from hospital and nursing home medical records.
- Is there any indication that the decedent may have been subject to undue influence in the making of the will or trust? You should discuss your concerns with your attorney, who will assist you in gathering evidence to prove or refute undue influence, as appropriate.
- The Probate Court will look for a number of factors in determining whether there was undue influence, no single factor being determinative. Those factors might include the following:

    1. Was the signer very old or mentally weak?
    2. Was there a change from a prior disposition of the property?
    3. Are there benefits flowing to a nonrelative?
    4. Was the beneficiary involved in having the person sign the new document?
    5. Were the people who would be the "natural objects" of the signer's bounty disinherited?
    6. Was there constant association and supervision by the beneficiary, as when the beneficiary lives with or cares for the signer? Was there a lack of opportunity for others to visit the signer?

If the original of a will or codicil cannot be located, should a copy be offered for probate? Under Michigan law, if the contents of the will are known or a copy is available a petition may be filed to probate the estate on the basis of a lost will.

Time Limits to Challenge the Will or Trust

Whether you are considering challenging the will or trust, or are named as the Personal Representative under the will, or Successor Trustee under the trust, and are wondering if you are settling the estate under a document which could later be challenged, you should be aware that there are time limits for challenging a will or trust.

Challenging a Will

The time limit for challenging a will depends on whether the will was *formally* or *informally* admitted to probate. (See Chapter 17, "To Probate or Not to Probate.")

If the will was *formally* admitted, as a general rule the will must be challenged within 21 days after the date of entry of the order admitting the will to probate. If the will was *informally* admitted, then there is no stated time period to object to its admission. However, the longer one waits to mount a challenge, the harder it may be to reach estate assets, which could be fully distributed to beneficiaries.

Challenging a Trust

In Michigan, a person may contest the validity of a trust that was revocable at the settlor's death no later than two years after the settlor's death, or six months after certain information is sent by the Trustee to the beneficiaries, whichever comes first.

That information includes a notice containing information required by statute to notify the beneficiaries of their interest and their rights as to the administration of the trust. See Chapter 16, "Keeping the Beneficiaries Informed."

Providing the required notice to trust beneficiaries thus cuts the time limit to challenge a trust down from two years after the date of death, to six months from the date of the notice.

Who Administers the Estate If There is a Will or Trust?

If there is a will, one or more Personal Representatives are usually nominated in the document. Alternates are often named in the event the primary nominees are deceased or decline to serve. If a probate estate will be necessary, the nominated Personal Representatives should ask the Probate Court to admit the will to probate and appoint them as Personal Representatives.

You have no authority to act in estate matters by virtue of being *nominated* as a Personal Representative in the will. You may not act in your official capacity until you are *appointed* by the Probate Court.

As a general rule, do not enter into any agreements on behalf of the probate estate until you have been appointed Personal Representative by the Probate Court. However, to get matters started you may consult an attorney and sign a retainer agreement with the attorney as nominated Personal Representative.

Further, your authority extends only to the probate estate. Many times, the decedent will have arranged his affairs so that the bulk of his property is held jointly or in one or more trusts, leaving little or nothing in a probate estate.

If there is a trust of which the decedent was Trustee, the trust agreement will usually designate one or more Successor Trustees to serve after the death of the decedent. If you are the designated Successor Trustee, you should notify the holders of the assets in the trust that the decedent Trustee has died and that you are the successor. Under Michigan law you are obligated to notify the qualified trust beneficiaries within 63 days of your acceptance of trusteeship, the trust's existence, the identity of the settlor (the person who created the trust), the court in which the trust is registered (if it is registered,) and the right to request a copy of the terms of the trust that describe or affect the trust beneficiaries' interests.

The Trustee also has the duty under Michigan law to keep qualified trust beneficiaries reasonably informed about the administration of the trust and of the material facts necessary for them to protect their interests. Also, the Successor Trustee must notify them in advance of any change in the method or rate of the Trustee's compensation, unless the trust provides otherwise.

If a bank or trust company has been named Personal Representative or Personal Co-Representative, or Successor Trustee or Successor Co-Trustee, request the assignment of an administrative officer. From that point onward you will have a contact person to either take over the administration of the estate or handle it with you.

A Trustee may resign, either with court approval, or by giving at least 28 days notice to the qualified trust beneficiaries, the holder of powers of appointment, and all other Co-Trustees.

A nominated Trustee who rejects the appointment as Co-Trustee may still act to preserve the trust property, inspect or investigate trust property to determine potential liability and compliance with environmental laws.

Who Administers the Estate If There is No Will or Trust?

If the decedent left no will, and if there is any property in the decedent's sole name, one or more Personal Representatives must be appointed to administer this property under the laws of *intestate succession*. An *intestate* estate is one in which the decedent died without a will.

One or more family members should petition the Probate Court to appoint one or more Personal Representatives. (See Chapter 17, "To Probate or Not to Probate.") Under Michigan law, persons seeking appointment as Personal Representative in an intestate estate have priority in the following order:

- The decedent's surviving spouse.
- Other heirs of the decedent.
- After 42 days after the decedent's death, the nominee of a creditor if the court finds the nominee suitable.
- The state or county public administrator (under certain circumstances).
- A person nominated by another person having priority, and if two or more persons share priority then they must concur in nominating another person to act for them.

Do You Really Want the Job?

You must appreciate that administering an estate of any size except the smallest is a major undertaking. It will probably require significant work on your part, may last for two years or even longer, and can put you at odds with members of your own family.

To get a sense of what is involved, take a few minutes to scan the remaining chapters of this book. You will find that you will be responsible for dealing with attorneys and other professionals, determining who is legally entitled to the estate, inventorying and valuing assets and liabilities, providing full information (including periodic accounts) to beneficiaries, complying in some cases with the requirements of the Probate Court, managing assets, settling claims, assisting in the preparation and filing of tax returns, dividing and distributing assets and funding trusts, and a host of other related and miscellaneous matters.

Your Fiduciary Duties

A Personal Representative or Trustee has a fiduciary relationship to the beneficiaries. You must be aware that as a fiduciary (one holding a position of great trust), you will not be allowed to handle the estate as you wish, as if the property were your own. Rather, you will have a number of duties or standards of behavior imposed by statute or common law, including:

- **Duty to Exercise Reasonable Care, Skill, and Prudence:** You must use your best efforts in the conduct of fiduciary affairs.
- **Duty of Loyalty:** You may be unable to serve if you have a conflict of interest. You may not engage in acts of self-dealing.
- **Duty Not to Commingle:** You must keep the property of the estate or trust separate from your own.
- **Duty to Preserve and Protect Fiduciary Property:** You must act to prevent loss to fiduciary assets.
- **Duty to Make Property Productive:** You must see that fiduciary assets are invested.
- **Duty Not to Delegate:** You are not relieved of your responsibility by delegation of your responsibilities to others. In Michigan, you may delegate investment and management functions only if you exercise reasonable care, skill, and caution in selecting an agent and establishing the scope and terms of the delegation. You must also periodically review the agent's actions in order to monitor the agent's performance and compliance with the terms of the delegation. In addition, if there is more than one Trustee, by agreement of the Trustees a Trustee may delegate to a Co-Trustee one or both of the following:
    - Any power permitted to be delegated under Michigan law to an agent not a Trustee; and
    - Any power that can only be performed by a Trustee, if notice of the delegation is provided to the qualified trust beneficiaries within 28 days.
- **Duty to Deal Impartially with Beneficiaries:** You must act impartially in managing and investing fiduciary assets. Typical situations which can result in a breach of this duty are where a fiduciary wants to buy an asset from the estate, or buy out a beneficiary's share of the estate so that the fiduciary will end up owning the entire asset. This is fraught with problems, which you should discuss with your attorney.
- **Duty to Keep and Render Accounts:** You must keep records and account to the beneficiaries of the estate or trust.
- **Duty to Furnish Information:** You must keep the beneficiaries of the estate or trust informed.
- **Duty to Pay Income:** You must pay the income of the estate or trust to those who are entitled to receive it.

- **Duty to Act as a Prudent Person Would in Dealing with the Property of Another**: You must follow the standards of the Michigan Prudent Investor Rule, unless the trust provides that this rule does not apply. If the Personal Representative or Trustee has special skills or is named Personal Representative or Trustee on the basis of representation of special skills or expertise, the Personal Representative or Trustee is under a duty to use those skills.
- **Duty to Expeditiously and Efficiently Administer the Estate:** You have the duty to settle and distribute the decedent's estate (after payment of taxes, expenses of administration and claims, if any) in accordance with the terms of the will or the laws of intestate distribution, or the trust, which are consistent with the best interests of the estate.

You will be responsible to the beneficiaries for meeting these obligations and for the proper administration of the estate or trust. We will discuss some of the above duties further in the context of the particular task to be performed.

In connection with the administration of the estate, a Personal Representative or Trustee may employ an attorney, accountant, investment advisor, or other specialized agent or assistant, and may compensate them for their services without court approval. However, this does not relieve the Personal Representative or Trustee of the other standards of care, discussed above.

Regardless of how conscientiously you think you are performing your job as fiduciary, there are no assurances that the beneficiaries will find your performance acceptable.

You may be questioned, challenged, and even sued. If the Probate Court finds that you did not properly perform your duties, and the estate suffered losses as a result, you may be required to *personally* repay the amount of the losses to the estate. (This is referred to as being *surcharged* by the court).

You could even be removed and someone else appointed in your place.

If the court finds that you embezzled or wrongfully converted or refused to transfer trust property without colorable claim, you may be found liable for *two times* the value of the property converted or wrongfully withheld (so-called "double damages").

Even the possibility that any of these things could happen may be very upsetting, and a person should carefully consider these aspects before accepting appointment as a fiduciary.

Making the Decision

You have the right to decline to serve, regardless of your relationship to the decedent. However, you should not decline merely because you lack expertise in legal and financial matters. If a bank or trust company will be serving as a co-fiduciary with you, it should handle the technical details. Your role will then be to represent the family and participate in the discussion and resolution of any major issues that may arise.

If the decedent did not provide for a bank or trust company to act as co-fiduciary, it may be possible to *add* one if you wish. Banks and trust companies have the staff and expertise to assist in even the most complex estates.

If the estate is too small to merit a corporate co-fiduciary, or if you wish to minimize fees, with competent professional assistance you will likely be able to administer the estate or trust without serious difficulty, notwithstanding your technical limitations. (See Chapter 12, "Where to Turn for Help.")

However, if you do not have considerable energy, interest, time and patience, you should consider stepping aside. You should also consider declining if you live in a distant state, if you travel frequently, or if there is a particularly contentious family situation. Finally, if multiple fiduciaries have been named and it is agreed that having less than all of them serve would be more efficient, some of them can decline to serve.

Before you back away from this responsibility consider carefully who may take your place, whether that person can meet the challenge, and whether there are ways that you could fulfill your obligations by enlisting the help of others.

Was It An Honor?

Sally was honored when she learned that her late aunt had named her Trustee of her trust. But when she talked to her attorney and learned all she would have to do, she changed her mind, declined to serve, and let the named Successor Trustee serve.

If You Do Decline

If you are named in the will as Personal Representative, or have priority for appointment in an intestate estate, or are named as a Successor Trustee, and decide you do not want the responsibility, you have several choices:

- You can simply decline to serve and let someone else with priority serve. If there is a will or trust, whoever is named your successor in the will or trust will generally be next in line to serve. In an intestate estate someone else with priority may be appointed.
- There may also be a procedure in the document indicating how your successor will be chosen. For example, a trust agreement may indicate that if there is no successor willing and able to serve, the person named may be entitled to select a successor, or the beneficiaries may select one.
- If you have priority to serve as Personal Representative and decline to serve, rather than simply allow your named successor to serve, you may be able to nominate a qualified person to act as Personal Representative. If two or more people have equal priority, any

who do not renounce their right to serve must agree in nominating another to act for them.

- You could try to reach an agreement with the beneficiaries as to who will serve and have that agreement validated by the Probate Court.

Dealing with Multiple Fiduciaries

The will or trust instrument may, and often does, nominate more than one fiduciary. As indicated above, some of those nominated may decline to serve. However, if two or more fiduciaries accept appointment, there is an obvious need for cooperation. One fiduciary cannot act independently of the other. Unless the will provides otherwise, if there are two or more Personal Co-Representatives then the concurrence of *all* of them is required on an act connected with the estate's administration or distribution.

If there are Co-Trustees then they act by majority, unless a Co-Trustee is unavailable due to absence, illness, disqualification or other temporary incapacity or fails or refuses to participate in the administration following notice from the other Co-Trustees. Then the remaining Co-Trustee or a majority of the remaining Co-Trustees may act for the trust.

If there is both a probate estate and a trust, it is possible for each to have different fiduciaries. For example, the decedent may have named his spouse as Personal Representative under the will, but provided for a bank to serve as Successor Trustee of his trust.

Objections to the Appointment

If you are unhappy with one or more of the nominated fiduciaries, you should immediately seek the advice of an attorney. It may be possible to get the nominee to decline to serve.

It is often better to have the attorney approach the nominee than to attempt it yourself, especially if the nominee is a family member.

If the person does not agree to decline to serve, objections may be made to the appointment in a Probate Court proceeding. This will be a rare occurrence. The attorney and those with knowledge of the circumstances will have to persuade the judge that the person should not serve. Each case turns on its own facts, but the following might justify not appointing someone with priority or nominated in the governing document:

- If there is a history of acrimonious relations between that person and some or all of the beneficiaries, so that having that person serve will give rise to continued disputes.
- If that person is involved in a dispute concerning estate assets which creates a conflict of interest. For example, if the decedent created joint property with rights of survivorship with the person seeking appointment, and there are reasons to believe that the joint property should be an estate asset, but the person refuses to pursue that position on behalf of the estate.
- If that person has a criminal record indicating that he or she should not be trusted with estate administration.

If an objection is made to the appointment of a Personal Representative, the court may appoint anyone with priority, but in certain circumstances may appoint someone else. For example:

- If the estate is large enough to meet exemptions and costs of administration but not large enough to pay anticipated unsecured claims, creditors may petition to appoint *any* qualified person.
- If a person who is left something under the will or an heir who appears to have a substantial interest in the estate objects to the appointment of a person whose priority is not determined by the will, the court may appoint someone else. The person appointed would generally have to be acceptable to the devisees and heirs whose interests in the estate appear to be worth in total more than one-half the probable distributable value. If there is no person acceptable to these people, then the court may appoint *any* suitable person.

Removing a Fiduciary

Once a fiduciary has been appointed, removal is more difficult. An action must be brought in Probate Court requesting the fiduciary's removal. Grounds for removal would include a breach of one or more of the duties of a fiduciary. The fiduciary may also be removed if removal is in the best interests of the estate, the Personal Representative or the person who sought their appointment intentionally misrepresented material facts in a proceeding leading to appointment, or the Personal Representative disregarded a court order, became incapable of discharging the duties of the office, mismanaged the estate, or failed to perform a duty pertaining to the office.

As a general rule, repeated, flagrant breaches of these duties would be required for removal, although each case turns on its own facts, which should be discussed with an attorney.

While removal is a possibility, it is also possible that the Probate Court might not remove the fiduciary if the breach of duty was done innocently and if it is promptly corrected. However, ignorance of the law is no excuse.

If an order of removal is obtained, there is generally a transition period, which may be relatively long, involving inventories and accounts by the old and new fiduciaries, as well as the physical transfer of the assets.

Not All Property is Subject to Control by a Fiduciary

A Personal Representative has authority over property in the probate estate. A Trustee is responsible for property in the trust. However, joint property and any property with a named beneficiary, such as life insurance, annuities, IRAs, and retirement plan benefits, passes by operation of law and no fiduciary is involved, unless the estate or trust is a beneficiary.

It is therefore possible that major assets pass outside the will, to persons not even named in the will, or in proportions totally different than indicated in the will. It is also possible that no assets at all pass under the will.

Contaminated Property

Under Michigan law, the Personal Representative and/or Trustee may refuse to accept property in the estate if the Personal Representative or Trustee determines that the property to be transferred to the estate either is or may be contaminated by a hazardous substance.

In a probate estate, the Personal Representative may exclude real estate or an ownership interest in a business entity from the scope of the Personal Representative's responsibility for up to 91 days. This can be done if the Personal Representative reasonably believes the real estate or other property owned by the business entity is or may be contaminated by a hazardous substance, or is or has been used for any activity directly or indirectly involving a hazardous substance, that could result in liability to the estate or otherwise impair the value of property held in the estate.

The Personal Representative must identify the real estate or ownership interest being excluded and specify the time period of exclusion in filing his or her Acceptance of Appointment. If the Personal Representative has identified excluded property in the Acceptance of Appointment, the Personal Representative's responsibilities extend to the excluded property at the end of the exclusion period or upon the Personal Representative's notice to the court of acceptance of that property.

However, the exclusion can be extended if, before the end of the exclusion period, the Personal Representative requests the court to appoint a Special Personal Representative with respect to the excluded property or to exercise administrative authority over the excluded property by direct judicial order.

The Court then may appoint a Special Personal Representative with the duty and authority to collect and manage the excluded property, but only to the extent necessary for proper settlement of the estate and to preserve, account with respect to, and distribute or otherwise dispose of the excluded property as directed by the general Personal Representative or other court order, or directly administer the excluded property by judicial order without the appointment of a Personal Representative with respect to the property.

Similar provisions exist under Michigan law with respect to Trustees of trusts which own property which is or may be contaminated, or interests in entities which own such property.

For example, a Trustee may refuse to accept property in trust if the Trustee determines that the property either is or may be contaminated by a hazardous substance or has been or is being used for an activity directly or indirectly involving a hazardous substance that could result in liability to the trust or otherwise impair the value of the trust property.

A Trustee may decline to serve or resign as a Trustee if the Trustee reasonably believes that there is or may be a conflict of interest between the Trustee in its fiduciary capacity and in its individual capacity because of a potential claim or liability that may be asserted against the Trustee on the trust's behalf because of the type or condition of property held in trust.

The Trustee may also appoint an independent Special Trustee to hold title to, and take a reasonably required action relating to environmental law in regard to property tendered to the trust, until the time that the Trustee determines that no substantial risk exists, if the tendered property becomes part of the trust property, or abandons the tendered property. ■

Notes

"Trust yourself.
You know more than you think."
— Dr. Benjamin Spock

CHAPTER 9
Social Security Benefits

If the decedent received Social Security benefits, those will now terminate. However, steps should be taken to determine if benefits are available for the survivors, including the spouse and children.

Most of us probably think of Social Security in terms of *retirement benefits* we will receive after a lifetime of work. However, a portion of our Social Security taxes in fact goes toward insurance for survivors. If the decedent has worked and paid into Social Security, survivors benefits may be payable to certain family members. These include widows, widowers, divorced widows and widowers, certain children, and dependent parents.

In this chapter we describe how those benefits are earned, who may receive survivors benefits, the amount of those benefits, and what you will need to make a claim. We also provide contact information and further resources. This information is based on **Social Security Administration ("SSA") Publication No. 05-10084** (July 2012). As the rules change frequently, we recommend you get the latest edition online, and contact Social Security if you have any questions.

We'll refer to the decedent as the *deceased worker*, and to the surviving spouse (or surviving divorced spouse) as *you*.

Steps to Be Taken Immediately

After the death of a person receiving Social Security retirement benefits, you or some other family member or other person responsible for the deceased worker's affairs should do the following as soon as possible:

- Notify the **Social Security Administration** of the death by calling their toll-free number, **1-800-772-1213**, or visit any Social Security office. Call between 7:00 a.m. and 7:00 p.m. on business days to speak with a service representative or make an appointment. The lines are busiest early in the week and early in the month, so try to call at other times. There is an automated phone service 24 hours a day, but call first thing in the morning or late afternoon to avoid busy signals. Have the deceased worker's Social Security number at hand. If you are deaf or hard of hearing, you can call **Social Security's toll-free TTY number, 1-800-325-0778**, during the same times.

- If monthly Social Security benefits were being paid by direct deposit to the deceased worker's bank account, you should notify the bank or other financial institution of the death. Request the bank or other institution to return to Social Security as soon as possible any funds received for the month of death and any later months. Social Security benefits are not payable for the month in which a beneficiary dies. Therefore, for example, if the person dies in July, you must return any payment received in July or later.
- If Social Security benefits were being paid by check, don't cash any checks received for the month in which the death occurred or thereafter. You should promptly return the checks to Social Security. If you do that by mail, keep copies of the checks and your correspondence. However, it is preferable to return the check in person and obtain a receipt.

The **Social Security Administration** maintains an excellent website from which you can obtain the publications referred to in this chapter, and many others: **www.socialsecurity.gov**

Your local bank branch is experienced in what has to be done with Social Security when a deposit holder dies. Take a certified copy of the death certificate and meet with a bank customer service representative. He or she will do what is necessary to reverse any direct deposit and return any overpayment to Social Security.

How Survivors Benefits Accumulate

If the decedent earned enough Social Security credits, certain family members may be eligible for Social Security survivors benefits. A worker can earn up to four credits per year.

The number of credits necessary to permit survivors to claim benefits depends on the age of the decedent at the time of death. A younger person would need less credits than an older person for family members to be eligible for survivors benefits. However, no one needs more than 40 credits, or 10 years of work, to be eligible for Social Security benefits.

In some circumstances, lower numbers of credits are sufficient: Benefits can be paid to children and to the surviving spouse who is caring for the children, even though the deceased worker did not have the number of credits normally required. These family members can receive benefits even if the deceased worker only had credit for one and one-half years of work in the three years immediately prior to death.

Who is Eligible for Survivors Benefits?

The following is a very brief overview of eligibility for survivors benefits. You will find it most useful to discuss your particular situation with a Social Security representative.

As of 2012, Social Security survivor benefits may be payable to the following categories of family members:

Widow or Widower

Full benefits are payable at age 66 for individuals born in 1945-1956, and will gradually increase to age 67 for individuals born in 1962 or later. If the widow or widower was born in 1945-1956, reduced benefits may be payable as early as age 60.

A disabled widow or widower may receive benefits as early as age 50.

The surviving spouse's benefits may be reduced if he or she also receives a pension from employment where Social Security taxes were not withheld. Further information on this reduction is available in **SSA Publication No. 05-10007 ("Government Pension Offset")** and **SSA Publication No. 05-10045 ("Windfall Elimination Provision")**, both of which are available on the Social Security website.

A widow or widower may be entitled to benefits at any age if he or she takes care of the decedent's child who is under age 16 or who is disabled and receives benefits.

Unmarried or Disabled Children

Unmarried children under age 18 (or up to age 19 if they are full-time students in elementary or secondary school) may be entitled to benefits. Also, children of the decedent may be eligible for benefits, regardless of age, if they were disabled before age 22 and remain disabled. Under certain circumstances, benefits can also be paid to stepchildren, grandchildren, step grandchildren or adopted children. Discuss these situations with a Social Security representative.

Dependent Parents

Dependent parents age 62 or older may also be eligible for benefits. To qualify as dependent parents eligible for survivor benefits, the decedent would have had to have provided at least one-half of their support.

Special One-Time Death Benefit

The surviving spouse or minor children of the deceased worker may be eligible for a special one-time death benefit of $255, if the deceased worker has enough work credits. This amount is payable to the surviving spouse if he or she was living with the deceased worker at the time of death. However, the benefit may still be payable if they were living apart and the surviving spouse was receiving Social Security benefits on the deceased worker's earnings record.

If there is no surviving spouse, the amount may be payable to a child who was eligible for benefits on the deceased worker's earnings record in the month of death.

Benefits Available for Surviving Divorced Spouses

If the deceased worker was divorced, the former husband or wife should be able to receive benefits as a widow or widower if the marriage lasted 10 years or more. However, the length-of-marriage rule will not apply if the former spouse is caring for a child of the deceased worker under age 16 or disabled and who is also receiving benefits on the deceased worker's Social Security record. The child must be the natural child of the former spouse, or legally adopted by the former spouse.

Any benefits paid to a surviving former spouse who is age 60 or older (50-60 if disabled) will not affect the benefit rates for other survivors who may be receiving benefits. However, if you are the surviving divorced mother or father who has the deceased worker's child under age 16 or disabled child in your care, your benefit will affect the amount of the benefits of others on the worker's record.

Applying for Benefits

How a survivor should apply for survivors benefits depends on whether the survivor is receiving other benefits from Social Security.

Survivors Not Already Receiving Social Security

A survivor who is not already getting Social Security benefits should apply for survivors benefits promptly because, in certain cases, benefits will not be retroactive, i.e., they will be paid from the time of application, not from the date the worker died. You may apply by calling Social Security or at any Social Security office. Local offices are listed in your telephone directory in the Government Offices section.

Certain information and documents will be required to process the application. While it will be helpful if you have everything at the time of application, don't delay just because you're missing something. Social Security will work with you to get the process started, and you can provide the missing documents later. You will need either original documents or copies certified by the agency that issued them.

The information you will need includes the following:

- Proof of death (either a death certificate or proof of death from the funeral home).
- Social Security numbers of the deceased worker and the survivor.
- The survivor's birth certificate.
- Marriage certificate, if the survivor is a widow or widower.
- Divorce papers, if the survivor is applying as a surviving divorced spouse.
- Dependent children's Social Security numbers and birth certificates, if available.
- The deceased worker's W-2 forms or federal self-employment tax return for the most recent year.
- The name of the bank or other financial institution and account number to which the benefits can be directly deposited.

Survivors Already Receiving Benefits

If the survivor is already receiving benefits as a wife or husband on the deceased worker's record at the time of death, report the death to Social Security and they will change the payments to survivors benefits. They will contact you if they need further information.

If the survivor is receiving benefits on his or her own work record, it will be necessary to complete an application for survivors benefits. It may be possible to obtain increased benefits as a widow or widower. Ask about this when you call or visit the Social Security office. The deceased worker's death certificate will be necessary to process the claim.

Benefits for any children will automatically be changed to survivors benefits after the death is reported to Social Security. They will contact you if they need more information.

What is the Amount of Benefits?

The amount of the benefits that family members can expect to receive from Social Security will depend on the deceased worker's average lifetime earnings: The higher the earnings, the higher the benefits. A Social Security Statement sent annually to each worker age 25 or older provides an estimate of survivorship, retirement and disability benefits together with other important information.

The amount of the benefits is a percentage of the deceased worker's basic Social Security benefit, based on age and the type of benefit for which the worker was eligible. Here are some typical percentages:

- Widow or widower, at full age of retirement age or older, generally 100%
- Widow or widower, age 60 or older, but under full retirement age: 71½% to 99%
- Widow or widower, any age, with a child under age 16: 75%
- Children, under the age of 18 (19 if still in elementary or secondary school) or disabled: 75%

There are disadvantages and advantages to taking your survivors benefit before your full retirement age. The advantage is that you collect benefits for a longer period of time, but the disadvantage is that your survivors benefit may be permanently reduced.

Contact a Social Security representative to discuss the amount of benefits in your specific situation.

Are There Maximum Benefits Payable to a Family?

There is a maximum amount of Social Security benefits that can be paid to a survivor and members of the family each month. The limit varies, but as a general rule will be about 150%-180% of the deceased worker's benefit rate. If the sum of the benefits payable to the family members exceeds the limit, benefits will be reduced.

Retirement Benefits for Widows and Widowers

If a widow or widower (including a divorced widow or widower) is receiving benefits, it is possible to switch over to his or her own retirement benefit as early as age 62. The person must be eligible and his or her retirement rate must be higher than the widow or widower rate. It may even be possible for a widow or widower to begin receiving one benefit at a reduced rate and then switch to the other benefit at an unreduced rate at age 65.

The rules are complicated and vary depending on the situation, so the best thing to do is discuss the matter with a Social Security representative.

Effect of Survivor's Earnings on Benefits

A person can receive survivors benefits and work at the same time. But if the person receiving survivors benefit is younger than full retirement age and earns more than certain amounts, the survivors benefits will be reduced.

If a person was born between January 2, 1943 and January 1, 1955, then full retirement age is 66. If the survivor works and is full retirement age or older, the person may keep all of the survivors benefits, no matter how much he or she earns. If the survivor is younger than full retirement age, there is a limit to how much he or she can earn and still receive full Social Security benefits.

For example, if a person is younger than full retirement age during all of 2013, Social Security will deduct $1 from the person's benefits for each $2 earned above $15,120. If the person reaches full retirement age during 2013, Social Security will deduct $1 from Social Security benefits for each $3 the person earns above $40,080 until the month he or she reaches full retirement age.

Also, the survivor's earnings will reduce only survivors benefits; they will not reduce the benefits of other family members.

For further information and examples, see the current edition of **SSA Publication No. 05-10069 ("How Work Affects Your Benefits")**.

What if the Survivor Remarries?

As a general rule, you cannot receive survivors benefits if you remarry before age 60. However, remarriage after age 60 (age 50 if disabled) will not prevent benefit payments on your former spouse's record. Also, at age 62 or older you may get benefits on the record of your new spouse if they are higher.

Dealing with Social Security

The Social Security Administration has made every effort to streamline the process by use of toll-free telephone numbers and offices located across the nation. They also have a website (www.socialsecurity.gov) from which you can download important information, including the publications mentioned in this chapter.

If you ask someone to contact Social Security on your behalf, you should know that since your personal information is involved, Social Security will be concerned with preserving your confidentiality. It is best that you be on the phone with them to give your permission to discuss your situation. If you have someone visit a Social Security office on your behalf, send a written consent in a simple letter. Otherwise, the Social Security representative will be unable to discuss the specifics of your situation with that person.

In the case of a minor child, the natural parent or legal guardian can act on the child's behalf in dealing with Social Security with regard to the child's benefits.

Do You Need Help?

In most cases you will be able to satisfactorily process your claim to Social Security benefits on your own.

However, if you have serious concerns about how your claim is being handled, or if you disagree with a decision on your claim, you can appeal. The necessary steps are explained in **SSA Publication No. 05-10041 ("The Appeals Process")**. You may want to consult an attorney specializing in Social Security matters. More information can be found in **SSA Publication No. 05-10075 ("Your Right to Representation")**. Ask the attorney assisting with estate administration or your local bar association for a referral. ■

Notes

"The test of our progress is not whether we add more to the abundance of those who have much; it is whether we provide enough for those who have little."

— Franklin Delano Roosevelt

CHAPTER 10

Veteran's Benefits

Various types of benefits may be available for survivors of veterans. Here we provide an overview of an extremely complex system, and sources of further information and assistance.

Survivors of veterans may be entitled to various burial-related benefits. Survivors' benefits are also available, but in relatively limited circumstances. In this chapter we provide a general overview of benefits available, eligibility, and sources of further information and assistance in filing applications for benefits.

For the most part, veteran's benefits are not paid automatically, but only upon filing a claim. Claims must generally be filed within two years after permanent burial or cremation.

The following information is based upon the **Department of Veterans Affairs (VA) manual, "A Survivor's Guide to Benefits"** (February 29, 2012), the latest edition of which may be obtained from the VA or downloaded on the Internet. The burial benefits available will differ based on whether the burial occurs in a national cemetery or a private cemetery. In most instances veterans are entitled to a government headstone, a burial flag, and a Presidential Memorial Certificate. To confirm eligibility for burial in a VA national cemetery you must call your local VA regional office.

You may also call the **VA toll-free at 1-800-827-1000** to discuss survivor benefits.

Burial Flag

A United States flag is available for most veterans at no cost. The flag may be given to the next of kin or friend of the decedent. Reservists entitled to retired pay are also eligible to receive a burial flag.

When burial is in a national, state, or post cemetery a burial flag will be provided by the cemetery. When burial is in a private cemetery, burial flags may be obtained through VA regional offices, national cemeteries, and most U.S. post offices by completing VA Form 21-2008, ***Application for***

United States Flag for Burial Purposes, and submitting it with a copy of the veteran's discharge papers (such as a DD Form 214 , or verification of service from the veteran's service department or VA) at any of these locations.

If the decedent was a veteran, your funeral director may be able to assist you in obtaining a burial flag.

Veteran's Benefits Resource

The **Department of Veteran's Affairs** website is located at **www.va.gov.** The full text of the VA manual, "**A Survivor's Guide to Benefits**" may be downloaded free.

The VA has a one-stop service inquiry page: **https://iris.custhelp.com/**

This provides information on where to get forms, whom to contact on specific issues, and answers to frequently asked questions on veteran's benefits. Search for "survivor benefits".

Presidential Memorial Certificate

A Presidential Memorial Certificate is an engraved paper certificate, signed by the current President, to honor the memory of honorably discharged deceased veterans.

Eligible recipients include the next of kin and loved ones of honorably discharged deceased veterans. More than one certificate may be provided.

Eligible recipients, or someone acting on their behalf, may apply for a certificate in person at any VA regional office or by U.S. mail or toll-free fax. Requests cannot be sent by email. You should enclose a copy of the veteran's discharge and death certificate to verify eligibility. Submit copies only, not originals, as any original documents will not be returned.

VA Form 40-0247, ***Application for Presidential Memorial Certificate***, is used to apply and is available on the VA website, with instructions on how to submit the form. Search for 40-0247. You may also call 1-202-565-4964 for further information.

Reimbursement of Burial Expenses

Federal Benefits

VA burial allowances are partial reimbursements of an eligible veteran's burial and funeral costs. When the cause of death is not service-related, the reimbursements are generally described as two payments: (1) a burial and funeral expense allowance, and (2) a plot or interment allowance.

Eligibility

You may be eligible for a VA burial allowance if *all* of the following requirements are satisfied:

- You paid for the veteran's burial or funeral;
- You have not been reimbursed by another government agency or some other source, such as the deceased veteran's employer; and
- The veteran was discharged under conditions other than dishonorable.

In addition, *at least one* of the following conditions must be met:

- The veteran died because of a service-related disability; or
- The veteran was receiving VA pension or compensation at the time of death; or
- The veteran was entitled to receive VA pension or compensation, but decided not to reduce his or her military retirement or disability pay; or
- The veteran died while hospitalized by the VA, or while receiving care under VA contract at a non-VA facility; or
- The veteran died while traveling under proper authorization and at VA expense to or from a specified place for the purpose of examination, treatment, or care; or
- The veteran had an original or reopened claim pending at the time of death and has been found entitled to compensation or pension from a date prior to the date or death; or
- The veteran died on or after October 9, 1996, while a patient at a VA-approved state nursing home.

Amount of Benefits–Service-Related Deaths

The VA will pay up to $2,000 toward burial expenses for service-related deaths on or after September 11, 2001. The VA will pay up to $1,500 for deaths prior to September 10, 2001. If the veteran is buried in a VA national cemetery, some or all of the cost of transporting the deceased may be reimbursed.

Non-Service-Related Deaths

For deaths on or after October 1, 2011, the VA will pay up to $700 toward burial and funeral expenses (if hospitalized by the VA at time of death), or $300 toward burial and funeral expenses (if not hospitalized by the VA at time of death), and a $700 plot-interment allowance (if not buried in a national cemetery).

For deaths on or after December 1, 2001, but before October 1, 2011, the VA will pay up to $300 toward burial and funeral expenses and a $300 plot-interment allowance. The plot interment allowance is $150 for deaths prior to December 1, 2001.

If the death occurred while the veteran was in a VA hospital or under VA contracted nursing home care, some or all of the costs for transporting the veteran's remains may be reimbursed. An annual increase in burial and plot allowances, for deaths occurring after October 1, 2011, begins in fiscal year 2013 based on the Consumer Price Index for the preceding 12-month period.

There is no time limit for filing reimbursement claims of service-related deaths. In other deaths, claims must be filed within two years after permanent burial or cremation. Burial expenses paid by the decedent's employer or a state agency will not be reimbursed.

How to Apply

VA Form 21-530, ***Application for Burial Benefits***, is used to apply for these benefits. Attach a copy of the veteran's military discharge document (DD 214 or equivalent), death certificate, funeral and burial bills, which should show that they have been paid in full. This form may be downloaded at www.va.gov/vaforms.

State Benefits

Many states provide benefits to veterans. To find out more about what is available from a particular state, go to the following website: www.va.gov/statedva.htm

There you will find a list of states and territories, and by clicking on a particular state or territory you will be directed to a website which generally describes services provided and benefits available, along with contact information.

County Benefits

Additional burial-related benefits may be available through the Veterans Affairs office in the county of residence. You should determine if these benefits are available by contacting the county office.

Sometimes county offices handle not only county benefits, but VA benefits as well. Personnel in these offices are very experienced and knowledgeable. In addition, various veterans organizations have service officers who will provide assistance with benefits. Contact information is available at the VA website indicated under "State Benefits" above.

Survivors' Benefits

Veterans' survivors are provided benefits in relatively limited circumstances. These are administered by the Veterans Benefits Administration (VBA), part of the U.S. Department of Veterans Affairs. The rules are relatively detailed and are subject to change. The following information was obtained from the VBA web site.

Dependency and Indemnity Compensation

Dependency and Indemnity Compensation (DIC) payments may be available for surviving spouses who have not remarried, unmarried children under 18, helpless children, those between 18 and 23 if attending a VA-approved school, and low-income parents of deceased service members or veterans.

Eligibility

To be eligible, the death must not have been the result of willful misconduct and must have resulted from one of the following:

- A disease or injury incurred or aggravated while on active duty or active duty for training;
- An injury incurred or aggravated in the line of duty while on inactive duty training; or
- A disability compensable by the VA.
- If a spouse remarries, eligibility for benefits may be restored if the marriage is terminated later by death, divorce, or annulment.

DIC payments also may be authorized for survivors of veterans who were totally service-connected disabled at the time of death, but whose deaths were not the result of their service-connected disability. The survivor may qualify if:

- The veteran was continuously rated totally disabled for a period of ten or more years immediately preceding death; or
- The veteran was so rated for a period of at least five years from the date of military discharge.
- Payments under this provision are subject to offset by the amount received from judicial proceedings brought on account of the veteran's death. The discharge must have been under conditions other than dishonorable.

DIC Payments to Surviving Spouse

Benefits are payable to eligible surviving spouses of veterans. The current rate is $967 per month. This amount may increase if there are dependent children. You may call 1-800-827-1000 for information about rates paid to eligible children.

DIC Payments to Parents and Children

The monthly payment for parents of deceased veterans depends upon their income. There are additional DIC payments for dependent children. A child may be eligible if there is no surviving spouse, and the child is unmarried and under age 18, or if the child is between the age of 18 and 23 and attending school.

Special Allowances

Surviving spouses and parents receiving DIC may be granted a special allowance to pay for aid and attendance by another person if they are patients in a nursing home or require the regular assistance of another person.

Surviving spouses receiving DIC may be granted a special allowance if they are permanently house bound.

Survivors Benefit Plan (SBP)

DIC payments are affected by the receipt of SBP benefits. Consult a benefits counselor at the VA Regional Office that serves your area for more details.

How to Apply

Obtain a copy of VA Form 21-534, ***Application for Dependency and Indemnity Compensation, Death Pension and Accrued Benefits by a Surviving Spouse or Child (Including Death Compensation if Applicable)***, from the VA or the website. Fill in the required information and mail the form to the VA Regional Office that serves your area.

Your VA benefits will generally relate back to the date the VA receives your application for benefits. Your date of application is therefore important to you, and you should apply as soon as possible, even if you do not have all the required supporting evidence or documents. You can complete your file later.

The following supporting evidence and/or documents should be submitted with your application, if available:

- **Dependency Documents**: Original or a copy of birth and marriage certificates and copies of divorce/death records terminating all prior marriages for veteran and spouse. Parents applying for DIC should furnish the original or a copy of the veteran's birth certificate.
- **Military Discharge**: DD Form 214 (Copy 4–Member Copy). Those applicants who have a copy of their DD Form 214 are encouraged to provide a copy with their claim to expedite processing. Otherwise, the VA will attempt to obtain verification from the service department. Copies of missing DD Forms 214 may be obtained from the National Personnel Records Center in St. Louis, Missouri through the **National Archives and Records Administration** (NARA) website, **www.archives.gov.**
- **Certification of Death**: Copy of the veteran's death certificate.

Veteran's Aid and Attendance Benefit

In some cases, the surviving spouse of a veteran may be entitled to additional monthly benefits under the Veterans' Aid and Attendance Benefit to help pay medically-related expenses associated with the need for the regular assistance of another person to maintain their safety and general welfare.

This assistance or care can be provided in one's own home (or the home of a family member), or even an independent living facility.

In order to qualify, the veteran must have served a minimum of 90 days in active duty, with one of the 90 days of active duty served during wartime, and the survivor must meet certain income and asset criteria. Generally, applicants must have less than $90,000 in assets, excluding their home and vehicles. This amount is subject to change.

The surviving spouse of the veteran must meet certain disability requirements to qualify:

- The aid of another person is needed in order to perform personal functions required in everyday living, such as bathing, feeding, dressing, toileting, adjusting prosthetic devices, or protecting himself or herself from the hazards of his/her daily environment; or
- The claimant is bedridden, in that his or her disability or disabilities require that the claimant remain in bed apart from any prescribed course of convalescence or treatment; or
- The claimant is in a nursing home due to mental or physical incapacity; or
- The claimant is blind, or nearly blind, as defined under the applicable rules.

Determining eligibility and the amount of the benefit is complicated. You should consult with a VA accredited attorney or contact the VA to determine whether the surviving spouse may qualify based on income and assets, and if so, the level of Veterans' Aid and Attendance Benefit.

VA Accredited Counsel

The VA requires that anyone who assists a veteran or family member with the preparation, presentation and prosecution of a claim for benefits be accredited by and through the VA before they can legally provide assistance.

Thus, to protect yourself while going through the VA process, make sure you are using an accredited person. To check if a person is accredited, go to: www.va.gov/ogc/apps/accreditation/index.asp and type their name for confirmation.

A one time agent – usually a family member – does not need to be accredited. ■

Notes

"The willingness with which our
young people are likely to serve
in any war, no matter how justified,
shall be directly proportional to
how they perceive veterans of early wars
were treated and appreciated by our nation."

— George Washington

CHAPTER 11
Life Insurance

Death benefits under life insurance can provide much needed cash. However, it's not always easy to find the insurance or to determine who is legally entitled to the benefits.

What Life Insurance Is In Effect?

There is no centralized agency or database that tracks life insurance sold in the United States. Unfortunately, life insurance beneficiaries cannot make a claim without at least knowing the name of the company that issued the policy. The insurance company has no way to know that the insured died, and you should not expect that the insurance company will contact the beneficiaries. Consumer Reports magazine reported in February, 2013 that at least $1 billion from misplaced or forgotten life insurance policies is waiting to be claimed by beneficiaries, and that the average unclaimed life benefit is $2,000 – with some payouts as high as $300,000.

Hopefully, the decedent left a complete schedule of life insurance policies, with company name, policy number and the amount of the death benefit. In that case, it will be very easy to locate all of the life insurance policies and certificates of group insurance on the life of the decedent. If not, you may have to do some detective work or find someone to help you.

In this chapter we provide you tips on how to discover whether there is life insurance, including information on companies which will search for life insurance on your behalf. We also address important questions to consider before submitting a claim for benefits.

To locate all life insurance on the decedent, including policies which appear to have lapsed, consider the many sources we have listed on the following pages.

- Your first source of information about life insurance on the decedent will probably be the family. If they don't know about insurance, they may use the same insurance agent as the decedent.
- Contact the life insurance agent of the decedent. Look in the decedent's address book or phone number list for contact information. The agent who wrote the auto, home, or health insurance may also have sold a life insurance policy. Look for calendars and other logo-bearing items (such as pens and refrigerator magnets) that may have been provided by an insurance agent and contain contact information.
- Contact the decedent's current and prior attorneys, accountants, trust officers, and financial planners, any of whom may have information on insurance on the decedent's life.
- Contact the decedent's employer or former employer or employers. Insurance may have been provided as an employee benefit, sometimes through a group insurance policy. Sometimes a group policy is converted to permanent insurance after employment is terminated.
- If the decedent was a business owner, contact the person responsible for paying the company's bills and determine if the company was paying for life insurance, which may be payable to the company or to others.

Finding Lost Life Insurance with Policy Locators

There are many companies which will search for life insurance policies for a fee. These incude **www.findlostlifeinsurancepolicy.com**, 888-428-4868 ($25.00 per search), which claims to search 90% of all life insurance policies issued in the United States; **www.lostpolicy.com** ($79.95 per search), which claims that their database accounts for more than 95% of all individual life insurance actually issued; **www.l-lifeinsurance.com**, 804-594-2359 ($98.50 per search), which advertises that they will contact over 450 life insurance companies on your behalf; and **www.policyinspector.com**, 802-355-6649 ($99.00 per search), which advertises that they will contact 400+ insurance companies.

The Policy Locator Service of **MIB Solutions. Inc.**, **www.mib.com/lost_life_insurance.html,** does not actually search for policies. According to their website, for a $75.00 fee they will search their policyholder database of over 180 million records for individually underwritten life insurance policy applications processed since 1996. The application may have resulted in the issuance of a policy.

None of these services will guarantee that they can find a policy. Published reports indicate that users of these types of services experience response rates in the range of 25%-30%.

We have not investigated any of these services, are not recommending any of them, and expressly disclaim any liability for your use of such a service.

Finding Life Insurance: Additional Resources

For additional help in locating life insurance, contact the office of the insurance commissioner in the state where you feel the policy may have been issued. The **National Association of Insurance Commissioners** maintains a web site, **www.naic.org/state_web_map.htm**, with a search tool to provide you contact information for the insurance commissioner in any state and the U.S. territories. The state insurance commissioner should be able to provide you list of admitted carriers in their jurisdiction so you can contact the insurance companies directly. Some states will forward the inquiry to the insurance companies for you.

The **Michigan Department of Licensing and Regulatory Affairs** maintains a toll-free hotline at 877-999-6442 and can assist you in locating the appropriate insurance company for a Michigan insured.

You should also search for unclaimed property in the states where the decedent lived. The decedent may have had a policy which escheated to the state, or may have been a beneficiary on someone else's policy and did not claim the benefits. There are organizations which will do this search for you, for a fee, but often you can do it yourself online. For the **Michigan Department of Treasury's free online search tool**, go to **www.michigan.gov/unclaimedproperty**. To search for unclaimed property in other states, go to the website of the **National Association of Unclaimed Property Administrators, www.unclaimed.org/**

Finally, **MarketSphere** is teaming up with **LexisNexis**, one of the largest providers of public data, to assist life insurance companies in finding the beneficiaries of billions of dollars in unclaimed insurance benefits. A 2012 news report indicates that LexisNexis will obtain lists of policyholders from the insurers that subscribe to the LexisNexis/MarketSphere service, draw from more than 10,000 sources to determine those who have died, and then use its "linking" technology to identify beneficiaries by cross-referencing or doing a "relative search." MarketSphere will then send letters notifying the beneficiaries that they can claim what is owed. If you receive a letter from MarketSphere, don't throw it away without opening it!

- Review any estate planning files of the decedent for checklists and other documents which may contain life insurance information.
- Check the decedent's safe deposit box.
- If you find one life insurance policy (even one which has lapsed), review the application, which generally will disclose other policies in effect on the proposed insured at the time of the application. Those other policies may still be in effect.

- Examine bank statements and check registers and canceled checks for the past two years for evidence of payments issued to life insurance companies. They may provide clues as to what insurance companies received premium payments, and may also include policy numbers. Life insurance payments may be made through automatic withdrawals, and these payments would appear on monthly bank statements, even if no checks are issued.
- Review any divorce documents for evidence of obligations to maintain life insurance.
- Review any trusts created by the decedent, particularly irrevocable trusts, which may own insurance on the decedent's life.
- Review credit card agreements for life insurance which may exist to pay off the credit card balance, or accidental death benefits. If in doubt, call the credit card company.
- Review mortgage payment stubs and mortgage closing papers for insurance which may pay off the mortgage balance. If in doubt, call the mortgage company.
- Review any consumer loan documentation (e.g., auto and boat loans) for insurance intended to pay off the loan balance in the event of death. If in doubt call the bank or finance company which made the loan.
- Check the mail for a year. Premium bills and policy-status notices are usually sent annually.
- Review income tax returns for the past two years for income as a result of group-term insurance premiums. A portion of each payment is considered compensation and is often reported as miscellaneous income, sometimes with a description referring to group term life insurance.
- Contact clubs, fraternal and other associations and trade unions in which the decedent was a member to determine if membership included any life insurance benefits.
- Contact the decedent's health insurance company. Sometimes health plans have a death benefit rider.
- Contact the administrator of the decedent's retirement plan. Some plans provide life insurance, or permit life insurance to be purchased as an investment within the plan.
- If the decedent died while traveling, check with the travel agent, airline and credit card company for travel insurance that may have been purchased, or may be provided as part of the travel package or with a credit card purchase as an included benefit.
- If the decedent had an email account, check for messages from an insurance agent or company.
- Contact the state insurance commission or whatever state bureau regulates life insurance companies in the state where the decedent resided, and ask for a list of companies licensed to write life insurance in that state. Contact those companies to see if they issued life insurance on the decedent. Somes states have programs where they forward inquiries to life insurance companies licensed in their state (e.g., New York and Missouri), but in most cases you will have to do the follow-up yourself.
- Engage a private company which, for a fee, will check with a certain number of life insurance companies on your behalf. Make sure you understand the services that will be provided and exactly what you will be charged. The fee should be fairly nominal, and should not be a percentage of the death benefits. The search company should *not* need the decedent's full Social Security number. Generally, all that will be required is the last

four digits of the Social Security number, name, date of birth, and the last city and state of residence, along with information on your relationship to the decedent. (See further information in the box on the second page of this chapter.)

- If you think the life insurance may have been purchased in Canada, contact the Canadian Life and Health Insurance Association, 1-800-268-8099.
- Sometimes an insurance company may have changed its name, merged with another company, or transferred its policies to another company. If you have a problem determining which company is currently responsible for a policy, contact the insurance commissioner of the state where the policy was purchased. If you can provide them the full legal name of the insurance company which issued the policy, which should be written on the policy itself, the state in which it was purchased, and the date the policy was issued, they may be able to advise you what company is currently responsible for the policy.

Before Claiming Benefits...

Don't rush to file claims for life insurance benefits. Contact each insurance company, on a preliminary basis, to determine what benefits are payable and who are the beneficiaries. Prior to filing the actual claim, review the information in this section to see if there are issues which could affect whether benefits are due, the amount of those benefits, and the proper beneficiaries.

- Determine if any premium payments were overdue at the date of death and if those premiums should be paid immediately to prevent lapse.
- Examine the circumstances of death to determine if accidental death benefits may be claimed.
- Determine if any policy was recently issued on the life of the decedent, so that the incontestability period has not yet run. This is often two years. If circumstances suggest that the insurance company may refuse to pay benefits, contact an attorney to evaluate whether options are available to avoid this defense.
- If the life insurance is owned by a partnership or corporation in which the decedent was a partner or stockholder, determine to whom the benefits should be paid. They may be payable to the company, a named beneficiary, the estate, or a co-owner as part of a buyout of the decedent's interest in the company.
- Determine if any beneficiary wants to *disclaim* all or any portion of the benefits to which he or she may be entitled. A *disclaimer* is, in effect, a refusal to accept the benefits, which would cause the disclaimed amount to pass to the person who would take the benefit if the primary beneficiary predeceased the insured without creating a taxable gift from the one who disclaimed. There are strict time limits and other rules which must be met for a qualified disclaimer. If you are involved in making the claim you or your attorney should advise the beneficiary about the possibility of a disclaimer before submitting a claim for benefits.
- Determine if a change of beneficiary should be given effect, or if the position should be taken that it is ineffective. Reasons why it might be ineffective might include failure to sign the form or to file it with the insurance company, or lack of competence at the time

of signing the change of beneficiary form. On the other hand, sometimes an "unsigned" change of beneficiary form can be given effect. (See the story in the box below.)

- If a prior spouse is named as a beneficiary, review divorce decrees and property settlement agreements to determine if the prior spouse is entitled to retain policy proceeds payable to him or her. In some cases the proceeds will have been intended only to secure a balance due under a divorce decree, the insurance may not have been reduced over time as initially contemplated, and the amount due under the divorce decree may already have been paid in full. In other cases, an old beneficiary designation may have been unintentionally left in place and may have been automatically voided by operation of law at the time of the divorce. The result will vary depending on applicable state law and, in some cases, federal law. (See the story in the box at the end of this chapter regarding a federal law claim by an ex-spouse to life insurance provided under a retirement plan, even though she had waived the insurance benefits under the divorce judgment.)
- If the decedent was a party to a prenuptial or postnuptial agreement, separation agreement, or divorce decree under which the decedent was entitled to insurance proceeds on the life of the other party, determine if the estate will be entitled to those benefits.
- Consider if the facts support a claim that the person named in the beneficiary designation was not intended by the owner of the policy to be the true beneficial owner of the insurance proceeds. In appropriate cases, it may be possible for a court to impose a *constructive trust* on those benefits, and deem that they are to be held for the benefit of someone else.

The "Unsigned" Beneficiary Designation

Chester, newly divorced, submitted a form changing the beneficiary on his life insurance from his former wife, Rose, to his father. He printed his name at the top of the form, but forgot to sign on the signature line, although two witnesses did sign it.

After Chester died, Rose claimed the purported change was ineffective because it wasn't signed. Under applicable state law, divorce did not automatically void a prior beneficiary designation in favor of an ex-spouse.

The father's attorney argued that the attempted change should be effective because the rules applicable to the policy did not require signature in any particular place on the form, and that Chester had printed his name in a space at the top of the form, with the intent to sign it.

The two beneficiaries reached a settlement.

Claiming Life Insurance Benefits

After you determine what insurance is in effect, who are the proper beneficiaries, that there is no desire on the part of a beneficiary to disclaim benefits, and that the beneficiaries do not desire to make the claim themselves:

- Make copies of all policies, including the application, any beneficiary designations, and assignments of the policies, for your file, before submitting the policies for payment.
- If there are any outstanding policy loans, consider whether they should be repaid rather than deducted from the death benefits, if that will result in an increased amount of benefits under the settlement options.
- Submit claims for death proceeds, preferably by certified mail, return receipt requested.
- Request that payment be made in a lump sum or under any other method of payment which is available, and which the beneficiary desires.
- Insurance companies will sometimes insist on opening a checking account for the beneficiary with the death benefits, rather than providing a check for the lump sum proceeds. If a lump sum is desired, request a check for the total benefits. If you forget to ask for a check for the total benefits, or if the checking account is opened notwithstanding your request, then write a check on that account for the full balance. Deposit the check to the desired account, and close the checking account with the insurance company.
- Request each insurance company to provide U.S. Treasury Form 712, ***Life Insurance Statement***, with regard to each policy, as well as copies of any assignments of the policies. Form 712 is necessary to prepare the federal estate tax return. The assignments may be needed to show that the insurance was transferred by the decedent more than three years prior to death, and thus excludable from the gross estate for federal estate tax purposes.

Other Issues Related to Life Insurance

- If the insurance proceeds are significantly less than what was expected, consult an attorney. Provide the attorney all the information and documents which cause you to believe there should be more insurance. Ask the attorney to thoroughly review the situation.
- Some polices provide for a double benefit in case of accident, and you may have to fight for it. For example, the insured may have had a heart attack, and then crashed the car. The insurance company may say the heart attack was the cause of death, although it could be argued that the heart attack caused the accident, and that the death was caused by the accident. An autopsy may be required to establish the cause of death.
- Consider whether beneficiaries of the life insurance benefits need investment advice.
- If there is insurance on the lives of others, payable to the decedent, consider if it is necessary to change the beneficiary on such insurance.
- If there is insurance in effect which was intended to protect the decedent, consider if that insurance should remain in effect. Such insurance may be on the life of the surviving

spouse, other family members, or business associates. In some cases that insurance should be retained, for the benefit of others, but in some cases it will be just as well to dispose of it by terminating the policy or in some other manner.

- Consider if new insurance should be obtained on the surviving spouse, to provide liquidity to pay estate taxes at the time of that spouse's later death.
- If the decedent owned life insurance on the lives of others, consider what should be done with that insurance. It may be appropriate to cash it in, let it lapse, distribute the policies to the beneficiaries of the estate, or take other action.
- Life insurance proceeds will generally be payable to named beneficiaries without regard to claims of creditors of the decedent. However, if the insurance is payable to the estate, the proceeds will be subject to claims. (See Chapter 19, "Dealing with Creditors.") ■

Getting Around a Beneficiary Designation

Michael was a participant in a qualified retirement plan. He used some of his account balance to purchase life insurance on his life. He later divorced, and unexpectedly passed away without changing his beneficiary designation. His ex-wife was still the beneficiary, even though under their divorce judgment she had waived the right to any benefits under the retirement plan.

Michael's daughter, as Personal Representative of his estate, asked the plan administrator to distribute the funds due under the plan to the estate, and provided a copy of the divorce judgment. The Plan Administrator refused, citing federal law, which required that the judgment meet certain requirements to effectively take the benefits away from the ex-spouse. The judgment did not meet the technical requirements of a Qualified Domestic Relations Order, or "QDRO."

After unsuccessful attempts to negotiate a settlement, the daughter's attorney filed an action to have a QDRO entered in the divorce case, which was retroactive to the date of the original divorce judgment. It met all the legal requirements, and allowed the Plan Administrator to pay the benefits to the estate, and not to the ex-spouse.

Another alternative would have been to allow the insurance benefits to be paid to the ex-spouse, then file a petition for a constructive trust, to seek reimbursement after she received the distribution. However, at that point the money might already have been spent.

The divorce attorney should have assured that benefit waivers arising out of the divorce were reflected in updated beneficiary designations, and not just in the divorce decree. However, this story highlights why it is important to consult a knowledgeable attorney to explore all of the options when faced with what seems to be an unfair situation.

CHAPTER 12
Where to Turn for Help

*Settling an estate can be overwhelming.
Help is available, from a range of service providers,
to get you through the process, cost effectively,
efficiently, and avoiding mistakes.*

Should You Go It Alone?

The administration of estates is inherently complex. It encompasses elements of law, taxation, accounting, asset management, and other disciplines. It is a rare individual who possesses a level of knowledge in each of these areas sufficient to handle an estate, from beginning to end, without help.

In some cases, the estate may appear to be small and the administration may seem "simple." Appearances can be deceptive. Within a seemingly "simple" estate there can be any number of issues having to do with property rights, valuation, taxation, and the creation and funding of trusts or other entities. Those responsible are subject to personal liability for mistakes or missteps. Ignorance of these issues is not an acceptable excuse.

You may be tempted to try to "get by" on your own. You may be concerned about fees. You may be reluctant to involve outsiders in what you believe are private family matters. Nevertheless, we urge you to seek professional assistance.

In this chapter we review the types of help you should consider, how to locate the right people for your estate, and how they are generally compensated. Finding the right people can make your job much easier and can actually save the estate money that might be lost if mistakes are made or opportunities missed.

People Who Can Help

Attorneys

The administration of an estate is, first and foremost, a legal matter. It is therefore essential that you have competent legal advice. We recommend that you have an initial consultation with an attorney who practices in the area of estate planning, probate, and trust and estate administration. Since this is a highly specialized area of law, you should seek an attorney with a primary focus in this area.

Where do you find such an attorney, and how do you determine if you have the right attorney? Following is a checklist of steps you might consider.

- If the decedent had an attorney, you may want to start with this individual since he or she will be most familiar with the decedent's affairs.
- If the decedent's attorney does not feel comfortable handling all aspects of the estate, he or she may want to locate another attorney to assist and act as co-counsel in certain areas which require particular expertise.
- If the decedent did not have an estate planning attorney or if you do not wish to work with that person, then you should look for one.
- Most major law firms have such individuals and there are smaller firms and sole practitioners with expertise in this area.
- You may ask for referrals from the trust department of your bank or from your state or local bar associations.
- Recommendations from your own attorney, accountant, financial advisor, or insurance agent may also be helpful.
- You can find biographical information on many attorneys in the **Martindale-Hubbell Law Directory, www.martindale.com.** Alternatively, for a more select group of attorneys who are recommended by their peers, who concentrate in trusts and estates, and who have practiced in this area for at least ten years, look for attorneys who are **Fellows of the American College of Trust & Estate Counsel ("ACTEC")**. You can find a state-by-state listing at **www.actec.org**, under the "Fellows" tab. Also look at the website for the attorney or the law firm.
- Do not hesitate to ask the attorney to summarize his or her experience in probate, and trust and estate administration. If the attorney admits that he or she only occasionally handles estate administration and has no one else in the firm who is active in this area, seek another firm.

Who is the Client?

The client of an attorney is the person who engages or hires the attorney. In an estate, the Personal Representative, Trustee, or other fiduciary engages the attorney, and the attorney represents the fiduciary, not the estate as such or the beneficiaries.

If you are a beneficiary or family member but are not the fiduciary, you are not the client, and the attorney for the fiduciary is not representing you, even though you may participate in meetings with or receive correspondence from the attorney.

If you feel your interests are not being properly addressed by the fiduciary's attorney, you should first discuss the matter with the fiduciary. If this does not result in a satisfactory resolution of your concerns, you should consider retaining separate counsel to represent you.

- Try to determine whether you will need assistance in Probate Court matters, in estate tax return preparation, or general administration. The attorney should be able to assess your needs at the first interview. Seek to match your needs with the attorney's skills.

For example, if you anticipate a will contest, you need a litigator, an attorney who tries cases. If you do not have a probate estate, but have thorny estate tax issues, seek someone who has that background even if he or she never gets to Probate Court.

- If the estate is large enough to involve estate taxes you should inquire if the attorney has advanced training in this area, such as a Master of Laws (LLM) degree in taxation.
- You should also ask to meet the associate attorney or legal assistant, or estate administrator who will be working on the estate. It is important to you that the firm have administrative staff to handle administrative matters for the estate, since the hourly rate for administration should be less than for highly qualified attorneys. You generally do not want the senior attorney to be handling every detail of administration.

If you are satisfied with the competence of the attorney, you should give some thought to the chemistry of the relationship:

- Do you feel that you will be comfortable working with this firm?
- Do you sense that the people you met will be responsive?
- Did you understand what they were saying to you or did they talk over your head?
- Were they patient if you asked for additional explanation?

The attorney will ask that you bring various documents to the initial consultation. He or she will review these documents and ask you questions to determine what must be done to administer the estate and the issues that will be involved.

The documents listed in Chapter 7, "Gather Important Documents," would be useful, but you may not have them all for the first meeting. In general, however, at a minimum it would be helpful to have the death certificate, legal documents such as the will, any codicils, trusts and any amendments, handwritten or typed lists disposing of personal property, any prenuptial agreement, information about life insurance, and information about assets and liabilities.

Also, prepare a list of contact information for all interested persons of the estate. This should include name, Social Security number, address, email address, phone number, and relationship to the decedent. Interested persons may include the surviving spouse; surviving children; descendants of deceased children; surviving parents of the decedent; the decedent's brothers and sisters; and children of deceased brothers and sisters. Also include any beneficiaries under the will, trust, or life insurance, whether or not related to the decedent.

The attorney will then discuss with you the steps that must be taken and any areas of special concern.

You can then decide if you want to engage the attorney to advise you, if you want to consult with another attorney, or if you believe you can handle the estate without the assistance of an attorney. Ultimately, you yourself will have to assess the qualifications of an estate attorney to whom you are referred, unless your own attorney is assisting you in locating an attorney to help with the administration of the estate.

If you decide to engage the attorney, there should be a discussion of which tasks you or other family members will perform, and which tasks will be handled by the attorney's office. The attorney may have an estate administration checklist to review for this purpose, or you may want to use this book as a guide.

The attorney should discuss the fee arrangement after reviewing the type of work which will have to be done to administer the estate. Fees will generally be charged on an hourly basis, but the attorney may be able to give you a rough estimate of total fees and expenses, and advise you whether fees will be billed monthly or at certain stages in the administration. Any estimate will obviously be based on certain assumptions as to what work will have to be done, and if the scope of the work increases significantly you should expect that the actual fees will be higher.

In any event, make it clear that you would like to receive detailed periodic billing statements, with a description of the work done, date, by whom it was done, and the amount of time for each task. This will help you evaluate the services and also the progress that is being made. This is desirable from the attorney's perspective as well, because it will help you appreciate the myriad of details being addressed and what it takes to accomplish seemingly simple tasks.

Also ask about the possibility of a fixed fee, which can sometimes be arranged if the work to be done is very predictable. You should recognize, however, that estate administration often takes twists and turns, and that it is usually difficult for an attorney to agree to a fixed fee, and sometimes difficult even to estimate what the overall fees will be. Much will depend on the issues (many of which cannot be anticipated at the outset), how much conflict there is among beneficiaries, and how responsive you are to the attorney's requests for information.

The attorney should then confirm the proposal or agreement in an engagement letter.

Accountants

You may be required to file a variety of tax returns, for the decedent and for the estate or trust. (See Chapter 21, "The Tax Man Cometh.") If there is a probate estate or a trust, you will have to provide accounts to the beneficiaries. If the decedent had an IRA or was a participant in a qualified retirement plan, you may need a computation of the required minimum distribution from the IRA or plan for the year of death and future years.

Virtually all estate planning attorneys are able to prepare the federal estate tax return, and state estate tax or inheritance tax returns. Some attorneys will also prepare fiduciary and individual income tax returns, prepare accounts, and calculate IRA and retirement plan distributions. Other attorneys will ask that you engage an accountant to provide these services.

Individual income tax returns for the decedent, or for the decedent and surviving spouse, are probably best done by the decedent's regular tax preparer because of that person's familiarity with the decedent's income and deductions. The decedent's regular tax preparer may also be able to compute required minimum distributions from IRAs and retirement plans.

However, if fiduciary income tax returns and accounts will be required – and they will generally be required if there is a probate estate or a trust – you should engage an accountant who is experienced in these specialized areas. Your attorney should be able to recommend several accountants who are qualified to do this work.

Before engaging an accountant, you should inquire about the experience of the accountant and any staff members who will be working on your behalf. You should confirm what work is to be done, what information you will have to provide, when you will have to provide it, and when the work will be completed. You should also reach an agreement on the fee arrangement. In some cases, there will be a flat fee for each return or other work product. In other cases, fees may be charged on an hourly basis. All of this should be memorialized in an engagement letter.

Getting Out of the Middle

Mildred was appointed Trustee of her late brother's trust, but quickly realized that the attitude and demands of the beneficiaries (her adult nephews) would make her job difficult. As Trustee she would have to make decisions with regard to discretionary distributions of principal and income. Her nephews were already starting to ask for distributions, and she found it difficult to say "no." However, she knew that the distributions probably should not be made in the amounts and for the reasons requested.

Mildred decided to resign as Trustee, and allow a bank to take over as Successor Trustee. In doing so, she did not consider that she was backing away from her responsibility. Rather, she felt the responsible thing to do was keep out of the middle and have an independent third party make the right decisions.

The accountant should be brought into the picture early because there are typically several income tax issues to be considered, and the sooner these are addressed the better.

Bookkeeping Services

You may be able to handle details of bill paying, check writing, and balancing the checkbook for the estate account yourself, or you may prefer to have those types of services performed by someone else.

These services do not require an accountant, though the accountant may have staff who can provide bookkeeping services for you. You can also seek an outside bookkeeping service based on recommendations from your accountant, your attorney, or friends.

In any event you must keep impeccable records on behalf of the estate. Do not simply continue to use the decedent's accounts, nor should you commingle or mix monies of the estate with your own. If you inadvertently deposit estate funds to your own account, or pay an estate expense from your own funds, correct the error as soon as you discover it and write a memo to document what happened.

Financial Advisors: Stockbrokers, Financial Planners, and Investment Advisors

If there are marketable securities, such as stocks, bonds, and mutual funds, you must see that they are properly managed. (See Chapter 18 "Protect and Preserve Estate Assets.") Alleged mismanagement of investments is a major area of liability exposure for fiduciaries. Unless you have extensive experience in this area, you should seek a competent financial advisor.

We use the term *financial advisor* to include the entire spectrum of professionals who offer services related to the management of investments. This includes, but is not limited to, stockbrokers, financial planners, and investment advisors.

The services that are available from financial advisors range from general advice to specific recommendations to full portfolio management. Therefore, you must first decide on the level of assistance you desire or, to say it differently, the degree of involvement the financial advisor is to have. You should then look for someone who is capable of providing the services you want.

You should consider continuing to use the decedent's stockbroker or financial advisor. However, do not feel obligated to do so if you have reservations about his or her ability to meet your needs. Your attorney will probably know of several financial advisors and will likely be familiar with the investment style and performance of each.

If significant assets are involved, you should interview several financial advisors and make a decision based not only on past performance, but also on accessibility and the "chemistry" of the relationship. You may not be a financial wizard yourself, but the financial advisor should not talk down to you. All your questions should be answered completely and politely.

Before committing to a financial advisor, you should have a clear understanding of the services he or she proposes to provide, the fees, and any restrictions or limitations on the advisor's authority.

If the advisor is to have full portfolio management responsibility, you should ask for materials which show the advisor's performance in managing portfolios of similar size and complexity. Results should be shown for the past one-year, three-year, five-year, and ten-year periods, and should include comparisons to industry benchmarks such as the Dow Jones Industrial Average and the Standard & Poors 500 Stock Index.

You should also have some idea of what the prospective portfolio manager has in mind. If, for example, the intention is to immediately sell everything and start over, you should know this up front and not have it come as a surprise when you see the activity on the account statement. You should also be aware that your job as a fiduciary is not necessarily to maximize returns, but to preserve the estate for the period of administration.

Finally, be sure you understand how the financial advisor will be compensated. Various arrangements are possible, sometimes involving fees based on a percentage of the assets, sometimes commissions, and sometimes a combination of the two. You should shop the quoted rates to see if they are competitive. If they are not, you may be able to negotiate a reduction. Be wary of a compensation structure that is weighted too heavily toward commissions, as this could result in excessive buying and selling, a practice known as *churning*.

The entire agreement should be set forth in one or more letters or forms which you will be asked to sign. You should have your attorney review them before you sign.

If significant assets are involved, you should bring a financial advisor on board as soon as possible. The financial markets can be extremely volatile. Allowing investments to go for even a couple of weeks without someone "minding the store" can result in serious losses, which could result in personal liability to you as the fiduciary.

Banks and Trust Companies

If you have a bank or trust company serving along with you as a co-fiduciary, that institution should assign an officer who is experienced in estate administration. That person will, in turn, be supported by specialists in tax, fiduciary accounting, asset valuation, and investment management.

If a bank or trust company is not presently serving, you may wish to add one as co-fiduciary in order to secure the full range of services that such an institution can provide. However, this may require going to Probate Court to change or reform the will or trust.

If you do not want the bank or trust company to have a fiduciary role, you can engage the institution in an agency capacity. All of the institution's resources will be available to you, but the institution will serve as your agent and will be subject to your direction.

As an alternative, you can hire a bank or trust company to be custodian of the assets of the estate. The institution can either manage the assets or provide investment recommendations to you. If you do not need investment counseling, the institution can simply hold the assets in safekeeping, collect the income, and maintain transaction records. Fees will vary depending on the role which the bank or trust company assumes.

Banks and trust companies acting as fiduciaries typically charge for estate administration services based on a percentage of the assets in the estate or trust, and there is sometimes a minimum fee. There may be additional fees for account maintenance, for tax return preparation, and for certain other services.

Your attorney should be able to refer you to several banks or trust companies with which he or she is familiar.

Appraisers and Valuation Services

Valuation may be important in connection with an estate tax return, possible sale of an asset, or in connection with distributions. In those cases it is generally not sufficient to estimate values yourself.

An appraiser may be needed to value personal property if an estate tax return is required, or where personal property is distributed to satisfy a specific request in a fixed dollar amount, or if personal property is to be divided equally. An appraisal may also be required if there are unusual items, antiques, art work, jewelry, or collectibles. An appraiser may also be required for real estate. If the decedent owned a closely held business or an interest in such a business, a qualified appraiser is a must if an estate tax return is required, and may be needed for other purposes.

Your attorney can recommend one or more appraisers who are qualified to appraise the type of property in question.

The appraiser may charge a fee based on the time required to complete the appraisal, but for some types of appraisals will be able to quote a fixed fee.

Listed securities will be easier to value, but date-of-death values and alternate values are required for estate tax purposes. Those values do not correspond exactly to the values shown on the brokerage statements. Valuation services provide values for listed securities based on the proper valuation method, based on mean market prices, and will also provide any accrued dividends and interest, as required for tax purposes.

The attorney can put you in contact with one or more of these services. However, if the attorney is handling preparation of the estate tax return he or she will probably determine how to value listed securities and obtain the necessary valuations for you.

A Worthwhile Appraisal

Michael was Trustee of his uncle's estate, which included a residence which his uncle left to him and which Michael did not intend to sell.

Initially he hesitated to get an appraisal, thinking it would be too costly. He was surprised to find that in his area a formal residential appraisal only cost $250-$500.

He got the appraisal, and the value of the residence was much less than he had thought. The IRS approved the valuation of the residence at the appraised value for federal estate tax purposes.

A valuation service valuing marketable securities will charge a few dollars for each value provided. You can look up and compute these values yourself, if you have retained the *Wall Street Journal* for the dates required, or by using online services referenced in Chapter 13, "Inventory the Assets.". However, if many securities are involved it may be well worth the modest fee to obtain the information from one of the valuation services.

Estate Liquidators

Estate liquidators will typically come to the decedent's residence, prepare the house for an estate sale, establish the prices, and hold the sale. Because they know the values of these objects, they may be able to get more than you thought the items were worth. They may arrange for articles not sold to be donated to charity or otherwise disposed of. They may also offer to buy whatever is left for a fixed price.

In addition to the convenience they offer, estate liquidators spare you the emotional stress of selling the decedent's personal property to strangers, who may denigrate the items in an effort to buy them for less.

Your attorney, friends or family members may be able to recommend one or more estate liquidators. If not, you should be able to find one through the Internet or the Yellow Pages of the decedent's telephone directory, through ads for estate sales in the local newspaper, or by watching for estate sale signs on the weekend.

You want to find an estate sales company that you like, one that you can trust, and one that has a history of providing their clients with excellent service. You also want one that can price the estate sale right, so that as much as possible will sell, but not lose money by pricing too low.

What You Should Expect

A professional estate sales service will assess the value of the items in the household and make price recommendations. A good service will come prepared with antique reference books, a camera, and an average household item price sheet for your review.

Most professional services will want to be fully responsible for the event, including a certain amount of house cleaning. Other services may break down the costs based on what they will be responsible for. However, a really good service will be interested in how the estate sale is presented and will want most of the control. Reputable services have regular customers who appreciate the standards that their service provides.

Estate liquidators generally charge a commission based on a percentage of the sales proceeds. Check with several to determine the going rate in your area. They will want to visit the residence to see whether there is enough personal property to conduct an estate sale. If not, they may be able to integrate some or all of the items into another sale.

Commissions can run between 25%-35% or more of the total sales proceeds. The rate can be expected to vary by region and by community.

Ask questions and avoid working with any service that cannot answer your questions directly and point you to the place in the contract that covers the questions you have. Consider several services, but don't automatically choose the one with the lowest rate. A low percentage may not be in your interest if they price the items too low, or if they do not provide the services you need.

Conduct a Phone Interview

Prior to hiring a company to do an estate sale, conduct a phone interview. Get a sense of how they treat you, whether they are responsive or curt, and whether they are willing to be transparent in how they do business. Consider the following questions:

- How long have you been in business?
- How many sales a month does your company conduct?
- Can you provide references for sales you have conducted? Check their references.
- Are you insured and bonded? Will you provide proof of that?
- What commission do you charge?
- What must I do to prepare for you to begin?
- Would your schedule permit you to handle an estate sale within my time frame?
- Can I remain on-site while you prepare the sale?
- How many days will it take you to set up for the sale?
- Do you price every item?
- How do you keep track of what items sell for?
- How many days do you hold the sale?
- How do you handle discounts or negotiations?
- May I see a copy of your contract?
- Do you charge extra to clean up prior to the sale, as well as post-sale?
- How much do you charge to clean out the residence, leaving it empty?
- Do you ever buy from your own sales or pre-sell to dealers?

Personal Interview

Once you make a tentative decision on a couple of possible estate liquidators, have separate personal meetings with them on the premises where the estate sale will take place. Before they arrive, separate the estate's valuable items and remember to point them out during the visit.

At this meeting you can ask any of the above questions that you didn't get to during the phone interview. Also ask the following:

- What sort of security do you provide?
- How many people will you use to staff the estate sale?
- How will you advertise the sale? Do you have email lists of regular buyers and, if so, how many people are on that list?
- How do you handle high value items? Do you send them to an auction, or sell them through the estate sale? (If you have any high value items, make sure they are as well versed with auction house strategies as they are with their estate sale strategies or, in the appropriate case, consider having the high value items sold by someone else at auction.)
- How does your firm account for each estate sale item sold?
- Do you provide a written item by item post-sale inventory?
- How long do you take to reconcile your books and send a check to the estate? Some liquidators will provide payment immediately after the sale.
- What do you do with the estate sale remainders? Do you donate them to charity and, if so, do you provide a written valuation and a receipt?
- Do you leave the house broom clean?

Visit an Estate Sale

Once you have narrowed the field to a few potential candidates, visit their estate sales to see how they actually operate them. Here are some things to look for:

- Did you see professional signs directing you to the location?
- Was it professionally advertised in the local newspapers in your city and surrounding area?
- Were you greeted upon entering the premises?
- Did it feel like a garage sale rather than an estate sale?
- Was security provided to help direct cars and secure valuables?
- Were enough people on hand to answer potential buyers' questions?
- Were the items organized, well displayed, and clearly priced? Was someone periodically keeping things in order?
- Did the service seem to have an awareness to how things were priced to avoid being taken by price switchers?
- Were display tables provided to help display large collections of glass and collectibles?
- Was glassware clean, knickknacks dusted, linens folded?
- Was the money collected in a systematic way and secured?

Prepare the Home for the Estate Sale

Once you have hired the estate sale company, make sure you do not throw away any items until their representative has walked through the home and you have discussed details of the sale and how you should prepare for it. There are many items which could appear to have little value, but could be of great value:

- Old magazines
- Children's games and dolls
- Logo-type ashtrays (such as ashtray from casinos that no longer exist)
- Sports memorabilia
- Gaudy costume jewelry
- Vintage clothing and accessories (shoes, hats, gloves)
- Books, music albums, 8-track cassettes, video gaming systems and games
- Old photographs
- Dated kitchen utensils, bowls, everyday dishes
- Chipped, broken dishes or glassware (which could be of interest to craft people)

Remove personal papers from the home, as well as items of great value, unless they are included in the sale. Assume that there will be shoplifters. Lock off or otherwise prohibit access to areas not involved in the sale.

If antiques or collectibles will be included in the sale, compare the prices that the estate sale service is suggesting with antique and collectible books or Internet sites such as eBay for ideas on what things sell for (not just what they appraise for), and verify that the service is close to the same estimates. In some cases an estate sale service will over-price an item so that they can take advantage of the total buy out agreement if the item does not sell during the sale.

Get at least two separate appraisals on valuables that you will be selling. Many appraisers own antique stores and they may be interested in purchasing items or auctioning them off after the estate sale has ended.

Make certain to read the estate sale service contract before you agree to sell anything independently before the sale. They may be assuming that certain items will be part of the sale, and if you remove them you could be violating your agreement.

After the Sale is Over

Professional services often offer a cash buyout on items not sold at the sale. Do not expect top dollar for the leftovers. Most sales offer major discounts on the last day that the event is held. If the items did not sell during that time, the value of what is left is not going to be great. The buy out is usually based on a percentage of the selling price and should be discussed prior to signing the contract.

Real Estate Brokers

If the decedent left real estate and you have decided to sell the property, a real estate broker can be of assistance. You should look for a broker who is familiar with the real estate market in the area where the property is located, and the particular type of property, e.g., personal residence, commercial property, manufacturing property, rental property, vacant land, or vacation property.

If the broker is successful in selling the property, he or she will receive an agreed percentage of the sales price as a commission. Ask your attorney what commission is typically charged in your area. Commissions will vary depending on whether commercial or residential property is involved, and may also vary depending on the value of the property. Even though there may be a "standard" brokerage commission in a community, commissions are sometimes negotiable, so you may want to talk with several brokers.

Try to get an idea of how much effort they will put into trying to sell the property. If it's commercial property, will they take professional photos and how will they market it? How much advertising will they do? How long do they estimate it will take to sell the property, and do they have a study showing how long other similar properties have taken to sell, and at what selling price compared to the listing price?

Do not hire a real estate agent merely because that agent suggests the highest listing price. If that is not a realistic position, the property could remain on the market a long time. The longer it remains on the market, the more likely it is that prospective buyers will feel it is a distress situation, particularly because an estate is involved. You may end up with a much lower price than if it has been priced "right" in the first place.

If you have obtained some prospective buyers yourself, make sure that a special arrangement is made with the broker to either exclude those buyers from the commission arrangement, or for a reduced commission. Your attorney should be able to assist you in working through the details of a listing agreement with the broker.

A real estate broker can also help if you are not selling the property but wish to know its approximate value. For a nominal fee, or perhaps on a complimentary basis, the broker can provide you with a *market analysis* and a range of prices within which the property might sell. (Note, however, that this is not the same as, or equivalent to, an appraisal by a qualified appraiser.)

Specialty Purchasers of Esoteric Items

If the decedent left a rare violin, an original letter written by George Washington, a collection of stamps, coins, guns, or Civil War artifacts, to mention a few examples, you may have to educate yourself in marketing that type of item in order to obtain the best price. You should expect that a sale to a dealer will be for substantially less than what you might obtain from an individual buyer, if you could find one.

You may want to use a dealer's offer as a base price, on which you should try to improve. Your attorney may know of a dealer who would be interested in the item in question, or you may be able to locate one through the Yellow Pages, on the Internet, or in a specialty magazine. If the decedent belonged to an organization or club of collectors, ask those people for suggestions as to how to sell these items.

You may want to try to market the item on **eBay (www.ebay.com)** or **Craigslist (www.craigslist.com)**, either directly or through a local company which helps people sell items on the Internet. You might also consider searching eBay or Craigslist to determine the approximate market value for certain items.

Finders of Missing Heirs

In most estates, you will know the family or the beneficiaries and where they are located. In some cases, however, beneficiaries may be estranged or for whatever reason may have had no contact with the family for many years, and their whereabouts may be unknown. In other cases, heirs may have died and their descendants may be entitled to a share of the estate. Less frequently, you know the family but may be uncertain whether there are other family members who are legally entitled to share in the estate, but who are unknown to you.

In these cases it may be useful to engage a genealogical search firm to do a diligent search for the heirs. Look for a firm that will quote you a reasonable fee, either based on time charges or an agreed fee based on the work done, rather than one which will charge a percentage of the estate. Seek a firm that will guarantee its results. In some cases an heir search firm will not charge the estate anything, but will negotiate a percentage fee with the heir, which can range as high as 40%. For further discussion of heir finders, see Chapter 15, "Who Shares in the Estate?"

Fees in Perspective

As this book illustrates, and anyone who has ever administered an estate can tell you, there are many things to be done in even the very smallest estate.

The professionals you engage to perform or assist with these tasks are just that – professionals. They have invested a great deal of time and money to earn advanced degrees, professional certifications, and state or federal licensure, and they generally pursue continuing professional education to keep their skills up to date.

They have the knowledge and experience to get you successfully through the challenges of estate administration. When viewed in relation to the services they are able to render, their fees are reasonable and necessary.

Indeed, for those who are accustomed to working with professionals, the fees incurred in the administration of an estate will not seem out of line. For the uninitiated, however, the idea of paying thousands of dollars in fees may be deeply disturbing.

Most professionals strive to minimize fees that must be charged by operating as efficiently as possible and by assigning work to staff members at the lowest level who can competently do the work, with lower billing rates. Most professionals will also advise you of things that you can do yourself.

Any responsibilities that you can take on will reduce fees, and the resulting savings can be significant. On the other hand, if you have other obligations competing for your time, it may be best to simply let the professionals do their job. If you take on too much, there is a danger that you may not finish your tasks on a timely basis, which can cause further problems and possibly even increase the fees.

Despite all of your best efforts, it is likely that fees will amount to a major expenditure. You must understand and accept this at the outset if you are to see the administration through to a successful conclusion.

Consider professional fees an investment to get the job done properly, without mistakes, unnecessary liability on your part, or additional costs for which you could be held personally liable. There is perhaps also some comfort in knowing that professional fees may be deductible for tax purposes.

The Team Approach

It is important that the professionals you employ not "do their own thing" in isolation, but work together as a team. A team approach minimizes duplication of effort and allows for sharing of information and collaborating on decisions.

As but one example, in an estate large enough to be subject to federal estate tax, expenses of administering the estate may be deducted either on the federal estate tax return or on the fiduciary income tax return for the estate or trust. The preparers of the different returns should jointly decide how these deductions can be used to greatest overall advantage.

You should see that each member of the team has the names, telephone numbers, and email addresses of the other members. You should also make it clear that they have your permission to exchange information pertaining to the administration of the estate.

When all of the team members work collaboratively, the estate will be settled more efficiently, and with fewer mistakes. ■

CHAPTER 13

Inventory the Assets

One of your first major tasks is to determine what is in the estate, which may not be as simple as it might appear. Some assets will not pass through the probate estate or trust, but by joint ownership or beneficiary designation. Valuation can also be an issue.

Taking Stock

Before you can administer the estate, you must know exactly what assets the decedent owned or in which he had an interest. General, approximate, or summary knowledge is not sufficient. You must develop a written, itemized list of each and every asset or property interest. This list is called an *inventory*.

You will have to provide the inventory to beneficiaries and possibly to the Probate Court. The inventory will also be used in the preparation of tax returns. It is difficult to overstate the importance of a complete and accurate inventory.

In this chapter, we discuss the steps involved in compiling an inventory and valuing the assets.

Where to Get the Information

Where do you get the information for the inventory? Most of the decedent's assets will normally be identified in the course of gathering the decedent's important documents. (See Chapter 7, "Gather Important Documents.")

Others may be discovered by reviewing the decedent's checking account activity for the year prior to death. Still others may come to light as dividend checks, brokerage account statements, tax bills, premium notices, proxy statements, and other correspondence arrives in the mail. Some assets may only be discovered by contact with the family, the decedent's accountant, attorney, business partners, or employer.

For example, if the decedent loaned money to a family member, and didn't obtain a promissory note, you may only learn about that by talking to the person who borrowed the money, or perhaps from other family members. Likewise, the decedent may be entitled to certain benefits from his employment, such as accrued vacation pay, and you may learn about that by contacting the employer. Both the loan receivable and the accrued vacation pay may be assets in which the decedent had an interest, and thus part of the estate.

Assets in Which the Decedent Had An Interest

The assets to be inventoried are not only those which are titled in the decedent's sole name. All assets in which the decedent had any interest, whether outright or in trust, including any joint interest (even if joint with a spouse), must be listed. Any *In Trust For, Payable on Death,* or *Transfer on Death* accounts must also be shown. These assets may not be part of the probate estate, but you should still list them and decide what to do with them, although generally they will pass to the surviving joint owner (for joint property) or the named beneficiary.

If the decedent made any transfers in which he retained any type of interest, these may be includible for federal estate tax purposes and should be discussed on a case-by-case basis with your attorney.

Although all assets must be inventoried, it is advisable to make separate inventories for each type of ownership, e.g., assets held in sole name, held jointly, held in the name of a trust, and having a designated beneficiary. This will facilitate notification of beneficiaries, probate filings, periodic accounts, and preparation of tax returns.

What is in the Estate?

What is in the "estate" depends on what "estate" you are talking about: The probate estate, the taxable estate for estate tax purposes, or the overall estate which must be administered.

Here we start with the broadest concept, the overall estate. After you have determined absolutely everything in which the decedent had any interest, you can address each item separately and determine if it is necessary to include it in the probate estate or in the taxable estate.

Example: Life insurance, payable to a named beneficiary, may be an asset in which the decedent had an interest, and thus part of the overall estate which must be administered. It may also be included in the taxable estate. However, if the proceeds are payable to a named beneficiary it will not be part of the probate estate.

The Question of Ownership

For each asset, you must make a positive determination of how it was owned (titled) at the decedent's death. Do not make any assumptions in this regard.

You may think that a bank account was in the decedent's name alone, when in fact there was a relative who was a joint owner, or designated as a beneficiary under a *Payable on Death* (POD), *Transfer on Death* (TOD) or *In Trust For* (ITF) account. A husband and wife may have thought that their house was owned jointly when, for whatever reason, it was titled in the husband's name alone.

For bank accounts, look at the most recent account statement or ask the bank to check its records. Do not rely on the names or other information printed on the checks. You may believe that a bank account was owned jointly with someone who had signature authority over the account, but it may actually have been owned by the decedent, and the co-signer may have only been acting under a power of attorney.

If an account is owned jointly with rights of survivorship, ask the surviving owner if he or she claims ownership in the account. If not, he or she may have been named on the account "for convenience only." In that case, the account should be treated as belonging to the decedent.

If you believe the joint account was a convenience account only, and not true joint ownership, and if the alleged joint owner takes the position that it was true joint ownership, then the Personal Representative should immediately petition the court seeking to have the account deemed part of the probate estate. Otherwise, the estate may never recover the funds or spend additional time, money and effort in attempting to collect from an uncollectible defendant.

For individual securities, look at the actual stock or bond certificate, if certificates exist. Do not rely only on notes that may be found in the decedent's records or even financial statements, which may have been prepared to show the financial condition of husband and wife, without consideration of who actually owns which assets.

For brokerage accounts, check the most recent account statement. If there are any doubts about the accuracy of the title on the account as reflected on the statement, investigate thoroughly. It is possible that the statement is incorrect.

The Vanishing Annuity

Making a correct determination of who owns an account may require going beyond the reporting on the brokerage statement and digging into the underlying facts.

In one case Harriet firmly believed she owned an annuity, but it was shown on the brokerage statement of her husband's trust.

When asked about this, the account executive explained: "That's just where we put it to get it on the statement."

Harriet was able to support her position that the annuity was hers, and the necessary correction was made.

For real estate, if there is any doubt how it is owned based on the records you locate, you should have a title search done by a title company. You may also want to have a title search done just to confirm that title is actually as you expect. Sometimes people operate for years under incorrect assumptions as to who has title.

Assets to Be Inventoried

The following is a basic checklist of the principal types of assets to be included. Consult your attorney if questions arise about whether an item is part of the estate for various purposes.

- Cash (including currency and coin of the United States and foreign countries, as well as collectible coins and currency).
- Bank accounts and accrued interest, whether the accounts are in the decedent's name alone or owned jointly with others.
- Securities of any type, whether in certificate form, held in brokerage accounts, mutual funds, or in dividend reinvestment programs, as well as accrued dividends and interest on those securities.
- Annuities, even if payable on death to a named beneficiary.
- U.S. and foreign government, corporate, and municipal bonds, and accrued interest.
- Accrued wages, accumulated vacation and sick pay, fringe benefits, and benefits under state worker's compensation laws.
- Retirement benefits, including those in employer sponsored plans, self-employed persons' plans and IRAs, even if the benefits are payable to a named beneficiary.
- Real estate, whether commercial, investment, or residential, and whether owned solely by the decedent or in joint ownership or partnership with others.
- Property (including but not limited to real estate) in another state or country, including ownership in vacation time-shares.
- Life insurance, whether on the life of the decedent or owned by the decedent on the life of another.
- Motor vehicles, boats, and airplanes.
- Personal property, including furniture, household furnishings, jewelry, art work, and collectibles.
- Business interests, including partnership, limited liability company, and closely held corporate interests.
- Debts owed to the decedent.
- Lottery winnings, even if not payable until a future date.
- Safe deposit box contents.
- Interests passing under someone else's will or trust (for example, the balance under a marital trust, which passes on the decedent's death to someone else).
- Rights under pending litigation, even if the amount ultimately to be collected, if any, will not be known until a future date.
- Miscellaneous assets, including frequent flyer miles.

Valuation

Each asset on the inventory must be valued. Values will be needed for the federal estate tax return, if a return is required to be filed, or filed even if not legally required. They will be needed to establish a new *basis* in the assets for income tax purposes, even if no federal estate tax return is filed. If there is a probate estate, values will be needed for the probate inventory. Finally, values may be needed to equalize distributions to different beneficiaries.

Values are normally determined under the rules set forth in the Internal Revenue Code and Treasury Regulations. In this chapter, we address only the most basic and most commonly encountered valuation rules, and there will be exceptions. For example, *alternate values* (see below) are not allowed on a probate inventory.

Each asset must be valued at its fair market value as of the date of the decedent's death. If federal estate tax will be due, the assets should also be valued six months after the decedent's death or, if distributed or sold within the six-month period, on the date of distribution or at their sale price. This so-called *alternate value* may, subject to certain rules, be used for federal estate tax purposes instead of date-of-death values. (See Chapter 21, "The Tax Man Cometh.")

For federal estate tax purposes, property is generally to be valued at its *highest and best use*. To illustrate, if a tract of farm land on the outskirts of an expanding suburb is worth $500,000 if used in agriculture but would fetch $20 million if sold to a condominium developer, then the highest and best use of the property is for the construction of condominiums and its value is $20 million. (In this situation, the property might qualify for valuation under a special method, called *special use valuation,* for federal estate tax purposes.)

There are valuation rules for each type of asset. For example, listed securities (stocks and bonds which are listed on an exchange, such as the New York Stock Exchange) must be valued at *mean market value*, which is the average of the high and the low for the date of death or six month after the date of death. Interest must be accrued through date of death and shown separately. Dividends are to be shown separately if the date of death was between the record date and the payment date. If the date of death was between the ex-dividend date and the record date, the dividend is not shown separately, but is added to the value of the stock.

In valuing some types of property interests, various premiums and discounts may have to be taken into account. A fractional interest in real estate may be discounted for lack of marketability, lack of control and cost of partition. Discounts may also be appropriate if there are transfer restrictions, if the land is not contiguous, or if there are other conditions which would tend to decrease its utility. A business interest may command a premium if it is a controlling interest or represents a swing vote. On the other hand, discounts for lack of control and lack of marketability may be indicated in the case of a minority interest in a closely held business.

Obtaining Values: Who and How?

One of the questions to be decided early in the administration of the estate is who will obtain asset values. You may wish to undertake this task yourself in order to save professional fees. Alternatively, you may prefer to have your attorney or accountant do so. In the latter case, you may be asked to sign a letter authorizing the attorney or accountant to receive this information.

If a federal estate tax return will be required, generally the person who is preparing that return will determine how values are obtained and will obtain the necessary valuations.

How asset values are obtained varies with the type of asset. Some of the more common types of assets and method of obtaining values are set forth below.

Bank and Savings and Loan Accounts

Values for bank or savings and loan accounts and accrued interest may be obtained directly from the financial institution. Write a letter asking for account balances and accrued interest as of the date of death.

Individual Stocks

If securities are held in a brokerage account, it may be possible to obtain mean market values and accrued dividends and interest from the brokerage firm. However, some brokerage firms will provide only closing or month-end values. If the brokerage company is unable to furnish the required values, you will have to get them yourself.

Detailed price information for individual stocks will be found in financial newspapers such as the *Wall Street Journal*. This data includes the high and low for the day, from which you can compute the mean market value. Since newspapers report prices from the prior business day, you should get and keep a copy of a newspaper from the day *after* the decedent's death.

If death occurred over a weekend or on a holiday, it is necessary to average the mean market values for the days which precede and follow the weekend or holiday. You will need copies for the Monday and Tuesday following the weekend or for the two days following the holiday.

Dividend information can be obtained from *Standard & Poor's Dividend Record,* which can be obtained at many public libraries. Dividends should be shown separately if the date of death was between the record date and the payment date. If the date of death was between the ex-dividend date and the record date, the dividend is not shown separately, but is added to the value of the stock.

Stock Values

Historical stock values may be obtained on the Internet for no charge at **www.bigcharts.marketwatch.com/historical**, or search for "historical stock prices" on **www.yahoo.com**, or go to **www.dailyfinance.com/historical-stock-prices/**

A very economical and perhaps the easiest way to obtain mean market values of stocks and bonds, including ex-dividend adjustments, accrued dividends, or interest, is to order them from a valuation service. One such service is "**Appraise**," provided by **Evaluation Services, Inc., www.appraisenj.com**, (888) 374-4706.

Corporate and Government Bonds

Detailed price information is available for corporate and government bonds in the *Wall Street Journal* and other financial newspapers. Pricing is per $100 of face value.

Example: A Ford Motor Company 7.45% bond maturing July 16, 2031 is priced at 95.701. A $10,000 bond is thus valued at $10,000 x 95.701%, or $9,570. However, accrued interest is not included in the price and must be computed.

Tax-Free Municipal Bonds

Values of tax-free municipal bonds are not listed in financial newspapers. Obtain the value, as well as accrued interest, from a stockbroker or a valuation service.

Mutual Funds

The typical *open-end* mutual fund is valued at its *net asset value*, or NAV. The NAV at the date of death or alternate valuation date may be obtained from the fund company, the stockbroker if the fund is held in a brokerage account, from financial newspapers, or on the Internet.

So-called *closed-end* mutual funds, of which there are relatively few, are really not mutual funds but are investment companies whose shares are traded on the stock exchange like stocks. Obtain the value of closed-end funds in the same manner as publicly traded stocks.

Household Effects and Personal Property

You may determine values for household effects and personal property yourself, if the items are of minimal value, or you may have values determined by an appraiser who specializes in household inventories. However, if there are unusual items, antiques, art work, jewelry, or collectibles, you should have the articles appraised by a qualified appraiser.

Real Estate

Real estate should be appraised by a real estate appraiser who is familiar with the market where the property is located and the type of property. In cases where the estate is small or a precise value is not needed for tax, probate, or determination of property rights, an estimate of the value by a real estate broker or even a value based on the state assessment of the property for real estate tax purposes may suffice. In Michigan, for certain purposes the value of real estate may be estimated at two times the State Equalized Value (SEV) of the property. Although SEV is determined for real property tax purposes, it is supposed be 50% of fair market value, and thus two times SEV is often used as an estimate of value.

If an asset is sold within a reasonable time after death, or if it had been purchased shortly before death, the sale or purchase price may be the best indication of value, assuming the transaction was at arm's length and absent any intervening change in the market. What may be considered a reasonable time depends on all the facts and circumstances. However, a general rule of thumb is that one year is a reasonable time.

Fractional Interest Discounts

Jack inherited an undivided one-third interest in lake front property from his father many years ago. His two siblings inherited the other two-thirds.

When Jack died, his Trustee had the property appraised for $300,000. However, since Jack's one-third interest could not be readily sold to a third party, the appraiser discounted the one-third interest for federal estate tax purposes.

Though fractional interest discounts vary and must be supported by competent appraisal, in that case the appraiser applied a substantial discount and valued the one-third significantly less than $100,000, saving considerable estate tax.

Life Insurance

For federal estate tax purposes, the value of life insurance on the life of the decedent is the amount received by the beneficiary. This even includes individual term life insurance, as well as group-term insurance provided by an employer. This amount is reported by the insurance company on Form 712, which you should request from the company.

Note that such insurance is an asset of the estate only if the decedent possessed, at death, one or more *incidents of ownership* over the policy. Incidents of ownership is an expansive concept which you should discuss with your attorney if you feel that insurance proceeds should be excluded from the gross estate because the decedent did not own the policy.

The value of life insurance on the life of another which was owned by the decedent is generally the replacement cost of the policy.

IRAs, Retirement Plans, and Annuities

The value of IRAs, retirement plans, and annuities is the amount payable to the beneficiary or beneficiaries as of the decedent's death.

Business Interests

If the decedent owned a sole proprietorship, a professional practice, or an interest in one or more partnerships, closely held corporations, limited liability companies, or other business entities, you should consult with your attorney and with the business' accountant to determine how the decedent's interest should be valued.

There may be a buy-sell agreement which may but will not always fix the amount that is to be paid for the interest. (Such an agreement is controlling for federal estate tax purposes, however, only if it complies with specific provisions of the Internal Revenue Code and Treasury Regulations.) Unless the decedent's interest can be valued by other means, you should obtain an appraisal from a professional appraiser who specializes in the type of business in question.

Valuation and Basis

The basis of an asset is its value for determining gain or loss on sale for accounting and income tax purposes. If you sell an asset for $500 and its basis is $300, your gain is $200.

Under federal tax law in effect at the time this book is being written, each asset of the estate that is includible in the decedent's gross estate for federal estate tax purposes will generally receive a new basis equal to its value for federal estate tax purposes. (Check with your attorney or accountant to see whether this step-up in basis is in effect for the estate your are settling.)

This is true even if no federal estate tax return is filed. The assets of the estate get a step-up in basis, assuming they have increased in value since the decedent purchased them. For example, if the decedent had purchased stock many years ago at a cost of $100 and that stock is worth $2,000 at his death, its basis "steps up" to $2,000. Therefore, the value you determine for an asset becomes its basis.

If only part of an asset is includible in the gross estate, then only that part receives a step-up in basis. If the decedent and his spouse owned their home as tenants by the entireties (joint tenancy between husband and wife), only one-half of the value of the home would normally be includible in the decedent's gross estate.

Thus, one-half of the property (which would be deemed to have passed to the spouse from the decedent) would have a basis equal to one-half of the value of the property for federal estate tax purposes. The other one-half of the property (which would be deemed to have belonged to the spouse) would have a basis equal to one-half of the cost of the property, with no step-up in basis.

However, if the property was acquired by husband and wife prior to 1977, owned by them jointly, and the decedent paid for it 100%, an exception may apply, and there could be a 100% step-up in basis in the first estate. Ask your attorney if the decision in *Gallenstein v. United States*, 915 F.2d 876 (6th Circuit, 1992) applies.

Under the law in effect for 2010 decedents, IRS Form 8939, ***Allocation of Increase in Basis for Property Received from a Decedent,*** had to be filed to obtain a step-up in basis, under complex rules in effect for that year.

Implications of Valuation

There may be significant implications in using one value as opposed to another for a particular asset.

Lower values will result in lower estate tax and may eliminate estate tax altogether. A low value for something which is actually worth more may also increase the amount of property passing to a particular beneficiary, since the person will receive the item but it may be counted as less of his or her share of the estate. Higher values will cause assets to have a higher basis, which will result in lower income tax on the sale of those assets.

You may be tempted to "skew" valuation in a certain direction to achieve a certain outcome. You may also be subjected to subtle or not-so-subtle pressure from beneficiaries to do so. For many assets, there is a range of values which might be considered reasonable. You cannot be faulted for selecting a value at the upper or lower end of this range, depending on your objective, as long as you can make a case for doing so.

As a fiduciary, however, you are legally obligated to value the assets correctly and fairly. There is a difference between an aggressive position and a blatant valuation misstatement. Such misstatements could result in tax penalties or even penalties for fraud. You could be compelled to reimburse the estate or trust for these penalties. For these reasons, you should consult with your attorney on all major valuation issues.

Lifetime Gifts

The federal transfer tax system is a unified system that imposes a single tax on the total of taxable gifts made during life and property transferred at death. Therefore, in addition to taking inventory of the decedent's assets, you must determine if the decedent made any taxable gifts during life.

Depending on the value of the gifts, they may have been required to be reported on federal gift returns, and you may find one or more gift tax returns in the course of gathering the decedent's important documents. If so, copies of should be provided to whomever will prepare the federal estate tax return along with the inventories you compile.

If you are aware of any gifts of money or other property the decedent made to any person which exceeded the amount of the *annual gift tax exclusion* in any one year you should bring this to the attention of your attorney. The annual gift tax exclusion was $10,000 for 1997-2001, and increased to $11,000 for 2002-2005, $12,000 for 2006-2008, $13,000 for 2009-2012, $14,000 for 2013, and is subject to further increases. These are the amounts that could been given to any number of persons in the year in question, without gift or estate tax implications. If you become aware of large gifts, consult your attorney regarding possible gift tax consequences.

These taxable gifts will generally not have to be brought into the estate for administration. However, they may impact computation of the federal estate tax. ■

Inventory Tips

Preparing a complete inventory of the estate may be a major or minor task, depending on the size and complexity of the estate. Here are some tips to keep you on track:

1. Carefully review the decedent's important papers to determine what types of assets may be involved.
2. Prepare a preliminary listing and approximate values, if known.
3. Determine whether you will obtain the necessary values or, if not, who will obtain them.
4. Set target dates for obtaining the values, and periodically check the status and follow up if necessary.
5. Make sure you understand the implications of valuation of particular assets.

Unclaimed Assets

Millions of dollars of assets go unclaimed each year. Under the law, property must be turned over to the state after a certain number of years if it has not been claimed or if there is no activity on the account.

For example, it could be a rental or utility deposit, a refund, an uncashed check, the balance in a dormant bank account, or rights under a life insurance policy. These are assets which you will generally not discover by reviewing the decedent's financial records and tax statements.

In Michigan, you may search for unclaimed property online at **www.michigan.gov/unclaimedproperty**, or contact the **Unclaimed Property Division, Michigan Department of Treasury**, P.O. Box 30756, Lansing, MI 48909, 517- 636-5320.

However, you may also want to check with the unclaimed property departments of any other states where the decedent lived and where the decedent had a vacation residence, in case accounts were opened there and then went dormant. Websites of each of the states' unclaimed property offices are available through the **National Association of Unclaimed Property Administrators, www.unclaimed.org**.

Notes

"When looking for assets,
use Biblical methodology:
Seek and thou shalt find!"

— Anonymous

CHAPTER 14

Are There Liabilities?

Before distributing assets you must determine if there are liabilities. The amount of liabilities will determine how much can ultimately be distributed to beneficiaries.

You know that you must inventory all of the decedent's assets. You must also catalog the liabilities of the decedent, i.e., amounts owed by the decedent at the time of his death, or obligations for which he was legally liable at the time of his death. Hopefully there will be fewer liabilities than assets, but you must address them nonetheless.

What Are Liabilities?

Liabilities include not only those for which the decedent was solely responsible, but also any obligations for which the decedent was jointly liable with others.

As with the decedent's assets, any major liabilities will normally be identified in the course of gathering the decedent's important documents.

You will likely learn of others as bills and statements arrive in the mail. You may also be notified after publication of a notice to creditors. (See the discussion of the notice to creditors in Chapter 17, "To Probate or Not to Probate," and see the more detailed discussion in Chapter 19, "Dealing With Creditors.")

As a general rule, you may have to look a little harder for assets than for liabilities. People who feel a debt is owed often make their presence known quite quickly because they want to make sure the debt owed to them is paid. However, beware of false claims. It has happened, probably more than once, that a person fabricated a claim which was not really owing, hoping that the person charged with handling the estate would simply pay it.

By way of example, look for these typical and not so typical liabilities:

Typical Liabilities

- Charge account balances, including principal amount of the debt and finance charges.
- Income taxes of the decedent.
- Real estate taxes.
- Utility bills.
- Hospital and medical bills.
- Ambulance bills.
- Amounts owed to care givers.
- Principal and interest under mortgages or land contracts payable.
- Principal and interest under other loans payable.
- Charitable pledges; however, some may not be legally enforceable. Ask your attorney.
- Contractual obligations.
- Business expenses accrued as of the date of death.
- Judgments against the decedent.
- Interest and penalties on tax deficiencies.
- Claims of a prior spouse, including alimony, child support, and claims under property settlements.
- Amounts due at death to professionals, such as attorneys, accountants, and investment managers.

Not So Typical Liabilities

- Fees due to the Trustee of a trust the decedent created during his lifetime.
- Contingent claims (claims which will not become due until a future event either occurs or does not occur), including claims under pending litigation.
- Amounts owed under guarantees made by the decedent.
- Claims filed by the state for support of the decedent's child in a state institution.
- Claims for repayments of amounts received by the decedent to which the decedent was not legally entitled.
- Claims against the decedent for tortious acts committed during his lifetime. Claims against the decedent for Social Security taxes the decedent did not pay with regard to an employee's wages.
- Security deposits which are to be repaid in the future.

Valuing Liabilities

Like assets, the decedent's liabilities must be valued. Generally, this will be a simple matter. Though you may have to distinguish between liabilities accrued at the date of death and liabilities which accrue after death, the amount of the liability will generally be the amount payable.

For example, the liability under a loan is the principal balance due, which can be determined from the records of the lender (such as a bank) or the borrower (the decedent). Accrued interest at the applicable rate, as well as any late payment penalties, can be computed under the terms of the loan. If the loan will continue after the decedent's death, interest will continue to be owed under the note or other instrument evidencing the loan.

Sometimes valuing a liability is more difficult. What is the amount of a liability which will only be payable in the future, perhaps even several years down the road, and which provides for interest at a rate which is below the current market rate?

What is the amount of a liability which may or may not be owed? The decedent's liability may depend, for example, on whether certain things happen or don't happen. For example, if the decedent promised to pay someone else's debt, under a guaranty, if that person doesn't pay, the decedent is liable for that debt only on a *contingent* basis.

Contingent liabilities are important, because they could mature into current liabilities, and they cannot simply be ignored. You must provide actual notice to known creditors, and that includes creditors with contingent claims. See Chapter 19, "Dealing with Creditors."

If you encounter any liability which seems to be out of the ordinary, consult your attorney.

Why Are Liabilities Important?

Liabilities are important to the administration of the estate because they affect how much will ultimately be distributable to the beneficiaries. If the estate has assets valued at $100,000 and liabilities valued at $100,000 there will be potentially no estate to distribute to the beneficiaries after paying all the liabilities.

In other words, as a practical matter, you have to know who is entitled to the estate, and creditors generally – but not always – come before beneficiaries. (See the discussion of the priorities of claims in Chapter 19, "Dealing with Creditors," and the discussion of statutory rights of surviving spouses and other statutory rights in Chapter 20, "Putting the Horror Stories in Perspective.") Certain statutory rights of family members and some creditors have priority over the rights of other creditors.

Next, if the estate is a taxable estate, then liabilities will be important because in most cases they will be deductible in determining the amount of estate taxes due. Though the estate has to pay the liability, it will reduce the amount of estate taxes otherwise payable, so Uncle Sam may, in effect, be picking up part of the tab.

What if An Obligation Is Very Old?

Every state has laws generally referred to as the *statute of limitations*. The statute of limitations generally provides that a claim must be pursued within a certain period of time, or the rights to the amount claimed will expire.

Statutes of limitations differ depending on the type of claim. For example, under Michigan law the statute of limitations for bringing a suit under a contract is generally six years.

By comparison, under Michigan law an action for medical malpractice which is alleged to have occurred on or after April 1, 1994 may be brought within two years after the date of the act or omission giving rise to the claim, or six months from the date the claimant discovered or should have discovered the existence of the claim, if later, so long as it is brought within six years after the act or omission giving rise to the claim.

Minors have the benefit of these rules, but in addition a minor's action may be brought any time before the minor's tenth birthday (or fifteenth birthday for injury to the reproductive system).

The point is that if a liability is not recent, there may be a way to avoid it under the statute of limitations. (Also, if the decedent is the potential plaintiff, you should be aware of the need to act before the statute of limitations bars the claim.)

Rules vary depending on the type of claim. Consult your attorney, who can evaluate the facts and determine what statute of limitations applies under applicable law.

What Do I Do About Liabilities?

If the estate will be a taxable estate, you will want to make sure that the person preparing the federal estate tax return knows about all liabilities. In every estate you should address each liability and decide if and when it should be paid.

As a general rule you should not rush to pay any of the decedent's liabilities before determining the total amount of estate assets and liabilities, whether certain claims have higher priority than others, and whether there are any defenses to any of the claims. See Chapter 19, "Dealing With Creditors," for a full discussion of these topics. The present chapter has addressed primarily the need to identify liabilities.

Your attorney can be of great assistance to you in evaluating claims, defending against claims if necessary, and in cutting off your potential personal liability, as fiduciary, for claims. ■

In a Taxable Estate, Liabilities Can Save Money

When Norman's father died, Norman was very adamant that his father had paid all his debts on a current basis, and refused to admit even the possibility of any liabilities.

The estate's attorney managed to convince Norman that he should check his father's papers anyhow, and he found evidence of a significant debt to a friend.

Norman knew his father would have wanted to pay it off, and so he did. At the same time, however, the debt was taken as a liability on the federal estate tax return, and saved the estate significant taxes.

CHAPTER 15

Who Shares in the Estate?

Determining who actually shares in the estate may involve much more than simply reading the will or trust or state statute. There are many reasons why a person may not be entitled to what looks like his or her share of the estate.

Throughout this book we refer to the *beneficiaries*, often assuming that a decision has been made as to who they are. The beneficiaries are the parties who are entitled to share in the estate. To determine who they are should not be rocket science, you think to yourself. Just look at the will or trust, if there is one, and if not then look at the applicable statute or perhaps a beneficiary designation.

In this chapter we discuss how you determine who will actually share in the estate. The estate, in this context, includes the probate estate, any trusts of the decedent, *In Trust For* accounts, securities registered in *Payable on Death* or *Transfer on Death* form, property which the decedent owned jointly with others with rights of survivorship, insurance on the decedent's life, annuities, IRAs, retirement plans, and trusts created by others of which the decedent was a beneficiary.

In more cases than you would suspect, people who appear to be beneficiaries may not receive what was provided under the documents. In other cases there are no documents and you will need to know what provisions the state has made to distribute property of a decedent who did not make a will.

Situations in Which a Beneficiary May Lose Out

A beneficiary may be an individual or an organization, such as a charity. The decedent's estate or trust may also be a beneficiary, for example, of a life insurance policy or an IRA.

Just because a beneficiary may appear to be entitled to share in the estate does not mean that the beneficiary will actually receive anything. The following are some examples of facts which could cause an amount not to be payable to a named beneficiary:

- An insurance company could refuse to pay a claim. This might occur, for example, if the decedent committed suicide during a contestability period, if questions were not answered honestly on the insurance application, if required premiums were not paid, or in some cases if the decedent was not in the same health condition at the time the policy was delivered as when the application was made.
- The beneficiary may not have survived the decedent for the time period required by the will or trust or by state statute.
- Specific property left to a beneficiary may not be in the decedent's possession at death, and the decedent may have clearly indicated that the bequest was to be made only if that property was still owned at death. This is known as *ademption*.
- The estate could be entirely consumed by debts and taxes.
- The decedent may be found to have been incompetent to make a will, or unduly influenced, or under fraud or duress. The decedent may have suffered from an insane delusion. For any of these reasons, the will or trust may not be legally effective.
- The will or trust may be challenged in Probate Court for lack of authenticity or other reasons. Beneficiary designations on insurance policies, IRAs, and retirement plans may also be challenged.
- The amount provided for the beneficiary may be found to have been satisfied by lifetime gifts.
- The amount payable to the beneficiary may be offset by debts owed to the decedent by the beneficiary.

A Taxing Experience

Lorraine left her cottage and a small business to her elder son, Leon. She wanted Leon to have the business because he worked there with her. She left the balance of her estate, principally her splendid residence, to her younger son, Simon, who looked forward to living in the residence. The estate was large enough to be subject to estate tax, but there were no liquid assets.

There was no tax allocation clause in the will. Under current Michigan law, estate taxes on the entire estate are therefore payable only out of the residue, which in this case is Simon's share. Simon has no other funds and must sell the residence to pay the estate taxes.

Equally important, not all those who appear to be beneficiaries will be able to successfully defend their entitlement to share in the estate. The following are some situations in which a beneficiary might be disqualified from taking the share provided for him or her:

- A beneficiary may be found to have caused the will or trust provision to be included through undue influence, duress or other improper means.
- The bequest may be contingent on the beneficiary meeting certain requirements, such as marrying within the faith, or not belonging to a cult, or being the decedent's spouse, and the beneficiary may not meet the particular requirement.
- The will or trust may contain a forfeiture clause, which causes a beneficiary to lose his or her share if the beneficiary challenges the will or trust. However, this type of provision may not be enforceable. Under Michigan law, such a clause is unenforceable if the beneficiary has probable cause for the challenge. Consult your attorney if such a clause is involved.
- A bequest to a charitable organization may be conditioned on the organization meeting certain tax exemption requirements, which it may not satisfy; or it may be required to do something specific with the bequest, which it may not agree to do, or may not be able to do, perhaps within a certain time frame; or the organization may no longer exist in the form originally specified and no successor may be provided.
- The beneficiary may be disqualified because the beneficiary intentionally killed the decedent.
- Under Michigan law, a surviving spouse may be disqualified from receiving an intestate share if the surviving spouse was willfully absent from the decedent or deserted the decedent for one year or more prior to the death.
- A spouse may not be entitled to death benefits under a retirement plan if the marriage occurred less than a year before the death of the plan participant. This will depend on the terms of the retirement plan.

Therefore, when making the initial determination of the beneficiaries, you should bear in mind that they are as yet only the *presumptive* beneficiaries. In this chapter, we explain how these *presumptive* beneficiaries are determined.

If There is a Will or Trust

Where There is a Will

If there is a will, and the decedent owned property which is subject to the will, then the beneficiaries of that property are those named in the will. This may seem obvious, but it is not that simple.

The will must first be determined to be valid. This is accomplished by a proceeding in Probate Court. (See Chapter 17, "To Probate or Not to Probate.") Until the will is admitted to probate, it is not the decedent's will, it is just a purported will, which may or may not be given legal effect.

The will may be contested by persons who, for one reason or another, do not want the will to take effect. It may be found to have been revoked, or invalid for various reasons. If these parties prevail, the will may be set aside.

If there is a will, the beneficiaries named therein, along with those who would inherit if there were no will, are the interested persons entitled to notice of proceedings and information

The Beneficiary Died First

Barry's will provided for his brother, Kevin, to receive a cash bequest of $50,000.

Kevin died before Barry.

Kevin's two children, Lisa and Amanda, were living at Barry's death.

Under Michigan law, Lisa and Amanda would each receive $25,000. This law is referred to as the "anti-lapse statute," which applies absent a contrary provision in a will or trust.

regarding the administration of the estate. The will is then admitted to probate. Normally the beneficiaries under the will would then be entitled to the probate estate. However, there can be complications

The will may provide that personal property is to be distributed according to the terms of a separate writing or memorandum which the decedent may have left, and that property will therefore not be distributed under the will. That document will override the will.

A beneficiary named in the will may not be living at the testator's death. At common law, the bequest to that person *lapses*. That is, it becomes void. Michigan and most other states have *anti-lapse statutes* under which the bequest may, under certain circumstances, pass to the deceased beneficiary's descendants.

The will may direct that a beneficiary is to receive a *specific bequest* of a particular item, such as the decedent's antique desk. However, if the decedent did not own the item at his death, the beneficiary cannot receive it. The decedent may have sold the item, lost it, or given it away during life. In some cases the beneficiary may get something of equal value, but not in all cases.

The decedent may have already given the item to the beneficiary, an act referred to as *ademption by satisfaction*.

The will may provide for two beneficiaries to each receive a cash bequest of $50,000. But if the estate amounts to only $80,000, then each beneficiary can receive only $40,000. This is called *abatement* and each bequest will *abate* or be reduced. The order in which beneficiaries' interests abate is determined by state law.

The decedent may have married after the execution of the will. Likewise, a child may have been born or adopted after the will was signed. Under Michigan law and the laws of many other states, a spouse or child can receive a share of the estate under specified circumstances, even though not provided for under the will.

If there is a surviving spouse, the spouse may, under the laws of Michigan and most other states, elect to either take under the will, i.e., to accept what is provided for in the will, or to take against the will. In the latter case, the spouse can receive a portion of the decedent's property that is fixed by statute. This portion is known as the *elective share, forced share,* or *statutory share.*

Most states have statutes designed to provide some protection to a surviving spouse, minor children and, in some cases, dependent adult children. In Michigan, a spouse and each minor and each dependent child are entitled to a homestead allowance, a family allowance, and certain exempt property. Those rights are in addition to whatever they are entitled to under the will.

See Chapter 20, "Putting the Horror Stories in Perspective," for a discussion of the various rights of the surviving spouse and children.

There could be a prenuptial or postnuptial agreement that limits the rights of the surviving spouse, but the validity of such an agreement could also be challenged.

If the decedent and a spouse or other beneficiary died in a common disaster, where the order of their deaths cannot be determined, it must be decided who died first. This must be determined by reference to the provisions of the will and rules of survival under state law.

A beneficiary could be named in the will whom you do not know or whom you are unable to contact.

There could be a charitable bequest where the exact beneficiary cannot be determined, e.g., a bequest to the "Children's Home," with no indication as to the specific organization which the decedent had in mind.

If the decedent owned no property subject to the will, the will generally will not be offered for probate and will be a moot issue.

Where There is a Trust

If there is a trust, and the trust holds property or is to receive property from another source, such as life insurance proceeds or the residue of the decedent's estate, then the beneficiaries of that property are those named in the trust agreement.

As with a will, there can be complications. Many of the issues discussed above with respect to a will can also apply to a trust agreement.

A trust does not necessarily terminate at the death of the grantor or settlor (the person who created the trust). The trust may continue, with provisions for distribution of income and/or principal to beneficiaries, and ultimate distribution to remainder beneficiaries.

If the trust holds no property, i.e., is *unfunded*, and will not receive any assets as a result of the decedent's death, the trust is a *dry* trust. Even though the trust names beneficiaries, the trust agreement may only become significant when property flows to it, perhaps from the probate estate, life insurance or another trust.

If There is No Will or Trust

Where There is No Will

If there is no will, and the decedent owned property in his sole name, then the beneficiaries of that property are the decedent's *heirs-at-law* determined under the state's laws governing *intestate succession*.

Many people assume that if the decedent left a surviving spouse, the spouse will be entitled to the entire estate. As you will see, depending on the size of the estate, this may not be the case under Michigan law. In Michigan, the laws of intestate succession provide for the following pattern of distribution, depending on who survives the decedent:

Intestate Share of a Surviving Spouse

The intestate share of a decedent's surviving spouse, for decedents dying in 2013, is one of the following.

- The entire intestate estate if no descendants or parents of the decedent survive the decedent.
- The first $210,000, plus one-half of any balance of the intestate estate, if all of the decedent's surviving descendants are also descendants of the surviving spouse and there is no other descendant of the surviving spouse who survives the decedent.
- The first $210,000, plus three-quarters of any balance of the intestate estate, if no descendant of the decedent survives the decedent, but a parent of the decedent survives the decedent.
- The first $210,000, plus one-half of any balance of the intestate estate, if all of the decedent's surviving descendants are also descendants of the surviving spouse and the surviving spouse has one or more surviving descendants who are not descendants of the decedent.
- The first $210,000, plus one-half of any balance of the intestate estate, if one or more, but not all, of the decedent's surviving descendants are not descendants of the surviving spouse.
- The first $140,000, plus one-half of any balance of the intestate estate, if none of the decedent's surviving descendants are descendants of the surviving spouse.

These dollar amounts are to be adjusted in future years for changes in the cost of living, and were different in earlier years. See Appendix C for a schedule of amounts which applied in prior years. Consult your attorney as to the amount for the year relevant to your situation.

Distribution of Balance of Estate or Entire Estate if No Surviving Spouse

Any part of the intestate estate that does not pass to the decedent's surviving spouse, or the entire intestate estate if there is no surviving spouse, passes in the following order to the following individuals who survive the decedent:

- The decedent's descendants by representation.
- If there is no surviving descendant, the decedent's parents equally, if both survive, or to the surviving parent.
- If there is no surviving descendant or parent, the descendants of the decedent's parents or of either of them by representation.
- If there is no surviving descendant, parent, or descendant of a parent, but the decedent is survived by one or more grandparents or descendants of grandparents, one-half of the estate passes to the decedent's paternal grandparents equally if both survive, or to the surviving paternal grandparent, or to the descendants of the decedent's paternal grandparents or either of them if both are deceased, the descendants taking by representation; and the other one-half passes to the decedent's maternal relatives in the same manner. If there is no surviving grandparent or descendant of a grandparent on

either the paternal or the maternal side, the entire estate passes to the decedent's relatives on the other side in the same manner as the one-half.

Prior to making distributions, there should be a proceeding in Probate Court to determine that the decedent did not leave a valid will and to determine the identity of the decedent's heirs-at-law.

If the decedent owned no property in his sole name, then intestate succession is not an issue and there is no need to go to Probate Court on the matter.

Where There is No Trust

Generally, if there is no written trust, then there are no trust beneficiaries. However, the lack of a separate trust document or the fact that there are no assets titled in the name of a trust does not necessarily mean that there is no trust.

The decedent may have provided for a trust in his will, i.e., *a testamentary trust*. Also, in some cases a trust may be established orally (without a written trust document). Further, in an appropriate case a court may impose a *constructive trust*, when the court feels it would be equitable to do so.

Constructive Trust

Carl purchased insurance on his life, which he intended to be used for his children's education. He named his brother, Dwight, as the beneficiary, and advised family members, including Dwight, of the purpose for the insurance.

Carl died several years later, and Dwight made a claim to the proceeds, as the named beneficiary of the policy. The children also made a claim to the insurance, on the theory that it was intended for their educational expenses, and that Dwight was merely to receive the proceeds for their benefit.

Dwight received the insurance proceeds from the insurance company. But even though there was no trust document, the court imposed a constructive trust on the insurance proceeds, and required that they be used for the children's education.

Property Passing Outside the Will or Trust

Jointly Owned Property

Property that the decedent owned jointly *with rights of survivorship* automatically becomes the property of the surviving joint tenants. A will or trust instrument has no impact on this. A major exception is if the property was jointly owned *for convenience only*. In this case, the property will be treated as if it were owned by the decedent in his sole name and it will pass either under the terms of the will or under the laws of intestacy if there is no will.

Property that the decedent owned with others *as tenants in common* (as contrasted with *joint ownership with rights of survivorship*) does *not* become the property of the surviving owner. Instead, the decedent's undivided interest passes under the terms of the will or under the laws of intestacy.

Beneficiary Designations

Property that has a designated beneficiary or beneficiaries will generally pass to the beneficiary or beneficiaries named. Again, a will or trust instrument has no impact on this.

Common examples of property that has a named beneficiary are life insurance policies, annuities, IRAs, retirement plans, and U.S. savings bonds. In some cases, a spouse will be entitled to qualified retirement plan benefits even if someone else is named beneficiary.

Property Passing Under Someone Else's Will or Trust

The decedent may have been a beneficiary of a trust created under someone else's will or trust. The most common example would be one or more trusts established by a predeceased spouse, parent, or grandparent of the decedent. The trust may have been for the decedent's benefit during the decedent's life.

To determine the disposition of the trust following the decedent's death, it is necessary to consult the governing instrument for the trust. This may be a trust agreement or, in some cases, a trust may be established under a will, and the terms of the trust are found within the will.

The decedent may have had the right to designate who would receive the balance of that trust on his or her death (a *power of appointment*). The decedent may or may not have exercised that power of appointment and, if not, the will or trust should provide where the balance of the trust will go.

Rights Under Trusts of Another

Gordon's wife, Rachel, died several years before him. Under her estate plan a marital trust and a family trust were established. Gordon received all the income from the marital trust. Income from the family trust could be paid either to Gordon or to the couple's children.

When Gordon died, both trusts terminated and were distributed, in accordance with their terms, to their children.

Other Issues

Disclaimers

Persons who are named to receive property are not bound to accept it. The intended recipient may *renounce* or *disclaim* the property, in whole or in part. In effect, the person is declining property that would otherwise pass to him or her.

There are several reasons why one might want to do so. One common reason is to allow the property to pass to down to the beneficiary who would take if the person who is disclaiming (the "disclaimant") died before the decedent. If the Internal Revenue Code requirements for a *qualified disclaimer* are met, the distribution will not be treated as a gift from the disclaimant for gift tax purposes. One of these requirements is that any disclaimer must be made within nine months of the decedent's death.

Example: Grandfather dies and leaves property to his wealthy son, who doesn't need it and would prefer that it pass to his own children. The son executes a qualified disclaimer, and the property passes under the will as if he predeceased Grandfather, directly from Grandfather, not a gift from son. If the son does not execute the qualified disclaimer and accepts his inheritance, it will either be includible in his own estate, or he will have to deal with the gift tax rules to give it to his children during his lifetime.

Timing of Disclaimers

A qualified disclaimer can permit a beneficiary to allow property to pass to another beneficiary, without creating a taxable gift.

However, qualified disclaimers must be made within certain strict statutory time limits, the person who is disclaiming must not benefit from the property to be disclaimed, and the disclaimer must meet a variety of other IRS requirements.

Make sure you understand how disclaimers might work in this estate, and that each beneficiary is made aware of the deadline and the other requirements for a qualified disclaimer. Ask your attorney to explain the applicable rules and deadlines early in the estate administration process, and before any distributions are made.

Altering Shares in an Estate

Will or Trust Contests

Although one way to alter shares of beneficiaries of an estate is to challenge the will or trust in Probate Court, the result of such an undertaking is uncertain. The court might construe or interpret the will or trust in accordance with the decedent's original intent. The court might set aside the will or trust and rule that the estate should pass under a prior will or trust or by intestate succession. It is unlikely, however, that the court will change the dispositive provisions, as courts in Michigan and most other jurisdictions are loath to rewrite the decedent's will or trust.

Agreements Among Beneficiaries

If the interested parties agree on a modification of their respective shares, it may be possible for them to enter into an agreement among themselves to alter their respective shares. This may or may not require court approval. State law will vary on this, so check with your attorney.

Under Michigan law, in a probate estate (not a trust), whether there is a will (a testate estate) or no will at all (an intestate estate), heirs or devisees may agree to alter their respective shares under what is known as the "Dodge Act." Subject to the rights of creditors and taxing authorities, interested persons may alter the interests, shares, or amounts to which they are entitled in any way that they agree in a written agreement executed by all who are affected by the changes. This does not require Probate Court approval.

There are some exceptions, such as where an interested person is a minor or incapacitated person. In that case, the agreement will require court approval, and if a beneficiary cannot be located that will be a problem. In the absence of these complication, however, if all interested persons agree, the beneficiaries of a probate estate can change their shares in a private agreement signed by all of the interested persons.

If a trust is involved, the rules are different, and what law will apply depends on when the trust became irrevocable.

For trusts that were or became irrevocable before April 1, 2010, the Estate and Protected Individuals Code ("EPIC") governs how affected parties may modify an irrevocable trust. Under EPIC, the interested parties could enter into an agreement which modifies their respective shares, subject to certain restrictions involving minors or unascertained interested persons, but in any event the agreement must be submitted to the Probate Court for approval. If the interested persons make an agreement but it is not approved by the court, the Trustee is not bound by the agreement, nor is anyone else who may be affected by the agreement but was not a party to it. Therefore, a Trustee would generally not want to make any distributions pursuant to an agreement by beneficiaries to alter their interests in pre-April 1, 2010 irrevocable trusts without seeking prior court approval, because of the potential liability for breach of the Trustee's duty under the terms of the trust.

The Michigan Trust Code ("MTC") applies to irrevocable trusts which became irrevocable on or after April 1, 2010. The MTC does not give the beneficiaries the power to alter their respective shares by agreement, but it does provide several ways that the shares of a noncharitable trust may be modified:

First, it may be modified by the court, with the consent of the Trustee and the qualified trust beneficiaries, if the court concludes that the modification is consistent with the material purposes of the trust.

Next, if there is a "trust protector" who has the power under the trust to grant, veto, or withhold approval of a modification of the trust, the trust may be modified with the consent of the qualified trust beneficiaries and the trust protector.

Finally, if there is a Trustee or trust protector to whom a power to direct modification of the trust has been given by the terms of a trust, then that person can modify the trust.

If the Trustee fails or refuses to consent, or fewer than all of the qualified trust beneficiaries consent, to a proposed modification of the trust, the modification may be approved by the court if the court is satisfied that (a) the trust could have been modified if the Trustee and all of the qualified trust beneficiaries had consented; and (b) the interest of a qualified trust beneficiary who does not consent will be adequately protected.

The MTC does provide for what is referred to as a *non-judicial settlement agreement* among interested persons, with respect to any matter involving a trust, provided that it does not violate a material purpose of the trust and includes terms that could be properly approved by a court. However, the statute specifically prohibits use of a non-judicial settlement agreement to modify the terms of a trust. On the other hand, such an agreement could arguably be used if the matter involves interpretation or construction of the terms of a trust, which are matters specifically mentioned in the statute which can form the basis of such an agreement. A non-judicial settlement agreement does not require court approval, but may be submitted to the court if desired.

There are also practical ways to modify shares. For example, it is certainly possible for beneficiaries to alter their shares by taking what is left to them under the terms of the trust, and then making gifts from one or more beneficiaries to the others to achieve the desired allocation. They could even enter into an agreement among themselves, and then direct the Trustee to make the desired distributions, to avoid successive transfers of property.

The Trustee should consider seeking releases and indemnification, and the parties should be mindful of potential income and transfer tax consequences of arrangements which result in the shares of some beneficiaries being reduced while the shares of others are increased. The parties should also ensure that representation exists where it is necessary or appropriate to have a beneficiary bind one or more individuals.

Reformation of Trusts and Wills

If there is evidence that dispositive or other provisions of a trust instrument are incorrect, it is possible to petition the Probate Court to reform or modify the document in a court proceeding.

Michigan law allows the Probate Court to approve reformation of the terms of a trust, even if unambiguous, to conform the terms to the settlor's intention if it is proved by clear and convincing evidence that both the settlor's intent and the terms of the trust were affected by a mistake of fact or law. The court may also modify the terms of a trust in a manner that is not contrary to the settlor's probable intention to achieve the settlor's tax objectives. A petition may be filed to reform a trust even if all the interested parties do not agree.

Also, if the trust is being construed or interpreted, or a Trustee appointed, those things (among others) can be accomplished in a non-judicial settlement.

It may also be possible to reform a will, particularly if a mistake can be proven, or if the matter arises out of something which can be resolved as a matter of construction.

Decanting of Trusts

Laws of several states, including Michigan under legislation enacted at the end of 2012, permit a Trustee to distribute the assets of a trust to another trust, which will generally be on the same basic terms, but conceivably could permit some terms to be different. This is referred to as *decanting*.

In Michigan, unless the terms of the trust expressly provide otherwise, if an irrevocable trust includes a discretionary trust provision (meaning that the Trustee has the authority to distribute out all the trust assets), the Trustee can distribute all or part of the trust property to the Trustee of a second trust, provided two conditions are met:

First, the terms of the second trust must not materially change the beneficial interests of the beneficiaries of the first trust.

Second, if the first trust indicates that it is to qualify for a tax benefit, or if appears that the first trust was designed for a tax benefit, the second trust must not be inconsistent with the tax planning of the first trust.

Also, the distribution to the second trust must not increase or change the compensation of the Trustee unless all the beneficiaries consent; must not result in a charge of fee for the transfer, unless the beneficiaries consent; may not reduce the standard of care applicable to the Trustee's actions or expand the exoneration of the Trustee; and may not reduce the authority of a person who has the power to direct or remove the Trustee.

Locating Beneficiaries: Heir Search Firms

If beneficiaries cannot be located, you should consider engaging a missing heir search firm to find them. You cannot simply administer the estate as if the beneficiary did not exist.

You may want to obtain a Probate Court order authorizing engagement of a particular firm and payment of fees for its services. If the beneficiaries do not turn up or cannot be located in a reasonable time, consult with your attorney about what to do with the property that is

Finding Missing Heirs

There are many firms that will offer to help you locate missing heirs, and they charge differently for their services. Some will locate heirs at no charge to the estate, but will charge a percentage fee to the heir. Other firms will charge the estate or the heir a flat fee or an hourly fee unrelated to the amount of assets involved.

One firm which advertises that it has non-percentage based fees and will provide an up-front fee quotation is **International Genealogical Search, Inc., www.heirsearch.com**, 1-800-663-2255.

You can learn a great deal about how these firms work and the relative advantages and disadvantages of each of them by contacting representatives of several firms.

distributable to these beneficiaries. You may not be able to simply allocate that property among the other beneficiaries. In Michigan there is a procedure to deposit the missing beneficiary's share with the county Treasurer's office.

Dealing with Contingent Fee Heir Finders

The Personal Representative of an estate, or Trustee of a trust, has an obligation to locate the rightful beneficiaries. What happens if no one is administering an estate, and as a result the decedent's property reverts to the state after a period of time, after which it is listed on the state's rolls of "unclaimed property"? You may be contacted by an "heir finder" whose business consists, in whole or part, of finding the heirs to these otherwise lost or abandoned fortunes.

For example, a long lost relative may have had bank accounts or perhaps U.S. savings bonds, either in joint name with another relative, or perhaps payable on death to that other relative. Both may have died, as a result the bank accounts or savings bonds may have become the sole property of the last of them to die. When that person died, he or she may not even have known of the existence of that property.

After a period of years, under the applicable state unclaimed property statute, the account would have been paid over to the state unclaimed property fund. It doesn't belong to the state. It is just waiting for the rightful heir to claim it. What if you were an heir at law of the last of them to die? You would be entitled the property, and might not even know that it exists.

You may have absolutely no idea you had these relatives, or that they left an estate to which you are entitled. You may receive a letter or a phone call from an attorney or investigator, maybe even from another state, telling you that the money is there, and all you have do is sign up and he will take it from there. You won't have to pay a thing. All the expenses will come out of the inheritance, and he will guarantee the results. You will pay nothing up front, and he will be entitled to only a contingent percentage fee when the money is payable to you.

What do you do?

On the one hand, if he's right, this is "found money" you never imagined you would ever get. On the other hand, a large contingent fee may be unreasonable.

Our advice is to proceed with caution, and try to learn as much as you can about the alleged inheritance so you can check it out yourself. If you feel it's worth paying someone, consider either a flat fee or an hourly fee based on the actual amount of time spent, not a percentage fee which could be unreasonable if a large inheritance is involved. In any case, if you decide to work through an heir finder, do not pay anything until your receive the inheritance.

Is a Percentage Contingent Fee Heir Finder Agreement Voidable?

What if you are reading this too late and have already agreed to a contingent fee heir finder agreement for a high percentage, say 40%. Can you get out of it?

Generally a contract is legally binding, and you will be obligated to pay the fee to which you agreed. However, in some limited cases it may be possible to either cancel the contract, or if you refuse to pay and are sued on the contract, have the court void the contract.

We suggest that you immediately contact an attorney to thoroughly analyze the facts and the law to see if there is some basis for either negotiating a different fee basis or avoiding the contract completely. Among other things, the attorney should consider the following:

1. If the agreement is oral (there is nothing in writing, or there is a written proposal but you have not signed it or agreed to it in writing, such as by email), it may not be enforceable under applicable state law. Some states view oral contracts with disfavor.

If the heir finder is an attorney, check the Rules of Professional Conduct applicable to attorneys in the state in which he is licensed to practice law. Some states require that contingent fee agreements be in writing.

Also, check your state law and the law of the state which is holding the funds to see if either state regulates heir finders by statute and/or regulation. If so, the law may require that the contract be in writing to be enforceable. Even if the law of the state which is holding the funds does not regulate heir finders, if your state does and requires that their contracts be in writing, then consider invoking your state's strong public policy to defend against the claim under an oral contract.

2. If you have already signed an agreement, have the attorney check the law in your state and the state holding the funds. Some states which regulate heir finders require that they register with the state, that their agreements contain certain specific provisions, and that the contingent fee not exceed a certain percentage. The heir finder might not be in compliance. If your state has such a law, but the fund is being held by another state which does not regulate heir finders, your attorney could still invoke the strong public policy of your state in defending a suit by the heir finder to collect his fee.

3. Check your state's consumer protection laws. Some states allow consumers to cancel certain contracts, including those signed at home, for a certain number of days after they are signed. Others permit cancellation of agreements which are unconscionable.

4. If the percentage fee is very high, or if the value of the assets to be recovered is very high and the proposed percentage, when translated into dollar terms, would appear to be unreasonable, consider petitioning the Probate Court in the state where the decedent died to have the contract deemed unenforceable because it is unreasonable.

Michigan Ethics Opinion RI-193 (March 2, 1994), dealt with a lawyer who located potential heirs, and addressed whether the lawyer could charge a contingent fee. The panel found no *per se* limitation on what could be charged (the case involved a proposed 40% contingent fee), but reviewed various generally applicable factors to determine whether the contingent fee was reasonable.

It held that the lawyer may only obtain a modest fee: "Since the lawyer knows the prospective client is entitled to the escheated funds, there is no 'contingency' or risk that the lawyer will 'lose' the case. Therefore, the lawyer may charge a modest hourly or flat fee for the services, which fee may be paid from the escheated funds."

The lawyer had already done the research, at his own risk and expense, to find the heir, and the only thing that remained to be done was to submit the papers to claim the funds.

Even if your case does not deal with a Michigan attorney, there could be similar rulings in the state where the attorney is licensed, or the Michigan ethics opinion could be used for its reasoning, if not as authority, even in a case which does not involve an heir finder who is an attorney.

This is a developing area of the law, and your attorney should also research court cases to see if any have held contingent fees of heir finders unreasonable. Even cases in other states could provide some precedent to help a court in making its decision, or to help you negotiate a lower fee with the heir finder. ■

Finding Unclaimed Assets Yourself

When approached by an heir finder, some people will want to try to find the unclaimed funds themselves. You may have a good knowledge of your family tree, or may be willing to do your own genealogy research to identify your ancestors. You can then check their names on the websites of each of the states' unclaimed property offices, available through the **National Association of Unclaimed Property Administrators, www.unclaimed.org.**

If you are successful, you may be able to save the heir finder's fees, which could range from 10% to 40%, and which in some cases are increased by out-of-state attorney's fees.

Notes

"If you want an audience, start a fight."

— Gaelic Proverb

CHAPTER 16

Keep the Beneficiaries Informed

What you tell the beneficiaries and when you tell them can make the difference between successful administration of an estate or a miserable experience plagued by distrust and lawsuits.

Information, Please

Aside from wanting a distribution, beneficiaries want information. They usually want as much information as they can get, and as soon as possible. To begin to understand the mind-set of a beneficiary, you must appreciate that you are merely the "collection agent," and your job is to collect the estate and pass it on to the beneficiaries.

It is *their* money. You may have to deal with a lot of details and thorny issues along the way, lose time from your "day job," have sleepless nights, and turn grey – and you may even be a beneficiary yourself. But as far as the other beneficiaries are concerned, you're working for them!

Some people don't realize this and assume that beneficiaries – particularly beneficiaries who are family members – don't need to be kept informed. Such a person may think:

"I've been given this responsibility by [Mom, Dad, Uncle Al, or whomever] and the beneficiaries should be delighted that I have accepted this tremendous burden and should simply let me get it all done. I'll do what I'm supposed to do and divide up the estate properly at the end."

As you will see, this type of attitude is based on incorrect assumptions, which can actually be hazardous to your emotional well-being and your financial health.

First, if you are the Personal Representative or Trustee, you are *legally obligated* to provide certain information. Under Michigan law, various types of information must be provided to beneficiaries of a probate estate or a trust, as well as to others, such as creditors and, in some cases, the State Attorney General. Legal implications of violating those obligations vary and should be discussed with your attorney.

Second, as a practical matter, problems with beneficiaries can usually be avoided, or at least minimized, if you are proactive, anticipate questions, and keep the beneficiaries fully informed at all times.

In this chapter, we first review the statutory requirements and then dispense some practical advice which should help you keep the beneficiaries happy.

You may have a dozen reasons why you honestly feel you don't need to provide information and should be allowed to go about your business of administering the estate without keeping others "in the loop." You may be:

- The oldest child.
- The only family member with any financial "savvy."
- The closest relative.
- The only relative.
- The only beneficiary who really knew and cared for the decedent.
- The only one who actually visited the decedent in his or her last years.
- The only beneficiary in town.
- The only beneficiary who doesn't spend his days at the bar.
- The beneficiary of the lion's share of the estate.
- The only individual beneficiary, with the rest going to charities.
- You may not have been invited to the weddings of the children of the other beneficiaries.
- You may not have spoken to the other beneficiaries in years, the last time may have been very unpleasant, and you may not care if you ever speak to them again.

We urge you to review this chapter carefully before you dig in your heels too far. Then have a heart-to-heart talk with your attorney about what you really should do in terms of providing information.

Requirements Under Michigan Law

If There is a Probate Estate

Within 28 days after his or her appointment, the Personal Representative must serve the decedent's heirs and devisees a notice of his or her appointment and duties. With 14 days after appointment of the Personal Representative, or retention of an attorney by the Personal Representative, whichever is later, the Personal Representative must mail the interested persons whose interests will be affected by payment of attorneys' fees a notice regarding the attorney fee agreement and a copy of the written attorney fee agreement.

Notice to creditors must be published and actual notice must be given to all known creditors.

Notice must be given to the surviving spouse of the rights of election, allowances, and exempt property within 28 days after the appointment of the Personal Representative.

An inventory of all of the assets of the probate estate must be served on all presumptive distributees within 91 days after appointment of the Personal Representative.

An account must be provided to all beneficiaries of the probate estate annually and upon completion of the administration.

All of this is explained more fully in Chapter 17, "To Probate or Not to Probate."

If There is a Trust

Within 63 days after the Trustee acquires knowledge that a *formerly revocable trust* has become irrevocable on the death of the grantor, or after accepting the position of Trustee, whichever is later, the Trustee must inform each qualified trust beneficiary of certain things, in writing.

The Trustee must inform each qualified trust beneficiary of the trust's existence, of the court in which the trust is registered (if it is registered), of the Trustee's name, address, and telephone number, and of the beneficiary's right to request and receive both a copy of the trust's terms that describe or affect the beneficiary's interest, and relevant information about the trust property.

The same information must be provided by the Trustee of an *irrevocable* trust within 63 days after acceptance of the trust.

In addition, upon reasonable request, the Trustee must provide a beneficiary with a copy of the trust's terms that describe or affect the beneficiary's interest and with relevant information about the trust property.

Unless the trust instrument directs otherwise, the Trustee must provide a statement of account to each qualified trust beneficiary at least annually and on termination of the trust or a change of the Trustee, and must keep each current trust beneficiary informed of the trust and its administration.

Unless the trust instrument directs otherwise, the Trustee must, on request, provide a statement of account to each qualified trust beneficiary who is not also a current trust beneficiary, and must keep each of those persons reasonably informed of the trust and its administration.

In the Trustee's discretion, the Trustee may provide a statement of account and other information to any beneficiary.

If there is no probate estate, the Trustee must publish a notice to creditors. The Trustee should also send actual notice to any known creditors. See Chapter 19, "Dealing with Creditors."

If There are Charitable Beneficiaries

Certain information must be provided to the Michigan Attorney General's Charitable Trust Section for a probate estate in which the residue is payable to a charitable beneficiary, or for a trust that has specific or residual charitable beneficiaries. Your attorney can tell you what must be done or you can contact:

Assistant Attorney General
Charitable Trust Section
P. O. Box 30214
Lansing, MI 48909
517-373-1152

Put it in Writing

All important information should be communicated to the beneficiaries in writing. All beneficiaries in a given category (i.e., beneficiaries of specific bequests and residuary beneficiaries) should receive the same form of letter. You may wish to customize letters for each beneficiary so they are advised only of their bequests and not what the others receive. Include a detailed list of whatever documents are being sent. This will reduce the possibility of misunderstandings and will eliminate any subsequent disagreement over what you did or didn't say, or what was or was not included in the package.

If you are going to use email, keep copies of whatever you send. Either add yourself as a "cc" or "bcc" person and print out the message as it comes back to you, or make a copy of your "sent" email message. However, discuss first with your attorney issues relating to lack of confidentiality of information sent over the Internet.

If you are sending faxes, keep copies of whatever is sent, and consider sending "hard copy" by mail as a general practice. Indicate on each letter or memo you are faxing or emailing that a copy is also being sent by mail.

Important letters or packages should be sent by certified mail, return receipt requested, or by overnight courier.

Discuss with your attorney whether he or she should receive copies of whatever you send to beneficiaries or others.

Keep meticulous files. At a minimum, file everything in chronological order. In more complex estates, you should also keep files by topic (e.g., various assets, liabilities, distributions, court filings, and so on). Avoid the tendency to simply jam everything into a file or box, or allow it to pile up on your desk, with the hope that some day you will have time to straighten it all out.

If you keep everything in order as you go, it will be easy. If not, you may never get to it, and some day you will have to find an important note, letter, memo, or other paper and you will spend hours searching for it.

Your First Communication

It is important to win the confidence of the beneficiaries at the very beginning, or you may find yourself on the defensive throughout the administration. With this in mind, beneficiaries should hear from you at the earliest possible date, ideally within two weeks of the decedent's death.

You may feel that this is too soon. You may still be involved with post-funeral tasks such as writing acknowledgment notes. You may feel that it is indecent to get into estate business so soon or you may just be inclined to put these matters off. You may find that you have no stomach for administering the estate, or that you are overwhelmed by your responsibilities.

If this is the case, you should – without delay – make arrangements either to step aside (decline to serve) or to get help. (See Chapter 12, "Where to Turn for Help.")

If you choose to serve as a fiduciary, the sooner you begin, the better. As explained above, there are statutory time frames that must be met, whether there is a probate estate or a trust. Just as importantly, a prompt commencement will be well received by the beneficiaries.

Your first formal communication should be a comprehensive letter, the exact nature of which will vary in each case, but in general at a minimum should:

- Begin by saying that you are writing in your capacity as Personal Representative and/or Trustee of the decedent, who died on a given date.
- Describe the decedent's estate planning documents. For example, the decedent may have left a last will and testament of a certain date and/or a trust agreement of a certain date, with codicils and/or amendments. Describe each document by name and date, and include copies or excerpts. Consult with your attorney as to whether full documents should be provided, or only that portion that relates to the particular beneficiary.
- Identify the beneficiaries and indicate what each is to receive, whether a specific bequest or percentage of the residue. (Discuss with your attorney how much information should be provided to people receiving specific bequests, i.e., bequests of specific property or fixed dollar amounts.)
- Enclose a preliminary inventory of assets, stating very clearly that this is preliminary and is subject to change as you learn more.
- Explain that the estate will be reduced to the extent of debts, expenses, and taxes.
- Explain that beneficiaries may disclaim (or turn down) all or any portion of what they would otherwise receive, how that would work, and the timing and implications of a disclaimer.
- If probate will be required, explain what is involved in this process, who the probate beneficiaries are, and what notices and other mailings these beneficiaries can expect to receive.
- List and discuss the main administrative tasks to be completed and the approximate time frame for each.
- Explain whether and when the federal estate tax and state estate or inheritance tax returns must be filed and when clearances may be expected.
- Discuss personal property. If it will be distributed to the beneficiaries, describe when and how this will be done. If it will be sold, describe when and how this will be accomplished.
- Explain that final distribution cannot be made immediately, although one or more partial distributions may be made.
- Discuss the management of the assets and what actions are planned to preserve and protect the assets, to diversify investments, and to obtain investment advice.
- State who is entitled to the income earned by the assets during the period of administration.
- Explain income tax matters, including the fact that taxable income of each residuary beneficiary will be shown on a Form K-1 to be sent to each residuary beneficiary after the end of the year, and that residuary beneficiaries must wait to finalize their personal income taxes until they receive the K-1.

- Discuss any related entities. (For example, there may have been a trust for the decedent's benefit which will now terminate and pass to other beneficiaries.)
- State whether or not you intend to charge a fee for your services as Personal Representative and/or Trustee and, if so, the manner in which the fee is to be determined. You must notify qualified trust beneficiaries in advance of any change in the method or rate of the Trustee's compensation, unless the trust provides that this is not necessary.
- Provide your contact information (telephone number, fax number, and email address) and solicit questions about the estate.
- Conclude with assurances that you will provide regular updates as administration of the estate progresses.

The first letter may well be the most difficult that you will have to write, simply because it includes so much information. However, a thorough first letter will give the beneficiaries confidence in you. Also, by laying out your timetable, you will forestall inquires from beneficiaries as to when they will receive their shares.

Depending on the size and complexity of the estate, your attorney may prepare a draft of this letter for your review, or you may prepare a draft for the attorney's review. Your attorney should in either case receive a copy of the final letter as sent to the beneficiaries.

If you are the only current beneficiary of the estate, then this letter would not be applicable. If the other beneficiaries are your children, you may decide that so formal a communication is not necessary. In other cases, however, we recommend that a letter of this type be used, although the specific contents will vary in each case.

The statutory requirements must be met in any event. Information regarding a trust must be provided to all *qualified* trust beneficiaries, not just *interested* beneficiaries. In other words, the trust agreement may provide that certain persons only receive assets from the trust at a future date, or after the death of someone else, but those people are still qualified beneficiaries and should receive a copy of the letter.

Progress Reports

After the first letter, you should provide the beneficiaries regular written progress reports. You should write periodically regarding the following:

- Any changes to the inventory.
- Sale of assets. (Enclose a copy of the closing statement or bill of sale, if applicable.)
- Appraisal of assets. (Enclose a copy of the appraisal.)
- Significant investment actions.
- Annual accounts. (Enclose a copy of the account. Consult with your attorney concerning what the account should contain to maximize its benefit to you as a fiduciary.)
- K-1s. (Enclose the K-1 and explain its significance.)
- Federal estate tax return and state estate or inheritance tax return, if applicable. (Enclose a copy of the returns.)

- Closing letter from the IRS, if federal estate tax was applicable, and from state tax authorities, if state death tax was applicable. (Enclose a copy.)

Always include a brief summary of what you are currently working on, such as assembling information for the federal estate tax return or for the fiduciary income tax returns. Beneficiaries want to know that you are working to move the administration forward.

In some cases you may want to solicit input from residuary beneficiaries on certain actions, such as sale of assets or selection of an investment advisor. By doing so, you may head off objections to what you did, which could come too late to change the outcome.

Protecting Yourself

You can expect to receive some sort of feedback from the beneficiaries. Ideally, you will get comments to the effect that you are doing a great job. You will appreciate knowing that your hard work has not gone unnoticed.

Unfortunately, this will not always be the case. Some beneficiaries may be critical of your efforts or may be generally hostile to you. If you sense that any beneficiary disagrees with your handling of a matter or with the administration generally, you should take appropriate steps to protect yourself. Discuss with your attorney whether, when, and how you should take any of the steps outlined in the following checklist. ■

Possible Methods to Protect the Fiduciary from Beneficiary Claims

- Obtain a **release** for an action you have taken which may give rise to complaints in the future, such as an investment decision.
- Obtain **consents** to an action you believe to be proper, but which might negatively impact one or more beneficiaries.
- Seek a **Probate Court order** with respect to a proposed distribution, particular question or issue. (This can be done even if there is no probate estate.)
- File an **account** with the Probate Court, which will include disclosure of the specific action or actions which might otherwise be challenged later, and specifically request approval of those actions in an **order approving the account.**
- Enter into a **settlement agreement** with the beneficiaries, approved by the Probate Court.

Notes

"People count up the faults
of those who keep them waiting."
— French Proverb

CHAPTER 17
To Probate or Not to Probate

What is probate, when do you need it, and what's the big fuss about probate anyhow? Here we provide straight answers to these questions, and an overview of various probate procedures, step-by-step.

Most of us have probably heard stories about what a dreadful experience it is to "go through probate." High expense, assets tied up for years, and lack of privacy are the traditional "evils of probate." The truth is that these alleged "evils" are generally grossly exaggerated and relate to laws and court practices of a bygone era, which have long ago been reformed in many states, including Michigan.

In this chapter, which deals specifically with current Michigan practice, you will learn what it really means to go through probate, when it is necessary, and when it is not. We will review expedited procedures available to small estates, and procedures which typically apply to other estates. In Appendix A we provide you samples of most of the basic Michigan probate forms developed by the State Court Administrative Office for use in Michigan Probate Courts, so you can see what is involved. In this chapter we discuss when those forms are used.

You may still conclude that probate of any size estate involves work which you would prefer to have handled by your attorney, but at least you will have a better appreciation of what it all really means.

What is Probate?

Probate of a decedent's estate is the court process which determines the validity of a will, or who the heirs are if there is no will, allows creditors an opportunity to file their claims, and provides for the remaining assets to be distributed to the rightful takers.

In some cases the Probate Court also supervises the affairs of minors and people who are incapacitated, and appoints guardians for those people and conservators for their property, a process which is sometimes referred to as *living probate* and can be quite burdensome.

The Probate Court also deals with other matters. However, our focus here is solely on the probate of decedents' estates.

When is Probate Necessary?

If the decedent owned any assets in his or her sole name, it is possible that probate proceedings will be required. This is true whether or not the decedent left a will. A will itself does not avoid the need for probate.

For example, if the house was left in the name of "William Jones," that would be sole-name property, and to be able to sell the house after his death, or transfer it to his heirs, probate would generally be necessary, regardless of whether William left a will.

By comparison, if he left his house in joint name with someone else, with rights of survivorship, then *probate of the house* would not be necessary.

For example, William may have put his house in joint name with his daughter during his lifetime. Title to the house would then read as follows: "William Jones and Elizabeth Jones, as joint tenants with rights of survivorship." (Real estate titled jointly with a spouse is called *tenancy by the entirety* instead of joint tenancy, with the same result.)

The house would then pass automatically to the survivor on the death of either William or Elizabeth. No probate of that asset would be required, just the recording of the death certificate of the first to die. However, if there are other probate assets, probate would be required of those assets, but not the house.

If the decedent owned sole-name real property in another state, as well as probate assets in the state of his domicile, it may be necessary to have probate proceedings in the other state as well. This is called *ancillary probate*. If the estate is being probated in another state, because the decedent resided there at the time of death, but there is real estate in Michigan, ancillary probate may be required in Michigan. (See the full discussion of ancillary probate at the end of this chapter.)

What is Not Subject to Probate?

Assets which are not titled in the decedent's sole name, or which have a named beneficiary, are not subject to probate. Examples of non-probate assets include:

- Joint property, i.e., property which is held jointly with rights of survivorship (sometimes indicated JTWROS).
- Property owned by a trust or a Trustee.
- Individual retirement accounts (IRAs).
- Pension, profit sharing, or other retirement plans.
- Annuities.

- Insurance policies.
- Savings bonds with *Payable on Death* (POD) designations.
- Accounts which are held *In Trust For* someone else (ITF accounts) or *Transfer on Death* (TOD).
- Any other asset payable to a named beneficiary.

None of these assets would generally have to be probated *unless they are payable to the estate.* There may be a specific beneficiary designation which says pay to "the estate," or there may be no beneficiary designated at all. If there is no beneficiary named, the terms of the contract, for example, may provide for payment to the estate. It is also possible that there is a beneficiary named but that beneficiary is deceased, and there is no other beneficiary named, and in that case the contract may require payment to the estate.

Avoiding Probate

A person can avoid probate at his or her death by ensuring that there is no property in the person's sole name.

The person accomplishes this by holding all assets jointly with others, in trust, or in assets which have named beneficiaries, such as life insurance, annuities, or retirement plans, or in accounts with "POD" (Payable on Death), "ITF" (In Trust For) or "TOD" (Transfer on Death) beneficiary designations. The person may also benefit from the exceptions to probate discussed in this chapter.

Exceptions to Probate

In certain situations, an asset which would generally be subject to probate can be distributed without probate, because of special rules. These are exceptions to the general rule that everything in the decedent's sole name requires probate. In Michigan, these exceptions include the following:

Transfer by Affidavit

If the decedent's probate estate (minus liens and encumbrances) does not exceed $21,000, as adjusted for cost of living, and does not include real property, a person entitled to certain assets of the decedent may claim them by providing the holder of the assets with a copy of the death certificate and an ***Affidavit of Decedent's Successor for Delivery of Certain Assets Owned by Decedent***, PC 598.

By law, the holder of the property must then pay or deliver the property to the claimant. More than 28 days must have passed since the decedent's death. This procedure cannot be used if an Application or Petition for the Appointment of a Personal Representative has been granted or is pending, or if a Petition and Order for Assignment (discussed below) has been filed.

The Affidavit is sent directly to the holder of the assets. It is not filed with the Probate Court, nor is it an order of the Probate Court. If this procedure and the Petition for Assignment are both available, the person holding the asset may not require the use of one proceeding rather than the other.

Although this procedure has been in effect in Michigan for several years, it is not yet widely understood. Be prepared to provide a copy of the statute supporting the form (MCL Section 700.3983) for review by the financial institution, especially if it is outside of Michigan. Some financial institutions may not honor the form, or they may refer it to their legal department for review, which could result in a delay of weeks to months. If you plan to use this procedure, you should be aware that you may encounter some difficulties. You may wish to call ahead to see what the particular financial institution may require before presenting the completed Affidavit.

Unpaid Wages

An employer in Michigan may pay the wages due a deceased employee to the employee's spouse, children, parents or siblings, in that order, unless the employee filed a request to the contrary with the employer. This avoids the need to open a probate estate just to cash the decedent's last paycheck.

Many employers are unaware of this and may therefore issue the last check in the name of the deceased employee, or issue it to "the estate." Mention this exception, and if they aren't familiar with it have the employer speak with your attorney.

Cash Up to $500 and Wearing Apparel

A hospital, convalescent or nursing home, morgue, or law enforcement agency in Michigan holding cash not exceeding $500 and wearing apparel of the decedent may deliver that property to the decedent's spouse, child, or parent who provides suitable identification.

The person claiming this property must also provide an affidavit which states the person's relationship to the decedent and that there are no pending probate proceedings for the decedent's estate.

Motor Vehicle Transfers

If the combined value of the decedent's motor vehicles does not exceed $60,000 and there are no probate proceedings for the decedent's estate, registration of title may be transferred by the Michigan Secretary of State to the surviving spouse upon submitting a death certificate, an affidavit of kinship, and the vehicle's original certificate of title. The surviving spouse may either title the vehicle, or reassign the surviving spouse's interest in the vehicle without first obtaining title. If the original title is not available, the surviving spouse must either title the vehicle in his or her name, or follow a special "duplicate/transfer" procedure.

If there is no surviving spouse, then title may be transferred to next of kin, i.e., to all children, equally; if no spouse or children, then to the parents of the deceased; if no spouse, children or parents, then to all brothers or sisters equally; and if none of the above, then to closest next of kin. If there is agreement among the next of kin (for example, several children or brothers and sisters) that the vehicle may be transferred to only one of them, then those who agree to waive their interest may do so.

The form to be used is Michigan Department of State TR-29, ***Certification from the Heir to a Vehicle.*** Waiver of an interest in the vehicle by next of kin is done on a Form TR-34, ***Certification***. That form should be used if there is more than one next of kin and the vehicle is to be transferred to only one of them. Both forms may be downloaded at **http://www.michigan.gov/sos/0,4670,7-127-1585_1587_1588-23308--,00.html.**

If the vehicle is being transferred from the decedent to an immediate family member, no use tax will be due. However, the next of kin may add a co-owner at the time of titling, and if that is done and if the co-owner is not an immediate family member of the deceased, the co-owner will be liable for use tax.

Call the **Secretary of State** in advance at **1-888-SOS-MICH (1-888-767-6424)** with any questions and to make sure the requirements can be met.

Watercraft Transfers

If the combined value of all of the decedent's watercraft does not exceed $100,000, and there are no probate proceedings for the decedent's estate, registration of title may be transferred by the Michigan Secretary of State to the surviving spouse or next of kin upon submitting a death certificate, an affidavit of kinship, and the certificate of title for the watercraft.

Income Tax Refunds

Income tax refund claims may be collected without probate by filing IRS Form 1310, ***Statement of Person Claiming Refund Due a Deceased Taxpayer.*** This form should be used unless the filer is a surviving spouse submitting a joint return, or if the filer is a Personal Representative filing Form 1040 for the deceased, in which case a copy of the letters of authority of the Personal Representative should be attached. Form MI-1040 is used to claim a refund of Michigan income tax due to a deceased taxpayer.

Travelers Checks

Under rules which are not specific to Michigan, many companies which issue traveler's checks will redeem them following the death of the owner, without requiring the appointment of a Personal Representative for the estate. Typically they will require that the checks be submitted along with a death certificate and an affidavit by the next of kin indicating to whom payment should be made.

In the case of American Express Travellers Cheques, which may be the most common form of traveler's check, the surviving spouse may take them and the death certificate to the bank and instruct the bank to call the **American Express Travellers Cheque Customer Service Centre,**

1-888-412-6945, for further instructions. We recommend making the call in advance of the visit to the bank, to make sure that the requirements can be met and the procedure is understood.

Why the Fuss about Probate?

Probate necessarily involves certain dealings with the Probate Court and this can take time and increase the costs of administering the estate.

Many years ago, the probate process involved payment of heavy fees for court-appointed appraisers, long delays, and filing of the probate inventory with the Probate Court, which resulted in a lack of privacy for the estate. Today in Michigan, and in many other states as well, the probate process can be relatively quick and painless, and involves minimal costs.

However, Probate Court filings are still required, and do take some time and involve some costs, however minor. If you had to do it several times, you would get the hang of it. But for anyone handling a probate estate for the first time, especially without an attorney drafting the papers and telling you what to expect, it can be a bit intimidating and even overwhelming.

For this reason, many people arrange their affairs so that probate will not be necessary upon their death. If the decedent did that, and had only non-probate assets, you're in luck. If not – even if there is only one probate asset – you will probably have the opportunity to find out what probate is all about.

Be patient, keep your sense of humor and your perspective, and hang on. This, too, will end.

The Typical Situation: A Pour-Over Will and a Fully Funded Revocable Trust

A decedent today might have both a will and a revocable trust.

The will would appoint a Personal Representative for the probate estate. The revocable trust, which becomes irrevocable on the death of the decedent, would name a Successor Trustee.

The will would provide that any assets in the probate estate would be distributed, or "pour over," to the Trustee of the now irrevocable trust, to be distributed in accordance with the terms of the trust. If all of the assets of the decedent were transferred to the trust during lifetime (i.e., the trust is "fully funded"), there may be no probate estate at all. The will would operate merely as a backstop, just in case there were assets in the probate estate.

The Probate Process

The purpose of probate is to see that claims against the estate are settled, and to distribute the decedent's assets to the beneficiaries under the will or, in the absence of a valid will, to the decedent's heirs. Remember that when we talk about the estate in this context, we mean the *probate estate*. The probate estate consists only of those assets, if any, that the decedent owned in his or her sole name and assets which, for some reason, are payable to the estate.

Probate proceedings take place in the Probate Court for the county where the decedent was domiciled at death. They are governed by state statute, court rules, and the practices of the local Probate Court. In Michigan, those rules can and do vary somewhat from county to county.

There is no requirement that probate administration be handled by an attorney. However, except in the smallest estates, most people would find it difficult, frustrating, and time consuming to attempt this without some degree of professional help.

Probate Court personnel are not allowed to give legal advice and, as a result, can provide only limited assistance. The amount of information you can obtain directly from the court will also vary, depending on the particular court. Larger, busier Probate Courts simply do not have the staff to deal with every inquiry or to provide much information over the telephone. They may have more information about the probate process, including current filing fees and blank probate forms available online.

Furthermore, probate administration does not take place in a vacuum. The appraisal and management of property and the handling of tax matters must be integrated into the process. Consequently, in most cases except the smallest estates it is advisable to engage an estate planning or probate attorney to handle or guide you through the probate administration.

Before You Leap...

In limited situations, it may be possible to transfer some sole-name assets which do not fall under the listed exceptions, without going through the hoops of probate, and you should at least consider this possibility. Here are a few examples:

Privately Held Businesses

If the decedent owned an interest in a privately held business, it may be possible to transfer the interest without probate. For example, if the decedent owned stock in a family-owned company, and the decedent's stock passes to family members, the surviving family members may be perfectly willing to transfer the stock without seeing formal letters of authority of a Personal Representative, issued by the Probate Court. If the stock can be transferred without probate proceedings, and if there are no other probate assets, then probate may be dispensed with.

Willingness to make a transfer of a business interest or investment may extend beyond strictly family relationships. For example, if the decedent owned a partnership interest in an investment partnership with other investors, the person in charge of recording transfers of those interests may not insist on having the partnership interest probated.

However, if stock is owned in a publicly traded company, New York transfer agents will always require the court appointment of a Personal Representative of the estate. This will require probate. That way, the transfer agent knows that the person instructing the transfer is authorized to do so.

Decedent with a Living Trust

If the decedent signed a revocable living trust which provides that all of his assets are deemed to be held in the trust, regardless of how they are actually titled, and did not actually transfer title to all of his assets to the trust, that broad language in the trust may, in some cases, help you avoid probate.

In most cases, if a third party is involved, and if the asset is not actually titled in the name of the trust or the decedent as Trustee, the third party will insist on probate.

In some cases, however, you may be able to convince the third party that the language of the trust was sufficient to transfer the asset to the trust, and no probate should be required. This is resolved on a case-by-case basis. If a large institution, such as a bank, brokerage firm, or publicly traded company is involved, it is unlikely the institution will acknowledge the effect of the language in the trust to actually transfer title to the trust. They will insist that the transfer must have been made during the decedent's lifetime on the books of the company.

On the other hand, if personal property is involved, such as jewelry or art work, a better case can be made that the language of the trust should be given effect. If the decedent actually signed an assignment of title to personal property to the trust, then that should suffice, even if the assignment remained in the decedent's files during his lifetime.

Your attorney can help you address your specific fact situation. The worst case is you try to transfer the asset without probate, your efforts are rejected, and you have to probate the asset. In most cases, this is what you should expect.

Remember that the person who allows the transfer, without probate, of an asset which should be probated is taking some risk that the transfer is not authorized. You should understand why your request is denied, then move on, calmly, and embark upon the probate process.

Probate Procedures

Michigan law provides for small estate procedures which can be used for estates of less than $21,000, adjusted for inflation, as well as the affidavit procedure discussed above. (All dollar amounts in this chapter are for 2013. See Appendix C for amounts for prior years. Check with your attorney or the Probate Court for dollar amounts in other years.

Normal procedures apply to estates over this amount. In the following pages, we provide an overview of the Michigan probate process as it applies to both the small estate and the estate which does not qualify as a small estate.

We also provide you references to the official Probate Court form numbers, so you can easily obtain those you need, by number, at the Probate Court or on the Internet. In Appendix A we have reproduced all of the probate forms referenced in this book, so that you can see what type of information they require. *Those forms have been reduced in size for printing and may thus not be completed and filed. You will need full-size forms.* **Michigan Probate Court forms** are available at any Michigan Probate Court. They are also available online, courtesy of the State Court Administrative Office at **www.courts.michigan.gov/scao/courtforms/probate/gpindex.htm**

Our explanation is not intended to make you an expert in this arcane area, but rather to give you an appreciation of the steps that must be accomplished in probate administration. Furthermore, the explanation in this chapter is limited to probate procedures per se. Matters such as inventorying the assets, protecting and preserving the assets, settling creditor claims, and filing tax returns are covered in other chapters.

Simplified Probate: "Small" Estates

Before beginning a "traditional" probate administration, whether supervised or unsupervised, in an informal or formal proceeding, consider whether either of two "small estate" procedures may be used. (We assume you have already considered availability of any of the other exceptions discussed above.) These small estate procedures may even be used in larger estates where most of the decedent's property passes outside of probate. For example, most of the property may be held in a revocable living trust, or consist of life insurance, retirement plan benefits, or joint property payable to a beneficiary or surviving joint tenant. One of these small estate procedures may even be used where the main goal is to retitle assets without the expense and delay of traditional probate proceedings.

Petition and Order for Assignment

If the total value of property (which may include real property and/or personal property) in the decedent's sole name remaining after payment of funeral and burial expenses does not exceed $21,000, as adjusted for cost of living, an heir or a person who paid for the funeral may file a ***Petition and Order for Assignment***, PC 556, with the Probate Court. You must also present a copy of the death certificate and the funeral bill, whether or not it has been paid. ***Testimony to Identify Heirs and Devisee Heirs***, PC 565, may also be required by some Probate Courts.

On the ***Petition and Order for Assignment***, you list the decedent's assets, date of death values, and the heirs who are entitled to them. You must pay a filing fee (currently $25), an inventory fee which is computed based on the total value of the assets, and a certification fee ($12 per copy) for the number of certified copies of the order desired. The Probate Court will assign a probate file number and complete the last section of the form (***Order Assigning Assets***), making it an order of the court. You can then obtain certified copies and present or send one to each holder of the decedent's assets with the request that they make distribution as specified in the order.

The court will order that the property be used to pay any unpaid funeral and burial expenses first, or to reimburse whoever paid those expenses. The court will order that the remaining property be assigned to the spouse or to the decedent's heirs if there is no spouse.

Note that under this procedure the decedent's assets are distributed to his or her *heirs*. Even if there is a will, it is not presented for probate, and the assets are not distributed according to the will. However, the will is filed with the court for safekeeping and future probate if the need arises. Inventories and accounts are not filed. A Personal Representative is not appointed, nor are letters of authority issued. No notice to creditors is published. The Order of Assignment simply assigns the assets to pay or reimburse funeral and burial expenses, and the balance to the heirs at law. Once the petition is filed and the order is entered (usually the same day), the file is closed.

An heir (other than a surviving spouse who qualifies for allowances, or minor children) who receives property through this procedure remains responsible up to the value of the property received for any of the decedent's unsatisfied debts for 63 days after the date the order is entered.

Summary Administration

If the value of the entire probate estate, less liens and encumbrances, does not exceed the homestead allowance, family allowance, exempt property, administration costs and expenses, funeral expenses, and expenses of the decedent's last illness, the Personal Representative may immediately distribute the estate and file a ***Sworn Closing Statement, Summary Proceeding, Small Estates***, PC 590, without publishing notice to creditors. To use this procedure the total allowances and above costs must equal or exceed the value of the decedent's estate, reduced by outstanding liens, mortgages and encumbrances.

The estate proceeding is started like a traditional estate, with an application or petition. The following forms will have to be filed:

- ***Application for Informal Probate and/or Appointment of Personal Representative (Testate/Intestate),*** PC 558, or ***Petition for Probate and/or Appointment of Personal Representative (Testate/Intestate)***, PC 559, with filing fee (currently $150)
- ***Testimony to Identify Heirs***, PC 565
- ***Supplemental Testimony to Identify Nonheir Devisees***, PC 566 (if there is a devisee who is not an heir of the testator, such as a trust)
- ***Renunciation of Right to Appointment, Nomination of Personal Representative and Waiver of Notice***, PC 567, from those with equal or greater right to appointment as Personal Representative.
- ***Notice of Intent to Request Informal Appointment of Personal Representative*** (if required), PC 557
- ***Register's Statement***, PC 568
- ***Acceptance of Appointment***, PC 571, and any required ***Bond of Fiduciary,*** PC 570
- ***Letters of Authority for Personal Representative***, PC 572
- ***Notice of Appointment and Duties of Personal Representative***, PC 573
- ***Notice Regarding Attorney Fees***, PC 576
- ***Notice to Spouse of Rights of Election and Allowances, Proof of Service and Election***, PC 581
- ***Inventory***, PC 577, and gross estate fee must be paid before the Closing Statement is filed.

- ***Account of Fiduciary, Short Form***, PC 583, or ***Account of Fiduciary, Long Form***, PC 584.
- ***Sworn Closing Statement, Summary Proceeding, Small Estates***, PC 590. This will be filed once the Personal Representative has fully administered the estate and distributed the remaining property to the persons entitled to it. The personal representative must have complied with the statements being made in the closing statement.
- ***Certificate of Completion,*** Form 592
- ***Personal Representative Notice to the Friend of the Court***, PC 618

After sending out the usual notices and preparing the inventory, the Personal Representative may immediately disburse the estate to the persons entitled to the estate. The Sworn Closing Statement must be sent to all distributees, creditors and other claimants known to the Personal Representative, whose claims are neither paid nor barred. If no objection to the Sworn Closing Statement is filed within 28 days, the Probate Register is to issue a Certificate of Completion.

The Seven Step Probate Process

1. Open the probate estate.
2. Provide required notices.
3. Prepare and serve the probate inventory.
4. Prepare and serve annual accounts.
5. File Notices of Continued Administration, if administration exceeds one year.
6. Make distributions to beneficiaries.
7. Close the probate estate.

Normal Probate (Except Small Estates)

The steps in the normal probate process, required in Michigan for all but the smallest estates, are set forth in the above box. (We deal with a special situation, *ancillary probate*, at the end of this chapter.)

Each of the steps in normal probate is explained below in general terms. The explanation, however, is intended only as background information. The precise actions to be taken may vary, depending on the circumstances and local court practice, and each involves a myriad of details which are beyond the scope of this book.

As you read through this discussion, remember that help is available from attorneys who are more familiar with this process than you would ever want to be. Your attorney can obtain the necessary information from you, and make recommendations as to the best way to proceed. Your attorney can then complete the forms, obtain your signature where required, file the forms, send out all the required notices, and assure the successful completion of the probate process. Remember, also, that even if the will nominated you as Personal Representative, you cannot act in this capacity until the estate has been opened and you have been appointed by the Probate Court.

1. Open the Probate Estate

At this point, you are certain that you need to open a probate estate. You have considered the possibility that assets can be transferred without probate, and you have also considered the small estate procedures discussed earlier in this chapter.

You should also consider that it may be necessary to *admit the will*, but it may not be necessary to *appoint a Personal Representative*. These two processes can be separated.

Under Michigan's tax apportionment rules (MCL Section 700.3920, *et seq.*), as a general matter death taxes are charged to the residuary estate unless the governing instrument (e.g., the will) directs otherwise. A provision in a will can direct that each beneficiary, even those receiving specific bequests, will be responsible for the share of the taxes generated by the bequest to the beneficiary. For that to be effective, however, the will must be admitted to probate.

If the estate is not large enough to generate estate taxes, then this won't be of concern. However, in a taxable estate you should ask your attorney whether the will should be admitted to assure that its tax allocation clause will be effective, even if it is not necessary to appoint a Personal Representative.

In some cases a decedent will hold a power of appointment under a trust created by someone else, which permits the decedent to direct how the balance of that trust will be distributed after the decedent's death. Often the trust will provide that the power of appointment must be exercised in the decedent's will admitted to probate. In this case as well, it is possible to admit the will, but not have a Personal Representative appointed.

Informal Proceedings. The probate estate can be opened under *informal* probate and appointment proceedings by filing a dual purpose form, ***Application for Informal Probate and/or Appointment of Personal Representative (Testate/Intestate)***, PC 558.

It is possible to file for only *one* of these purposes. For example, if the decedent had a power to appoint or designate who will receive certain property, which had to be exercised in a will admitted to probate, but there is no other reason to probate the will, application may be made only for informal *probate*. On the other hand, if the sole purpose is to investigate a wrongful death action, application may be made only for informal *appointment*.

The following additional forms must also be filed:

- ***Testimony to Identify Heirs***, PC 565
- ***Supplemental Testimony to Identify Nonheir Devisees***, PC 566 (if there is a devisee who is not an heir of the testator, such as a trust)
- ***Register's Statement***, PC 568
- ***Acceptance of Appointment***, PC 571
- ***Letters of Authority for Personal Representative***, PC 572

- ***Renunciation of Right to Appointment, Nomination of Personal Representative and Waiver of Notice***, PC 567, from those with equal or greater right to appointment as Personal Representative. (See Chapter 17, "Who Should Administer the Estate?" regarding priority for appointment as Personal Representative if there is no will.)
- ***Notice of Intent to Request Informal Appointment of Personal Representative***, PC 557. You may serve all persons with equal or greater rights to appointment as Personal Representative with a copy of the Notice together with a copy of the ***Application for Informal Probate and/or Appointment of Personal Representative (Testate/Intestate)***, PC 558, if waiver/consents or renunciations cannot be obtained. The Court will appoint the Personal Representative as requested in the notice in either 7 or 14 days (depending on whether service of the notice was personally served or served via regular first class mail), if no objections are received.

A filing fee (currently $150) must also be paid, to open the estate. There is an additional fee for every certified copy of the letters of authority, evidencing appointment of the Personal Representative by the Probate Court. This can vary, but is generally $12 per certified copy.

Formal Proceedings. Alternatively, the probate estate can be opened under *formal* testacy /intestacy and appointment proceedings by filing a ***Petition for Probate and/or Appointment of Personal Representative (Testate/Intestate)***, PC 559.

Formal proceedings to open an estate does not mean that the estate will remain supervised by the court for the administration of the estate. That will only happen if you request supervised administration. Supervised administration will result in the Probate Court's involvement in every step of the probate process and may be advisable if there are disputes, if disputes are contemplated, or if the Personal Representative wants protection for all major actions taken.

The following additional forms may also be filed:

- ***Waiver/Consent***, PC 561, from each interested person or, if Waivers and Consents cannot be obtained, then ***Notice of Hearing***, PC 562
- ***Testimony to Identify Heirs***, PC 565
- ***Supplemental Testimony to Identify Nonheir Devisees***, PC 566 (if there is a person receiving a bequest under the will, i.e., a devisee, who is not an heir of the decedent. For example, a trust receiving assets under the will would be such a person and would require filing of this form.)
- ***Order of Formal Proceedings***, PC 569
- ***Acceptance of Appointment***, PC 571
- ***Letters of Authority for Personal Representative***, PC 572

A filing fee (currently $150) must also be paid, as well as the fee for certified copies of the letters of authority ($12 each).

If a Petition for Formal Probate and/or Appointment has been filed, and Waivers and Consents have been obtained from all interested persons, the order may be entered immediately without a hearing. Otherwise, the procedure is as follows:

- The Probate Court sets a date and a time for hearing.
- The Petitioner must send copies of the petition, the will (if any), testimony forms, and the notice of hearing to the interested persons.
- A proof of service must be filed with the court. This certifies that the required notices and documents have been sent.
- If the petition is unopposed at the time set for hearing, the court may either grant or deny at the hearing.

Why Use Formal Proceedings? Is there any reason to open the estate under formal proceedings instead of the simpler informal proceedings? There may be.

First, if the will is admitted through informal proceedings, there is no statute of limitations on contesting the will. This means that at some point in the future, even after assets have been distributed and the estate is "closed," someone could challenge the will. Even where the sole purpose of admitting the will is to exercise a power of appointment, it would be prudent to have the will admitted formally. The time period to object to a will's admission under formal testacy proceedings is limited to the appeal period, 21 days after the order admitting the will is entered. There is no time limit to object to a will that has been admitted via informal probate.

Second, under informal proceedings, there is no formal determination of testacy or heirs. This means that there is no court order stating who is entitled to share in the estate. Cautious attorneys therefore advise that in each estate there should be a Probate Court hearing either at the beginning of the probate process, or at the end, for protection on these two important issues.

Finally, informal proceedings may be no "simpler" than formal proceedings. If waivers and consents can be obtained from all interested persons in a formal proceeding, the protection of a formal proceeding can be obtained and a hearing can be avoided.

2. *Provide Required Notices*

In each type of probate proceeding, whether formal or informal, certain information must be provided.

Notice to Interested Persons. The Personal Representative must, within 14 days after appointment, serve interested persons with a ***Notice of Appointment and Duties of Personal Representative***, PC 573, with copies of:

- Last will and testament, and codicils, if any
- ***Application for Informal Probate and/or Appointment of Personal Representative (Testate/Intestate)***, PC 558, or ***Petition for Probate and/or Appointment of Personal Representative (Testate/Intestate)***, PC 559
- ***Testimony to Identify Heirs***, PC 565
- ***Supplemental Testimony to Identify Nonheir Devisees***, PC 566 (if applicable)
- ***Notice Regarding Attorney Fees***, PC 576. It is not necessary to file a copy of the notice or a proof of service with the court. Local court practice may require that a copy of the attorney's fee agreement letter or engagement letter be sent with the notice.

Notice to Creditors. The Personal Representative must publish a notice notifying creditors of the estate to present their claims within four months after the date of publication or be forever barred. This is done by preparing a ***Notice to Creditors, Decedent's Estate***, PC 574, and ***Notice to Known Creditors***, PC 578.

Courts vary in their procedures for getting the Notice to Creditors to the local legal newspaper for publication. The Probate Court will advise you whether they will automatically forward the notice to the newspaper or whether you have to do it. After publication, the legal newspaper will send you the Affidavit of Publication for filing with the Probate Court. If there is no Personal Representative, but the decedent had a revocable trust, then the Trustee of the decedent's trust must publish the necessary notice.

The Personal Representative must give actual notice to all known creditors within the four-month period following publication. "Actual notice" means that the notice must be sent to the creditor, not merely published in the legal newspaper. ***Notice to Known Creditors***, PC 578, must be sent to each creditor of whom the Personal Representative has knowledge, or whose existence is ascertainable from the decedent's records. If actual notice is not given to a known creditor, the creditor will be able to assert a claim against the estate after the expiration of four months from the date of publication of the notice to creditors.

The four-month period is thus a shorter time period for claims which applies only if certain requirements are met. Otherwise, the creditor can assert the claim at any time within the applicable statute of limitations, which could be several years, depending on the nature of the claim.

Also, if the decedent had a trust, the Trustee must be notified of the four-month claims period. This notice must be given within the four-month period. This can be accomplished by sending the Trustee a copy of ***Notice to Creditors, Decedent's Estate***, PC 574.

A more detailed treatment of the requirements for giving notice to creditors is found in Chapter 19, "Dealing with Creditors."

Notice to Surviving Spouse. The surviving spouse must be given notice of the rights of election, allowances, and exempt property, within 28 days of the Personal Representative's appointment. The form used for this purpose is the ***Notice to Spouse of Rights of Election and Allowances, Proof of Service, and Election***, PC 581. No notice need be given if the spouse is the Personal Representative or one of the Personal Representatives.

Notice to Friend of the Court. ***Personal Representative Notice to Friend of the Court***, PC 618, must also be sent to the Friend of the Court in the county where the estate is being administered. If a devisee or heir listed in the notice is in arrears in child support, the Friend of the Court will typically put a lien on the devise or inheritance.

3. Prepare Probate Inventory

An inventory of all of the assets in the probate estate must be prepared and served on all presumptive distributees (but not to other interested persons, unless they request it) within 91 days of the Personal Representative's appointment. This is done on an ***Inventory*** form, PC 577.

The original inventory *may* be filed with the court, but does not have to be, and is generally not filed with the court unless the administration is supervised. Proof of service of the inventory *may* be filed with the court, but does not have to be. If you wish to close formally or seek and order of discharge, you will be required to file the inventory rather than merely present it.

In either case, the inventory must be presented to the court for computation of a fee known as the *gross estate fee*, or sometimes simply as the *inventory fee*. The fee must be paid before closing the estate or within one year after appointment of the Personal Representative, whichever is earlier.

4. *Provide Annual Accounts*

Unless otherwise provided in the will, an account must be provided to all interested persons annually and upon completion of the administration. Interested persons include creditors as well as devisees or heirs at law. The ***Account of Fiduciary*** form, PC 583 or PC 584, may be used for this purpose. If the estate is supervised, the account must be filed with the court and allowed on waivers and consents or after hearing.

5. *File Notices of Continued Administration*

Each year, within 28 days after the anniversary of the appointment of the Personal Representative, a ***Notice of Continued Administration***, PC 587, must be filed with the court and a copy provided to interested persons, including creditors, if the probate estate has not yet been closed.

6. *Make Distributions to Probate Beneficiaries*

Unless the estate is supervised, or letters of authority have been restricted, distributions to beneficiaries of the probate estate may be made without a court order.

The Personal Representative *may* deliver a written proposal for distribution to all persons who have a right to object. Any distributee who does not object within 28 days gives up the right to do so.

The Personal Representative may also defer some or all distributions until the estate is to be closed and submit a ***Schedule of Distributions and Payment of Claims***, PC 596, to the court for approval.

Methods to Close the Probate Estate

The probate estate may be closed by any of the following four methods which apply:

- **Summary Administration for Small Estates**
- **Sworn Statement**
- **Petition for Complete Estate Settlement**
- **Petition for Settlement Order**

7. *Close the Probate Estate: Four Methods*

Method #1: Summary Administration for Small Estates

If the value of the entire probate estate, less liens and encumbrances, does not exceed the homestead allowance, family allowance, exempt property, administration costs and expenses, funeral expenses, and medical and hospital expenses of the decedent's last illness, the Personal Representative may immediately distribute the estate and file a ***Sworn Closing Statement, Summary Proceeding, Small Estates***, PC 590.

No notice to creditors need be provided prior to the Personal Representative distributing the estate. However, the closing statement must be sent to all estate distributees and to all creditors and other claimants of whom the Personal Representative is aware, whose claims are neither paid nor barred. A full written accounting of the estate administration must be provided to each estate distributee whose interests are affected.

If no objection to the closing statement is filed within 28 days, the Personal Representative is entitled to receive a ***Certificate of Completion***, PC 592, from the court.

Method #2: Sworn Statement

Unless the estate is supervised, the probate estate can be closed by filing a ***Sworn Statement to Close Unsupervised Administration***, PC 591. This may be filed no earlier than five months after the date of the Personal Representative's appointment.

In the sworn statement, the Personal Representative represents that he or she has done the following:

- Determined that notice was published and the time limit for presentation of creditors' claims has expired.
- Fully administered the decedent's estate by making payments, settlement or other disposition of all claims that were presented, administration and estate expenses, and estate, inheritance and other death taxes, except as specified in the statement, including distribution of estate property to the persons entitled. If a claim remains undischarged, the statement must state whether the Personal Representative distributed the estate subject to possible liability with the distributee's agreement, or describe other arrangements that have been made to accommodate outstanding liabilities.
- Sent a copy of the statement to all estate distributees and to all creditors or other claimants of whom the Personal Representative is aware, whose claims are neither paid nor barred.
- Furnished a full accounting of the Personal Representative's administration to the distributees whose interests are affected by the administration. The accounting must clearly state the amount paid out of the estate in fiduciary fees, attorney fees and other professional fees.

Since the accounting does not have to be filed with the court, no particular form is required. However, a Personal Representative can use ***Account of Fiduciary, Short Form***, PC 583, or ***Account of Fiduciary, Long Form***, PC 584.

If no objection to the closing statement is filed within 28 days, the Personal Representative is entitled to receive a ***Certificate of Completion***, PC 592, from the court.

Absent fraud, misrepresentation, or inadequate disclosure, and unless previously barred by adjudication, an action against the Personal Representative for breach of fiduciary duty must be commenced within six months after the filing of the sworn statement.

Method #3: Petition for Complete Estate Settlement

The method which offers the greatest protection is the ***Petition for Complete Estate Settlement***. Depending on whether testacy has previously been adjudicated, either the ***Petition for Complete Estate Settlement, Testacy Previously Adjudicated***, PC 593, or the ***Petition for Adjudication of Testacy and Complete Estate Settlement***, PC 594, is filed.

This is a formal proceeding which offers an opportunity to settle all issues in closing an estate, providing the Personal Representative the protection of a court order. It is available for all estate proceedings, whether or not the estate was begun by informal or formal proceedings.

If formal testacy has not been determined, such a determination may be requested if it is desired before final distribution. The petition may also request the court to consider the final account, to compel or approve an accounting and distribution, to construe a will or determine heirs, and to adjudicate the estate's final settlement and distribution.

If there is a request for an adjudication of testacy, there must also be a determination of heirs.

As part of this estate settlement procedure, the Personal Representative will generally request to be discharged. Michigan Court Rules require that a Personal Representative making this request must also file additional papers with the court, so the court can make a determination that the estate has been properly administered. Those papers, and the proofs of service for them, are as follows:

- Inventory
- Accountings
- Notice of Appointment
- Fees notice
- Notice to spouse
- Notice of continued administration
- Affidavit of any required publication
- Tax information concerning inheritance or estate tax
- Any other papers the court may require

In addition to the petition, the following additional forms must also be filed:

- ***Waiver/Consent***, PC 561, from each interested person, or ***Notice of Hearing***, PC 562
- ***Schedule of Distributions and Payment of Claims***, PC 596 (if needed)

A filing fee (currently $20) must be paid. The court may approve settlement, direct or approve estate distribution, and discharge the Personal Representative from further claim or demand of an interested person. On waivers and consents or after hearing, the court will issue an ***Order for Complete Estate Settlement***, PC 595.

How to Bar Future Claims from Beneficiaries

When Barry and Harry's mother passed away, a meeting was held at the family attorney's office to review the assets and the will. The assets consisted of stock in a brokerage account, and bank accounts. Under the will, the estate was to be distributed to Harry, Barry, and Barry's children. Harry had no children. Harry, Barry, and Barry's children were all present.

At the meeting, it was disclosed that some bank accounts were held in joint name with Harry, Barry and their mother. Therefore, they passed automatically, by operation of law, directly to Harry and Barry, not under the will. There was discussion about compensating Barry's children for their share of the jointly held bank accounts, but there was no agreement.

An inventory was filed including only the assets in their mother's sole name. No objections were filed. The estate was then closed in what is known as the *informal* method. Barry voluntarily gave his children a portion of the joint accounts, because he felt this was his mother's intent. Harry did not give them anything.

Over a year later, Barry's children filed a petition to re-open the estate, alleging that the joint accounts were not true joint property, but held jointly "for convenience," and since they were joint for convenience only, they should have been included in the inventory of the probate estate. Eventually, the parties reached a settlement.

From the point of view of the Personal Representative, this problem could have been avoided if the estate had been closed *formally,* obtaining a court order preventing the later filing of a petition to re-open the estate. Instead, it had been closed *informally*, and that allowed the later objection which resulted in the children receiving more than just their share of the probate assets.

From the children's point of view, since it had not been closed formally, they had an opportunity to petition to have the estate re-opened so they could assert their claim.

Another method to achieve finality and protect the fiduciary is to file a petition for Probate Court approval of an accounting. The court order effectively bars claims which could otherwise be raised in the future on matters disclosed in the accounting. Otherwise, the statute of limitations on a claim by a beneficiary against a Personal Representative is generally six months after filing of a closing statement, and for a claim against a Trustee can be as long as five years after the termination of the trust.

Method #4: Petition for Settlement Order

The estate may also be closed under a ***Petition for a Settlement Order.*** This procedure is very similar to the Petition for Complete Estate Settlement. However, it is only available where the estate is being administered under a will admitted to probate informally. Also, it may not be used if any part of the estate is intestate.

The petition may not contain a request for a determination to adjudicate testacy. The petition may, however, request the court to consider the final account, to compel or approve an accounting and distribution, to construe the will, or to adjudicate the estate's final settlement and distribution. The Personal Representative may also request to be discharged, and in that case will have to submit additional papers to permit the court to determine that the estate has been properly administered. (See the list under Method #3 above.)

The Personal Representative may petition at any time, and a devisee may petition after one year after the original Personal Representative's appointment. However, the court may not accept a petition under this procedure until the time has expired for presenting a claim that arises before the decedent's death.

There are no forms for this procedure. The petition will have to be individually drafted.

Ancillary Probate

In some cases a person dies a resident of one state, but has property in another state. For example, a Michigan resident may die with a vacation home in Florida, or a Florida resident may die with a home in Michigan. Two complete probate processes are not always necessary. The probate process in the state of residence (the *domiciliary state*), may be the full probate process, but the one in the other state where only certain property is located may be subject to a second, sometimes abbreviated process, where the authority of the Personal Representative granted by the state of domicile to deal with the property in the other state is acknowledged based on what was done in the domiciliary probate.

If the decedent resided in Michigan and the estate is probated in Michigan but there is property is another state, consult an attorney in that other state about ancillary probate in that state.

If the decedent resided outside Michigan and the estate is probated in that other state and there is property in Michigan, the process depends on the type of property involved and the law provides alternatives:

Personal Property. If personal property is located in Michigan, or if someone in Michigan is indebted to the nonresident decedent, at any time after the expiration of 63 days after the nonresident decedent's death, anyone who is indebted to the nonresident decedent, or who has personal property belonging to the decedent, or an instrument evidencing a debt, obligation, stock, or right to bring a lawsuit on behalf of the nonresident decedent, may pay the debt or deliver the personal property or the instrument to the Personal Representative in the other state (the *domiciliary foreign Personal Representative*), upon receipt of the following:

1. Proof of the domiciliary foreign Personal Representative's appointment, which would typically be a certified copy of his or her letters of authority issued by the Probate Court in the other state; and

2. A sworn statement made by or on behalf of the domiciliary foreign Personal Representative stating (a) the date of the nonresident decedent's death; (b) that local administration, or an application or petition for local administration, is not pending in Michigan; and (c) that the domiciliary foreign Personal Representative is entitled to payment or delivery.

This would protect the person who delivers the property to the domiciliary foreign Personal Representative, without requiring anything to be filed in the Probate Court in Michigan. There would be no probate at all in Michigan, not even ancillary probate.

Real Estate. If the property in Michigan is real estate, and the estate was already probated in another state, an ancillary estate proceeding in Michigan may be commenced by informally probating the will in Michigan. An interested person may file a written application for informal probate in the Probate Court where the real estate is located, together with deposit of an authenticated copy of the will and of the statement probating it from the office or court where the will was first probated. This would entail filing of authenticated copies of the Personal Representative's appointment, bond, order appointing Personal Representative, and letters of authority from the other state. Before the Probate Court in Michigan will issue letters of authority it is likely that the remaining documents, i.e., testimony of interested persons, supplemental testimony interested persons testate estate (if applicable), register's statement, and acceptance of appointment, must be filed.

This process would be essentially the same as proceeding in a domiciliary estate, i.e., where the decedent died as a Michigan resident.

However, there is a simpler ancillary probate process allowed by Michigan statute: The foreign domiciliary Personal Representative merely files authenticated copies of the Personal Representative's appointment and any bond filed in the foreign domiciliary proceedings. Those documents are filed in the Probate Court in the Michigan county where the decedent's real property is located. On filing the appropriate papers, under the law the foreign Personal Representative has all of the powers of a domiciliary Personal Representative. No additional documents are filed in the Michigan Probate Court, and no letters of authority are issued in Michigan.

If the real estate is to be sold, contact the title company which will insure title in the purchaser, and make sure they are comfortable with the simpler procedure. ■

NOTES

"The so-called 'evils of probate'—
long delays, high costs, and lack of privacy –
– relate to a bygone era, at least in Michigan.
But it's still a process which baffles most mortals."

— ANONYMOUS LAWYER

CHAPTER 18

Protect and Preserve Estate Assets

Once you have identified estate assets, you need to manage them during the period of administration. Failure to do so could result in losses, and personal liability for the fiduciary.

If you are the Personal Representative, you have a duty to protect and preserve the property in the probate estate. If you are the Trustee, it is incumbent on you to safeguard the assets of the trust. The decedent's property, in other words, is in your hands.

While you must guard against loss, that is not sufficient. You are also expected to make the property productive. It is anticipated that the assets will earn income and appreciate in value while in your custody as a result of wise investments on your part.

This is an awesome responsibility, and one which must not be taken lightly. Should you fail to meet the standards set forth in the will or trust, or established by state statute or case law, you could be personally liable to the beneficiaries for any damages.

In this chapter, we discuss the concerns that should be addressed in managing the most common types of estate property.

What Are Your Duties?

If you are a fiduciary, a number of duties or standards of behavior are imposed by statute or common law. Some of these are summarized in an earlier chapter. (See Chapter 8, "Who Should Administer the Estate?") Many of these duties or standards relate directly or indirectly to the management of property and you should familiarize yourself with them.

One of your first and most obvious duties is to avoid conflicts of interest. As a fiduciary you should be very careful to avoid putting your own interest ahead of that of the beneficiaries. For example, buying an asset from the estate could create a conflict of interest. Simply getting an appraisal and buying at the appraised value may not be sufficient to avoid a claim that you breached a duty to the other beneficiaries. Buying out another beneficiary's share so that the fiduciary can own all of a given asset may likewise create a conflict of interest. Discuss with your attorney how certain transactions could create conflicts of interest, and how you should deal with them.

The will or trust instrument may impose specific duties related to property management. You should read these documents carefully to determine what directions they may contain.

Under Michigan law, except as otherwise provided by the will, the Personal Representative must take all steps reasonably necessary for the management, protection, and preservation of the estate in the Personal Representative's possession.

Unless otherwise provided by the governing instrument, *all* fiduciaries – Personal Representatives and Trustees – are bound by Michigan's Prudent Investor Rule.

Property which the decedent owned jointly with others with rights of survivorship automatically passes to the survivors by operation of law, and neither the Personal Representative nor the Trustee is responsible for it. However, to prevent any misunderstanding, we recommend you notify the survivors that the property is now theirs and that they are responsible for its management.

Before you do so, however, make sure the property was truly joint and that the survivors claim ownership. It may be that an asset was held jointly for convenience only. This is often done with bank and brokerage accounts. In that case, the asset should be treated as belonging to the decedent and the Personal Representative should manage it as part of the probate estate. (See Chapter 13, "Inventory the Assets.")

The decedent's trust, or possibly his probate estate, may be the beneficiary of pensions, retirement plans, IRAs, and various types of annuities. If you are the fiduciary, you may be responsible for making investment choices for an account. You may also have to select a settlement option, a matter which we take up in a later chapter. (See Chapter 23, "Transfer Remaining Assets to Beneficiaries.")

If other beneficiaries are named, then the Personal Representative or Trustee has no responsibility. Nevertheless, it would be a good idea for you to notify the beneficiaries, provide them with relevant information, and give them at least a general warning about the advisability of seeking professional advice before making any elections. Their decisions may have significant tax and legal implications.

Setting Priorities

The first step is to determine priorities and make note of any items which may be time sensitive. The following are some examples:

- If the decedent owned perishable items, these should be attended to before they become worthless.
- If property or casualty insurance is expiring, it must be renewed without delay.
- If investments such as certificates of deposit are maturing, they may be automatically renewed unless action is taken.
- The decedent may have owned high concentrations of certain investments; lack of diversification could expose the estate or trust to significant risk.
- Stock options may have to be exercised by a given date.

- Contractual obligations may have to be fulfilled immediately or on a specified future date, or may be accelerated as a result of the decedent's death.
- Leases may have to be renewed, or lease options exercised; or leases may automatically renew if an election not to renew is not made by a certain date.
- A right to sell stock or other business or investment interests under a buy-sell agreement, or a partnership or other agreement may have to be exercised by a certain date.
- Notify the credit reporting agencies of the death, to prevent identity theft. (See Chapter 5, "Notify Key People.")

Establishing Authority

The decedent's assets may be in various entities with different types of ownership. Before you can act with respect to any asset, you must establish your authority to do so.

Assets in Decedent's Name

For assets owned in the decedent's sole name, you will likely have to present your *letters of authority*, issued by the Probate Court, evidencing your appointment as Personal Representative. (See Chapter 17, "To Probate or Not to Probate.") You may also have to retitle sole-name assets in your name as Personal Representative.

For sole-name assets which pass under the will to a beneficiary or which "pour over" to a trust, it may be possible to leave the assets titled in the name of the decedent until the time comes to transfer them to the beneficiary or the trust. This will avoid the need to retitle the asset twice.

Assets in Trust Name

For assets in the name of a trust, you will have to show that you are the Successor Trustee. Providing a copy of the trust or certain relevant provisions and a death certificate may suffice. However, you may also be asked to provide a *certificate of trust existence and authority,* which your attorney can prepare for you. You will have to notify the qualified trust beneficiaries of your appointment and provide certain information about yourself and the trust, your acceptance of the Successor Trustee position and the terms of the trust, the beneficiaries' interest under the trust and possibly accountings.

Joint Assets

For assets owned jointly by the decedent with others with rights of survivorship, all the survivors normally need to do is provide proof of the decedent's death and identify themselves as the survivors. However, you should consider whether the jointly held asset may have been a convenience account or whether a name was added under duress, fraud, or undue influence.

In cases where you suspect there are reasons to challenge a joint account, the bank or brokerage firm may initially take the position that you have no right to information about the account because, from their point of view, the surviving joint owner automatically inherited it at the first owner's death. See your attorney for guidance. It is imperative that you obtain the information necessary to determine whether this was true joint ownership, and it is possible to do so, even though you may initially be rebuffed by the bank or brokerage firm.

Retirement Accounts

For assets held in an IRA, pension, or profit sharing plan, or other retirement account, if there is a named beneficiary that person is the only one with authority over that account, although a spouse sometimes has rights even if not a named beneficiary.

The Personal Representative or Trustee will generally not have authority over these accounts, unless the estate or trust is the beneficiary.

If you are challenging a beneficiary designation, see your attorney for guidance.

Bank Accounts

Opening New Accounts

In order to make deposit, disbursements, and other cash management functions over the course of administration of the estate, it will be necessary to open one or more new bank accounts.

If there is a probate estate, accounts should be opened in the name of the Personal Representative and the estate. (For example: "Mary A. Jones, Personal Representative/Estate of John R. Jones, Deceased.")

A taxpayer identification number (TIN), also called an Employer Identification Number (EIN), will have to be obtained for the estate from the Internal Revenue Service. This may be accomplished by filing IRS Form SS-4 with the IRS online, by facsimile, by phone or by mail. It is easiest to obtain the TIN online (www.irs.gov), or you may ask your attorney or accountant to prepare Form SS-4 for you.

The TIN should be obtained and the new accounts opened as soon as possible. Banks will sometimes open an account indicating "applied for" where the TIN has not yet been obtained, but more often they will insist on having the number at the time the account is opened.

If the decedent had a revocable living trust, it became irrevocable – and became a separate entity for legal and tax purposes – at the decedent's death. Accounts should be opened in the name of the Trustee and the trust.

A taxpayer identification number will have to be obtained for the irrevocable trust. There are different ways of titling such a trust after the decedent's death, with some attorneys preferring to add the date of death, when it became irrevocable, after the trust name. For example: "Mary A. Jones, Trustee/ John R. Jones Irrevocable Trust UTA [date of death]." This distinguishes the trust from the one which existed prior to death and bore the date of its execution. Some will use the original trust name and date. Follow your attorney's advice on this point.

At a minimum, there should be a checking account. If there is both a probate estate and a trust, there should be a checking account for each. All cash and checks received should be promptly deposited to the checking account for the probate estate or the trust, as appropriate, and all disbursements for that entity should be made from this account.

Because most financial transactions flow through the checking account, keeping separate checking accounts for the probate estate and the trust will facilitate the record keeping which is required of you as Personal Representative of the estate and/or Trustee of the trust.

Unless otherwise provided in the governing document, you must provide accounts to beneficiaries at least annually. (See Chapter 16, "Keep the Beneficiaries Informed.") You must also provide information required for the preparation of the various tax returns. Your records must be sufficient for both of these purposes.

If significant funds accumulate in the checking account, consideration should be given to putting some of the excess into a money market account, certificates of deposit, or other fairly liquid, secure investments. If the amounts are very large, you should consider whether multiple accounts should be opened with different institutions to benefit from federal insurance of the accounts.

Why Separate Accounts?

If you are not detail oriented by nature, you may question the need for separate accounts and meticulous records. You may think it would be simpler to just run everything through your own personal accounts and keep any relevant information "in your head."

As a fiduciary, you are simply not allowed to commingle or mix funds of the estate or trust with your own funds.

Also, a probate estate and a trust are separate entities for legal and tax purposes. It would be quite time consuming and expensive for an attorney or accountant to comb through your personal records to ferret out the transactions that apply to the probate estate or the trust.

Furthermore, without separate records, it would be more difficult for you to defend yourself against a charge of financial malfeasance or to prove figures on a tax return to an auditor.

If you are not of a temperament to observe formalities, recognize distinctions between entities, and keep complete records, you should enlist a family member or an outside professional to handle the details of the administration for you. As an alternative, you may wish to add a bank or trust company as co-fiduciary, agent, or custodian. Finally, you may want to step aside in favor of someone who is more suited to this type of work.

Existing Accounts

Accounts in Decedent's Name

Accounts in the decedent's sole name should be retitled in the name of the probate estate. Accounts should not remain in the decedent's name and you should not write checks or withdraw funds under a power of attorney since your authority to act under the power expired at the decedent's death.

Accounts in Trust Name

Accounts in the name of a trust that was revocable by the decedent should be retitled. The pre-death trust was not a separate taxable entity. All transactions of the trust were attributed to the decedent. The trust probably used the decedent's Social Security number as its taxpayer identification number. By contrast, the post-death trust is a separate taxable entity, and it must have its own taxpayer identification number. Our practice is to include the word "irrevocable" in the name of the trust on accounts after the decedent's death, and to include the date of death as the date of the trust.

Joint Accounts

Accounts that were joint with rights of survivorship should be retitled in the name of the surviving joint tenant or joint tenants. If the account was joint for convenience only and the surviving tenant does not claim ownership, the account should be treated as being in the decedent's sole name and retitled in the name of the probate estate.

Certificates of Deposit

If there are certificates of deposit, the Personal Representative, Trustee, or surviving joint owner should be aware of the terms and the maturity dates. There is no need to prematurely cash in a certificate of deposit which is paying an attractive rate of interest.

However, if it is desired to withdraw the funds prior to the maturity date of a CD, banking regulations generally allow early withdrawal without penalty in the case of death of the account owner. Check with the bank.

Other Financial Assets

Other financial assets typically include stocks, bonds, and mutual funds. They may be held individually (in certificate form), or in one or more brokerage accounts.

Securities in Certificate Form

Securities owned by the decedent or his trust in certificate form (not held in a brokerage account) may remain in that form until a decision is made as to who should receive that security or if it is to be sold. There is generally no need to retitle those securities prior to distribution.

Securities in Brokerage Accounts

Securities in a brokerage account in the decedent's sole name should generally be transferred to a new brokerage account in the name of the Personal Representative of the estate. Securities in a brokerage account in the name of the decedent's revocable trust, which became irrevocable upon his death, should generally be transferred to a new brokerage account in the name of the Trustee of the irrevocable trust. The procedure in both cases is the same as for bank accounts, discussed above. This involves more than a change in the name of an existing account. New accounts are opened, and the securities are actually transferred from the old account to the new account.

Jointly Owned Securities

If it is determined that the joint account is a true joint account and was not established as a joint account merely for convenience, securities owned jointly by the decedent and others as joint tenants with rights of survivorship may generally be transferred to the surviving joint owners, in the same manner as a joint bank account, as discussed above. If the securities are in a brokerage account, a new account may be opened by the surviving joint owners and the securities transferred to it. If the securities are in certificate form, contact the issuing company, agency, or a stock brokerage firm for guidance as to how to retitle the security.

Mutual Funds

Mutual fund shares are held in accounts, either directly with the issuing mutual fund, or by a stock brokerage firm in an account which may hold several mutual funds and other securities.

In either case, mutual funds in the decedent's sole name should generally be transferred to a new brokerage account in the name of the Personal Representative of the estate.

Mutual funds in the name of the decedent's revocable trust, which became irrevocable upon his death, should generally be transferred to the name of the Trustee of the irrevocable trust.

Contact the brokerage firm, if the mutual fund is held in a brokerage account, or the mutual fund directly, if the mutual fund is held at the issuing mutual fund company. You will need to establish your authority in either event, and provide a new taxpayer identification number for the estate or irrevocable trust. Titling of the account will be the same as the bank accounts, discussed above.

IRAs and Other Retirement Accounts

Many types of securities, including stocks, bonds, and mutual funds, may be held in IRA or other kinds of retirement accounts.

However, even though you may see the decedent's name in the title of the IRA or other retirement account, you should *not* retitle those accounts in the name of the Personal Representative. Unless the estate is the beneficiary of the account, those accounts do not belong to the estate and should remain titled as they are, until action is taken by the beneficiary. Disposition of these accounts will generally be governed by a beneficiary designation, not by the will or trust, unless the beneficiary designation directs the account back to the estate or trust.

Education Savings Plans

An education savings plan (also referred to as a Section 529 plan), may have been established by the decedent, as the *account owner*, to help fund higher education for a child, grandchild or other family member, as the *beneficiary*.

All 50 states have set up one or more Section 529 plans. Since they welcome non-residents, you may well be dealing with a plan outside the decedent's or the beneficiary's state of residence. These plans are administered by money management firms, such as Fidelity, Vanguard, TIAA and Merrill Lynch, and state law and the rules of these plans differ.

A *contingent owner* should have been designated, to have the rights of the account owner with regard to the account at the account owner's death. Check with the company that sponsors the plan to see if this was done and, if so, determine who is the contingent owner.

The Michigan Education Savings Program rules, for example, provide that the account is not a probate asset and the contingent account owner automatically takes over the account on the death of the account owner. However, prior to taking any action regarding the account following the death of the account owner, the contingent account owner must provide a certified copy of a death certificate identifying the deceased account owner by name and Social Security number, and/or other proof of identity recognized under applicable law and acceptable to the program.

Management of Financial Assets

If you are the Personal Representative or the Trustee, you must see that the financial assets of the probate estate or trust are properly managed. If the probate estate or trust is the beneficiary of a retirement plan, IRA, or annuity, and you as fiduciary are empowered to choose investments for the account, you must see that this is done wisely.

If you are the surviving joint owner of an investment portfolio, you owe it to yourself to look after these assets for which you are now responsible.

If you are the beneficiary of a retirement plan, IRA, or annuity, and you have authority to select investments, it is in your interest to do so in a manner which best suits your needs.

If you are not experienced in investment management, you should seek a competent advisor. (See Chapter 12, "Where to Turn for Help.")

Whether you work with an advisor or on your own, there are certain things to keep in mind as you decide what to do with the investments.

Estimating Cash Needs

To prepare an estimate of the cash that will be required, ask your attorney or accountant to prepare a projection of the estate taxes, if any, that will be due. This will require an estimate of the gross estate, as well as information about prior taxable gifts and use of the lifetime gift tax exemption, as well as an estimate of amounts deductible for estate tax purposes. (For over 99% of estates, under the current estate tax exemption there will be no federal estate tax.)

To the amount of the estimated estate tax, add estimated fees, funeral and administration expenses, debts (including unpaid income taxes), and claims.

Finally, add any cash bequests that must be paid under the will or trust.

How Much Cash is to be Raised?

Cash will be needed to pay debts of the decedent, claims against the estate, funeral expenses and expenses of administration, income taxes, and possibly federal estate taxes and state death taxes. If you are unable to develop an estimate of these amounts on your own, you should work with your attorney to come up with an estimate of the amount that will be required to discharge these obligations.

If the will or trust provides for cash bequests, funds will be needed to pay them.

Beyond these needs for cash, you may wish to liquidate all or a portion of the securities. You may be concerned about potential fiduciary liability in the event of a market downturn, especially in today's extremely volatile markets. You may be the sole beneficiary or the surviving joint tenant and you may not wish to hold the securities going forward.

In any event, before you sell, make sure you have the requisite authority. Normally this is not a problem. Many wills and trusts give the fiduciary broad authority to sell assets and to make distributions to beneficiaries in cash or in kind, or partly in each.

Nevertheless, Michigan law requires that, unless the will indicates a contrary intention, a decedent's probate estate should be distributed *in kind* to the extent possible. That means the securities themselves would be distributed to the beneficiaries, and not the cash resulting from the liquidation of the securities. Also, beneficiaries may have strong feelings on the matter and should be consulted or at least advised before you embark on a liquidation program.

When it is determined how much cash is to be raised, plans must be made to do so. It must be decided what securities will be sold and when this will be accomplished. Your investment advisor can help you with this.

You should ask the brokerage firm holding the securities what they will charge to sell them. If the portfolio is large, you may want to check with one or two reputable discount brokerage firms to see what they would charge. Sometimes the difference will be significant.

However, you should also consider that it could take some time to transfer the securities to another firm (1-2 weeks would not be unusual). If the stock market drops significantly during that time period, you may lose more in market value that you would have saved in commissions by moving to another firm. If that is a concern, consider discussing the situation with the beneficiaries, so that they understand and appreciate what you are trying to do, the potential commission savings, and the risks. In any event, attempt to negotiate a better rate with the first firm based on the information you have about what the other firm would charge.

The proceeds of sales of securities should be placed in a money market account so that a market rate of interest can be earned with minimal exposure to loss of principal.

What is the Extent of Your Investment Authority?

Many wills and most trusts give the Personal Representative or Trustee authority to invest in such assets as they deem advisable. This seemingly broad authority may be limited, however, by the requirement that the fiduciary invest and manage assets as a prudent investor would.

In Michigan, this requirement has been codified as the Prudent Investor Rule. The statute sets forth duties with respect to portfolio strategy, risk and return objectives, diversification, loyalty, impartiality, investment costs, and delegation of investment and management functions.

The Prudent Investor Rule may be expanded, restricted, eliminated, or altered by the will or trust instrument.

We recommend you seek the advice of your attorney concerning the extent of your investment authority in light of the language in the will or trust and the requirements of the Prudent Investor Rule.

Even if you believe you have full authority, you should consider getting approval of major investments, or of the overall investment plan, from the beneficiaries. By getting the beneficiaries to sign off, you will be better able to defend yourself from "Monday morning quarterbacks" who might criticize your actions if the investments go awry.

If investments have passed to you as the sole surviving joint tenant, or if you are the sole beneficiary under the will or trust, you have complete authority with respect to those assets.

What Types of Investments Make Sense?

For investments in the probate estate or the trust, which are held in a fiduciary capacity, safety is paramount. Speculative or very risky investments should be avoided.

If you are the Personal Representative or Trustee, you must decide how much safety is required. Must everything be reduced to cash and held in federally insured bank accounts? Must the money be spread among different financial institutions so that the amount on deposit in any one institution is within the federal deposit insurance limit?

Are U.S. government securities acceptable? Mutual funds with high yield foreign government bonds? High-grade corporate bonds? "Blue chip" stocks?

Your decision should take into account the expectations of the beneficiaries as well as your own risk tolerance.

Tax-exempt investments may or may not be desirable for the probate estate or for the trust, depending on the tax situations of the estate or trust and the beneficiaries. This should be discussed with your accountant.

The needs and investment objectives of the beneficiaries should also be considered in deciding what investments make sense. How long do you anticipate being involved as fiduciary? Is there a need to generate income for the beneficiaries during this period?

Are there or will there be continuing trusts which will go on for years after administration of the estate, and should investments be made with a view to satisfying the objectives of those trusts and their beneficiaries?

Your attorney and investment advisor should be able to assist you in this regard.

What is the Overall Plan?

Keep in mind that investments may be found in the probate estate, in one or more trusts, and in retirement plans, IRAs, or annuities. These various "pots" of investments should not be dealt with in isolation. All of them should be taken into account in designing a comprehensive financial plan.

Where possible, assets within a single entity (e.g., the probate estate or the trust) should be consolidated for convenience. Assets held individually or in multiple small brokerage accounts may be consolidated into a single brokerage account.

How Will Assets Be Managed Going Forward?

When the administration of the estate is concluded, there may be some investments for which you are responsible. There may be investments which you received from the decedent's probate estate or trust, or which became yours as the surviving joint tenant. There may be investments in a continuing trust of which you are Trustee.

These assets will have to be managed going forward. You will have to decide how much responsibility you want to take on yourself, and how much you are willing to delegate to a professional money manager.

Sometimes you can hold assets individually, in certificate form, but most people find this cumbersome, and certificates are less common today than they were years ago. A popular alternative is to hold the assets in a brokerage account. You can manage the account yourself or you can allow the broker or other money manager to do so. You can, if you wish, require that they obtain your approval prior to any transaction.

Banks and trust companies provide another alternative. It is a popular myth in some circles that "stodgy bankers" are overly conservative and produce mediocre investment returns. You may be surprised by the investment track records that some banks and trust companies have compiled.

We recommend you interview several brokerage companies, money managers and banks and trust companies, to understand the services they provide, how they charge, and how they differentiate themselves from the others. Your attorney can refer you to several of each.

Tangible Personal Property

Tangible personal property is property that is moveable, and can be touched or felt. It is to be contrasted with real estate (land and buildings), which is *real* property, not *personal* property. Tangible personal property includes items such as furniture, clothing, artwork, jewelry and household goods. Strangely enough, tangible personal property includes pets. In some cases, tangible personal property requires title evidencing ownership, such as motor vehicles, boats, and aircraft.

If there is a surviving spouse, tangible personal property will typically pass to the spouse, either because the spouse is considered to have owned it jointly with the decedent with rights of survivorship, because the will or trust instrument leaves it to the spouse, or the surviving spouse may elect household goods as part of the exempt property spousal election. If this is the case, the spouse will normally assume responsibility for the property and there is no need for the Personal Representative or Trustee to be concerned about it.

If there is no surviving spouse, or if the spouse does not receive all of the tangible personal property, as in a second marriage, the situation is different. Any property which is determined to be joint with rights of survivorship is the responsibility of the surviving joint owner or owners. (An automobile, for example, may be registered jointly. Also, it is possible that the decedent executed an assignment making his children, or others, joint owners of all or part of his tangible personal property.) The decedent may also have left a written memorandum directing distribution of certain tangible personal property to certain people. Under Michigan law, that will generally be given effect. However, the Personal Representative or Trustee must take charge of any remaining tangible property.

If the Personal Representative and Trustee are not the same person, it must be decided who is responsible for the tangible personal property. Discuss this with your attorney.

If you are responsible for the decedent's tangible personal property, you must assure that it is safeguarded. Consider taking the following steps immediately:

- If the property is in a home or apartment, make sure the premises are secure. If there is any question about the number or identity of people who have keys, consider changing the locks.
- Arrange for a prompt inventory of all items. (See Chapter 13, "Inventory the Assets.") A written inventory, in addition to its other uses, is an important control which will enable you to keep track of all of the items and make a claim against the insurance if something is stolen, or lost in a fire, flood or other disaster. Also consider taking photos and/or making a video of the tangible personal property, and possibly even have that done by a professional to provide added authority.
- Be sure all family members and friends who have access to the premises understand who is entitled to the property and when and how it is to be distributed. Otherwise, they may mistakenly believe they are free to take whatever they wish. You may wish to have the locks changed to prevent this type of situation.
- Valuable items, such as fine jewelry, artwork, or collectibles, should be placed in safe storage. You should also check to make sure these items are properly insured.
- Potentially dangerous items such as guns or drugs require special handling.
- Make sure proper attention is given to pets, and if there is a separate plan for the care of the decedent's pets, which could be included in a Pet Trust, make sure that it is respected. Do not simply let someone who shows an interest in the pet take it without considering the matter with those who would inherit it. If there is no plan, do not simply have the pet euthanized without exploring alternatives for the pet's adoption. Contact the pet's veterinarian, local animal shelters, animal rescue groups, friends and neighbors.

Financial Records

Consider removing the decedent's financial records from the premises if you are the fiduciary and you will not be living there. This should certainly be done if the premises will be vacant.

In any event it will be easier for you to work with those records if they are at your home or office, or the office of your attorney or accountant.

If the residence is going to be sold, you certainly don't want people passing through to be able to see these records when they open drawers.

Real Estate

Who is responsible for real estate will depend on how it was titled.

Real estate that was owned by a husband and wife as tenants by the entireties passes to the surviving spouse and is the responsibility of the spouse. Property that is joint with rights of survivorship is the responsibility of the surviving joint tenant or joint tenants. Real property that is subject to probate administration or part of the trust estate is the responsibility of the Personal Representative or the Trustee, as the case may be.

You should verify how the property is actually titled since it may be titled differently than you or other family members may have thought.

In the case of a partial or fractional interest in real estate, or a home held in a personal residence trust or other trust, you should consult with your attorney to determine the responsibilities for the property following the death of the decedent, or what happens to the property under the terms of the trust.

Safeguarding Real Estate

If you are responsible for a residence or other real property, whether in Michigan or in another state, you must see that it is safeguarded and maintained until it is either sold or deeded to a beneficiary. If there is a leased residence, it will need to be safeguarded until the lease is terminated. Review the lease to determine the decedent's obligations and make necessary arrangements with the rental management.

Be sure there is adequate homeowner's or renter's insurance in force. The existing policy may have lapsed with the decedent's death. You should check with the insurance agent to determine what coverage there is, if it is effective if the premises are vacant, or not owner-occupied, and how long it can be continued. Continuing homeowner's insurance on a residence which is owned in a trust can be a challenge, although a few companies will write this type of coverage, on a case-by-case basis.

If a residence or apartment is vacant, consider living in the home temporarily to "house sit" or having another family member or other person do so. If this cannot be arranged, you or another family member should look in on the premises regularly. If there is a security system, make sure it is working. If there is no system, consider having one installed.

Consider notifying the neighbors and police that the house is vacant. Whether or not the house is occupied, you should continue the utilities, arrange for landscaping and snow removal. Be sure that the bills for these services, as well as those for property insurance, property taxes, and any mortgages or home equity loans, are paid promptly, subject to consideration of options if the property is "under water," i.e., the debt exceeds the value of the property.

Underwater Real Estate

Try to determine the value of real estate which is subject to a mortgage as soon as possible, and the amount of the mortgage balance. If there is no equity in the property, i.e., if the value of the property is less than the outstanding mortgage or mortgages (i.e., the property is "underwater"), discuss your options with your attorney.

In some cases it may be better to walk away from the property, i.e., either let it go in foreclosure or deed it back to the lender in lieu of foreclosure, rather than continue to make mortgage payments and pay taxes, utilities and other expenses of keeping up the property. It is possible, in some cases, to give up the property without any liability for a deficiency, even if the estate or trust has ample assets to pay the mortgage. For further discussion on this topic, see the section on Underwater Real Estate in Chapter 19, "Dealing with Creditors."

You should develop a strategy on this quickly. If you let months go by and continue to make payments on the mortgage and pay real estate taxes, and later decide that you should not have done this, you will have wasted estate assets.

Sale of Real Estate

If the property is to be sold, you should meet with a real estate broker as soon as possible and take steps to place it on the market.

If the property is in the probate estate and the letters of authority have been restricted, the Personal Representative may have to get permission from the Probate Court to make the sale.

You may want to get a court order even if it is not required, and even if you are dealing with a trust, to protect yourself against charges that the property should not have been sold, or that it was sold at too low a price. As an alternative, you could obtain the written agreement of the beneficiaries to sell at the proposed price. However, a court order will provide greater protection.

Any proposed sale should be reviewed by your attorney before you sign any documents. This is especially true if the sale is to be made to a family member or other "insider" at a below-market price. Such a sale involves a potential conflict of interest, as well as a host of property rights issues and potential gift tax questions which must be sorted out before a deal is finalized.

Potentially Contaminated Property

If any real property is suspected of being contaminated by environmentally hazardous substances, and if you are the Personal Representative or Trustee, you should consult with your attorney before taking any action with respect to the property. Ideally, this should be done even before you agree to serve as a fiduciary. See the discussion of contaminated property in Chapter 8, "Who Should Administer the Estate?"

Once you become an "owner" of the contaminated land, you may be financially liable for its cleanup. The cost of remediating the site to the satisfaction of state and federal authorities could exceed the value of the land itself. Your attorney will advise you how best to handle the matter, and you or your attorney may have to engage a specialist in environmental law.

Rental Property

If the probate estate or the trust contains rental property, the Personal Representative or Trustee must see to the collection of rents, the maintenance of the property, and compliance with all the landlord's obligations. You will also have to file a fiduciary income tax return to report the income. You should consult with your attorney or tax preparer regarding tax consequences of ownership of rental property.

If the decedent was managing the property, you may need to engage a third party property manager to take over this responsibility.

At some point you will have to decide whether to retain the property, for ultimate distribution to the beneficiaries, or to sell it. You should seek the assistance of a real estate broker for evaluation of the market, and consider involving the beneficiaries in this decision.

Business Interests

If the decedent had a business interest in his sole name or in his trust, the Personal Representative or Trustee is responsible for preserving this interest.

If the decedent was in business with others, the surviving owners may decide to terminate the enterprise or to continue it. Either way, there could be a buy-sell agreement or other document which spells out how this is to be done and sets forth the rights of the decedent.

You should obtain copies of any such documents and have them reviewed by your attorney. You should then monitor the actions of the surviving owners to ensure that they comply with the terms of the agreement and that the decedent's probate estate or trust gets the settlement to which it is entitled.

If the decedent or his trust was the sole owner of a business, the Personal Representative or Trustee will have to see to the continuation of the business until arrangements can be made to sell it or transfer ownership to the beneficiaries.

A fiduciary does not automatically have authority to continue a business. Authority is often granted in the will or trust instrument. If it is not, you must look to state law.

In Michigan, a Personal Representative may continue a sole proprietorship or partnership for four months, but must then either reorganize the sole proprietorship or partnership as a corporation or limited liability company, if none of the probable distributees objects, or obtain Probate Court approval to continue in business beyond the four month limit. A Trustee, on the other hand, is permitted to continue a business in any form and for any length of time.

If the decedent was a licensed professional, such as a lawyer, doctor or certified public accountant, there are special rules which apply to the continuation of the practice. Much will depend on whether there are other professionals in the practice, or outside the firm, who have agreed to take over the practice pursuant to a succession plan.

Do not assume, for example, that a spouse can simply step into the shoes of the deceased professional. There are also confidentiality rules which apply to client records. Consult your attorney.

If you are the fiduciary, unless you feel that you are capable of running the business yourself, you must make sure that there are people in place to handle day-to-day operations. If there is no one inside the business who can be relied upon to do so, you should consider bringing in someone from the outside to provide the needed management.

If you are considering selling the business, bring in professionals to help you determine the value, locate potential buyers, and work out terms which are reasonable and will not expose you to claims by the beneficiaries. In many cases, beneficiaries will feel that you should have obtained a higher price, or better terms. If you sell to a buyer who cannot pay cash, be careful about getting adequate security to secure the balance, and consider not only getting formal approval of the transaction from the beneficiaries, but Probate Court approval as well. ■

A Probate Court Order Would Have Avoided Personal Liability

John's father sold his business several years before he died. The buyer paid a down payment, with the balance payable over a period of years, with interest. When John's father died, John was appointed Personal Representative of the estate.

John decided to negotiate with the buyer to pay off the installment note early, at a steep discount. He did not obtain a formal appraisal of the note receivable, or ask for current financial information of the buyer. He had heard that the buyer was in financial difficulty, and thought it would be better to get cash for the note, even if substantially less than the full balance.

John and his sister agreed to this arrangement. However, his sister later learned that the buyer's financial condition was far better than John initially thought. His sister hired an attorney who filed a petition in Probate Court to "surcharge" John for the difference between the discounted amount the estate has previously received for the note (and which she had approved at the time) and the full outstanding balance. The court granted the surcharge petition, and John had to pay, even though his sister had previously agreed to the transaction.

John should have obtained an appraisal of the note, and sought a Probate Court order approving his cashing out of the note at a discount.

CHAPTER 19
Dealing with Creditors

Knowledge of the claims process will enable you to pay proper claims, avoid those which need not be paid, and avoid personal liability for claims.

Should you be under the impression that estate administration is only about gathering assets and distributing them to beneficiaries, we must remind you of another major aspect of handling an estate: The second admonition in the standard definition of estate administration is to "pay debts, expenses, and taxes." Almost every estate will have some creditors, and most will have expenses of administration and funeral expenses.

The debts of the decedent must be settled; they are not automatically extinguished on death. Creditors must be reckoned with, and you and family members need assurances that all liabilities of the decedent have been put to rest and are behind you. You do not want to receive unpaid bills long after the estate has been distributed.

The legal, moral, and ethical thing to do, if there are enough funds in the estate, is to pay all creditors in full. If you know with certainty who all the creditors are and have estate funds to pay them, that's fine. However, you may not be able to pay them all, and you may not be 100% certain that a claim won't be filed which would come as a complete surprise to you.

In this chapter you will learn:

- Why you should not rush to pay liabilities of the estate from personal funds.
- The various types of creditors' claims and how they differ.
- What your legal obligations are to notify creditors of the decedent.
- When creditors must present claims and what happens if they fail to file a claim or file late.
- Which types of claims are entitled to priority, if estate assets aren't sufficient to pay everyone.
- How you, as the fiduciary, may be personally liable if you don't handle claims properly.
- How you can avoid personal liability for claims.
- When revocable trust assets and other non-probate assets may be subject to claims.
- What types of assets are generally not subject to claims.

While you may think that topics such as will contests would fill the court dockets, claims against estates are a more frequent source of Probate Court litigation. As you will see, this is an area in which the support and guidance of an attorney are usually required. Note, also, that the law with regard to probate practice and claims will vary from state to state.

Which "Estate" is Subject to Claims of Creditors?

As you know from other chapters, the term "estate" has different meanings, depending on the context.

In the context of our discussion of claims, we are generally referring to the decedent's probate estate.

It is the probate estate that is generally subject to claims. It is the Personal Representative who generally has the responsibility of dealing with creditors.

In Michigan, however, a decedent's revocable trust may also be liable to pay claims. Also, if there is no probate estate, the Trustee is responsible for the notification of creditors and payment of claims. In some cases, if there is no probate estate and no trust, nonprobate assets may be subject to claims.

Are There Other Sources of Payment?

Before your start to tally estate assets and potential claims, consider whether other sources of payment exist. In some cases certain of the decedent's debts may be covered, at least in part, by other sources, so that you need not pay them in full from the estate.

Consider the following possible sources of payment of the decedent's debts and obligations:

- The decedent may have prepaid funeral expenses in what is known as *pre-need* planning.
- The decedent may have left life insurance for the specific purpose of paying funeral and burial expenses. This may provide a source of cash, but if payable to the estate will become an estate asset and subject to the claims rules discussed in this chapter.
- Burial assistance may be available from the Veteran's Administration. (See Chapter 10, "Veteran's Benefits.")
- The decedent may have had credit life insurance, which would pay the balance on the home mortgage, car or boat loan, credit card accounts, or an automobile lease.
- Medical bills may be covered by health insurance, Medicare, or in some cases by automobile or homeowners insurance.
- Estate taxes may be reimbursable from trusts which are included in the decedent's gross estate and the assets of which give rise to those taxes.

Why is the Claims Process So Important?

The claims process can protect the interests of the family, creditors with priority, and other creditors as well. Aside from validating the will, and determining who are the beneficiaries of the estate, determining what claims should be paid prior to distribution to beneficiaries ranks high on the list of reasons why the probate process exists.

Consider the following case in which proper use of the claims process was essential to the well-being of the decedent's family:

Thelma's husband, Edgar, died suddenly. This was a second marriage and the couple kept their financial affairs separate and filed separate tax returns. Thelma had no knowledge of Edgar's finances.

Edgar didn't have a will or trust, and Thelma had herself appointed Personal Representative. She spent a considerable amount of time diligently searching his records for assets and liabilities. To her surprise and great chagrin, she found that Edgar owed $120,000 back taxes to the IRS and the state taxing authorities, going back many years, including interest and penalties. She also determined that Edgar had virtually no assets.

Edgar's employer did provide $100,000 of group term life insurance on his life, which Edgar had always assured Thelma would pass to her. However, the employer couldn't find any beneficiary designation, and so it paid the $100,000 to the estate rather than to Thelma.

Thelma was prepared to pay the funeral expenses out of her own funds, and use the insurance money to pay $100,000 of the $120,000 back taxes. There would be nothing left for her.

However, after consulting an attorney Thelma learned that certain claims had priority. She paid the funeral expenses from the estate's funds. She exercised her rights as surviving spouse and took her lawful homestead, family allowance, and exempt property. She paid herself a reasonable Personal Representative fee, and paid a reasonable fee to the attorney and accountant. She then paid the small balance to the taxing authorities.

Without knowledge of the claims process, Thelma would have used the insurance money to pay the back taxes, paid the funeral and other expenses from her own pocket, and would have had very little left for herself. What Thelma did was just what the law allowed her to do, and was approved by the Probate Court every step of the way.

Pay Estate Liabilities From Estate Funds

A Personal Representative is generally not personally liable either for the decedent's obligations, or for obligations incurred by the Personal Representative during administration of the estate. Before you rush to pay any of these from your own funds, consider why you want to do that.

The Claim Had to Be Paid, and the Money Was Gone!

When Helen's husband, Bruce, died, Helen became Successor Trustee of his trust. She didn't consult a lawyer, didn't publish a claims notice, and didn't send actual notices of claims to known creditors. She paid all the bills she knew about, and distributed the remaining estate to Bruce's children by a prior marriage, according to the trust.

A year later, a home health care company learned, after an audit of its records, that Bruce still owed them $12,000. They demanded the payment from Helen, as Successor Trustee, and she had no choice but to pay it, out of her own funds because Bruce's children had already spent their inheritance. Had Helen followed the proper claims procedure and given actual notice to all the known creditors, the claim would either been timely submitted and paid, or it would have been barred.

If there is a timing issue, you may ask the creditor to wait until you can liquidate estate assets. If the decedent's debts are large, you may have to sell assets to raise the cash to pay them. However, those types of decisions should be made as part of an overall plan, with an understanding of what is needed and when. (See Chapter 18, "Protect and Preserve Estate Assets.")

You may even have to take loans against assets to pay obligations, including taxes.

If you are concerned that estate assets may be insufficient to pay the claim, then you certainly should know this:

As a general rule, neither the fiduciary nor survivors have any obligation to pay claims against the estate out of their personal funds.

As Personal Representative, you could be personally liable under a contract you enter into with regard to estate matters if you don't indicate that you are dealing on behalf of the estate. You could also be personally liable to creditors if you don't follow the priority rules for paying creditors, discussed below, or if you otherwise violate your fiduciary duties. Survivors may also be liable if they were also parties to a contract with the decedent, if joint obligations were involved, or they take joint property which is subject to a mortgage.

However, the general rule is that you are not personally liable for the obligations of the estate. If there is a trust, the trust may be liable for the decedent's debts, and if the estate is insolvent (i.e., liabilities exceed assets of both the probate estate and the decedent's trust), in certain circumstances non-probate assets will be liable for the decedent's debts. We will discuss insolvent estates further on in this chapter. We have also included a checklist for dealing with an insolvent estate at the end of this chapter

You May Be Able to Deal With Friendly Creditors

Some of the decedent's creditors may be willing to work out an arrangement. Before we embark on the formal claims process, we will review those possibilities:.

- Credit card companies will be happy to hear from you with a request for the final account balance and instructions to close the account. Carefully review the last bill and recent bills, especially those covering any period of incapacity, and the post-death period as well. Try to identify any charges that may have been made without the decedent's authorization. If the estate is cash poor, offer to settle for a percentage of the balance.
- Subscriptions to magazines can sometimes be canceled and a refund given for the balance of the subscription term. Some people have subscriptions to expensive newsletters which provide investment advice, and the subscription may be paid annually. See if you can cancel and get a prorated refund.
- Cable television, DVD rental contracts, Internet service, cable modem, telephone, and cellular telephone service contracts should be reviewed to determine whether and how they can be terminated. Often a telephone call to the company will result in immediate termination without penalty. If an amount has been prepaid, ask for a prorated refund due to death.
- Apartment rental contracts may be somewhat more difficult to terminate. Assisted living facility contracts may have a clause which provides for termination on death. Review the contract and discuss the matter with the landlord.

Dealing with the Landlord

Even if the estate is technically liable under the lease, the landlord has an obligation to try to rent the property and cannot merely sit back and collect rents from the estate for the remainder of the lease if you terminate early. If you are having problems with the landlord's position, see your attorney.

However, sometimes there is such demand for the unit that you will have to negotiate for time to move the furniture and personal belongings to another location.

- If a beneficiary is to receive the residence or other real estate, or if it is intended to keep it within the family, consider refinancing mortgages or other obligations, or paying them off, perhaps with insurance proceeds. Sometimes a "due on sale" clause will require that the balance be paid off.

Joint Debts; Obligations That Go With the Property

There may be debts for which the decedent and someone else were jointly liable. A loan taken out by both the decedent a child or business associate would be prime examples. Ask your attorney to closely examine current Michigan law to determine if the estate is liable on the joint debt, or if a claim may be made against the other person liable on the debt.

There may also be debts which are secured by property, and the property is to be distributed to a beneficiary. A mortgage on real estate would be an example. If the estate does not pay the mortgage debt, the real estate remains subject to the debt when the property is distributed to the beneficiary.

Taking Over the Home...with the Loan

George and Elise owned their residence as tenants by the entireties (joint tenancy between husband and wife).

There was a mortgage on the home in their joint names.

When Elise died, George became the sole owner of the property. George also remained liable on the mortgage debt.

Overview of the Claims Process

The claims process may be broken down into seven steps. (As indicated below, the same process may be applicable, with modifications, to the Trustee of the decedent's revocable trust.)

- The Personal Representative determines who are creditors of the estate. (See Chapter 14, "Are There Liabilities?")
- If the decedent died less than 3 years before the estate is opened, the Personal Representative *publishes* a notice to creditors that the decedent has died and the creditors must present their claims by a certain date or they will be barred.
- The Personal Representative provides *actual notice* to known creditors. (The notice process is discussed in detail below and is summarized in Chapter 17, "To Probate or Not to Probate.")
- The claimant either files a claim as directed in the notice, or begins a lawsuit to collect the claim within the time limit for presenting claims.
- The Personal Representative *allows* the claim (i.e., agrees with the claimant that the claim is owed and pays the full amount of the claim), *disallows* the claim in part, or *disallows* the claim in total (i.e., rejects the claim as not owed)

- If the Personal Representative has disallowed a claim in full or part and the claimant wants to pursue the claim, the claimant must file a lawsuit on the claim within 63 days of the date the Personal Representative mails the disallowance.
- If a claimant has submitted a claim late, the claim will generally be barred.

If a claim is valid, and if estate property has been distributed to beneficiaries prior to satisfying the estate's debts, those who received the property may have to give it back to the estate to satisfy the claim. If beneficiaries fail to return the distribution to pay the creditor's claim, the Personal Representative may be *personally liable* for the amount of the claim.

Various Types of Claims, With Different Implications

The definition of a *claim* under Michigan law is very broad. Claims include liabilities of the estate that arose before, at, or after the death of the decedent. Claims can be based on contracts (agreements that the decedent made or that the estate makes), or on a tort (something that the decedent did or did not do in violation of a duty, such as injuring someone in an accident, or failing to properly do something he had a duty to do). For further examples of the types of liabilities which may give rise to claims, see Chapter 14, "Are There Liabilities?"

Claims also include funeral and burial expenses and expenses of administration. They do not include estate taxes, which are subject to other procedures.

Complicating things further, different types of claims are subject to different claims procedures. It's also important to know the type of claim it is because the statute provides an order of priority for payment based on the category of claim.

Insolvent Estates: Priorities of Various Types of Claims

Michigan statute provides the following order of priority in which claims against the estate of a decedent must be paid if estate property is insufficient to pay all claims in full (i.e., an insolvent estate):

- Costs and expenses of administration.
- Reasonable funeral and burial expenses.
- Certain statutory allowances for the family (homestead allowance, family allowance, and exempt property, in that order). (See discussion of these family allowances below and also in Chapter 20, "Putting the Horror Stories in Perspective.")
- Debts and taxes with priority under federal law, including claims of the State of Michigan under Michigan's Estate Recovery Law, if the decedent received Medicaid long-term services after turning 55.
- Medical and hospital expenses incurred in connection with the decedent's last illness, including compensation of people who attended to the decedent.

- Debts and taxes with priority under Michigan law.
- Other claims.

The priority of administrative expenses, funeral and burial expenses, and family allowances is very important to the family. It means that even if there are not enough assets in the estate to satisfy all claims, the people administering the estate can be paid, the decedent can be buried, and the family can get certain amounts (defined by statute and adjusted for inflation), before anything is paid to creditors.

No preference can be given in payment of a claim over another claim of the same class, and a claim due and payable is not entitled to preference over a claim which is not yet due.

In certain circumstances, nonprobate property such as property in the decedent's revocable trust may be liable for claims. For example, if there are insufficient assets in the probate estate to pay all timely presented claims in full, or to satisfy homestead allowance, family allowance, and exempt property, the Personal Representative is required to certify the amount and nature of the deficiency to the Trustee of the decedent's revocable trust, who is obligated to pay those amounts out of trust assets.

If a Personal Representative is not appointed for estate, the Trustee is required to pay directly an enforceable and timely served claim of a creditor of the decedent (settlor of the trust), including a claim for the settlor's funeral and burial expenses. However, if a Personal Representative is not appointed for the estate within four months after the date of the publication of notice to creditors, the revocable trust will not be liable for payment of homestead, family, or exempt property allowances.

If the Personal Representative is aware of other nonprobate transfers that may be liable for claims and allowances, then, unless the will provides otherwise, the Personal Representative is to proceed to collect the deficiency, so that each nonprobate transfer, including those made under the revocable trust, bears a proportionate share or equitable share of the total burden.

Property subject to a general power of appointment, even if not exercised, could be subject to charges against the estate. Life insurance in certain circumstances may also be reached by the decedent's creditors. There could also be circumstances where a transfer is brought back into the estate as a fraudulent conveyance, under the Uniform Fraudulent Transfers Act. In some of those cases the Personal Representative may have an obligation to pursue collection of the equitable share of the claims from the nonprobate property.

We will now review the various types of potential claims and some of the characteristics of each.

Administrative Expenses

Administrative expenses are those which are necessary to administer the estate. They include reasonable attorney and accountant fees, court fees, costs of publication, costs for death certificates, and reasonable fiduciary fees. Many other types of expenses may also fall within this category. If you need to incur an expense to administer the estate, it's probably an administrative expense, and you should ask your attorney if in doubt.

It is generally not necessary to file a claim against the estate for administrative expenses. This is because payment of the various types of administrative expenses is specifically authorized by law and court rules.

That does not mean, however, that all administrative expenses will necessarily be allowed. There is always a means for someone to complain to the Probate Court about excessive or unnecessary administrative expenses.

For example, if the estate is in a supervised probate proceeding, or closed in a formal proceeding, the expenses will be included in an annual account, and will be subject to review by the Probate Court as part of that account. If, on the other hand, the estate is being administered in a nonsupervised probate, an account will have to be provided to interested persons, any of whom can ask the Probate Court to review the expenses and disallow them. A petition would have to be filed requesting a hearing, and notice would have to be given to the Personal Representative and all interested persons.

Fiduciary Fees

A Probate Judge once said that some Personal Representatives consider their letters of authority a "license to steal" by taking unreasonably high fiduciary fees.

Judges are aware of the tendency of some people to put their hands into the estate's "cookie jar." These people sometime rationalize excessive payments to themselves based on a close relationship with the decedent, years of service prior to the decedent's death without charging, or a desire to adjust their share of the estate because of a belief that the other beneficiaries are not worthy of their shares.

None of this has any place in determining reasonable fiduciary fees. (See discussion regarding fiduciary fees in Chapter 22, "Should You Take Fiduciary Fees?") The courts view fiduciary fees in the context of what would be reasonable if another fiduciary were handling the matter, generally without regard to all of the emotional or personal baggage a particular individual may bring to a situation.

You should therefore be aware that someone could be looking over your shoulder, and that you are always subject to "a higher authority" – the Probate Court.

Additionally, unless the trust provides otherwise, if you are a Trustee of a trust you are required to notify the qualified trust beneficiaries in advance of any change in the method or rate of the Trustee's compensation.

Attorney Fees

A Personal Representative may employ an attorney to perform necessary legal services or to assist the Personal Representative in the performance of the Personal Representative's administrative duties. The same rule applies to a Trustee. The attorney is entitled to reasonable compensation, which would include reimbursement of necessary costs.

Michigan court rules require attorneys to have written fee agreements with a Personal Representative of a probate estate. If a probate estate is involved, the attorney must serve all interested persons with a copy of the fee agreement, and a notice regarding attorney fees. (See the Probate Court form, ***Notice Regarding Attorney Fees***, PC 576).

Strictly speaking, the Successor Trustee of a revocable trust which became irrevocable on the decedent's death is not required to provide a copy of the fee agreement to the beneficiaries. However, if you are the Successor Trustee you should discuss with your attorney the advisability of providing the fee agreement in any event. It may be better to let the beneficiaries know up front how legal fees will be determined, rather than deal with objections after the fact from beneficiaries who are surprised by the extent of the legal services required and the basis upon which the Successor Trustee contracted for them.

Attorney fees are always subject to Probate Court review and must be reasonable. In appropriate circumstances, they may be adjusted by the court. There are various factors to be taken into account in determining the reasonableness of attorney fees; the number of hours of service is not the sole criterion. However, regardless of the fee agreement, Michigan court rules require that every attorney who represents a Personal Representative must maintain time records reflecting what was done, by whom, when, and how much time it took to perform the services. The same records should be maintained if the attorney is representing a Trustee.

Funeral and Burial Expenses

Normal Estate Administration

There will generally be no issue in determining what constitutes reasonable funeral and burial expenses. If the estate is insolvent, however, some courts outside Michigan have held that the rights of the estate's creditors should be taken into account in determining if the funeral and burial expenses are reasonable and therefore entitled to priority, and a Michigan court might do so as well.

This is an area in which common sense will take you far. If there's going to be an issue concerning the ability to pay all the creditors, or if you expect that some of the beneficiaries might complain, don't incur extravagant funeral or burial expenses. If the estate is going to be a taxable estate, don't assume that all the funeral-related expenses will be deductible on the estate tax return.

Even in large estates, where payment of creditors is not an issue, expenses for lavish funeral luncheons are a prime target for disallowance on IRS audits of estate tax returns.

Special Rules for Small Estates

If the value of the estate is $21,000 or less (for decedents who die in 2013, and subject to inflation adjustment) after payment of funeral and burial expenses, it can be handled under an expedited small estate proceeding. (See the discussion of small estates in Chapter 17, "To Probate or Not to Probate.")

Summary Administration

Another procedure, *Summary Administration,* can apply even if the value of the estate is over $21,000. This procedure allows distribution of the estate without giving notice to creditors, if it appears from the inventory and appraisal that the value of the entire estate, less liens and encumbrances, does not exceed certain expenses and statutory allowances.

To determine if the estate qualifies, the Personal Representative should first add up (a) administration costs and expenses, (b) reasonable funeral and burial expenses, (c) the statutory homestead allowance, (d) the exempt tangible property allowance, and (e) a reasonable family allowance for one year. (All of these allowances are discussed in detail in Chapter 20, "Putting the Horror Stories in Perspective.") The sum of total allowances plus costs must equal or exceed the value of the decedent's estate, as reduced by outstanding liens, mortgages and encumbrances. If the estate does qualify, the Personal Representative may distribute assets to the persons entitled to them.

The Personal Representative does not need to provide notice to creditors, and may immediately distribute the assets to those persons entitled to them and file a closing statement or, in some cases, may wish to file a final account. (See discussion at the end of this chapter as to why filing an account may be advisable.) Under this procedure, except for creditors holding mortgages, liens, and encumbrances, the assets are not subject to creditors' claims. (For further discussion of Summary Administration see Chapter 17, "To Probate or Not to Probate.")

Statutory Spousal and Family Allowances

Michigan statute provides for certain allowances to assure that the surviving spouse and children are not left totally without means. These statutory allowances, which are granted very high priority, are the following:

1. The homestead allowance.
2. The family allowance.
3. The exempt property allowance.

Administration costs and expenses, and reasonable funeral and burial expenses, have priority over these statutory allowances. The homestead allowance has priority over all other claims.

The family allowance has priority over all claims against the estate except the homestead allowance, and administration costs and expenses, and reasonable funeral and burial expenses.

Rights to exempt property (or other assets needed to make up any deficiency in exempt property) have priority against all claims against the estate, again with the exception of administration costs and expenses, and reasonable funeral and burial expenses. However, the right to assets to make up a deficiency in exempt property is reduced as necessary to permit payment of the homestead allowance and family allowance.

The amounts of these allowances and who may be entitled to them are discussed in detail in Chapter 20, "Putting the Horror Stories in Perspective."

Other Types of Claims

Claims for Taxes

Federal, state, and local governments do not have to file claims against the estate in order to pursue their claims for the decedent's tax obligations which accrued during his lifetime, nor to perfect their claims for income taxes for which the estate may be liable, nor for estate taxes.

The decedent's tax liabilities are certainly not wiped out as a result of death. On the contrary, if there are any deficiencies which arose during the decedent's lifetime, the taxing authorities can proceed against the Personal Representative of the estate.

Moreover, if the decedent made a taxable gift during his lifetime, or if there is estate tax due on the decedent's estate, a lien for those taxes automatically arises at time of the gift (for gift taxes), and at the date of death (for estate taxes).

The assets may be released from the lien if the assets are used to pay certain charges against the estate and reasonable administration fees, and in certain other circumstances. However, if the Personal Representative distributes estate assets without having first paid the tax, or without getting the property released from the tax lien, the Personal Representative may be held *personally* liable for the unpaid tax, interest, and penalties.

Secured Debts

The decedent may have given security for a debt. For example, a mortgage is security for a mortgage loan. A creditor whose debt is secured by mortgage, pledge, or other lien does not have to file a claim within the statutory claims period.

However, if the secured creditor has received actual notice (the "Notice to Known Creditors"), and if the secured creditor does not file a claim within the claims period, the rights of the secured creditor may be limited to the security. If the value of the security is less than the amount of the debt, the deficiency may be an unsecured claim which, because it was not presented during the claims period, may be barred. Consult your attorney for guidance.

Underwater Real Estate

Michigan law provides a way for a Personal Representative to dispose of real estate the value of which is less than the outstanding mortgage liability, i.e., "underwater" real estate. After the expiration of the statutory notice period, the Personal Representative may convey the real estate to the mortgage lender via quit claim deed. After the deed is recorded, the Personal Representative delivers the deed to the mortgage lender with a letter which states that the deliver of the deed constitutes a distribution of estate assets. This may be done whether or not the mortgage lender has presented a claim.

Whether the estate will be liable for the "deficiency," i.e., the difference between the mortgage balance and the value of the property, will depend on whether the mortgage lender has filed a timely claim. If it has not, then the claim for a deficiency is relegated to the status of an unsecured creditor and, since a timely claim was not filed, the claim should be disallowed and should be barred. This would be the case even if the estate has sufficient assets to pay the claim.

If a timely claim was filed, and if there are sufficient estate assets to pay the claim for a deficiency, then the estate may be liable to pay it, unless the Personal Representative can establish that the value of the property was equal to or exceeded the mortgage balance.

Unsecured Debts

Unsecured debts will include most of the debts of the decedent, as described in Chapter 14, "Are There Liabilities?" If a debt does not fall into any of the preceding categories, it is probably an unsecured debt without priority.

Those types of debts must be the subject of a claim filed within the statutory claims period. However, if the Personal Representative knows or should know of the creditor, then actual notice of the claims period must be given to the creditor; published notice will not suffice. See the discussion below regarding notice to creditors.

Claims Not Due and Contingent or Unliquidated Claims

Some claims are not due until a future date, or may become due only if certain things happen or do not happen. For example, an obligation under a promissory note due in five years is not presently due. Likewise, if the decedent signed a guaranty of a bank loan of a third party, the estate is not presently liable under the guaranty if payments under the loan are being made by the person primarily responsible for it. Additional examples which are commonly encountered today are where a parent or grandparent co-signs on a student loan or car loan to a child or grandchild, or signs a guaranty of those loans, and the parent or grandparent dies.

Persons with claims that are not presently due, or are contingent, or unliquidated (not presently representing a fixed amount) are still creditors of the decedent, even if the decedent was only a guarantor (signed a guaranty of someone else's obligation), or co-signed the note of another person. This is so even if the other person agreed to be primarily liable and was making all the payments.

Therefore, those creditors should be provided actual notice of the claims period. They are "known creditors" because their claims could be discovered if you searched the decedent's records. Once proper notice is given, the creditor must present a claim within the statutory time frame if the creditor wishes to preserve its rights, whether the claim is absolute or contingent.

If the creditor does not present a claim within the statutory time frame, and the Personal Representative has satisfied all the other requirements to close the estate, the Personal Representative may proceed to close the estate.

However, if the creditor properly presents a claim, in a timely fashion, Michigan law provides several ways the contingent claim may be satisfied in order for the Personal Representative to close the estate:

If the claimant consents, the Personal Representative may pay the claimant an amount which represents the present value of the claim, or an agreed value, taking uncertainty into account. Alternatively, an arrangement may be made for future payment, or possible payment, on the happening of contingency or on a liquidation by creating a trust, by giving a mortgage, by obtaining a bond, by obtaining security from a beneficiary who is receiving a distribution from the estate, or by entering into some other type of arrangement which satisfies the creditor.

As a practical matter, if the third party continues to make payments on the obligation, it is possible that the creditor will not make a claim against the estate. If the time for filing a claim passes after the creditor receives actual notice, and the creditor does not file a claim, then the claim will be barred. However, if the Personal Representative does not give actual notice, and the third party later defaults on the obligation, the creditor may be able to file a claim against the estate since the claims period would not have started to run as to that creditor, because the creditor did not receive actual notice.

If the decedent guaranteed or co-signed on an obligation of a third party, in some cases it may be possible for the estate to make a claim back against the third party. If that person is receiving something from the estate, an arrangement may be made to compensate the other beneficiaries from that distribution. If the creditor has security for the obligation (such as a mortgage on real estate, or a security interest in personal property which is often given when there is a purchase under an installment agreement), the Personal Representative should not pay the claim unless the creditor surrenders the security interest. The Personal Representative should take an assignment of the security interest, so that the estate can then step into the shoes of the creditor when the estate seeks reimbursement from the third party.

Contingent and unliquidated claims present complexities beyond usual claims for a fixed dollar amounts. Therefore, you should consult your attorney about any contingent or unliquidated claims.

Notice to Creditors

No Notice Required in Small Estates or Summary Administration

Estates which qualify for the small estate procedure (value of the estate under the current small estate amount after payment of funeral and burial expenses), as well as those which qualify for Summary Administration, don't have to publish a claims notice nor give actual notice to known creditors. This is sometimes referred to as the "total allowance procedure."

Also, estates which qualify for use of the ***Affidavit of Decedent's Successor for Delivery of Certain Assets***, PC 598 do not need to publish a claims notice or give actual notice to known creditors.

All other probate estates must publish a claims notice, unless the decedent died more than three years before the date of commencement of the probate estate.

Publication of Notice to Creditors

Except in the situations described above, the Personal Representative (or trustee of the decedent's revocable trust if there is no probate estate) must publish a notice which informs creditors that they have four months from the date of publication to present their claims or the claims will be barred.

Why Give Notice to Creditors?

There are several reasons why it is important to give notice of the claims period to creditors.

First, the Personal Representative or Trustee may be personally liable for debts of the decedent if assets are distributed without paying all proper claims.

Second, giving notice is required by law.

Third, and perhaps most important, properly giving notice to both unknown and known creditors significantly reduces the time period in which a creditor may file a claim against the estate or trust.

The statute of limitations applicable to the claim of an unknown creditor is reduced from three years after the decedent's death to four months.

For a known creditor, it is reduced from three years (or other applicable limitations period) to four months after the date of publication of the claims notice, or 28 days following actual notice to the known creditor, whichever is later.

However, if the claim is a secured claim (such as a mortgage loan or home equity loan secured by a mortgage on real estate), giving actual notice to the secured lender (e.g., the bank or mortgage company) could allow the estate or trust to escape liability for the loan in the event of foreclosure.

If notice is given to the lender (a known creditor), and if it does not file a claim within the claims period, it will be entitled to its security. However, any claim for an amount in excess of the value of the security (the "deficiency") will be relegated to the status of an unsecured creditor.

That means that if the value of the security (the real estate) is less than the amount of the debt, and if the claim is not filed within the claims period, the claim for any deficiency will be barred – even if the estate or trust has sufficient assets to pay it.

Consult your attorney for guidance.

The notice must appear once in a newspaper defined by court rules. Probate Court form, ***Notice to Creditors, Decedent's Estate***, PC 574 is used for this purpose.

The Personal Representative or Trustee does not have to publish notice if the estate has no assets, the decedent has been dead for more than three years, or notice was previously published in the Michigan county where the decedent was domiciled.

Actual Notice to Known Creditors and Trustee

The Personal Representative must also give actual notice to each known creditor. Notice must either be served personally or by mail.

A creditor is considered to be *known* to the Personal Representative if the Personal Representative has actual notice of the creditor or if the creditor's existence is reasonably ascertainable by the Personal Representative based on an investigation of the decedent's available records for the two years immediately preceding death and the decedent's mail following death.

When giving notices to known creditors, consider giving notice to all hospitals, physicians, and other health care providers who attended the decedent during his or her last illness and the two years prior to death. This notice will give them an opportunity to submit their bills within the claims period or be barred.

Actual notice should also be given by the Personal Representative to the Trustee of a revocable trust of the decedent.

Actual notice must be given within the four-month period following publication of the notice to creditors. However, if the Personal Representative first knows of an estate creditor less than 28 days prior to the expiration of this time period, actual notice may be given within 28 days after the Personal Representative first knows of the creditor.

Actual notice to known creditors and to the Trustee can be given by sending a copy of Probate Court form, ***Notice to Creditors, Decedent's Estate,*** PC 574.

Generally there is no personal liability of the Personal Representative or the estate's attorney for failure to give the required notice, if they believe, in good faith, that notice to that person is not required. However, the estate may be liable for failure to give the notice.

Presentment of Claims

If a claim is presented to the estate the Personal Representative should determine whether the claim has been presented in a timely manner, properly stated, properly served, and represents a bona fide claim.

As this is a practical guide and not a legal treatise, we will not address those details here. The claim should be promptly forwarded to your attorney for a determination as to whether it should be allowed or disallowed (and possibly litigated), or an attempt made to settle the claim.

Timing is critical. If the Personal Representative fails to notify the claimant of any disallowance within 63 days after the expiration of the time for original presentation of the claim, or 63 days after appointment of the Personal Representative, whichever is later, the claim will be considered to have been allowed. Under the statute, the Personal Representative can later change the allowance to a disallowance, but we recommend taking the appropriate action within the initial time limits if possible.

Certain Claims Need Not Be Presented

Claims need not be presented in several circumstances:

- If a claim is being made in a proceeding against the decedent that is pending at the time of death, the claimant need not present the claim to the Personal Representative.
- A creditor who has a mortgage, pledge, or other lien on estate property can pursue the collateral without filing a claim.

- A creditor who wants to establish the liability of the decedent or the Personal Representative, where the liability is covered by insurance, can pursue the liability without presenting a claim, but only to the extent of the insurance coverage limits.
- Post-death claims for compensation for services rendered and reimbursement of expenses advanced by the Personal Representative or by an attorney, and certain others providing services to the Personal Representative, need not be presented at all. The statute specifically provides that this type of claim is not affected by the notice to creditors. However, these claims are subject to court review if there are objections.

When Are Claims Barred?

Pre-Death Claims

Claims may be barred at different times, depending on when the claim arose, and whether the required notices to creditors were given. Here are typical scenarios dealing with claims that arose before the death of the decedent:

- If the applicable statute of limitations has already run at the time of the decedent's death, the claim is barred. It is therefore important that any claims be referred to your attorney to determine if the statute of limitations had already expired when the decedent died.
- If the statute of limitations had not run as of the time of the decedent's death, it is suspended for four months after the decedent's death, after which time it starts to run again.
- If proper notice to creditors was given and the claim is not properly presented, in a timely manner, then the claim will be barred after the expiration of the claims period.
- If the requirements of the notice to creditors are not met, the claim will be barred three years after the decedent's death.

This means that if proper notice is not given, claims may be presented for up to three years after the decedent's death. Therefore, publishing notice to creditors and giving actual notice to known creditors will considerably shorten the period during which a creditor may make a claim. Once a claim is barred, the liability may not be asserted against the Personal Representative, the Trustee, the persons receiving the estate, or the persons who receive nonprobate assets.

Post-Death Claims

Claims arising after the decedent's death will be barred unless presented within certain time limits as well:

- Claims based on a contract with the Personal Representative must be presented within four months after performance by the Personal Representative is due.

- For almost all other claims, the claim must be presented within four months after the claim arises, or four months after the date of publication of the notice to creditors, whichever is later.
- There is no time limit for presentation of claims for compensation for services rendered and reimbursement of expenses advanced by the Personal Representative or by an attorney, and certain others providing services to the Personal Representative.

The Personal Representative May Be Personally Liable

The law requires the Personal Representative to pay claims in the order of priority provided by law. This is to be done after the expiration of four months after the publication date of the notice to creditors, and after providing for the statutory allowances (homestead and family allowance and exempt property), for claims already presented that have not yet been allowed or whose allowance has been appealed, and for unbarred claims that may yet be presented. The Personal Representative is also to provide for costs and expenses of administration.

At the same time, however, the Personal Representative is permitted to pay a claim that is not barred at any time, whether or not the claim is formally presented. However, if the Personal Representative pays a claim in any of the following circumstances, he or she may be personally liable to another claimant whose claim is allowed and who is affected by the payment:

- If payment of a claim is made before the expiration of the above time limit and the Personal Representative does not require the claimant who is paid to give adequate security for the refund of any portion of the payment necessary to pay another claimant; or
- If payment of a claim is made, due to the negligence or willful fault of the Personal Representative, in a manner that deprives another claimant of payment.

Further, a Personal Representative who does not comply with all of the statutory requirements with regard to allowances and priority of payment of claims, and distributes estate property in a manner which causes damages to anyone who would have been entitled to those allowances or payment of claims, could be held personally liable for breach of fiduciary duty.

Claims Against the Decedent's Revocable Trust

If no Personal Representative of the decedent's probate estate has been appointed, and if the decedent created a revocable trust, then the Trustee of that trust must publish the same notice to creditors, and give actual notice to known creditors, in the same manner as discussed above. There is no court form but a form similar to the one used by a Personal Representative may be drafted by your attorney.

If the property in the probate estate is insufficient to pay the following expenses, claims, and allowances, the property in the decedent's revocable trust (which became irrevocable on the decedent's death) may be subject to:

- The administration expenses of the decedent's estate.
- Funeral and burial expenses.
- Enforceable and timely presented claims of creditors of the settlor (the decedent).
- Homestead, family, and exempt property allowances.

Certain Property May Be Exempt From Claims

There are several types of property which may be exempt from claims of creditors:

Property Passing Under Beneficiary Designation

Certain assets pass on the decedent's death under a beneficiary designation, by operation of law. Those would include life insurance, IRAs, pension and profit sharing plan benefits, annuities, deferred compensation plans, and U.S. savings bonds with a Payable on Death or Transfer on Death designation. Generally those assets would not become part of the probate estate, and thus would not be subject to claims of creditors. However, in some cases the assets of an IRA or other type of retirement plan may not be subject to claims of creditors, even if paid to the estate or trust. Consult your attorney.

The Personal Representative or Trustee would generally not have any authority over the proceeds of those types of assets. In limited circumstances, however, the statute does allow a creditor to reach life insurance premiums paid if the creditor can show that the premium dollars were fraudulently transferred to an insurance or annuity policy.

Joint Property

Absent a fraudulent conveyance, and possibly other factors involved in the creation of joint accounts, property owned jointly with rights of survivorship will automatically pass to the surviving joint owner or owners upon the decedent's death. That type of property also passes by operation of law, outside the probate estate, and will not generally be subject to claims. The surviving joint owner would generally become the owner of the property free from the claims of the creditors of the deceased joint owner unless, for example, the property is subject to a mortgage, pledge, or other lien.

A transfer may be held to be a fraudulent conveyance if it is done with the intent to hinder, delay or defraud creditors. This is an expansive concept which you should discuss with your attorney.

Other Property

Other types of property may be exempt from claims of creditors under state law. For example, Michigan law provides a long list of exemptions, outside the probate and trust statutes, which can protect probate and trust property of a decedent. Life insurance proceeds paid directly to the Trustee of the revocable trust pursuant to a beneficiary designation may also be exempt. Consult your attorney.

Checklist for Dealing with An Insolvent Estate

If it appears that the debts of the decedent will exceed the assets of the estate (an insolvent estate), anyone responsible for settling that estate should consider the following action items, which are discussed more fully elsewhere in this chapter and are only highlighted here:

- **Small Estates.** In small estates or Summary Administration, the Personal Representative should follow the procedure described earlier in this chapter. For other estates, the Personal Representative should take the following steps:
- **Start the Claims Period.** Publish the notice to creditors and send the notice to known creditors to all known creditors. You can reduce the time that a known creditor has to file a claim to a maximum of one month if you wait until three months after the expiration of the general claims period to serve the notice to known creditors. Don't forget holders of mortgages and other security. Their claim may be limited to their security if they do not file a timely claim. This could allow the estate to avoid any deficiency.
- **Notify Friend of the Court.** Provide notice to the Friend of the Court in the county where the decedent resided. Probate Court form ***Personal Representative Notice to Friend of the Court***, PC 618 is used for this purpose. This permits the Friend of the Court to make a claim for child support against heirs and devisees.
- **Tally Up Assets and Liabilities.** Prepare an inventory of the estate's property, determine values, the amount of any liabilities, and whether they are secured by liens on property. Claims based on a contract with the Personal Representative must be presented within four months after performance by the Personal Representative is due.
- **Review Claims Priorities.** Closely review the priorities for payment of claims, make sure you understand them, and assure that if any amounts are going to be paid before the picture is clear, only higher priority claims are paid.
- **Consider Possible Medicaid Estate Recovery.** If the decedent received payments under Medicaid for long-term care services after attaining age 55, consider the State of Michigan a known creditor, and serve the State a notice to known Creditors. If they file a claim, consult with your attorney as to whether it should be disallowed.
- **Suspend Payment of Claims.** Do not pay claims, except the highest priority claims, or make distributions until the claims period has expired and the Personal Representative has determined the amount of all obligations and where each of them falls within the statutory list of priorities. Notify all creditors, beneficiaries and other interested persons that you will not be paying claims or making any distributions until the end of the claims period.

- **Look for Fraudulent Conveyances.** Review the decedent's transfers prior to death to determine if any of them could be considered fraudulent conveyances. This does not mean there was fraud involved, merely that the transfer was made without adequate consideration and, in this context, that it was made when the person was insolvent or that it made the person insolvent. It could, for example, involve a gift, or a transfer to joint ownership, and transfers between family members will be closely scrutinized by a court. The Personal Representative has the legal right to pursue these transfers and bring them back into the estate for payment of claims of creditors.
- **Look for General Powers of Appointment.** Determine whether the decedent had any powers of appointment under a trust created by someone else. The Personal Representative may be able to reach that property, even if the power was not exercised. This involves so-called "general" powers of appointment," not "limited" or "special" powers of appointment.
- **Consider Revocable Trust Assets.** Do not assume that only assets in the probate estate are available to creditors. If probate assets are insufficient to pay claims, assets in the decedent's revocable trust may also be used to pay claims. Consider both sources when determining if the "estate" is actually insolvent.
- **Consider Possible Tax Liens.** Tax liens can exist even if you have no actual notice of a lien. Tax liens automatically attach to property, for example, which is subject to federal estate or gift tax when a transfer is made or, for estate tax purposes, at the date of death. The person receiving the property may be personally liable for the tax due.
- **Consider All Claims Carefully.** Be meticulous in addressing all claims which are filed against the estate or trust. Disallow those which are not valid or which are not timely submitted.
- **File a Final Account.** It is possible to close an estate by merely filing a ***Sworn Statement to Close Unsupervised Administration***, PC 591. In this document, the Personal Representative affirms that, if required by law or court rule, notice to creditors has been published, the time for presentment of claims has expired, the assets of the estate have been distributed to those persons entitled to them, and a copy of the Sworn Statement has been sent to claimants whose claims are neither paid nor barred. However, we suggest that when you are ready to close the estate, you consider serving a final account on all interested persons, including any creditors who may not have been paid in full, and have the Probate Court approve the account. This should serve as *res judicata*. This means that the matter cannot be raised again, either in the same court or in a different court. A court will use the doctrine of *res judicata* to deny reconsideration of a matter. Having the account approved by the Probate Court may thus bring finality to the dispute and prevent the creditor from successfully suing on the claim at a later date. ■

Notes

"Running into debt isn't bad.
It's running into creditors that hurts."

— William Greider

CHAPTER 20

Putting the Horror Stories In Perspective

Horror stories about estates abound. In this chapter we shed light on the realities, which may not be nearly so adverse as you may have heard.

We have all heard stories about how someone died and the family couldn't touch the assets, that everything was "tied up" in Probate Court for years, and the family was in a desperate situation, even though the estate was ample. In another case, some property had to be sold and, as the story goes, that also dragged on for months or years. In another story, everything had to be sold to pay estate taxes. In yet another case, the creditors or the tax authorities got the entire estate and the family got nothing.

And how often do we hear of the second wife who was cut out by the husband's will, and his children by a prior marriage took the entire estate?

In every story there is probably a grain of truth, but the facts become distorted as the story is told and retold. Anyhow, it doesn't really matter what someone says happened in a case they heard about. What matters is that if you find yourself in a similar situation, here and now, you need to know what really can happen. It may not always be rosy, but often it's not quite as horrible as the folks will tell you.

Providing for the Family's Cash Needs

The first myth is that after someone dies everything is "frozen" – tied up in probate or with the IRS – and nothing can be touched, not a penny spent, until the process is completed years down the road.

The reality is that in most situations, even if there is a probate estate, the family's cash needs can be met from several sources, if not immediately then with only minor delays. Consider the following examples:

Joint Accounts

Joint accounts owned by the decedent and the surviving spouse automatically become the property of the surviving spouse and can continue to be accessed just as prior to the death.

Credit Cards

Credit cards owned by the surviving spouse can continue to be used to charge expenses. The decedent may have expired but if the card hasn't the survivor can generally continue to use either joint credit cards or credit cards in the surviving spouse's name alone. However, notice of the death of the joint account holder should be provided to the credit card company, and new cards may be issued in the surviving spouse's name alone.

Life Insurance

Often there will be life insurance payable directly to the surviving spouse or children. That has nothing to do with probate and the cash received by the beneficiaries can generally be spent. Insurance proceeds can usually be obtained within a couple of weeks after application is made.

Revocable Trust Assets

If the decedent had a revocable trust, the Successor Trustee can access the assets of that trust, including the trust's bank accounts, without any involvement with the Probate Court at all. However, the trust accounts should retitled in the name of the Successor Trustee of the now irrevocable trust, and a taxpayer identification number obtained and used for the new accounts.

Obtain Probate Authority

Finally, even if everything is in the decedent's sole name – there are no joint accounts, no credit cards, no life insurance, and no revocable trust assets – obtaining authority from the Probate Court will still not involve the draconian process so often described.

Please take a moment to peruse the small estate procedures outlined in Chapter 17, "To Probate or Not to Probate." These are truly expedited procedures. However, even if the estate does not qualify for any of these procedures, within a couple of days the necessary probate pleadings can be prepared, an estate opened, and letters of authority issued to the Personal Representative, who will then have very broad authority to use estate assets. Generally no court hearing is necessary and it's merely a matter of getting the documents together and the facts straight, and starting the process.

Sometimes the letters of authority will require Probate Court approval of sale of real estate, but not for other transactions.

Yes, it is true that in a taxable estate liquidity – cash – will have to be raised to pay estate taxes, due nine months after the date of death. However, estate taxes will only be due if the estate is very, very large, which under current law is limited to an extremely tiny fraction of U.S. estates. (See Chapter 21, "The Tax Man Cometh.")

The stories we have all heard paint a picture of a modest estate where, due to probate or the IRS, the poor widow is left without cash to buy a meal. This is simply not true.

The bottom line is that today, in Michigan at least, these horror stories just do not represent reality.

Estate Property Can Be Sold

A related story is that certain estate property has to be sold, and there is a buyer but the sale will fall through because of the delay in "going through probate."

Again, today this type of situation should generally not happen. The Personal Representative generally has the authority, under the law, to sell estate property, including both personal property and real estate, without permission or other action of the court in all types of probate administration, including supervised administration.

There could be an exceptional case where the Probate Court has restricted the ability of the Personal Representative to sell real estate or personal property. That type of restriction would appear clearly upon the letters of authority and would be the exception, not the rule.

Even if there is such a restriction, or if some interested person is objecting to the proposed sale, the Personal Representative may ask the court to confirm a sale of personal property or real estate in a formal proceeding. Interested persons would have to be given notice of the hearing, and the matter would be resolved by the court. It could take a few weeks to schedule a hearing. In most cases an interested buyer will understand this modest delay.

Estate Tax Liability Doesn't Freeze the Estate

Even in cases where the estate is so large that a federal estate tax return is required, this still doesn't freeze the estate.

The federal estate tax return is generally not filed until the due date, which is nine months after the date of death. That return is sometimes filed on extension up to six months later, or a total of 15 months after the date of death. It is true that a prudent Personal Representative

Expediting Partial Distributions

If partial distributions are contemplated, it is important to assemble the information needed to prepare the federal estate tax return as early as possible.

This is so the amount of tax can be estimated and it can be decided how much of the estate may be safely distributed.

should not distribute the entire estate until an IRS closing letter is received, which could take six months or more after the estate tax return is filed. This means that the Personal Representative will not be in a position to make final distribution until at least 15 months to two years after the date of death, maybe longer if there is a protracted audit.

However, this does not mean the estate is frozen during the period of administration. Partial distributions of estate assets can generally be made, and in most cases would be made if there is a surviving spouse or children. Even in other cases, once the estate assets are known and liabilities, including tax liabilities, are determined, the Personal Representative will have a sense of what can safely be distributed on an interim basis.

The Surviving Spouse and Children Generally Won't Be Left Penniless

It is possible that the decedent may have left no assets at all. In that case, of course, there will be nothing for the surviving spouse and children. But in almost all other cases the surviving spouse and children have certain rights which rank so high on the list of priorities that, whether there is a will or no will at all, they will get something.

What the statute allows for the surviving spouse and children may not seem like a lot, but everything is relative. If the concern is that creditors will take the estate and the surviving spouse and children will literally be thrown out into the cold, this is not quite so. Even if the decedent left the estate to others, the family still has certain rights.

The amounts mentioned in this chapter are based on statutory amounts under the Michigan Estates and Protected Individuals Code ("EPIC"), which applies to estates of individuals who died after March 31, 2000. The statutory amounts are subject to annual inflation adjustments, and the amounts mentioned in this chapter have been adjusted for 2013 decedents.

A complete schedule of adjusted amounts from April 1, 2000 through 2013 is contained in Appendix. C If a person died before April 1, 2000, you will need to refer to smaller amounts as provided under the Revised Probate Code which was in effect prior to that date. For deaths after 2013, consult the Probate Court or your attorney.

Also, the allowances and exempt property we describe are available for a decedent who dies while domiciled in Michigan. If the decedent died domiciled outside of Michigan, statutory allowances will be governed by the law of the decedent's domicile at the time of death.

Homestead Allowance

The surviving spouse is entitled to receive a homestead allowance of $21,000, subject to adjustment for inflation.

If there is no surviving spouse, the minor and dependent children of the decedent are entitled to a homestead allowance equal to $21,000, as adjusted, divided by the number of the decedent's minor and dependent children. A dependent child means an adult child who was dependent upon the decedent.

The homestead allowance has priority over all claims against the estate, including other allowances and other claims, with the sole exception of administrative costs and expenses, and funeral and burial expenses. Therefore, it is virtually the top priority for disbursement from an estate.

Also, the homestead allowance is in addition to any share passing to the surviving spouse or minor or dependent child under the decedent's will, unless otherwise provided, by intestate succession, or by elective share. We will discuss below what assets can be used to satisfy the homestead allowance.

Family Allowance

A reasonable family allowance is payable to the decedent's surviving spouse and minor children whom the decedent was obligated to support, and children of the decedent or another who were in fact being supported by the decedent. The family allowance is intended to provide support and maintenance for these people during the period of estate administration.

If the estate is inadequate to discharge allowed claims, the family allowance is not to continue for a period of more than one year. It is payable to the surviving spouse, if living, for the use of the surviving spouse and minor and dependent children. Otherwise, it is payable to the children or persons having their care and custody.

The statute does not set an amount for the family allowance. It simply says that a "reasonable" family allowance is payable, either in a lump sum or in installments. The Personal Representative may determine the family allowance in a lump sum not exceeding $26,000 (as adjusted) or periodic installments not exceeding 1/12 of that amount per month for one year. This amount is adjusted annually for inflation.

The Personal Representative may disburse the funds of the estate to pay the family allowance in that amount or a lesser amount without court order. It is possible that a greater amount of family allowance may be payable, but only if approved by the Probate Court. If someone who is entitled to family allowance dies, that person's rights to any allowance which has not yet been paid terminate. However, remarriage does not cut off rights to unpaid family allowance.

The family allowance has priority over all claims against the estate, except administrative costs and expenses, funeral and burial expenses, and the homestead allowance. It is not chargeable against a benefit or share passing to the surviving spouse or children by the will of the decedent, unless otherwise provided, by intestate succession, or by way of elective share.

Exempt Property

The decedent's surviving spouse is also entitled to household furniture, automobiles, furnishings, appliances, and personal effects from the estate up to a value not to exceed $14,000 (as adjusted) more than the amount of any security interests to which the property is subject. If there is no surviving spouse, the decedent's children are entitled jointly to the same value. All children are allowed to receive this allowance, not just minor or dependent children.

If encumbered assets (assets subject to a security interest) are selected and the value in excess of security interests, plus that of other exempt property, is less than $14,000, or if there is not $14,000 worth of exempt assets in the estate, the spouse or children are entitled to other assets of the estate, if any, necessary to make up the $14,000 value. Rights to exempt property and assets needed to make up a deficiency of exempt property generally have priority over all claims. However, the right to assets to make up a deficiency of exempt property may have to be reduced to permit payment of homestead and family allowances.

The rights to exempt property are in addition to a benefit or share passing to the surviving spouse or children by the decedent's will, unless otherwise provided, by intestate succession, or by elective share. A specific devise of personal property to the spouse or children without a further indication that it replaces this exemption is not to be interpreted as within the phrase "unless otherwise provided."

What Assets Are Used to Satisfy the Allowances?

If the estate is otherwise sufficient, property specifically devised is not to be used to satisfy rights to homestead allowance or exempt property. Subject to this restriction, the surviving spouse, fiduciaries, or others who have the care and custody of minor children, or children who are adults, may select property of the estate as homestead allowance and exempt property.

Selection can be made using a Probate Court form, ***Selection of Homestead Allowance and Exempt Property, and Petition and Order for Family Allowance***, PC 582. The Personal Representative may make those selections if the surviving spouse, the adult children, or those acting for the minor children are unable or fail to do so within a reasonable time. The Personal Representative may execute a deed of distribution or other instrument to establish the ownership of property taken as homestead allowance or exempt property.

If an interested person is not satisfied with the selection, determination, payment, proposed payment, or failure to act with respect to any of these allowances, that person may file a petition in the Probate Court for appropriate relief.

Property in the decedent's revocable trust may be reached to satisfy homestead, exempt property, and family allowance.

Spousal Elections

The surviving spouse of a decedent who was domiciled in Michigan and who dies testate (with a will) may file with the court an election in writing that the spouse elects one of the following:

- That the spouse will abide by the terms of the will.
- That the spouse will take one-half of the sum or share that would have passed to the spouse had the decedent died intestate (without a will), reduced by one-half of the value of all property derived from the decedent by any other means other than testate or intestate succession upon decedent's death. The property "derived by the surviving spouse from the decedent" includes the following:

1. A transfer made within two years before the decedent's death to the extent that the transfer is subject to federal gift or estate tax.
2. A transfer made before the date of death subject to a power retained by the decedent that would make the property, or a portion of the property, subject to federal estate tax.
3. A transfer effectuated by the decedent's death through joint ownership, tenancy by the entireties, insurance beneficiary, or similar means.

- If a widow, that she will take her dower right as provided by law. The dower election, which is available only to a surviving widow, entitles her to use, for her lifetime, one-third of the land her husband owned at the time he died.

Spousal Election Not Applicable to Revocable Trust

Under current Michigan law, the property subject to the spousal election is only the property subject to the will, i.e., the probate estate. Thus, for example, property the decedent may have transferred to his or her revocable trust during lifetime will not be subject to the spousal election.

This is to be distinguished from homestead, exempt property and family allowance, which may be satisfied from revocable trust assets.

Within 28 days after the Personal Representative is appointed, notice must be given to the surviving spouse of the rights of election, allowances, and exempt property.

The Probate Court form ***Notice to Spouse of Rights of Election and Allowances, Proof of Service, and Election***, PC 581, may be used for this purpose.

The court rules provide that proof of service of the notice does not need to be filed with the court, and that no notice need be given in the following situations:

- The right of election is made before notice is given.
- The spouse is the Personal Representative or one of the Personal Representatives.
- There is a waiver of the rights and allowances.

If the spouse exercises the right of election, the spouse must serve a copy of the election on the Personal Representative personally or by mail. The same form used to notify the spouse of his or her spousal rights (PC 581) may be used to make election. The election must be made within 63 days after the date for presentment of claims or within 63 days after the service of the inventory upon the surviving spouse, whichever is later. The election may be filed with the Probate Court, but that is not required unless the estate is in supervised administration.

If the spouse dies before making the election, the election may no longer be exercised. This may seem obvious but would otherwise be an issue where one death followed the other closely in time, and the estate of the second to die wanted to exercise the election in the first estate.

If the surviving spouse fails to make an election within the time specified, it is generally presumed that the surviving spouse elects to abide by the terms of the will or to accept his or her intestate share. However, that presumption will not apply in the following cases:.

- Assets are discovered after the estate has been closed.
- If the spouse petitions during estate administration for allowance of claims against the estate, because of estate litigation, or other good cause.

Possible Reduction in the Spouse's Elective Share

At the time Sidney died he was in the middle of a divorce with his third wife, Evelyn. However, because the divorce was not finalized they were still legally married and Evelyn had all the rights of a surviving spouse.

A few days before Sidney died he wrote a new will, in which he left everything to his children by his first marriage.

After Sidney died, Evelyn made an election against the will, hoping to take her elective share of a relatively large estate. However, Evelyn was the beneficiary under Sidney's profit sharing plan beneficiary designation, which Sidney could not change. Under federal law such a change required his wife's consent, and in view of the pending divorce Sidney didn't even bother to ask Evelyn to consent.

In computing the amount of Evelyn's elective share, the profit sharing account was considered as part of "property derived by the spouse from the decedent by any means other than testate or intestate succession upon the decedent's death."

As a result, Evelyn's elective share was reduced by one-half the profit sharing plan balance she received, substantially reducing the amount of her elective share of estate assets.

Effect of Prenuptial or Post-Nuptial Agreement

If there was a valid prenuptial or post-nuptial agreement between the decedent and his or her spouse, all of the spouse's statutory rights discussed above may have been waived.

Several conditions must be met for a prenuptial or post-nuptial agreement to be enforceable. If there is a such an agreement in your case, consult your attorney to determine whether it is valid or should be challenged. Under Michigan law, for a prenuptial agreement to be valid it is generally required that each party be represented by a separate attorney, that there be full financial disclosure by both parties, and that the agreement be fair, among other things.

Rights of a Spouse Who Was Omitted in a Premarital Will

What happens if a person makes a will and then marries, and the spouse is not mentioned in the will? Under Michigan law, there is some relief for the spouse who was omitted from the premarital will (a *pretermitted spouse*).

If the spouse of the testator (the person who made the will) marries the testator after the testator executes his or her will, the surviving spouse is entitled to receive, as an intestate share, not less than the value of the share of the intestate estate the surviving spouse would have received if the testator had died without a will (the intestate estate) as to that portion of the testator's estate, if any, which does not fall into either of the following categories:

- Property devised to a child of the testator who was born before the testator married the surviving spouse and who is not the surviving spouse's child.
- Property devised to a descendant of such a child.

However, this rule will not apply in three situations:

- If it appears, either from the will or other evidence, that the will was made in contemplation of the testator's marriage to the surviving spouse.
- If the will expresses the intention that it is to be effective notwithstanding the subsequent marriage.
- If the testator provided for the spouse by transfer outside the will, and the intent that the transfer be a substitute for leaving something in the will can be established by statement of the testator, or can be reasonably inferred by the amount of the transfer or other evidence.

Remember that even if this election is not worthwhile, either because of the exclusion of amounts left to children and descendants from the estate for these purposes, or because it just doesn't apply in view of the above conditions, the surviving spouse can still elect against the will and take the elective share.

Rights of Children Omitted in a Parent's Will

As a general rule, a parent has no obligation to leave anything to a child, and a child who receives nothing under the parent's will has no right to any of the estate. However, there are exceptions where the child is born or adopted after the execution of the will (a *pretermitted child*).

If the testator does not provide in his or her will for a child who is born or adopted after the execution of the will, the omitted after-born or after-adopted child will be entitled to a share of the estate unless:

- It appears from the will that the omission was intentional. (For example, a person might specifically say that he intends to leave nothing to any after-born or after-adopted children, or that the only children who are to take under the will are those who are in being at the time of execution of the will.)

- The testator provided for the omitted after-born or after-adopted child by transfer outside the will and the intent that the transfer be a substitute for leaving something in the will can be established by statement of the testator, or can be reasonably inferred by the amount of the transfer or other evidence.
- The will left all or substantially all of the estate to the other parent of the omitted child and that other parent survived the testator and is entitled to take under the will.

If none of the above apply, the omitted child is entitled to a share, generally determined as follows:

- If the parent had no child living when the will was executed, the omitted child will receive an intestate share.
- If the parent had one or more living children at the time the will was executed, and one or more of them was left something under the will, the omitted child is entitled to the same share as the child to whom a bequest was made.

In other words, the omitted child is written into the will, in the same manner as the other children. ■

CHAPTER 21

The Tax Man Cometh

Under current estate tax law, most estates will not be subject to federal estate tax. But you should still be aware of the basic gift and estate tax rules, and income taxes will still need attention.

Death and Taxes

It has been said that the only two certainties in life are death and taxes. Today the federal estate tax will not impact the vast majority of estates, because of the extremely high exemption, but there could be many other tax returns that have to be filed.

We will discuss the federal estate tax in detail later in this chapter, but for now we ask you to consider the broad range of returns which, in some cases, will have to be filed:

- Federal, state, and local individual income tax returns for years prior to death.
- Federal, state, and local individual income tax returns for the year of death.
- Federal and state fiduciary income tax returns for the probate estate.
- Federal and state fiduciary income tax returns for any trusts.
- Federal gift tax returns.
- Federal estate tax return.
- State estate or inheritance tax returns.
- Generation-skipping transfer tax returns.
- Tax returns for household employees.
- Business tax returns.

Taxes are best taken seriously. The federal government has super-preferred creditor status and takes priority over most other claimants. Taxes must be paid or provided for before any distributions are made to beneficiaries. If you are a fiduciary, you may be *personally liable* for unpaid taxes to the extent of any distributions to beneficiaries. If you are a beneficiary, you may be liable for unpaid taxes to the extent of any property you received.

If you are a fiduciary, the filing of timely, correct, and complete returns and the payment of tax when due is one of your most important responsibilities. You need not prepare the returns yourself. However, you should have a general understanding of each return, what it shows, and when it is due. You should also be aware of any elections that have been made and any questions or issues and the positions that have been taken with regard to them.

In this chapter, we explain the basics of each tax and highlight the things you must do or consider to discharge your duties as Personal Representative or Trustee.

For each tax, we identify some of the elections or issues that should be considered. Many of these elections are subject to time limits. If you think any of the elections or issues may apply to the decedent's situation, you should bring this to the attention of your attorney at once. To be safe, you should have the attorney review this list and tell you which of the elections or issues may apply to your situation, and whether there are any other elections.

Also ask your attorney if you should file IRS Form 56, ***Notice Concerning Fiduciary Relationship***, to let the IRS know you have been appointed Personal Representative or Trustee and establish your authority to deal with them on tax matters and to receive tax information.

Individual Income Tax Returns

Federal, state, and local individual income tax returns must be filed for the year of death and for any prior year for which the decedent had not filed. Returns may have to be filed for more than one state or locality, depending on where the decedent resided and the sources of the decedent's income.

Individuals with other than salary income, which is subject to withholding tax, are normally required to make installment payments of the tax that is expected to be due. However, the IRS has indicated that such payments need not be continued after death, although payments would still be required of a surviving spouse.

The federal income tax return (Form 1040) is generally due on April 15 of the year following the tax year. The Michigan income tax return (Form MI-1040) is also generally due on April 15. The dates for local returns may vary, but many are due on either April 15 or April 30. Due dates for income tax returns in other states and localities may vary. Make sure you know what state or local returns are required, and when they are due.

An automatic six-month extension of the federal income tax return may be obtained. Additional extensions may be requested, but are at the discretion of the IRS. An extension of the due date for filing the federal return automatically extends the due date for the Michigan income tax return to the new federal return due date. If you have not been granted an extension for the federal return, it is still possible to obtain an extension of 180 days for the Michigan individual income tax return, or 150 days for fiduciary income tax returns, upon request.

An extension of time to file does not extend the time for paying the tax. An estimate of the tax due should be paid with the extension form to avoid the running of interest.

Returns should be signed by the Personal Representative, if there is one. Otherwise, the Trustee or anyone who is in charge of the decedent's property may sign.

If there is a surviving spouse, he or she may file a joint return with the decedent for the year of death (if the surviving spouse did not remarry in that year) and for any prior year. The surviving spouse signs the return, and if there is a Personal Representative, the Personal Representative must also sign. If there is more than one Personal Representative, all should sign.

The decedent's regular tax return preparer may be the best one to prepare these returns because of his or her familiarity with the decedent's income and deductions.

If there are liabilities on the decedent's income tax returns that are due to income of the decedent alone, the surviving spouse may not want to file a joint return. He or she should evaluate the situation with legal counsel.

In estates where an estate tax return will be filed, there are at least two elections that should be considered:

Medical Expense Deduction

Medical expenses of the decedent paid after death may be deducted on the decedent's final federal income tax return. However, if these expenses are deducted on the income tax return they cannot also be deducted on the decedent's federal estate tax return. Since for most estates today there will be no estate tax return, medical expenses will generally be taken on the income tax return.

U.S. Savings Bond Interest

Accrued interest on Series E or EE U.S. savings bonds owned by the decedent may be reported on the decedent's final federal income tax return. In some situations, this could result in less income tax being paid. For example, if the decedent had excess charitable contributions in the year of death, or carried over from prior years, accelerating the income onto the decedent's final return is a way to get some benefit from those charitable deductions.

It may also result in the income tax being paid by the estate, rather than the beneficiaries who receive the bonds, the implications of which should be considered in each case. If an estate tax return is being filed, the income tax may be deductible for federal estate tax purposes.

Fiduciary Income Tax Returns

What and When to File; Extensions

If there is a probate estate or a trust, a federal fiduciary income tax return must generally be filed for the estate or trust for the years it is open. One or more state fiduciary income tax returns must generally be filed as well. A Michigan return must generally be filed for an estate or trust which is considered a Michigan resident, or an estate or trust with income from Michigan sources. Filing requirements for other states may vary.

Like individuals, estates and trusts must make installment payments of the tax that is expected to be due. However, estates are excused from this requirement for tax years ending less than two years after the decedent's death. A trust which was revocable by the decedent and which received the residue of the decedent's probate estate is likewise allowed a two-year reprieve.

The federal fiduciary income tax return, Form 1041, ***U.S. Income Tax Return for Estates and Trusts***, is generally due on April 15 of the year following the tax year. The Michigan fiduciary income tax Michigan, Form MI-1041, ***Michigan Fiduciary Income Tax Return***, is also generally due on April 15. If an estate or trust has adopted or elected a fiscal year (discussed below), returns are generally due the 15th day of the fourth month after the close of the tax year.

An automatic five-month extension of time to file the federal return for an estate or trust may be requested by submitting federal Form 7004, ***Application for Automatic Extension of Time To File Certain Business Income Tax, Information, and Other Returns.***

An extension of the due date for filing the Michigan fiduciary income tax return may also be requested. Send the Michigan Department of Treasury payment of the estimated tax liability with a copy of the approved federal extension, and the Treasury will grant a 150-day extension for fiduciary returns. The Michigan Department of Treasury will not notify you of approval. If you do not have a federal extension, file a Michigan Department of Treasury Form 4, ***Application for Extension of Time to File Michigan Tax Returns***, with the payment

An extension of time to file does not extend the time for paying the tax. An estimate of the tax due should be paid with the extension form to avoid the running of interest.

Returns for the estate must be signed by the Personal Representative. Returns for the trust must be signed by the Trustee. If there is more than one Personal Representative or Trustee, only one is required to sign. However, ask your attorney if both should sign.

While the decedent's regular tax accountant may be best able to prepare the individual returns, the fiduciary returns are another matter. Fiduciary income tax is a specialized area and most tax return preparers have had only limited exposure to it. Even at the risk of bruised feelings, you should insist that the fiduciary returns be prepared by someone who is experienced in this field.

An estate or a trust is a separate entity for tax purposes and must have its own Taxpayer Identification Number (TIN). Taxpayer Identification Numbers are usually obtained for the probate estate and/or the trust early in the administration in order to open bank, brokerage, and other accounts in the name of the probate estate or trust. However, if a TIN has not already been obtained, a number will have to be secured before a fiduciary return can be filed.

What's on a K-1?

The most common items of income shown on a K-1 are interest and dividends, which the beneficiary is instructed to report on Schedule B on the beneficiary's federal income tax return.

Short-term or long-term capital gain may also appear.

The K-1 for the final year of the estate or trust may indicate deductions or loss carryovers which may be used by the beneficiary.

A fiduciary income tax return is a hybrid type of return that attributes taxable income either to the estate or trust or to the beneficiaries. Income and, in some cases, capital gains, can either be taxed to the estate or trust or "carried out" to the beneficiaries.

A special form, known as a K-1, is prepared for each beneficiary as part of Form 1041. The K-1 notifies the beneficiary of the amount of income and capital gains that the beneficiary must include in his or her federal taxable income for the year. A similar form is used with the MI-1041 to notify beneficiaries of items that must be included on their Michigan returns.

You or your attorney should advise the beneficiaries that their tax situation will be slightly different because of the estate or trust, and particularly:

- A portion of the income and capital gains of the estate or trust may be taxed to them.
- They will be receiving a K-1 after the end of the estate or trust's taxable year, which they must give to their tax preparer so that it may be taken into account in preparation of their individual income tax returns. If the estate or trust will be on a fiscal year (a tax year ending on a date other than December 31), let them know what fiscal year has been elected and approximately when they can expect to receive their K-1s.
- They cannot finalize their own taxes until the K-1 is received.
- They cannot determine the amount to include in income by simply adding up the distributions they received for the year. This will not, except by coincidence, equal the figure on the K-1.

Make sure to tell them that none of this is your fault, or the fault of your attorney or accountant. It's simply the system which the Congress has put into place and the IRS administers.

Some of the issues that should be considered in connection with the fiduciary income tax returns include the following:

Adoption of Fiscal Year for Estate

An estate may adopt a fiscal year (i.e., a year ending other than on December 31), and this may present opportunities for tax planning. It may be possible to defer the liability of the beneficiaries for taxes on the estate's income which is allocated to them. It may also be possible to reduce taxes by spreading income over two fiscal years.

Election to Treat Trust as Part of Estate

An election may be made to treat the trust as part of the estate for income tax purposes for two years after the decedent's death. (If there is no probate estate, the election may still be made.) This effectively allows a trust's income to be reported on a fiscal year basis, but only for two years. It may also allow timely filing of the return where the original due date has been overlooked.

Where to Deduct Administration Expenses

Most administration expenses may be taken on the fiduciary income tax return in the year paid. However, any such expenses deducted for income tax purposes cannot be deducted on the decedent's federal estate tax return. It must be decided which is more advantageous in those rare cases where an estate tax return will be filed.

Avoiding Taxation at Estate or Trust Level

The fiduciary tax brackets are severely compressed and most of the income of an estate or trust is taxed at the highest rate. For example, for the 2012 tax year a married couple filing jointly would need $388,350 of taxable income to reach the 35% marginal federal income tax bracket, while a trust would reach that bracket with only $11,650 of taxable income.

Therefore, if taxes are the primary concern, plans should be made to distribute enough to the beneficiaries to ensure that all the income of the estate or trust is "carried out" to the beneficiaries so that it will be taxed to them instead of the estate or trust. This assumes that the marginal tax rates of the beneficiaries are lower than that of the estate or trust, which is often the case.

Plan for the Final Year

You should ask for bills for anticipated legal and accounting work that will be done after the final year of the estate or trust, e.g., preparation of fiduciary income tax returns for the year. These bills should be paid before the end of the year so they can be deducted on the final return.

Federal Gift and Estate Tax

Overview of Current Status of Gift and Estate Tax

Back in 1789, Benjamin Franklin said "...in this world nothing can be said to be certain, except death and taxes." Maybe so, but death taxes are becoming less likely, and for most readers of this book federal estate tax will not be due in connection with the estate you are settling.

The short story is that if the decedent died in 2011 there was a $5 million federal estate exemption. That means that if the taxable estate, i.e., the "gross estate" and certain taxable gifts, less applicable deductions, was less than $5 million, there was no federal estate tax due. For 2012 deaths, the exemption was increased to $5,120,000. Further, as will be discussed below, the estate tax exemption and the gift tax exemption was the same in 2011-2012, which means that a person could either give the exemption amount away or leave that amount on death, and there would be no gift or estate tax.

That regime was scheduled to expire as of the end of 2012. Effective January 1, 2013 the $5,120,000 estate tax exemption was to automatically roll back to $1 million, and the gift tax exemption was to go down to $1 million. However, that did not happen. Instead, Congress enacted the American Taxpayer Relief Act of 2012. As of this writing (early 2013) the federal estate tax and gift tax exemptions remain at their 2012 level, but further increased by indexation to $5,250,000. However, we can provide no assurances that some future law might not change these exemptions, upward or downward.

We could simply say, "Check with your attorney to determine if the estate could be subject to estate tax." That's probably what you should do in any event. You could also go to the IRS website, www.irs.org, in the "Forms and Publications" section, and look for the instructions to Form 706, the ***United States Estate (and Generation-Skipping Transfer) Tax Return*** (referred to in the form list as "Inst 706"). The instructions will indicate who has to file.

That will provide you the filing threshold, but you could still benefit from some discussion of what is included in the "gross estate" and other topics related to the estate and gift tax. To that end, we offer the following very brief overview of an extremely complex series of topics.

Gift and Estate Tax Systems Are Unified

The estate tax system and the gift tax system are "unified." That means they work together. If a person makes taxable lifetime gifts, those gifts use up part or all of the person's estate tax exemption available to the estate when the person dies. Otherwise, a person could avoid estate tax by simply giving away all of his or her estate to family members.

The Personal Representative (or the Trustee of the decedent's revocable trust if there is no probate estate and no Personal Representative) must therefore review all gift tax returns which have been filed, and inquire into whether returns ought to have been filed just in case part of the exemption was used on lifetime gifts. Once the estate exceeds the exemption, the federal estate tax is imposed at a flat rate of 35% under the law in effect for estates of decedents dying in 2011 or 2012, and 40% for 2013 and beyond (subject to future changes in the law).

Portability of the Estate Tax Exemption

A married person who dies in 2011 or after can pass along his or her unused federal estate tax exemption so that it can be used by the surviving spouse. The Executor of the first spouse to die must file an estate tax return in the first estate – even if no return would otherwise be required – to elect to use the exemption in the second estate, and there are strict time limits for filing this return.

This is referred to as "portability" of the estate tax exemption. Portability is new and is now allowed only for estates of decedents dying in 2011 or after. It allows the use of both spouses' estate tax exemptions without having to set up special trusts. It can double the exemption even if all property passes outright from the first to die to the surviving spouse under a simple will, joint property with rights of survivorship, or beneficiary designations.

What About Deaths in 2010?

In 2010, there was a dual system, where an estate could be totally exempt from estate tax, or opt back into the system and be subject to a $3.5 million exemption, with differences in whether the income tax basis of the estate's assets would be fully stepped up. If you are involved with an estate of a 2010 decedent, you should have already addressed this situation with your attorney. Form 8939, ***Allocation of Increase in Basis for Property Received from a Decedent***, may have been required in that estate.

Most Estates Are Not Subject to Federal Estate Tax

Under the current (2011 and after) exemption, very few estates are subject to the federal estate tax. The number of estate tax returns filed decreased from more than 108,000 in 2001 to fewer than 34,000 in 2009 (when the exemption was $3.5 million), and of those only 15,000 were taxable. (A return can be filed with no tax due, as is the case where the entire estate, or everything in excess of the exemption amount, passes to the surviving spouse or charity.)

As we will see below, this decrease in estate tax returns filed tracks the increase in the estate tax exemption. There were 2,437,163 deaths in the United States in 2009. If only 15,000 taxable estate tax returns were filed, that represents only about 6/10 of 1% percent of the deaths.

Nonetheless, there are still estates which exceed the exemption, even after the meltdown in the stock and real estate markets. Anyone settling an estate needs to know that there could be an estate tax, understand what makes up the gross estate for estate tax purposes, and know the current estate tax exemption.

So that you have a sense of the roller coaster that we have been on over the years, here is a schedule of the federal estate tax exemption which has been in effect for various years since 1998:

Year	Exemption	Year	Exemption
1998	$625,000	2006-2008	$2,000,000
1999	$650,000	2009	$3,500,000
2000-2001	$675,000	2010	Repealed*
2002-2003	$1,000,000	2011	$5,000,000
2004-2005	$1,500,000	2012	$5,120,000

*For deaths occurring in 2010, there was the possibility of opting back into the estate tax with a $3.5 million exemption, and modified step-up in basis.

The $5,120,000 exemption in effect for 2012 has been increased by indexation to $5,250,000 for 2013, and will be subject to further adjustment in the future. The gift tax exemption is currently the same amount as the estate tax exemption, but this has not always been so. If you discover large gifts were made by the decedent, consult an estate planning attorney to help you figure out what exclusions or exemptions may have applied during the years the gifts were made.

We will first discuss the federal gift tax return, then move on to the estate tax return.

Federal Gift Tax Returns

Is a Return Required?

Much of what we are about to say about the filing of a federal gift tax return may be academic for most estates, in the context of a very large lifetime gift tax exemption. However, you still need to be aware of the rules, and make sure you are aware of the lifetime estate and gift tax exemption amount for your decedent.

Although the exemption is $5,250,000 in 2013, that figure is subject to change, so consult your attorney or the IRS website as to the exemption in effect in your case. In very large estates, the gift tax return will still be very relevant.

If the decedent made any taxable gifts during his or her life, federal gift tax returns may have to be filed. Generally no returns are required for gifts to qualified charities, outright gifts to a U.S. citizen spouse, or gifts that are within the annual gift tax exclusion, which was $10,000 per donee per year, and has been increased by indexation over the years. The annual gift tax exclusion is currently $14,000 per donee per year (beginning in 2013). Certain other gifts for the payment of educational tuition and medical expenses may also be exempt if statutory requirements are met.

The Gifts That Weren't

At his attorney's urging, Sam made a large number of $10,000 gifts to all of his children, their spouses, and their children, just a few days before he passed away.

These gifts were each intended to qualify for the $10,000 annual gift tax exclusion which was then in effect. By removing this money from Sam's gross estate for federal estate tax purposes, his family would have saved a huge amount of taxes.

Unfortunately, many of the family members felt it was inappropriate to cash the checks while Sam was so ill. So they held onto the checks and cashed them after he passed away.

The IRS took the position that the gifts were not completed gifts, because Sam could have stopped payment on the checks.

The money represented by the checks uncashed at the date of death was included in Sam's gross estate, and federal estate tax had to be paid on those amounts.

If the decedent was married at the time of the gift, the annual gift tax exclusion exemption may be doubled, and under current law that means it could be $28,000 per donee per year (starting in 2013). This requires that the gift be made from an account jointly owned by husband and wife or each from their own separate property, or that a federal gift tax return be filed and that "gift splitting" be elected in that return, so that the gift is deemed to be made one-half from each spouse.

However, the definition of a gift in the Internal Revenue Code and Treasury Regulations is very broad and there are some transfers which you might not think are gifts which are considered gifts for gift tax purposes.

There may also be a question as to whether gifts made at the end of the decedent's life were complete as of the date of death. Consequently, any transfers made by the decedent should be reviewed by your attorney.

Only a handful of states have a *state* gift tax, and Michigan is not among them.

What and When to File; Extensions

The federal gift tax return is officially known as the ***United States Gift (and Generation-Skipping Transfer) Tax Return, Form 709.*** The form is also used to compute generation-skipping transfer tax (GST) on those gifts which are also generation-skipping transfers, and to allocate GST exemption.

The decedent's final gift tax return is due by April 15 of the year following the year of death or, if a federal estate tax return must be filed, the due date (with extensions) of the federal estate tax return, *whichever is earlier*. If the decedent made any gifts in years prior to his or her death which were not reported on a gift tax return, the necessary returns must be filed as soon as possible.

Any gift tax liability must be paid no later than the due date of the return. However, since each person can make a certain amount of taxable gifts during his or her lifetime (i.e., gifts beyond the annual gift tax exclusion and other exclusions), unless the lifetime exemption is exceeded there will be no gift tax liability.

There are two methods of extending the time to file a federal gift tax return, neither of which extend the time to pay the gift tax, if any is due.

The first method is to extend the time to file the income tax return. Any extension of time granted for filing an individual income tax return will also automatically extend the time to file the gift tax return. Form 4868, ***Application for Automatic Extension of Time to File U.S. Individual Income Tax Return,*** or Form 2350, ***Application for Extension of Time to File U.S. Income Tax Return***, is used to apply for income tax extensions. These forms may only be used to extend the time for filing the gift tax return if you are also requesting an extension of time to file the income tax return.

The second method can be used if you do not request an extension for the income tax return. Use Form 8892, ***Application for Automatic Extension of Time to File Form 709 and/or Payment of Gift/Generation-Skipping Transfer Tax*** to request an automatic six-month extension of time to file the gift tax return.

Remember, however, the due date of the gift tax return may not be extended beyond the due date (with extensions) of the federal estate tax return, if a federal estate tax return has to be filed. Also, since an extension of time to file does not extend the time for paying the tax, an estimate of the tax due should be paid with the extension request to avoid the running of interest.

Gift tax returns should be signed by the Personal Representative, if there is one. If not, the Trustee or anyone who is in charge of the decedent's property should sign.

If the decedent's regular tax accountant has prepared gift tax returns in the past and is comfortable doing so, you may wish to have the accountant prepare the final gift tax return and any gift tax returns that may be required for prior years. If the accountant is not accustomed to gift tax returns, we recommend you ask the attorney to either prepare the gift tax returns, especially if the attorney will be preparing the estate tax return or, at a minimum, to review the drafts prepared by the accountant prior to filing.

What Should Be Reflected on the Gift Tax Return?

Although what is a taxable gift may appear to be a very basic question, sometimes the answer is not so simple, and may be counter-intuitive.

Lending money to a family member and then discharging or forgiving the loan is a taxable gift. Giving money to a family member which the family member then uses to pay medical expenses is a taxable gift, although paying the medical expenses directly to the medical service provider may qualify for an unlimited gift tax exemption.

Giving a child money to pay a grandchild's college or private elementary or secondary school tuition is a taxable gift, although paying that tuition directly to the school may qualify for an unlimited gift tax exemption.

Giving someone expensive jewelry is a taxable gift. Buying someone a car or a house is a taxable gift. Signing a guaranty of a loan which permits the person to buy the car or house is not a taxable gift until you actually have to pay under the guaranty.

In many cases these gifts will be valued under the annual gift tax exclusion amount (currently $14,000), and so no gift tax return would be required if there were no other gifts to the person in the same year which brought total gifts over $14,000. Also, if the decedent was married at the time of the gift, the decedent's spouse's annual $14,000 gift tax exclusion may also be available.

The best approach is to discuss with your attorney all significant transactions made by the decedent and let the attorney advise you as to which would have required a gift tax return, especially since the annual gift tax exclusion was $10,000 for many years, and gradually increased to $14,000.

Should Gift Splitting Be Elected?

Splitting gifts with the spouse has the effect of doubling the amount of the annual exclusion that is available. The spouse must consent to this treatment by signing the decedent's return to consent to gift-splitting. The spouse may also have to file a gift tax return. Should gifts made by the decedent be split with the decedent's spouse?

If the gifts exceed the annual gift tax exclusion, and use part of the decedent's lifetime gift tax exemption, gift-splitting will result in using part of the spouse's lifetime gift tax exemption as well. This could be a problem if the spouse has a large estate and if the gifts were made to people to whom the spouse would not have made gifts. This could be the case, for example, in a second marriage where the gifts were made to the decedent's children who are not also the spouse's children.

There are other situations where gift-splitting is not advisable, particularly if the decedent entered into advanced planning strategies in his or her final year. We therefore recommend you consult with the gift tax return preparer or an estate planning attorney before electing gift-splitting.

Should GST Exemption Be Allocated?

Here we tread on really esoteric ground, but extremely relevant to some estates:

Transfers which skip a generation, including transfers to trusts which ultimately will make distributions to persons in generations which are more than one generation below the person who made the transfer, can be subject to yet another tax, the generation-skipping transfer tax (sometimes referred to as the "GST").

Currently the GST exemption is the same amount as the gift and estate tax exemption. In most estates, this tax will have no impact. However, in very large estates, it can be extremely relevant.

If the decedent has a large estate, and made large gifts which have to be reported on a gift tax return, whoever prepares the return should consider whether a portion of the decedent's generation-skipping transfer tax exemption should be allocated on the return. It could help shelter future distributions from trusts, for example, to grandchildren and others in lower generations.

This will affect larger estates only and deals with transfers which currently or in the future may benefit persons more than one generation below the decedent, e.g., grandchildren and below. It can also affect gifts to non-relatives who are a certain number of years younger than the decedent.

Federal Estate Tax Return

Who is Responsible for the Return?

The *Executor* is responsible for the return and signs the return for the estate. The Executor is also responsible for paying the tax. The Executor is a defined term in the Internal Revenue Code. If there is a Personal Representative who has been appointed and is acting, then the Personal Representative is the Executor. If there is no Personal Representative, then any person in actual or constructive receipt of property of the decedent, including but not limited to the Trustee of the decedent's trust, is an Executor.

When to File; Extensions

Transfers at death are reported on Form 706, ***United States Estate (and Generation-Skipping Transfer) Tax Return***. Form 706-NA, ***United States Estate (and Generation-Skipping Transfer) Tax Return / Estate of Nonresident Not a Citizen of the United States***, is filed for estates of nonresident aliens.

The return is generally due nine months from date of death. An automatic six-month extension of time to file may be obtained by filing Form 4768, ***Application for Extension of Time to File a Return and/or Pay U.S. Estate (and Generation-Skipping Transfer) Taxes***, by the due date of the return.

An additional, special extension was available to estates of married individuals with assets of less than $5 million, but only if the decedent died in the first six months of 2011, and the Executor filed Form 4768 requesting an extension no later than 15 months after the decedent's death. IR-2012-24; IRS Notice 2012-21.

This extra time was available to an estate if the estate did not request an automatic six-month filing extension on Form 4768 prior to the regular nine-month filing deadline. This was intended to give 15 months after the date of death, rather than nine months, to make the portability election by filing an estate tax return on Form 706.

An extension of time to pay may also be requested on Form 4768, but that extension is not automatic and is discussed further below. Any tax estimated to be due should be paid by the nine-month date, even if an extension of time to pay is requested and granted. While the granting of an extension of time to pay will not avoid interest on payments made after the nine-month date, it should avoid assessment of penalties.

Significance of the Federal Estate Tax Return

In the relatively rare case where a federal estate tax return is to be filed, you will find that it "drives" the administration of the estate. Required information must be gathered. Assets must be valued. Issues and questions involving the interpretation of federal and state law must be addressed. Available elections must be considered. Cash must be raised to pay the tax. All of this must be completed in time to meet the filing deadline.

After filing, the administration of the estate is to a certain extent on "hold" until the Internal Revenue Service reviews the return, which normally does not occur for approximately six months. At that time, the IRS may either issue a closing letter indicating the return has been accepted as filed, or send correspondence advising that the return has been selected for audit. In the meantime, cautious Personal Representatives or Trustees may make partial distributions to beneficiaries in modest amounts which will clearly leave sufficient liquid assets which could be used to pay an estate tax deficiency if the IRS adjusts the return. In fact, some banks and trust companies administering an estate might even wait until the estate tax liability is known before making any substantial distributions to beneficiaries.

In general, if the estate was large enough to require a federal estate tax return, your chances for an audit are very good. The audit could take anywhere from a week to several months, or even longer. The audit could result in changes to asset values, inclusion of additional assets, or disallowance or changes in the amount of deductions.

If the estate's representatives disagree with the audit changes, they may appeal to the IRS Appeals Office. If this does not resolve the matter, the estate's representatives may take the case to a federal court. Consequently, it could be years before a final determination of federal estate tax liability is obtained.

We hasten to reassure you, however, that this is a worst case scenario. Many returns are accepted as filed. Where there is an audit, it sometimes amounts only to a request for additional information, and once that information is provided the return is accepted. In other cases, where issues are raised by the auditor, a satisfactory settlement can usually be negotiated.

The receipt of a closing letter from the IRS means that the asset values reported on the return, or as adjusted on audit, are the values "as finally determined for federal estate tax purposes." The will or trust instrument may direct that bequests or *spin off* trusts be funded using these values. Also, these values are presumed to be the new income tax basis for the assets included in the gross estate.

Who is Subject to Federal Estate Tax?

The federal estate tax is imposed on the taxable estate of every decedent who is a citizen or resident of the United States. U.S. citizens and resident aliens are taxed on their worldwide assets. That means, for example, that if the decedent owned a vacation home in France, or a Swiss bank account, and if he or she was either a U.S. citizen or a resident alien, those assets are includible for federal estate tax purposes.

The tax may also be imposed on the part of a nonresident alien's gross estate which is "situated" in the United States. Determining what property is "situated" in the United States may be more complicated than it would appear. For example, stock issued by a U.S. company is considered situated in the United States, even if the certificates are held abroad. People who are not U.S. citizens, and have never set foot in the United States, but have an account with a U.S. brokerage firm in which they own U.S. securities may thus find their estates subject to federal estate tax on those securities.

Note that nonresident aliens do not benefit from the same estate tax exemption as U.S. citizens and residents. Their exemption covers only $60,000 of property. Treaty provisions may significantly affect estate, gift, and income taxation of persons who are not U.S. citizens or who hold dual citizenship, so treaties should always be investigated in the case of a resident alien or nonresident alien decedent.

Valuation Dates

Generally, value for estate tax purposes is the fair market value as of the date of death. However, the Executor may elect to value the property as of the "alternate valuation date," which is six months after the date of death (or the date of sale or distribution of the property, if earlier), if the election will decrease both (1) the value of the gross estate, and (2) the amount of tax due.

Thus, alternate valuation cannot be elected on a return if there is no estate tax due using date of death values. Alternate valuation is intended to provide relief from downturns in the market. If property is distributed, sold, exchanged, or otherwise disposed of within six months after death, the alternate value is the sales price or the value at the time of disposition.

In the estate of a U.S. citizen or resident alien, farm property or real estate used in a trade or business may qualify for "special use valuation" if detailed requirements are met. If the property qualifies, it may be valued at its "actual use value" rather than at its highest and best use, which would be the usual guideline for determining fair market value.

What Property is Subject to Estate Tax?

The estate tax is imposed on the "taxable estate" of a U.S. citizen or resident alien. The "taxable estate" is the "gross estate" less certain allowable deductions. "Gross estate" means the value of all property, real or personal, tangible or intangible, wherever situated, in which the decedent had an interest at the time of death.

The purpose of the following discussion is merely to give you an idea of how broad the notion of "gross estate" is for federal estate tax purposes. While initially you might think that determining a decedent's gross estate would be a simple matter – for example, tallying up bank balances, value of brokerage accounts and real estate – the concept reaches much further. We will not delve into the details, but just give you an overview.

Property in Which the Decedent Had An Interest. It may seem obvious that a decedent's gross estate includes all property in which the decedent had an interest at the time of death. Examples would be cash, stocks, bonds, notes, real estate, business interests, artwork, and tangible personal property which the decedent owned, either in sole name or the name of the decedent's revocable living trust.

In most cases, real estate, closely held business interests, artwork, tangible personal property, and other hard-to-value assets should be appraised, even if the gross estate doesn't reach the level where an estate tax return would be required. This is because, under current law, those assets will receive a new income tax basis as of the date of death, and that will be the fair market value of the assets.

In general, publicly-traded stocks and bonds are valued using the mean of the highest and lowest quoted selling prices on the date of death or, if the decedent died during a weekend, holiday, or other extended period when the markets are closed (such as the post-9/11 closure), the average of the highest and lowest selling prices on the nearest dates before and after the date of death that the markets were open.

Certain Gifts Made within Three Years of Death. Prior to the 1981 Tax Act, gifts made within three years of death were brought back into the decedent's gross estate. These gifts were referred to a "gifts in contemplation of death." This general rule was repealed for decedents dying after December 31, 1981. However, the "three-year rule" was retained for the following:

- Transfers of property in which the decedent had a life estate;
- Transfers of certain property in which the decedent had a reversionary interest;
- Transfers of certain property the enjoyment of which the decedent had a power to alter, amend, revoke or terminate;
- Transfers of life insurance policies insuring the decedent's life; and
- Gift taxes paid on gifts made within three years of death.

The most common example of the operation of this provision is when a person has transferred a life insurance policy on his or her life to an irrevocable life insurance trust. If the person dies within three years of the transfer, the death benefits are included in his or her gross estate.

The rule even applies if the person doesn't actually own the insurance but merely has certain rights in the policy, such as the right to name a beneficiary, which is considered an "incident of ownership." Thus, for example, if a person has an employer-paid group term life insurance policy, which he does not actually own, transfers all rights in that policy to an irrevocable trust, and dies within three years of the transfer, the death benefits are includible in his gross estate.

Transfers With Retained Life Estate. The gross estate includes the value of any property which the decedent transferred without full and adequate consideration and in which the decedent retained (1) the possession or enjoyment of, or the right to the income from, the property, or (2) the right, either alone or in conjunction with any other person, to designate the persons who shall possess or enjoy the property or the income therefrom.

The most common example is a decedent's transfer to his or her own revocable living trust in which he or she has retained the right to income. Revocable trusts do not avoid estate tax. Another common example is where a decedent transfers his or her home to a child or children but either retains a legal life estate or just continues to live in the home without paying rent. While the transfer prevents the home from being subject to probate, it does not remove the property from the decedent's gross estate.

Transfers Taking Effect at Death. The gross estate includes the value of any property which the decedent transferred without full and adequate consideration and in which the decedent retained a reversionary interest, but only if: (1) possession or enjoyment of the property can be obtained only by surviving the decedent, and (2) at the time of the decedent's death the value of the reversionary interest exceeds 5% of the value of the property.

The term "reversionary interest" includes a possibility that property transferred by the decedent may return to him or his estate and a possibility that property transferred by the decedent may become subject to a power of disposition by him. The 5% requirement is determined actuarially.

Example: The decedent transferred property in trust with the income payable to his wife for life and with the remainder payable to the decedent or, if he is not living at his wife's death, to his daughter or her estate. The daughter cannot obtain possession or enjoyment of the property without surviving the decedent. Therefore, if the decedent's reversionary interest immediately before his death exceeded 5% of the value of the property, the value of the property, less the value of the wife's outstanding life estate, is includible in the decedent's gross estate.

Revocable Transfers. If a decedent transferred property, in trust or otherwise, without full and adequate consideration but retained the power, exercisable by the decedent alone or in conjunction with any person, to alter, amend, revoke or terminate the enjoyment of the transferred property, the value of the property is included in the gross estate.

The most common example of property included under this provision is a transfer to a revocable living trust of which the decedent is both settlor and Trustee (which trust, in most cases, would also be includible under another provision because the decedent retained the right to income).

This provision applies to any power affecting the time or manner of enjoyment of the property or its income, even if exercise of the power does not benefit the donor directly and even though the identity of the beneficiary is not affected. For example, it is applicable to a power reserved by the grantor of a trust to accumulate income or to distribute it to another person, and to distribute trust principal to that other person, even though the remainder is vested in the other person or his estate and no other person has any beneficial interest in the trust.

Annuities. The gross estate includes the value of any annuity if:

- The decedent has a right to receive the annuity for any period that does not end before his death; and
- A payment is receivable by any beneficiary by reason of surviving the decedent.

The amount includible is the portion of the amount receivable as is proportionate to the part of the purchase price of the annuity contributed by the decedent (or the decedent's employer).

This provision covers many types of arrangements, including IRAs and other retirement plans in which the decedent is the participant, as well as other "payments receivable" such as payments under a salary continuation agreement with an employer. Inclusion in the gross estate is not contingent on whether the decedent was actually receiving payments at the time of his death, so long as he had an enforceable right to receive payments at some time during his life.

Property Held Jointly with Rights of Survivorship. For estate tax purposes, there are generally two kinds of jointly held, survivorship property. The first is property held jointly with a spouse, and the second is property held jointly with one or more persons other than a spouse or with a spouse and one or more other persons.

Property held jointly with a spouse is called a "qualified joint interest" and is any interest in property held by the decedent and the decedent's spouse as tenants by the entirety, or joint tenants with right of survivorship, but only if the decedent and the spouse are the only joint tenants.

Note that this does not include property owned with a spouse as *tenant in common* (where there is no right of survivorship). In that case, the decedent's interest is included in his gross estate under other general rules.

In the case of a qualified joint interest, as a general rule only one-half of the value of the property is included in the estate of the first to die, regardless of how the tenancy was created or which spouse contributed the consideration for the property. Because the property passes to the surviving spouse by operation of law, it qualifies for the estate tax marital deduction if the surviving spouse is a U.S. citizen.

For property held jointly with a person other than a spouse (or with a spouse and a third person or persons), the entire fair market value is generally included in the decedent's gross estate, except to the extent that the decedent's Executor can prove that the property originally belonged to (or the consideration for the property was furnished by) the surviving joint tenant. To the extent that the property was acquired by the decedent and other joint owners by gift or inheritance, only the decedent's fractional share of the property is included. Basis is stepped up to the extent of the decedent's proportionate contribution.

Example: John and Bill own a residence as joint tenants with right of survivorship. When they purchased the home in 1980 for $150,000, John contributed 60% of the down payment and Bill contributed 40% of the down payment. They have continued to make the mortgage payments, and to contribute to any capital improvements, on the same percentage basis, and have kept meticulous records which reflect this.

John dies in 2012 when the fair market value of the residence is $500,000. Because John's Executor can prove that Bill provided 40% of the consideration, only 60% of the value of the residence, or $300,000, is included in John's gross estate. The property passes to Bill by operation of law, but there is no marital deduction because John and Bill are not married.

For income tax purposes, Bill's new basis in the home is $360,000, computed as follows: $60,000 for Bill's carry-over basis in 40% of the property, plus $300,000 for John's stepped-up basis in 60% of the property.

Powers of Appointment. A power of appointment is the power which is sometimes given to the beneficiary of a trust to designate who will receive the trust property, generally after the beneficiary's death, but sometimes it may be exercised during the beneficiary's lifetime. Some powers are "limited" or "special" powers of appointment. Others are "general" powers of appointment. The general rule is that the gross estate includes the value of any property over which the decedent had a general power of appointment. A general power of appointment is defined as "any power of appointment exercisable in favor of the decedent, his estate, his creditors, or the creditors of his estate."

Example: Father creates an irrevocable trust for the benefit of his son for life. At the son's death, the son may appoint the remainder to any person, or to his own estate, by his will. To the extent that the son does not exercise the power, the remainder passes to the son's children. The son has a general power of appointment, and the value of the trust at the son's death is includible in the son's gross estate (even if the son does not exercise the power). By contrast, if the son had only a special or limited power of appointment (meaning that he could not appoint to himself, his creditors, his estate, or the creditors of his estate), the property subject to the power would not be included in his gross estate.

Example: Father creates an irrevocable trust for the benefit of his son for life. At the son's death, the son may appoint the remainder to or among any of the son's descendants by his will. To the extent that the son does not exercise the power, the remainder passes to the son's children. Because the permissible appointees are limited to the son's children, and do not include the son's creditors, his estate or the creditors of his estate, the value of the trust is not includible in the son's gross estate.

If a power given to the decedent to consume, invade, or appropriate income or corpus, or both, for the benefit of the decedent is limited by an "ascertainable standard" relating to the health, education, support, or maintenance of the decedent, then that power is not deemed a general power of appointment for estate tax purposes.

Example: At death, husband creates a trust for the benefit of his wife, who survives him. The wife is the Trustee of the trust. She is entitled to all of the income from the trust, and has the power to make distributions of principal to herself for her health, maintenance and support. The wife has a limited or special power of appointment and, upon her death, the remaining corpus of the trust is not included in her gross estate.

Proceeds of Life Insurance. First, the gross estate includes all proceeds of insurance under policies on the decedent's life "receivable by the Executor" of the decedent's estate. The word "receivable" means that the gross estate includes not only the value of insurance proceeds paid to the estate as named beneficiary, but also the value of proceeds paid to another who has a legal obligation to pay such proceeds to the estate.

For example, assume the decedent creates an irrevocable life insurance trust and transfers a policy insuring his life to the trust more than three years before his death. If, pursuant to the terms of the trust, the Trustee is required to pay to the Executor funds for taxes, debts, or other charges enforceable against the decedent's estate, then the amount of the proceeds required to be paid to the Executor to satisfy this obligation is includible in the decedent's gross estate.

Second, the gross estate includes the amount receivable by all other beneficiaries as insurance under policies on the life of the decedent with respect to which the decedent possessed "incidents of ownership." "Incidents of ownership" is not limited to ownership of the policy in the technical legal sense, but refers to the right of the insured or his estate to the economic benefits of the policy. It includes the power to change the beneficiary, to surrender or cancel the policy, to assign the policy, to revoke an assignment, to pledge the policy for a loan, and to obtain a loan from the insurer against the surrender value of the policy. Therefore, a policy provided by the decedent's employer is generally included, even if the decedent is not the owner of the policy, because the employee/decedent has the right to designate beneficiaries of the insurance.

The Executor should request IRS Form 712, ***Life Insurance Statement***, from any insurance company which has issued a policy on the decedent's life, as well as on any policy over which the decedent had incidents of ownership, whether on the decedent's life or on the life of another.

This form should be attached to the federal estate tax return, or held even if no return is required, as it contains valuable information about the insurance.

Even if the proceeds are not includible in the gross estate (e.g., a policy owned by an irrevocable trust, over which decedent had no incidents of ownership, and which was not transferred within three years of death), the policy should still be noted on the federal estate tax return. Form 712 should be obtained from the insurance company, and the policy should be shown at zero value and an explanation provided as to why the proceeds are not included.

Deductions from the Gross Estate

The "taxable estate" is determined by reducing the gross estate by a number of deductions.

Deduction for Expenses, Indebtedness, and Taxes. The general rule is that the value of the taxable estate is determined by deducting from the value of the gross estate amounts for:

- Funeral expenses;
- Administration expenses;
- Claims against the estate; and
- Unpaid mortgages or other indebtedness on estate property

"Funeral expenses" include the usual charges associated with a funeral, such as the fee to the funeral home, the cost of flowers, honoraria for clergy and musicians, interment fees and the like. They also include a reasonable expenditure for a tombstone, monument, or mausoleum, or for a burial plot, either for the decedent or his family, including its future care, if such expenditure is allowable by local law.

"Administration expenses" include expenses that are actually and necessarily incurred in the administration of the decedent's estate, i.e., incurred in the collection of assets, payment of debts, and distribution of property to the persons entitled to it. Examples of such expenses are:

- Probate fees;
- Personal Representative's and Trustee's fees;
- Attorney and accountant fees;
- Appraisal fees;
- Storage charges and expenses of maintaining and selling estate property.

On the other hand, expenditures not essential to the proper settlement of the estate, but incurred for the individual benefit of the heirs, legatees, or devisees, may not be taken as deductions.

"Claims" for which a deduction is allowed are those which represent personal obligations of the decedent existing at the time of death, including interest accrued on those claims as of the date of death. Examples include the following:

- Income taxes, including taxes for the year of death;
- Property taxes that were an enforceable obligation at the time of death;

- Unpaid gift taxes on gifts made by a decedent before death;
- Medical bills not covered by insurance;
- Other debts, such as utility bills and charge card bills; and
- Claims arising from litigation.

Interest accrued on unpaid taxes after the date of death may be deductible in certain circumstances, particularly if the estate does not have sufficient liquidity to pay the tax. Penalties may also be deductible.

A deduction is allowed for the full unpaid amount of a mortgage on any property included in the gross estate (including interest accrued to date of death) if the decedent's estate is liable for the amount of the mortgage.

Medical expenses paid after death may be deducted on either the federal estate tax return (as debts) or on the decedent's final income tax return, but not both.

Deduction for Losses. A deduction is allowed for losses occurring as a result of fires, storms, shipwrecks, other casualties, theft, etc., when such losses are not compensated for by insurance or otherwise. If insurance is received but the value of the proceeds is less than the value of the loss, the excess (i.e., the amount not reimbursed by insurance) is deductible. Such losses also qualify as deductions against the income of the estate or trust; however, the deduction must only be taken once.

Transfers for Public, Charitable, and Religious Uses. As a general rule, a deduction is allowed for the amount of all bequests, legacies, devises, or transfers to a qualified tax-exempt organization or to a governmental entity for exclusively public purposes. There are no percentage limitations such as those that apply to the income tax charitable deduction.

In the case of U.S. citizens or residents, the deduction is not limited to transfers to U.S. charities; gifts to foreign charities may qualify as well.

The deduction is allowed only if the transfer was made by the decedent during his lifetime or at death pursuant to a will or other governing instrument executed by the decedent. If there is a dispute among the heirs and, as part of a settlement, they decide that some amount will be donated to charity, that amount will generally not qualify for the estate tax charitable deduction because it was not made pursuant to the decedent's will or trust.

The Marital Deduction. In general, a deduction is allowed for the value of any interest in property which is included in the gross estate but passes from the decedent to a surviving spouse who is a U.S. citizen.

Property which passes outright to the surviving spouse clearly qualifies for the marital deduction. Examples include outright transfers by will or trust, property passing by right of survivorship, property passing by beneficiary designation, and property passing by virtue of state law, such as dower, elective share, and spousal allowances.

Property which does not pass outright to the surviving spouse but instead passes to a marital trust for the surviving spouse may also be deductible, but only if the trust satisfies certain technical requirements.

Exception if Surviving Spouse is Not a U.S. Citizen. As a general rule, if the surviving spouse is not a U.S. citizen, then the decedent's gross estate is not entitled to a marital deduction for property passing to the surviving spouse, whether outright, by survivorship, or by beneficiary designation. However, the marital deduction is allowed if the surviving spouse becomes a U.S. citizen before the date the decedent's federal estate tax return is filed, and the spouse was a U.S. resident at all times after the date of the decedent's death and before becoming a U.S. citizen.

The marital deduction also is allowed if the property passes to the non-citizen spouse in the form of a "Qualified Domestic Trust" (QDOT). The QDOT may either be established by the decedent or by the surviving spouse after the decedent's death, and must meet extremely detailed statutory provisions and regulations.

Credits Against the Estate Tax

Certain credits are also allowed against the estate tax, including a credit for gift taxes before 1977; a credit for prior transfers (which provides some relief where there are several deaths in relatively close succession); and a credit for foreign death taxes.

Should You File a Return if Not Required?

A federal estate tax return *must be filed* for a decedent who died in 2012 where the gross estate, plus adjusted taxable gifts and specific exemption, is more than $5,120,000. That figure is $5,250,000 for 2013. "Adjusted taxable gifts" refers to taxable gifts made by the decedent after December 31, 1976. The "specific exemption" is a gift tax exemption which was allowed under prior law for gifts made by the decedent after September 8, 1976.

A federal estate tax return *may be filed* even if the value of the gross estate, plus the adjusted taxable gifts and specific exemption, is under the filing threshold. Why would you do so? Reasons for filing include:

- Values for some assets, such as real estate or closely held business interests, may be uncertain. Filing the return and obtaining an IRS closing letter may help fix the value.
- Filing generally starts the three-year statute of limitations running.
- Filing avoids a failure to file penalty in the event that additional assets or taxable gifts are discovered which would put the estate over the filing threshold.
- The return establishes basis in the hands of the beneficiaries for the assets reported.
- The fiduciary will receive a closing letter from the IRS and therefore finality.
- For a married couple where a death occurs in 2011 or thereafter, filing of a return is required in the first estate to elect "portability," i.e., use of the estate tax exemption from the first estate in the estate of the second spouse to die.

Unlike a simple income tax return, the federal estate tax return is not something you should prepare on your own. As you can see from the above overview, even determining what is included in the gross estate requires considerable understanding of the law. Valuation issues abound, and if the estate is large enough to merit filing a return, you should consider preparation of the return a post-death planning opportunity, not merely filling in blanks on a tax form. It is your fiduciary duty to seek out an attorney or accountant who has significant experience in preparing estate tax returns.

Deferred Payment

Various methods are available to defer the payment of the federal estate tax. The principal Internal Revenue Code provisions which permit deferral of the estate tax are Sections 6159, 6161, 6163 and 6166.

If your estate is large enough to require payment of estate tax and if you have liquidity issues such that you need to consider deferral of the payment of the tax, you clearly should be consulting an attorney who specializes in this area. The following is therefore only a very brief overview of some of the options.

Section 6159 Installment Agreement. Section 6159 applies to any tax, not just the estate tax. The IRS is authorized to enter into a written agreement with a taxpayer to satisfy a tax liability by installment payments, if the Service determines that an installment arrangement will facilitate collection of the tax. It will generally remain in effect for the term specified in the agreement, but can be terminated if the IRS determines that collection of the tax is in jeopardy.

The Service can also terminate the agreement for other reasons, including failure to pay an installment when due, failure to pay any other tax liability when due, failure to provide financial information when requested by the Service, or if the Service determines that there is a significant change in the financial condition of the taxpayer. The Service may also modify the agreement, rather than terminate it, in any of these circumstances.

Short Extensions. Section 6161(a)(1) allows the Service the discretion to extend the time for payment for up to 12 months. The Regulations add a requirement of "reasonable cause."

"Reasonable Cause" Extensions. Section 6161(a)(2) permits a much longer extension of payment, up to 10 years. In this case the statute itself includes a reasonable cause requirement, which requires that you show why payment is impossible or impractical at the normal due date.

This extension is not automatic, and the estate must pay interest on the balance due for the extension period. To apply for an extension, Form 4768, ***Application for Extension of Time to File a Return and/or Pay U.S. Estate (and Generation-Skipping Transfer) Taxes,*** must be filed early enough to allow the IRS time to consider the application and reply before the initial nine-month period expires. An application for an extension of time to pay estate tax applied for after the estate tax due date will generally not be considered by the IRS. If an extension of time to pay is granted, the Executor may be required to furnish a bond.

Form 4768 requires a detailed written statement explaining why you cannot pay the estate tax when originally due. The following are examples of what may constitute reasonable cause:

- Assets are located in several legal jurisdictions outside your immediate control.
- Assets consist of rights to receive payments in the future, such as royalties, annuities and accounts receivable.
- The value of the estate cannot be determined by the date due or assets cannot be collected without a lawsuit.
- You have made a reasonable effort and are unable to convert assets into cash.
- To borrow to pay the tax, you will have to pay an unusually high interest rate.

Reversions and Remainder Interests–Section 6163. If the value of a reversionary or remainder interest in property is included in the gross estate, that portion of the estate tax which is attributable to that interest may be deferred under Section 6163, at the Executor's election, until six months after termination of the interest which precedes the reversion or remainder interest.

The IRS may grant an additional extension, for no more than three years after the end of the above six month period, for reasonable cause.

Closely Held Business Interests–Section 6166. Internal Revenue Code Section 6166 grants an extension of time for payment of estate tax where the estate consists largely of an interest in a closely held business.

If the value of an interest in a closely held business which is included in the gross estate of a U.S. citizen or resident decedent exceeds 35% of the adjusted gross estate, the Executor may elect to pay part or all of the estate tax in two or more (but no more than 10) equal installments. Payment of principal may be deferred for five years, with only the interest on any unpaid balance payable during such deferral period.

Section 6166 deferral is available only to delay payment of taxes on closely held business property. The business must be engaged in productive activities. It cannot simply manage assets. The deceased must have been a U.S. citizen or resident at the time of death to use Section 6166.

Further, deferral is available only for the federal estate tax due on the portion of the estate that consists of closely held business property. For example, if 50% of the estate consists of closely held business property, then only 50% of the estate taxes may be deferred by electing Section 6166. The remaining estate taxes are due within nine months of the decedent's death and are subject to interest and penalty for late payment.

Consult your attorney with regard to the details of these tax deferral provisions, including applicable interest rates, security, and events which could terminate deferral.

Amended Returns

The regulations do not permit amending the federal estate tax return (Form 706) after the due date (including extensions), but "supplemental information" may be filed. If information or changes come to light after a return has been filed, the instructions to Form 706 indicate that you should file another Form 706; write "Supplemental Information" across the top of page 1 of the form; and attach a copy of pages 1-3 of the original Form 706 that has already been filed. We suggest you include a letter of explanation. If the return has already been selected for examination, this should be provided directly to the office conducting the examination.

If a refund is requested, Form 843, ***Claim for Refund and Request for Abatement***, should also be submitted.

Who Should Prepare the Return?

The federal estate tax return can be very complex. Moreover, it is outside the scope of experience of most tax practitioners. It is the province of estate planning attorneys. a few accountants, and bank or trust company tax departments who deal on a regular basis with the preparation of these returns and the issues that relate to them, as well as arguing these issues with the IRS in audits.

It would be a serious mistake to allow an inexperienced practitioner to prepare this return and an even more serious mistake to try to do it yourself. Missing a single election could cost the estate thousands of dollars in taxes.

Generation-Skipping Transfer Tax

The federal generation-skipping transfer tax (GST) is a tax which is imposed on transfers to persons who are more than one generation below the person making the transfer. It is separate from, and in addition to, the other two federal transfer taxes – the federal gift tax and the federal estate tax.

While there is an entire lexicon of specialized terms associated with the GST, some basic terminology is essential to even a rudimentary understanding of this tax. A few of the key words are as follows:

Transferor: A person transferring property which may be subject to federal gift or estate tax.

Skip Person: A person who is more than one generation below the transferor, such as a grandchild.

Direct Skip: Any transfer subject to federal gift or estate tax which is made to a skip person.

Taxable Distribution: Any distribution from a trust to a skip person prior to a taxable termination. (Both terms are misnomers, since tax does not necessarily have to be paid on a taxable distribution or on a taxable termination.)

Taxable Termination: A transfer to a skip person which occurs when all other interests in a trust come to an end.

GST Exemption: An amount, which is indexed for inflation, which an individual may transfer free of GST. For 2011, the amount was $5 million, and this was increased to $5,120,000 million for 2012, and $5,250,000 for 2013. A person may allocate all or a portion of the exemption to a transfer which has GST implications in order to protect the transfer from GST, either currently or in the future. If no allocation is made, automatic allocation rules will apply.

Summary of GST Return Requirements

Generation-skipping transfers made by a decedent, during life or at death, are reported – and GST exemption allocated – on returns which have been discussed above. Therefore, our treatment here will be brief.

Lifetime direct skips and other lifetime transfers with GST implications are reported on a federal gift tax return.

Direct skips at death and other transfers at death having GST implications are reported on Schedule R of the federal estate tax return.

If the decedent was a beneficiary of a trust created by another, the decedent's death could result in a taxable termination with respect to that trust. If so, the Trustee of that trust will have to file Form 706GS (T), ***Generation-Skipping Transfer Tax Return for Terminations.***

If, following the death of the decedent, a taxable distribution is made from a trust of which the decedent is the transferor, the Trustee of that trust must prepare Form 706GS (D-1, ***Notification of Distribution from a Generation-Skipping Trust.*** Copy "A" of this form is filed with the IRS; Copy "B" is sent to the distributee. The distributee is then responsible for filing Form 706 GS (D), ***Generation-Skipping Tax Return for Distributions.***

State Death Taxes

State Estate and Inheritance Taxes

In addition to the federal estate tax, some states impose a state estate tax and/or inheritance tax. Michigan imposed these types of taxes in the past, but does not presently impose such a tax.

In the past, many states (including Michigan) imposed an estate tax which was equal to the state death credit allowed by the federal government against the federal estate tax. However, the state death credit was ultimately repealed, which left many states without an estate tax. Some states have since enacted their own estate tax, independent of the federal estate tax. In Michigan, there is no estate tax for decedents who died after December 31, 2004.

Other states have an inheritance tax, which is also imposed at the time of death but works differently from an estate tax. Some states have both types of taxes.

Chart of State Death Taxes

The law firm of McGuireWoods maintains a state-by-state chart which tracks state laws relating to state estate or inheritance tax. See www.mcguirewoods.com/news-resources/publications/taxation/state_death_tax_chart.pdf, and ask your attorney about the situation in your own state, as this area is in a constant state of flux.

State Generation-Skipping Transfer Tax

The Michigan generation-skipping transfer tax system depends on the federal generation-skipping transfer tax system. The Michigan GST equals the Michigan portion of the maximum credit allowable under the federal GST system for state generation-skipping transfer taxes. The Michigan GST applies to property in trust (and trust equivalents) that has a tax situs in Michigan.

For 2005 and thereafter, there is no Michigan GST. This is because the Michigan GST is a so-called "pickup" or "sponge" tax, designed to absorb the federal credit for state generation-skipping taxes. The credit for state GST paid, which was the basis for the Michigan GST, was eliminated , pursuant to a series of federal statutes, as from 2005.

As a result, there is no Michigan GST tax for deaths in 2005 and thereafter. Other states may impose a GST, and the GST may well come back into effect in Michigan in the future. Consult your attorney about possible GST in your state.

Tax Returns for Household Employees

If the decedent had any household employees, you should check with the decedent's accountant to make sure that Social Security, unemployment, and withholding taxes are remitted and the necessary returns are filed when due.

You may wish to consider making a special severance payment to these individuals, especially those with long service. Absent a contract, there is no legal requirement to do so. However, many families do this to express their appreciation to the employees and to help defray their expenses while they look for a new position.

Business Tax Returns

Tax returns for a business of the decedent are the responsibility of the managers of the business and are not discussed here. We will nevertheless mention one important election that is available to a partnership of which the decedent was a partner.

As a general rule, the income tax basis of partnership or limited liability company assets is not adjusted upon the death of a partner. However, a partnership may make an election under Internal Revenue Code Section 754 to adjust the basis of partnership property by the difference between the basis of a new partner's interest in the partnership and the new partner's proportionate share of the basis of the partnership property.

If the decedent owned partnership interests you should raise with your accountant or attorney the possibility of making Section 754 elections. If permitted by the partnership or limited liability company, these elections could result in increased depreciation and other advantages to those who inherit the partnership or limited liability company interest. ■

CHAPTER 22

Should You Take Fiduciary Fees?

Whether to take fiduciary fees, and how much to take, are thorny issues. Understanding how to approach these delicate subjects can help avoid disputes and preserve family relationships.

You Are Entitled to Be Paid

If you serve as a Personal Representative, you are entitled to a Personal Representative fee from the estate. If you serve as a Trustee, you are entitled to a Trustee fee from the trust. If you are acting in both capacities, you may take a fee for each.

In rare cases, the will or trust agreement may direct that the fiduciary serve without compensation. In these situations, it may still be possible to get permission from the Probate Court to pay fees, notwithstanding this direction.

In other instances, the will or trust may set forth an amount for compensation, or provide that the fiduciary may receive "reasonable compensation." If the fee specified in the will or trust, or the fee that the beneficiaries are willing to pay as reasonable compensation, is inadequate, you may request the Probate Court to approve fees. In either event, it is important to keep detailed records of your services provided as fiduciary, including the dates and time spent on each task, and a fairly detailed description of what you did.

You must first decide whether or not to take a fee, even if the document says you are entitled to reasonable compensation. This can be a question of family politics. If you decide to take a fee, you must then decide the amount to charge, which must be reasonable. In this brief chapter, we discuss the factors to be considered in coming to the right decision.

Should You Charge?

Personal Aspects

In deciding whether or not to take a fee, you should consider your relationship to the decedent and to the beneficiaries and your personal feelings about the matter.

In many situations, if a family member is serving as fiduciary he or she will feel no fees should be taken, that the work is just part of being family, and that it would be unseemly to take a fee. This is often a first reaction, before actually doing the work.

Often, after the fiduciary realizes how much work has been involved, and that he or she was doing all the work and other family members were merely sitting back and reaping the benefits, a fiduciary fee seems appropriate.

Sometimes, the decedent will have intended that the fiduciary was to be paid and may have made that intention known. If that is the case, the decedent's intention should be taken into consideration and may tip the scale in favor of taking fees.

You must be the judge of whether it is appropriate or will cause problems with other family members if you take fiduciary fees in a family setting. If possible, the matter should be discussed with the others involved, so that they know how you feel, and you have an opportunity to discuss the basis upon which you intend to charge and why you feel the proposed fees are fair.

Ask your attorney for some suggestions as to what would be a fair fee, given the factors discussed below. Give the other family members a copy of this book to peruse so that they can see what may be involved in administering an estate. This may make it easier for them to understand why they should insist that you take a fee.

When the fiduciary is the decedent's attorney or accountant, it is sometimes indicated that the person should be paid his or her regular hourly rate for providing professional services. This is intended to counter the argument that Personal Representative or Trustee services are "administrative" and not entitled to be compensated at the same rate as professional services.

What's Fair is Fair

The time involved and the effect on the fiduciary's "other" job cannot be ignored.

Steve, a litigation attorney, acted as his father's Personal Representative in handling a sticky estate with numerous issues arising on an IRS estate tax audit. However, he saw his income from his law practice drop significantly. He found himself spending as much time working on estate matters as on his own practice.

He kept track of his time, achieved a great result for the family, and ultimately Steve's estate attorney suggested that he take a reasonable fiduciary fee, to which his siblings gladly agreed. They received the benefits of his work, and felt it was only fair that he be properly compensated.

Uncle Sam Paid Part of the Fees

Larry didn't really want to take a fiduciary fee, but his attorney pointed out to him that it would save estate taxes.

The estate was a taxable one, with federal estate tax at the time being imposed at a 45% rate, and the fees were deductible on the estate tax return. Larry's personal income tax rate was only 15%.

Larry decided to take the fees, just to save estate taxes. Later he decided to make a gift to his siblings, who were the other beneficiaries, so each got their share of the after-tax amount he took as fees.

As fewer estates are subject to estate tax, the deduction for fiduciary fees on an estate tax return will become less important. However, the fees will still be taxable income to the fiduciary, and possibly subject to self-employment tax as well, so consider that aspect before converting a non-taxable inheritance into taxable compensation.

However, the professional is taking time which would normally be billed to other clients, and would probably not accept the appointment unless he or she was adequately compensated.

Charitable Beneficiaries

In the case of a Michigan estate, if there are charitable beneficiaries the Michigan Attorney General may be an interested person and may have something to say about what fiduciary fees are taken. This is an extra measure of protection for the charities.

Where charities are beneficiaries, make sure to ask your attorney about whether and when the Attorney General should be notified of the estate administration, and the extent to which the Attorney General will be involved in any fee issues. (See Chapter 16, "Keep the Beneficiaries Informed.")

Tax Implications

If you are a beneficiary and a fiduciary, you must also consider the tax implications of receiving a fiduciary fee. Any fee payment you receive will be taxable income to you in the year that you receive it. It may also be subject to self-employment tax. However, such a payment may be deductible by the estate in determining its federal estate tax or fiduciary income tax.

An analysis should be done which compares the options, taking into account the difference between your tax bracket and that of the estate or trust, to arrive at the best overall result. The estate's attorney or your own tax advisor should be able to assist you.

In some cases the estate's bracket is significantly higher than that of the fiduciary, and it makes sense to take the fees and benefit from the spread between the rates. This is clear in a taxable estate where there is only one beneficiary, who also happens to be the Personal Representative.

However, if there are several beneficiaries, then the personal aspects may come into play, and the tax saving objective may not be determinative.

Remember that regardless of the potential tax benefits, any fiduciary fee must still be reasonable.

What is a Reasonable Fee?

In deciding how much to charge, you should evaluate the following:

- The amount of time required, which will always be a significant factor. We therefore recommend that any fiduciary who is even considering asking for compensation keep a written log of the amount of time spent. This log should be kept daily, not cobbled together after a number of weeks or months. Each time entry should also include a detailed description of what was done.
- The nature, number and complexity of the estate assets. A fiduciary may be justified in receiving higher fees if the estate has many assets, or assets which are unique, as compared with an estate which is very simple and has only cash and marketable securities. For example, an estate with multiple real estate holdings, valuable art work and jewelry, or closely held businesses will take more to administer than a simple estate, and the fiduciary fee should reflect that complexity.
- Your experience and qualifications. Higher fees are justified to the extent the work done requires a greater level of expertise and skill, such as in managing securities or real estate, or tax planning. Lower fees are appropriate when little expertise or skill is necessary, or when much of the work requiring the higher skill level is performed by professionals, such as lawyers, investment advisors, or accountants, who charge the estate for their services. Also, even if you have expertise, you cannot expect to be paid your expert rate for doing a menial task which could be delegated to a lower level person.
- The makeup and temperament of the parties involved. A large number of beneficiaries and creditors will give rise to more questions, communication and coordination. While this may be reflected in the number of hours it takes to settle the estate, there may also be parties who are adversarial and uncooperative. Having to deal with them could, in certain circumstances, justify a higher fee than if everything went smoothly.
- The extent of the responsibilities and risks assumed. The total dollar value of the estate is an indication of the responsibilities and loss exposure assumed by a fiduciary, and should thus be considered in determining whether a fee is reasonable. All things being equal, a multi-million dollar estate merits a higher fee than a $50,000 estate. Taking on responsibility for the decedent's affairs before death may also support a higher fee than if only post-death administration is required.
- The results obtained may also be a factor. Competence is expected, but creative thinking and extremely favorable results in handling the investments and disposing of the decedent's properties, minimizing estate expenses, and/or avoiding or minimizing creditor claims, can support a higher fee.

- The fees customarily charged in the area should also be taken into account. Geography can make a difference. Consider what the Probate Court judge normally sees in estates where yours is located, and if it's a small town and you are working in a distant large city, what is "reasonable" in the community could be very different from the hourly rate in the big city.

No one factor is determinative. If the matter is to be submitted to the Probate Court, you should expect the judge to be very interested in how the fees were determined, which of the above factors support the fee that is being requested, and whether all the beneficiaries agree. There is no hard and fast rule and you should ask your attorney what would be considered reasonable in the particular case.

If you decide to take a fee, you should advise the beneficiaries as soon as possible, preferably in your first letter to them. As indicated earlier, you should keep a detailed record of time spent and services performed, as you may have to present that to justify your fees several years down the road, because the other beneficiaries have challenged them, because you have decided to seek Probate Court approval, or because the IRS is questioning the fee deduction on audit of an estate tax or income tax return. ■

Notes

"What brings many people into Probate Court is that some Personal Representatives consider that their letters of authority give them a license to steal from the estate."

— Anonymous Probate Court Judge

CHAPTER 23

Transfer Remaining Assets to Beneficiaries

Before transferring assets to the beneficiaries, take the time to review this chapter to be sure there are no outstanding issues to be resolved.

When and How? It Depends.

When and how assets are transferred to beneficiaries depends on a number of factors, such as whether or not there is a probate estate, whether or not estate taxes must be paid, how the assets are held, and what types of assets are involved.

In this chapter, we will explain how to fulfill your duty to transfer the assets to the beneficiaries while avoiding personal liability to beneficiaries, creditors, or taxing authorities.

Your Responsibility as Fiduciary

If you are the fiduciary, it is your responsibility to see that distributions are not made prematurely. Most beneficiaries, on the other hand, want to receive what is coming to them at the earliest possible moment. Many have no idea of the administrative steps that must be completed before you will be in a position to make distributions, or the time these steps will require.

Beneficiaries may naively believe that you can sit down and write them a check for the full amount of their inheritance within a week or two of the decedent's death, whereas the reality in some cases will be that this cannot occur for up to two years. It is imperative that you educate the beneficiaries in this regard. (See Chapter 16, "Keep the Beneficiaries Informed.")

Even if you explain all of the administrative constraints and provide a time line which indicates your best estimate of when distributions can be made, you may be pressured to make distributions sooner. Depending on the type of distribution being contemplated, you may need answers to the following questions before the distribution is made:

- Have all property rights been finally fixed? Is there a contest of the will or trust instrument pending? May the spouse elect against the will? Are disclaimers being considered?
- Have all assets been identified and valued?
- Is Probate Court approval required for the distribution that is contemplated and, if so, has it been obtained?
- If a federal estate tax return or state death tax return must be filed, are there any assets which should be retained for possible examination in connection with an audit of the return?
- If federal estate tax or state death taxes must be paid, must any of these taxes be apportioned to or recovered from beneficiaries? If that is so, then beneficiaries of specific bequests, for example, may not be entitled to the total dollar amount provided for them in the instrument.
- If any assets are to be distributed in kind, are all beneficiaries in agreement as to who is to receive what and how the various assets are to be valued?
- Have all creditors been paid?
- Is there pending litigation which could affect the amount of the estate which can be distributed? Are there disputes which could result in litigation?
- If federal estate tax and/or state death tax returns were required, have closing letters been received from the taxing authorities?
- If you are considering making any distributions before all creditors have been paid or before tax clearances have been received, you must be extremely careful. If you are a fiduciary, you have what is known as *fiduciary liability*. If liabilities to creditors or liabilities for taxes exceed the remaining assets in the estate or trust for which you are responsible, you could be required to pay these obligations out of your own pocket to the extent of any distributions you allowed to be made.

Partial Distributions

You may be able to make one or more partial distributions rather than waiting until all issues have been resolved. In fact, for income tax purposes, you should – if possible – distribute enough in each tax year to "carry out" the income of the estate or trust to the residuary beneficiaries, since this will normally result in the income being taxed at a lower rate.

However, you should be conservative and take care not to distribute too much until all tax and other liabilities have been finalized or you have been released from personal liability.

If the will or trust instrument provides for pecuniary bequests (e.g., gifts of a specified sum of money) and the aggregate of these amounts is modest relative to the total size of the estate, these bequests should be paid as soon as funds are available, to avoid the running of interest.

Fiduciary Liability After Audit Adjustment

John was Personal Representative of his uncle's estate. He made sure that all creditors were paid, and had his uncle's estate planning attorney prepare federal estate tax and state death tax returns. The combined tax on the two returns was $950,000. John filed the returns and paid the tax.

On audit of the federal estate tax return, the values of several limited partnership interests were significantly increased, which resulted in additional tax of $125,000 being assessed. John's attorney told him about the audit changes and the additional tax but John – distracted and not thinking clearly – believed that the attorney was going to "take care of it." Then, under pressure from two of his cousins, John distributed the remaining assets in the estate to the beneficiaries.

When John realized the additional tax hadn't been paid, he notified the beneficiaries and asked each of them to return a portion of their distribution to cover the $125,000 tax assessment.

One beneficiary told John he had already spent the money on his child's college tuition. Another replied that he was referring the matter to his attorney. John never heard from the other beneficiaries.

John was held personally liable for the $125,000. Neither the IRS nor the Tax Court bought into his defense that he thought the attorney was going to take care of paying the additional tax. He was therefore found to have distributed assets to beneficiaries while he knew there was tax due. Ultimately John was forced to liquidate most of his brokerage account and take out a second mortgage on his house to satisfy the debt to the IRS.

In Michigan, unless a contrary intent is indicated by the will or trust, a general pecuniary bequest bears interest at the legal rate, beginning one year after the first appointment of a Personal Representative or the Trustee's acceptance of appointment. Also, the earlier you can satisfy these bequests, the earlier the beneficiaries will stop contacting you to ask when they can expect to be paid.

Prior to payment, however, be sure to determine if estate taxes must be recovered from these amounts. You should also make sure that expenses and claims of creditors have been addressed.

What Do the Beneficiaries Get?

What a beneficiary receives is known variously as a *bequest*, a *legacy*, or a *devise*. The precise legal definitions of these terms differ, but in common everyday usage, they are treated as synonyms. We will use the term *bequest* in our discussion.

Fiduciary Left Holding the Bag After Distributing Without Considering Tax Allocation

Ruth was the Personal Representative of her aunt's probate estate. A business major in college, Ruth was intent on administering the estate as efficiently as possible. She quickly determined the assets of the estate and made an estimate of the federal and state estate tax that would be due. Satisfied that there would be plenty of money to cover debts, expenses, and taxes, she then mailed checks for $25,000 to the ten beneficiaries who were to receive cash bequests in this amount.

Several weeks later, Ruth received a call from an attorney representing one of the remainder beneficiaries of the estate, i.e., those who were to receive the balance of the estate after payment of the ten specific bequests of $25,000 each. The attorney told Ruth that her aunt's will directed that estate taxes be apportioned among *all beneficiaries* and that the $25,000 specific bequests should have been reduced by the amount of tax allocable to them. Ruth consulted an estate planning attorney who confirmed what the remainder beneficiary's attorney had told her.

Ruth was unsuccessful in recovering the taxes from four of the ten beneficiaries who had received the $25,000 payments, and she was forced to reimburse the remainder beneficiaries for these taxes from her own funds.

Specific Bequests

A *specific bequest* is a gift of some specific article or asset, such as "my antique desk" or "my IBM stock." If the decedent's will or trust instrument leaves such an item to a beneficiary, and the decedent or the trust owned it at the time of his death, then the beneficiary is entitled to it.

However, if the decedent or trust did not own the article, the beneficiary cannot have it, but may be entitled to something of equal value. (See the discussion of *ademption* in Chapter 15, "Who Shares in the Estate?")

If estate taxes must be paid, the will or trust instrument may direct that taxes be *apportioned*, meaning that taxes are to be allocated to all beneficiaries in proportion to their interests. If this is the case, specific and general bequests will bear their share of the tax and you must be sure to collect the tax from the specific beneficiaries or hold back part of their distribution to cover the tax.

General Bequests

A *general bequest* is a gift which is payable out of the general assets of the estate or trust. For example, "I give to my brother, Colin, the sum of $50,000." If the estate is not large enough for all general bequests to be made in full, a proportionate reduction must be made in each. (See the discussion of *abatement* in Chapter 15, "Who Shares in the Estate?")

Again, if estate taxes must be paid, the will or trust instrument may direct that taxes be apportioned. In that event, specific and general bequests would generally pay their portion of the tax and you must either withhold the tax from the payment or collect the tax from the beneficiaries.

Residuary Bequests

A residuary bequest is a gift of all or a part of the estate after debts, expenses, taxes, and specific and general bequests have been satisfied.

The direction in a will or trust instrument for the distribution of residue is typically fractional in nature, such as: "My residuary estate shall be distributed one-half to my daughter, Mary, one-quarter to my son, John, and one-quarter to my son, William."

Distribution may be made prorata, meaning that each residuary beneficiary is given his or her proportionate share of each of the assets comprising the residue. This method is unquestionably fair since it treats all residuary beneficiaries equally. In Michigan, absent a contrary provision in the will or trust instrument, prorata distribution is not mandatory. Disproportionate shares or different kinds of property may be distributed to different beneficiaries.

So, if Mary wants the IBM stock, John wants the municipal bonds, and William wants the house, this can be accommodated. To protect yourself, however, you should have all of the remainder beneficiaries agree to such a distribution in writing. If you have liquidated the estate and only cash remains, then the prorata versus non-prorata issue is moot.

Advancements

It is possible that a beneficiary may have received all or part of his or her bequest as a gift from the decedent during the decedent's life. You may hear this referred to as an *advancement* although, strictly speaking, this term should be used only in relation to an intestate share. The correct word in the context of a provision in a will is *satisfaction*.

Whether or not lifetime gifts from a decedent to a beneficiary were in satisfaction of a bequest must be determined under state law. Michigan has a statute which addresses this question. If under the statutory guidelines a lifetime gift is determined to have been in total or partial satisfaction of a beneficiary's testamentary entitlement, then the gift must be taken into account in determining what the beneficiary is to receive.

Distributions in Cash or Kind

Many wills and trust instruments allow the fiduciary to make distributions in cash or *in kind*, or partly in each. A distribution is made in kind when the distribution is of property, such as securities, real estate, or personal property, rather than in money.

It should be decided early in the administration which assets are to be distributed in kind and which will be sold and the proceeds distributed in cash. This plan will then drive how the assets are managed over the course of the administration and how much cash is raised. (See Chapter 18, "Protect and Preserve Estate Assets.") When it comes time to make a distribution, the estate should consist of cash and other assets as you had planned.

If a pecuniary bequest is satisfied in kind, Michigan law provides that the property the fiduciary selects for that purpose must be valued at its value on the distribution date, unless the governing instrument expressly provides otherwise.

Loans Owed to Decedent by Beneficiaries

Unless the will or trust provides that a debt will be discharged, if a beneficiary owed an amount to the decedent the loan receivable should generally be distributed back to the beneficiary (the one who owed the money), including accrued interest, as part of (not in addition to) the beneficiary's share of the estate. The beneficiary should be advised that discharge of the debt in this manner generally does not constitute taxable income, but that the interest which is forgiven will be income to the beneficiary. If the debt exceeds the beneficiary's share of the estate you should talk to your attorney about how to deal with the excess.

Distributions Outright or in Trust

A beneficiary's distribution may or may not be outright. The will or trust instrument may direct that a beneficiary's share be held (or remain) in trust. The trust may continue until the beneficiary attains the age of majority, or there may be partial distributions at specified ages, or the trust may last for the beneficiary's life.

The Trustee may have discretion to make or not make certain distributions. There may be different provisions for different beneficiaries. (For example, Mary and John may receive their shares outright, while the share for William is to be held in trust.)

You must read the will or trust instrument very carefully to make sure you understand and comply with its terms. Ask your attorney to provide you a written summary of the terms of the trust so that you know you are interpreting them correctly. Your attorney should also advise you whether you should provide copies of the summary to the beneficiaries or the parents or guardians of minor beneficiaries.

If the will directs that one or more trusts be created, or if the trust instrument provides for the creation of one or more new, or *spinoff*, trusts, these trusts must be *funded*. There is more to this than meets the eye and you should have the assistance of your attorney in this process. (See Chapter 24, "Going Forward: Avoiding Loose Ends.")

Distributions to Minors

If any distribution is to be made outright to a minor, you should consult with your attorney. In Michigan, a minor is an individual under the age of eighteen years.

Wills and trust instruments often provide for amounts payable to minors to be held in trust until the individual attains majority, or sometimes give discretion to retain the amount in trust until that age.

If a distribution is to be made to a minor and no trust is provided, it may be necessary for a conservator to be appointed to receive the property for the minor. This will require a Probate Court proceeding.

Alternatively, a Personal Representative may also transfer the property to a custodian under the Michigan Uniform Transfers to Minors Act, if the will or trust instrument authorizes such transfers. However, even if the instrument is silent with regard to transfer of a minor's bequest to a custodian, the distribution may still be made to a custodian if (a) the Personal Representative or Trustee believes it is in the best interests of the minor, (b) the transfer to a custodian is not prohibited by or inconsistent with the provisions of the will or trust instrument, and (c) if the transfer exceeds $10,000 in value, the transfer is authorized by the court.

How Are the Assets Held?

In the Probate Estate

Cash distributions from the probate estate are accomplished by simply writing a check on whichever of the estate's accounts has check writing privileges.

Distributions in kind are more involved. Assets in the decedent's name go into the probate estate and, eventually, to the beneficiaries. The residue of the probate estate often "pours over" to the decedent's trust and ultimately passes to the beneficiaries of the trust. In theory, the assets must be retitled at every step:

- From the decedent's name to the probate estate.
- From the probate estate to the decedent's trust.
- From the decedent's trust to the trust beneficiaries.

In practice, it may be possible to bypass some or all of the intervening transfers. For example, assume that the decedent's probate estate, consisting of securities in a brokerage account, pours over to his trust. The trust then terminates and passes outright to the decedent's two children, Peter and Paul.

If the probate estate is ready to be closed, and if the Personal Representative of the probate estate and the Trustee of the trust are the same person or are otherwise agreeable, the brokerage firm could be requested to register the securities from the name of the decedent directly into the names of Peter and Paul.

This will not work in all cases. Holders of assets in the decedent's name may insist that they be retitled in the name of the probate estate. There may be a separate Trustee who would want to physically receive the assets into the trust. There may also be income tax complications.

To accomplish any transfer, contact the holder of the assets for forms and instructions.

Remember that it may be necessary or advisable to get Probate Court approval before making a distribution of probate assets.

In a Trust

Cash distributions may be made from the trust by writing a check on the trust's check writing account.

In kind distributions must be done by retitling the assets in the names of the beneficiaries. The necessary forms and instructions may be obtained from the holder of the assets.

As previously explained, you must make sure you understand the dispositive provisions of the trust or trusts with which you are dealing. (See above, "What Do the Beneficiaries Get?") A trust may terminate upon the decedent's death, but it need not. A trust may continue for any period that is within the limits of any applicable rule against perpetuities, which varies from state to state. Ask your attorney how this rule might apply in your situation.

Whether or not the decedent had a trust, there may be other trusts, such as a predeceased spouse's marital trust or family trust, from which distributions are to be made as a result of the decedent's death. This depends on the terms of the trust in question.

As mentioned, a trust may provide for distributions which create yet other trusts. (See above, "What Do the Beneficiaries Get?") There could be a marital trust for a spouse, a family trust (also called a credit shelter or bypass trust), or a trust for a child, grandchild, or other individual. The funding of such trusts requires specialized knowledge and you should enlist the assistance of your attorney. (See Chapter 24, "Going Forward: Avoiding Loose Ends.")

ITF, TOD, and POD Designations

One or more bank deposits may have been made by the decedent in trust for another. These accounts are sometimes called *Totten Trusts, In Trust For* accounts, or *ITF* accounts. Under Michigan law, these accounts are payable to the person for whom the deposit was made.

Michigan law also provides for the ownership of securities in *Transfer on Death* (TOD) or *Pay on Death* (POD) form. If the decedent owned securities which were titled in this fashion, the securities may be reregistered in the name of the beneficiary as they are not estate assets.

Joint With Rights of Survivorship

Property which was held jointly by the decedent and one or more others with rights of survivorship passes automatically to the surviving joint tenant or joint tenants. The survivors need only retitle the property. For bank and brokerage accounts, it will generally be necessary to present only the decedent's death certificate. Ask the bank or brokerage firm if other documentation will be required.

In the case of real estate, the survivors should record a certified copy of the death certificate with the Register of Deeds for the county where the property is located. This may be done by attaching a copy of the legal description of the property to the death certificate and submitting both documents for recording together.

It may be that an asset was held jointly for convenience only and the surviving joint owner does not claim ownership. This is often done with bank accounts. In this case, the asset should be treated as belonging to the decedent and distributed as part of the probate estate. (See Chapter 13, "Inventory the Assets.")

If estate taxes must be paid and the will directs that taxes be apportioned, the surviving joint tenants are responsible for their portion of the tax and you must collect it from them.

With Named Beneficiary

Life insurance proceeds will be paid by the insurance company to the beneficiary or beneficiaries named in the policy. If the beneficiary is the "estate" of the insured, this means the proceeds are payable to the Personal Representative of the probate estate. If the beneficiary is the decedent's trust and you are the Trustee, the money will come to you. Otherwise, a fiduciary is not involved with the distribution of life insurance proceeds.

Other assets which pass to the beneficiary or beneficiaries are pensions, retirement plans, IRAs, and various types of annuities. The decedent may have named a trust as beneficiary. It is possible though not usual for the decedent's estate to be the beneficiary. This may be intentional or could happen if no beneficiary is named at all, or if the named beneficiary predeceases the decedent. If the estate or trust is not the beneficiary, the benefits pass without the involvement of a fiduciary.

If you are the beneficiary of a pension, retirement plan, IRA, or annuity, whether in your individual capacity or as Trustee or Personal Representative, you must be aware that these vehicles typically offer different settlement options which may have widely different tax consequences.

This is an exceptionally complicated area which is governed both by the U. S. Department of Labor under the Employee Retirement Income Security Act of 1974 (ERISA) and by the Internal Revenue Code and Treasury Regulations. You should not make any election without competent advice, as most elections are irrevocable. You should seek advice from your attorney, who will review the documents and discuss the options with you.

Ask the attorney if he or she has substantial expertise in dealing with retirement plan benefits. If the attorney admits that this subject is not within his or her expertise, suggest that another attorney be consulted on this subject.

If estate taxes must be paid and the will directs that taxes be apportioned among all beneficiaries, including beneficiaries under retirement plan, the beneficiaries are responsible for their portion of the tax and you must collect it from them.

Retirement Plan Distribution Resource

There is an excellent book on the subject of planning for distributions from retirement plans, written for lawyers, which your attorney should have and which we highly recommend: **LIFE AND DEATH PLANNING FOR RETIREMENT BENEFITS,** by Boston-based attorney Natalie Choate, who is national expert on the topic (**www.ataxplan.com**).

Types of Property

Automobiles

If the decedent owned one or more cars in his or her sole name whose total value does not exceed a certain value ($60,000 in 2013), and there is no other property which necessitates the opening of a probate estate, the decedent's surviving spouse or next of kin may, under Michigan law, transfer the title at a Michigan Secretary of State's office by presenting a certified copy of the death certificate and Michigan Department of State Form TR-29, ***Certification from Heir to a Vehicle,*** which is available online at **www.michigan.gov/documents/tr-29_16195_7.pdf**

Make sure that title to the vehicle is actually transferred. If an accident occurs while the vehicle is still titled in the decedent's name, there could be liability to the estate.

Firearms

Before personally transporting any firearm to a beneficiary, research the law which applies to the type of firearm, the method of transport, and where you will be transporting it. Do not just put the firearm in the back seat and start your journey to deliver the bequest. All states and some municipalities have specific regulations concerning who can carry firearms and where they can be carried. The concealed carrying of guns is allowed in some states but not others. Different rules apply to antique firearms in some states, and even the definition of an antique firearm may differ.

If you are considering shipping a firearm to a beneficiary via a carrier such as the U.S. Postal Service, FedEx or UPS, contact them in advance to determine if they will accept the particular firearm and, if so, what requirements they may have, which could vary depending on the type of firearm and whether the shipment will cross state lines. Private party to private party shipments

Resources on Transporting Firearms

For articles and tables of laws relating to the transport of firearms, go to the **National Rifle Association Institute for Legislative Action (NRA-ILA)** website, **www.nraila.org**, and search under the tab "Gun Laws." You will find articles on "Interstate Transportation of Firearms," and "Airline Transportation of Firearms," a "Compendium of State Firearm Laws," as well as links to "Canadian Guns Laws" and the Bureau of Alcohol, Tobacco, Firearms and Explosives (BATF) periodic study of state laws and published ordinances on firearms.

Make a chart of the laws which apply in each jurisdiction through which you will travel, as they may differ, and make sure you comply with them. Keep copies of the state laws and ordinances with you, in case you are stopped and the officer does not know the law and mistakenly believes there is a requirement you are not following.

may not be accepted, and as concerns FedEx and UPS you will likely have to work through the main shipping center, not an authorized shipper in a mall or retail store.

You can find helpful articles on this subject by doing a Google search for "firearms shipping guide."

One way around most of the complexity is to find a gun dealer who will ship firearms for non-customers, which some will do for a fee in addition to the actual shipping costs.

Other Personal Property

Personal property that is specifically bequeathed, whether by a personal property memorandum, will, or trust instrument, should be delivered to the appropriate beneficiary.

If personal property is to be divided between or among two or more beneficiaries and the will or trust instrument does not specifically direct how this is to be done, the Personal Representative or Trustee must see that it is done fairly.

One method is to have the beneficiaries first draw lots to determine an order of selection and then have each beneficiary choose one item. This process is repeated until all items have been taken or until no beneficiary wants any of the remaining articles. Any articles not claimed are then sold.

A refinement of this approach is to value each item and make equalizing distributions in cash so that each beneficiary receives the same total amount of property and cash.

If a federal estate tax return must be filed, valuable items should not be distributed to beneficiaries until a waiver of inspection has been obtained from the IRS. This is especially true of valuable jewelry or artwork. Otherwise, if the estate tax return is audited, the agent could require you to make the property available for examination or appraisal by the IRS.

Real Property

Execute a Personal Representative's or Trustee's deed conveying real estate to the beneficiary. This type of deed is designed especially for fiduciaries and creates less liability for the fiduciary than a warranty deed.

In Michigan the transfer from the estate or trust to a beneficiary is exempt from state real estate transfer tax. However, the transfer may uncap the value of the property for Michigan real property tax, which means that the taxable value of the property could increase for tax purposes.

In any event, Michigan Department of Treasury Form 2766, ***Property Transfer Affidavit,*** must be filed by the beneficiary with the local tax assessor within 45 days after the transfer. The date of death – not the date the deed is signed or delivered – may be deemed to be the date of the transfer.

If the form is not filed timely, a penalty of $5 per day (maximum $200) applies for residential property. Penalties are substantially higher for industrial or commercial real property, depending on value. Further, if the transfer uncapped the taxable value, when the tax authorities find out about it they can go back and assess back taxes based on the uncapped value, for several years, plus interest.

You should have your attorney prepare the necessary deed and Property Transfer Affidavit, as certain exemptions from uncapping may be available and must be elected on the Affidavit if applicable. The form is available online at www.michigan.gov/documents/l4260f_2688_7.pdf

You may also need to file Michigan Department of Treasury Form 2602, ***Request to Rescind Principal Residence Exemption (PRE)***. This should be filed when a residence is no longer occupied by an owner as a principal residence. The exemption will be removed as of December 31 of the year in which the request is filed. The form should be sent to the township or city assessor of the community where the property is located. The form is available online at www.michigan.gov/documents/2602f_2607_7.pdf

The beneficiary should also be advised to consider purchasing title insurance insuring his or her title to the property. If you have located title insurance in the decedent's records you should pass it along to the beneficiary receiving the property. The old policy may be helpful to the title insurance company, and in some cases will result in a credit against the new premium.

Other Considerations

You should make sure that you are protected with respect to any distribution or decision to abandon real property which you authorize.

- You should ensure the distribution is regarded as proper. If a Probate Court order is required, be sure you have one. Even if a court order is not required, you may want to get one, or possibly a settlement agreement signed by all of the beneficiaries.
- You must be able to prove that the beneficiaries got what you say you gave them. You should get receipts. For distributions made by check, the canceled check will serve as a receipt, but if the distribution is intended to be a final distribution, then a receipt will say so and serve a purpose beyond a canceled check. A receipt and release will also serve to release you from further liability to the beneficiary.
- Consider taking steps to facilitate the recovery of the money, if need be, to pay additional debts, expenses, and taxes. The attorney can draft a refunding agreement for the beneficiaries to sign, in which they would agree to repay what they have received in certain circumstances. This is no assurance that the money will actually be repaid, but it may be better than no agreement at all.
- If real property is valueless or is so encumbered that it is of no benefit to the estate or trust, consider abandoning it. This can be the right decision in certain cases. Have the Probate Court approve a decision to abandon property.

In addition, consider the following additional steps when making distributions:

- If a federal estate tax return or state death tax return must be filed, make sure all property transferred to the spouse is of a type which qualifies for the marital deduction, if possible.
- Suggest to beneficiaries that they open a bank or brokerage account to receive the assets coming to them. If the amount is large, also suggest that they obtain competent investment advice.
- Even if you are making a "final" distribution, you should consider holding an amount in escrow to cover any unexpected additional liabilities. If the amount is relatively small, these funds should be in a non-interest bearing account so no additional fiduciary income tax returns will be required. When you are satisfied that there are no remaining liabilities, you may disburse the balance remaining to the beneficiaries.
- Do not leave assets in the decedent's name or in joint name with the decedent. ■

Notes

"If you see yourself as prosperous, you will be.
If you see yourself as hard up,
that is exactly what you will be."
— Robert Collier

CHAPTER 24

Going Forward: Avoiding Loose Ends

You're in the home stretch! Here are a few details to attend to as you approach the closing of the estate.

When you have grappled with all the tasks we have explored in the preceding chapters, you may believe that you are done. Beneficiaries are no longer calling you; your life is beginning to take on some semblance of normalcy. It has been a long time. You want to pack up all of the estate stuff in boxes and take it down to the basement.

Before you declare yourself finished, however, there are a few more matters that must be dealt with, as we explain in this chapter.

On the Business Side

Obtain All Tax Clearances

- If a federal estate tax return was filed, the Personal Representative should expect to receive an estate tax closing letter from the IRS about four to six months after the return is filed, if the return is accepted as filed and contains no errors or special circumstances. Returns that are selected for examination or reviewed for statistical purposes will take longer. If there is an audit, ask the auditor when you can expect the closing letter, which will reflect any audit adjustments.
- IRS Form 5495, ***Request for Discharge from Personal Liability under IRC Sections 2204 or 6905,*** may be filed either with the federal estate tax return or at any time during the three years after the form is filed. In that form the Personal Representative of the estate, or the Trustee of the decedent's trust, may request discharge from personal liability for the decedent's income, gift and estate taxes.

- A release for Michigan income taxes may likewise be requested. Send a letter to:
  Income Tax Division
  Michigan Department of Treasury
  Lansing, MI 48922
- If state death tax returns were filed, releases should be requested from those states. Michigan currently has no estate or inheritance tax, and therefore no releases need to be requested with regard to these taxes.
- If there is a probate estate, and you are the Personal Representative or a Personal Co-Representative, make sure you close the estate and receive the appropriate certificate of completion or settlement order. (See 17, "To Probate or Not to Probate.")
- If you were the guardian or conservator of the decedent, file a final report or account and obtain an order of discharge from the Probate Court.

Adjust Basis in Decedent's Assets

Each asset of the estate that is includible in the decedent's gross estate for federal estate tax purposes receives a new basis equal to its value for federal estate tax purposes. (See Chapter 13, "Inventory the Assets.") This is so even if no estate tax return is required to be filed.

It is important to know the new basis, as any gain on sale of inherited assets will be computed with reference to the new basis, not the decedent's original cost for the property. Therefore, make sure your records show the new basis, and that all beneficiaries are aware of the new basis in property they inherit. If the assets are reflected on a brokerage account or mutual fund statement which shows basis, verify that the basis shown on the statement agrees with your records. If not, ask the brokerage firm or mutual fund company to correct it. You should also furnish the new basis information to your accountant or tax preparer.

You must also retain documents which substantiate this new basis. If a federal estate tax return was filed, you should keep a copy of the return and any audit adjustments. If no return was filed, you should keep a copy of the inventory showing the date-of-death values.

If you have any question about which assets have a new basis or what that basis is, you should ask your attorney. You should do this without delay. If you sell an asset and the gain or loss for income tax purposes is figured using the old basis, the result will be incorrect and could cost you additional tax.

Funding of Trusts and Bequests

If the decedent had a revocable living trust, the governing instrument may provide for the creation of one or more new *spinoff* trusts. It is also possible for *testamentary* trusts to be created under the will. The decedent may of course also direct, in either a will or trust agreement, that one or more outright bequests be distributed.

A transfer in trust or an outright bequest may be pecuniary (referring to a dollar amount) or *fractional*, and it may be *formula* or *nonformula*. This results in four possible combinations:

Nonformula Pecuniary, such as "the sum of $100,000."

Nonformula Fractional, such as "one-quarter of my residuary estate."

Formula Pecuniary, such as "that amount which reduces federal estate tax payable as a result of my death to zero."

Formula Fractional, such as "a fractional share of my estate, the numerator of which equals that amount which reduces federal estate tax payable as a result of my death to zero, and the denominator of which equals the entire value of my estate."

Funding refers to the satisfaction of a transfer in trust or an outright bequest with assets. Funding of small nonformula pecuniary bequests is normally done in cash and presents no special problems. All other types of funding, however, raise important questions, such as:

- Should funding be done in cash or in kind? If in kind, what assets should be selected?
- Are assets to be valued as of date of death or date of distribution?
- In the case of a formula funding, what is the amount that results from the application of the formula?
- Will funding trigger gain for income tax purposes? Can this be avoided?
- What are the other income tax consequences of funding?
- What are the consequences of a partial funding?
- If funding is to be fractional, must it be *prorata* – must each and every asset be fractionalized – or may assets be selected on a *pick-and-choose* basis as long as the required fractional amount of the estate is allocated to the trust or bequest to be funded?

As these questions suggest, this is a complicated and highly technical area. Mistakes could have serious tax and property rights consequences. You should review any funding matters with your attorney, who will advise you concerning the requirements of the will or trust instrument, the rules imposed by the Internal Revenue Code, and possible tax savings strategies.

If a federal estate tax return was required, the funding of trusts and bequests is often deferred until the federal estate tax closing letter is received. This is because formula language often refers to values "as finally determined for federal estate tax purposes."

However, the creation and funding of spinoff trusts cannot be delayed indefinitely. To do so violates the terms of the instrument, which require creation of the spinoff trusts, if not at a specified time, then within a reasonable time. Long delays can result in significant adverse tax consequences.

For example, extremely long delays in creating a marital trust could jeopardize the estate tax marital deduction allowed on the decedent's federal estate tax return, make the accurate allocation of assets between the marital trust and other trusts a near impossibility, and create an income tax nightmare.

Trust Administration

If the decedent's trust continues, or if one or more new spinoff trusts are created, you may be the Trustee of these entities. You may also be Trustee of other trusts, for example, trusts of the decedent's spouse. If so, you are responsible for the ongoing administration of these trusts.

You will have to manage the investments and make distributions in accordance with the governing instrument. You will have to see that fiduciary income tax returns are prepared and filed. You will have to provide accounts to the beneficiaries at least annually.

Unless you are experienced in these matters, you should seek professional assistance. Your attorney can advise you regarding your responsibilities and can either prepare the required accounts and tax returns or refer you to an accountant who is experienced in this area.

Distribute Balance of Funds Held in Escrow

When the last distribution from the estate or trust was made, you should have held an amount in escrow to cover any unexpected additional liabilities. (See Chapter 23, "Transfer Remaining Assets to Beneficiaries.") When, in your judgment, sufficient time has passed and you no longer feel the need to hold this reserve, you should disburse the funds to the beneficiaries who are entitled to them. At the same time, you should obtain receipts for the final distribution and releases of the Personal Representative or Trustee from further liability.

Continuing Investment Management

If you have not yet been able to get to it, this is the time to think about the management of the investments for which you are now responsible. These include investments in your own name (or in the name of your own revocable living trust) which you received from the decedent's probate estate or trust, or which became yours as the surviving joint tenant, as well as assets you owned prior to the decedent's death. There may also be investments in a continuing trust of which you are Trustee.

For our recommendations in this regard, see Chapter 18, "Protect and Preserve Estate Assets," under the heading "How Will Assets Be Managed Going Forward?" Also see the tips in Chapter 25, "Financial & Estate Planning for the Survivors."

Decide What to Do About Pending Litigation

If the decedent was involved in legal proceedings at the time of his death, the Personal Representative stands in the decedent's shoes and is responsible for continuing the matter in the decedent's behalf. Even if no probate estate is otherwise necessary, if litigation is going to be continued you will generally need to have a Personal Representative appointed for this purpose.

If the decedent's death was, or may have been, the result of another person's action (or inaction), there may be grounds for the Personal Representative to bring a lawsuit for wrongful death. If you are the Personal Representative, you should discuss this with your attorney.

If you are a family member who might be entitled to damages under a wrongful death claim, you should discuss the possibility of a lawsuit with the Personal Representative. If the Personal Representative does not want to proceed, then you should discuss your options with your own attorney.

Not all litigation needs to be pursued. Sometimes people bring suits out of frustration, or out of "principle," and after their death an objective evaluation leads to the conclusion that it is just not worth the time, effort, and expense to continue the litigation. If you are the one responsible for the decision to continue, settle, or drop pending litigation, do so objectively.

If wrongful death litigation is to be pursued, be mindful of the possible estate tax consequences. If the alleged damages are based on the decedent's conscious pain and suffering, and if as a result a significant portion of the damages will go to the estate (and not directly to family members), those monies will be includible in the gross estate for estate tax purposes. Even if the gross estate was under the amount which would be subject to estate tax (see Chapter 21, "The Tax Man Cometh"), significant damages could bring the gross estate to the taxable level. The bottom line may be that a significant portion of those damages may go to the IRS for estate taxes.

On the other hand, sometimes damages can be payable on account of the losses suffered by close family members due to the death, and payable directly to them and not to the estate. Damages payable directly to the family members would generally not be part of the gross estate, and not subject to estate taxation. This should be taken into account in deciding whether and how to pursue the litigation, and how to structure a possible settlement in a manner that will yield the most to the family.

How Long Should You Retain the Files?

There are no hard and fast rules which dictate how long you must keep files pertaining to the administration of the estate. If there is no threat of litigation, you may consider discarding most files after five or six years. We recommend that you retain some items permanently.

These include the following:

- A copy of the will. (For a Michigan decedent, the original will should have been filed with the Probate Court in the county of the decedent's domicile at the time of death, for safekeeping even if there was no probate estate.)
- Executed (signed) copies of any trust agreements and Trustee appointment letters.
- All annual accounts for the probate estate or for any trust.
- A copy of the federal estate tax return and all state death tax returns.
- Closing letters for all federal estate tax and state death tax returns.
- Certificate of completion or settlement order from the Probate Court.
- Original of any settlement agreement or refunding agreement, and receipts and releases signed by beneficiaries.

On the Personal Side

Memorializing the Decedent

Many families compile memory books to preserve their remembrances of the decedent. These can range from simple scrapbooks or photo albums to elaborate full color publications which are given to all family members and friends as keepsakes.

We know of one case where a family member invested many hours of time to compile a twelve-page, single-spaced biography of the decedent, which he then sent to all members of the extended family. In addition to honoring and remembering the decedent, this biography will be very valuable to those recipients who are interested in their genealogy and family tree.

Today some families might do the same thing but post it on a family website so it can be easily accessed by friends and relatives around the country and around the world.

This is also the time to consider charitable giving in memory of the decedent. You may have already identified a charitable cause for memorial contributions at the time of the funeral. There are unlimited opportunities to create charitable funds in the decedent's honor, which can make a positive contribution to our community and society and keep the decedent's memory alive for future generations.

Perpetual Care of Grave Site

You should check with the cemetery regarding arrangements for perpetual care, which consists of cutting the grass and removing any debris. In addition, you may wish to visit the grave periodically to trim grass from around the monument and footstone, remove twigs, and satisfy yourself that everything is in order.

Most cemeteries have rules governing what decorations may be placed on the grave. Many cemeteries offer to place pine branch "blankets" on the grave in winter and remove them in the spring. The cemetery may also offer to place flowers on certain holidays.

A Final Word to the Beneficiaries

When the administration of the estate is complete, you have an opportunity to deliver a final message to the beneficiaries. You should take this seriously and consider carefully the thoughts you want to leave with them. You may want to offer words of conciliation, or you may feel moved to comment on some aspect of the decedent's philosophy.

One Personal Representative wrote to his brother and sisters as follows:

> With this distribution, the administration of mother's estate is complete. I now want to take off my "executor" hat and say a few words as your brother. As long as mother was alive, the four of us kept in touch through her. Now, however, if we want to have a relationship, we must communicate directly. This means making the occasional call, writing the occasional note or card, sending the occasional email, and visiting whenever possible. Is this important? I think it is, because we are a family. We go back a long way – longer than any friend, longer than any spouse. No one else knows, as just one example, all the things that went on at the dinner table on [street name]. We have the ability to share, from this unique perspective, one another's joys and sorrows, to provide support, to be there for each other. This is pretty precious and is something that I hope we will all want to preserve.

In another case, a Trustee shared thoughts of what his aunt and uncle had been trying to accomplish with their gifts and bequests, as an expression of their family's philosophy with regard to wealth. He wrote the beneficiaries in the following terms:

> "Since I expect this will be my last letter to you as Trustee, I feel that I should share with you something of the philosophy of Robert and Elizabeth in regard to their bequests to us. Robert and Elizabeth believed that our family should improve itself financially from generation to generation; that money should be kept in the family, invested, and made to grow; that it should be passed on to the next generation 'to see what they can do with it,' as Elizabeth put it.
>
> This philosophy goes back at least as far as Robert [family name], Sr., the grandfather of Robert and Elizabeth. It can be seen in the enclosed agreement penned by their father, Robert [family name], Jr., as he began to deed lots from [name] Subdivision to his children in 1940. It was the hope of Robert and Elizabeth that we would be good stewards of the funds entrusted to us, that they would multiply under our care and devolve upon future generations of our family."

We sincerely hope you will take a moment to reflect on these suggestions, and then move on to consider our final message in Chapter 25, "Financial & Estate Planning for the Survivors." ■

Notes

"I am of the opinion that my life belongs to the community...and as long as I live, it is my privilege to do for it whatever I can. I want to be thoroughly used up when I die, for the harder I work, the more I live. I rejoice in life for its own sake. Life is no brief candle to me. It is a sort of splendid torch which I have got hold of for a moment and I want to make it burn as brightly as possible before handing it on to future generations."

—George Bernard Shaw

CHAPTER 25

Financial & Estate Planning for the Survivors

Receipt of an inheritance is an event which should trigger a review of estate and financial planning for the beneficiaries. Getting your own house in order may even make it easier to settle your own estate.

Now is the time for you to get your own financial and estate planning house in order. Your situation has probably changed as the result of the loss you just suffered. Your family situation may be very different if you've lost a child, parent, or spouse. Your financial situation may be very different if you've received a sizeable inheritance. This may be the largest sum of money you will ever acquire at one time.

Equally important, if you've been involved in administration of the estate, you have probably learned the importance of proper estate planning. This may be because the decedent's estate was impeccably planned, in which case you can appreciate how much it helped you. Or perhaps the decedent's estate planning was sorely neglected, and it caused a myriad of problems – financial losses, family disputes, unnecessary taxes, frustration, delays, and expense – and you have learned the real cost of poor planning or no planning at all.

In any event, there is no time like the present for you to address your own planning. Since this book is not about financial and estate planning, but rather about estate administration, we'll only touch upon a number of the most important areas for you to address. We urge you to deal with them sooner rather than later.

Financial Aspects

In recent years people in the financial services industry have talked about trillions of dollars in wealth which will be transferred from the senior generation to the next generation over the coming decades.

Although the ups and downs of the stock market and the world economy have certainly changed whatever projections have been made, your inheritance may still be the largest amount you will ever have, perhaps aside from your own retirement nest egg.

Many people will simply take what they receive, leave it in the same form ("If that stock was good enough for Dad, it's good enough for me..."), or if it's in cash then they may put it in the bank. In many cases, that can be a terrible mistake, one you will only come to appreciate years down the road. Here are a few tips you should consider with your windfall.

X-Ray Your Securities

Whatever securities you have received, make sure you know what you have and make an affirmative decision, on a case-by-case basis, to either sell them or keep them. Don't let inertia govern.

You may have received individual stocks and bonds, mutual funds, money market accounts, certificates of deposit, or government bonds. The worst thing you can do is just sit on them.

Whether to hold onto them or sell them should be a financial decision, not an emotional one. Mom or Dad (or whoever was kind enough to leave them to you) may have bought them or held them for years for their own reasons, but your decision should be based on the here and now, and what's likely to happen tomorrow and in the years to come.

People often avoid selling appreciated securities because they do not want to trigger capital gains tax. For the moment, that's not an issue for you because you probably have a new cost basis (step-up in basis) to the date-of-death value.

A large concentration of a particular stock may have been acquired over many decades because of an employment relationship with the company, stock splits or stock dividends, or a dividend reinvestment program. Whatever the reason, we suggest you take a good, hard look at what you have and ask yourself this simple question:

If you had everything in cash, is this the portfolio you would create for yourself?

Look at each security. How has it performed over the last year, three years, and five years? If the returns are not consistent, are you comfortable with the volatility of the security?

If there are mutual funds in the basket, are they expensive to hold? How do their expenses and returns compare with others of the same type? Are there other alternatives which you presently own or can identify which have lower expense ratios or consistently higher returns?

Are the investments themselves sound? Are the industry sectors represented those which you feel will do well in the future? Are they sufficiently diversified, taking into account other investments you already have?

If the basket of investments includes individual bonds, you have even more thinking to do. If there are tax-free municipal bonds, does your personal income tax rate merit that type of investment? Is the state of the issuer such that you are also exempt from state income tax on the bond interest? Are you comfortable with the ability of the issuers of the bonds to pay the interest, and the principal at maturity?

Are the maturities acceptable to you? If they are very long term, you may be subject to more volatility in their values over time. If you can't handle that volatility, then consider selling some and investing in shorter-terms bonds or maybe stocks, depending on how they all fit in your asset allocation.

Dump the Losers

If the entire basket of securities is high quality, with great returns and even better prospects – stocks, bonds, and mutual funds you would buy today if you had the opportunity – you're in great shape. Most likely, however, there will be a few that you would rather not own.

Some may be hands-down dogs, and you should decide how quickly to sell them. Others may just not be what you would want to own. They may not be the best investments, but nothing to panic over. Put those securities on a watch list and take your time over the next year to make a decision about whether to sell those as well or continue to hold.

Evaluate What's Left, Based on Your Own Goals

Maybe the securities you've inherited would, on some sort of objective basis, be fine investments, but are they consistent with your own goals and objectives?

For example, Uncle Don was really into day trading high-tech stocks and left you a bundle of very exciting opportunities. You've looked at the charts on these stocks over the past couple of years, and the past few months, and your stomach fell as you watched the incredible volatility. You already have a fair amount in the same sectors and you don't feel you can handle much more.

You may decide to diversify the inherited securities in another sector or sectors to allow you to sleep better at night.

Another example: Grandma was a great believer in U.S. Treasury bonds. "You'll never lose a penny on these," she often told you. That's correct, but if you're young and looking for appreciation, a large concentration of fixed income securities – even the best quality – just won't meet your growth objectives.

You get the point: Even if what you inherited is high quality, it may not all be right for your goals, objectives, and investment personality. Decide which ones aren't a good fit and move them out.

Rebalance Your Entire Portfolio

After you've figured out what you're going to hold and what you're going to sell, and the tax consequences of any of that, make sure to consider your own investments as well.

Do you have an asset allocation? Have your investment goals, time horizon, or personal situation changed much since you originally set it up? At this time you'll need to reset the overall allocation for stock, bonds, and cash.

If you don't relate to this discussion – which is entirely possible since your inheritance may well be the first sum you've ever had to invest – then we strongly suggest you start learning about investments, from the ground up.

Every stock brokerage firm and online brokerage service will provide you brochures about the basics, and bookstores and public libraries are filled with books on investing as well. Take the time to read about investing , and then decide if you want to go on your own to seek professional guidance.

Consider Professional Investment Help

Not everyone who receives an inheritance, whether relatively small or very large, has the time or inclination to invest and manage it themselves. Many of those who might be so inclined still prefer to hire professionals to do the job for them.

A professional investment advisor can help you evaluate the portfolio, identify your goals and objectives, decide what to hold and what to sell, and help you set up the right portfolio for yourself and your family to give you a good chance to achieve financial success and security in the future. Revisit the discussion on financial advisors in Chapter 12, "Where to Turn for Help."

Estate Planning

Review Your Estate Plan

A death in the family is the typical trigger for a complete review of your estate planning. This is a major change in your family situation, and may also involve receipt of a substantial inheritance.

Many people believe that once they have signed their estate planning documents, they can put them in the vault and forget about them. Not so. They should be reviewed whenever there are significant changes in your family (which would include marriages, divorces, births, and deaths), changes in your assets, or changes in the tax law.

Services for Senior Citizens

If the survivors include senior citizens, a whole host of other issues will arise:

How long can the senior citizen stay in the family home, and what are the other options?

What charitable and volunteer organizations exist within the community to provide services to seniors?

What services are available for those with various disabilities? What should be done if the senior citizen is or may be suffering from Alzheimer's disease?

What organizations provide information on other specific health conditions?

Check with your local **Area Agency on Aging** for resources on services for senior citizens.

Estate Planning Checklist

The authors have prepared a detailed estate planning checklist, which may be obtained via a simple email request to **inquiries@carobtreepress.com**. Note "estate planning checklist" in the subject line .

Your attitudes toward family and charity may also change over the years. Planning techniques also evolve, and plans should be reviewed after major tax law changes. It's a good idea to have your plan reviewed every five years in any event, just to see if you still like it or want to make changes.

Certainly a death can cause you to rethink many aspects of your estate plan, and also to consider your plan more seriously, since death is no longer merely a theoretical possibility.

Who should receive what, how should they receive it, who has already passed away, and are relationships the same as they were the last time you reviewed your documents? Who should now serve under your Power of Attorney and Health Care Designation? These are but a few of the questions that will come up when you look at your existing estate planning documents.

If you have never addressed your estate planning, then now is the time. Remember, you do have an estate plan. It's either the one that you set up for yourself, or the one that the law provides for you. It's your choice.

Coordinate Your Estate Plan

Some people still forget that many arrangements "outside" their estate planning documents will override those documents, and need to be coordinated with the overall plan.

Joint ownership, beneficiary designations on life insurance, annuities, IRAs and retirement plans, and *Payable on Death* designations on government bonds, for example, all need to be reviewed. If the assets will pass in a way which is inconsistent with your will or trust, then changes may have to be made in the form of ownership or beneficiary designations.

Now is the time to check joint ownership and beneficiary designations. You may have been the surviving joint owner on property owned jointly with the decedent, and now have a decision to make as to how to deal with that property.

You may have been the primary beneficiary on IRAs or annuities, and now have to designate your own beneficiaries. If you have inherited some large IRAs you have some serious planning to do to maximize the tax benefits of those accounts and defer the income to the extent possible, if that's your game plan.

If the accounts were yours in the first place, and the decedent was your beneficiary, then you have to rethink your beneficiary designations also.

Whatever you do, you must make sure that you've covered all the bases and that your estate plan, which you took pains to have drafted, will work in the context of all the assets which make up your estate.

Share Information with Your Family

As you've just been involved in administering an estate, you know how important it can be to have complete information. Make sure that your family doesn't have to search for information when handling *your* estate.

Prepare a detailed checklist describing every asset and liability, locations of accounts, computer passwords, locations of safe deposit boxes and keys, and full life insurance and other insurance information. Make sure you have a digital asset plan (see Chapter 3, "Passing on Digital Assets").

Suffering the loss of a family member is traumatic enough without having to worry about how to pay bills, where accounts are located, how to access password-protected computerized records, whether there is a safe deposit box, and where the key might be.

Insurance companies won't seek out your beneficiaries to pay them benefits. To make a claim your beneficiaries will either have to know that there is insurance and with which company, or they will have to do an investigation to locate that information.

Plan Beyond Your Will or Trust

Many people often view their estate plan as what is found within their will or trust. A review of the documents may, in fact, reveal that the plan is fine, as far as it goes.

But many planning opportunities appear only after careful consideration of all of your assets and objectives with regard to those assets. Tremendous long-range tax benefits can be achieved by lifetime planning, annual gift programs, moving investments, business assets, personal residences, and other assets down one or more generations, at the least tax cost possible.

If you focus only on your will or trust, you may be overlooking tremendous planning possibilities. If your estate is a modest one, then this may not be a concern. But if your estate has grown over the years to the point where it may be taxable, then you really should begin to consider other options to minimize estate taxes.

Plan for Several Generations

If you have children or grandchildren, and a large estate, you ought to think about planning for more than one generation.

Most parents feel that if their children have reached a certain age, whether that be 35, 40, or even 45, they are comfortable leaving them their share of the estate outright, not in trust. This decision reflects a degree of confidence in the children – which is fine – but it overlooks estate tax problems your children may have in their own estates.

The tax law allows you to leave a certain amount of your estate – $5,250,000 ($10,500,000 for a married couple) under current (2013) law – in such a way that it can pass to your *grandchildren*, or even lower generations, free from estate tax in your *children's* estates.

This type of planning is obviously only for those with very large estates, and it won't save you any estate tax in your estate. But it will allow your *children's* estates to eventually avoid significant taxes, and your grandchildren may ultimately receive many millions more when your children pass on.

It can even be done in a way that allows your children use of the funds if they need them during their lifetimes. So you don't really have to bypass your children to provide them these potential benefits.

Consider Life Insurance

Not everyone needs life insurance. However, life insurance can be particularly useful in large estates to create additional tax-free wealth, outside the taxable estate, to replace all or part of the estate taxes.

A policy which pays on the last death (so called *survivorship* or *second-to-die*) insurance can be obtained even where one spouse has a poor health history. These types of policies are generally less expensive than insurance on the healthier spouse alone.

If you're single, don't rule out life insurance, even at an advanced age. Competition between insurance companies is such that a policy may be available for less than you think, though your health will obviously be a critical factor.

The insurance lobby is one of the most powerful in this country. The special tax-free treatment of life insurance proceeds – achieved through the efforts of that lobby – should not be overlooked.

The premiums on a large policy may appear to be high. But the ultimate benefit to your family could be even greater, in dollars, and also in terms of investment return for your premium dollar. If properly structured, it can also be totally free from income and estate taxes.

Start Planning Early

If your estate is now at the taxable level – currently $5,250,000 (in 2013) and double that for married couples – you should be thinking about ways to limit the estate tax burden. Most planning techniques will benefit from an early start. So it's really not in your interest to procrastinate.

For example, you can give away $14,000 each year ($28,000 per year for married couples), to as many people as you choose, without incurring gift tax and without using up any of your lifetime estate and gift tax exemption. This is your annual gift tax exclusion (as from 2013), and it expires on December 31 of each year. It's a "use it or lose it" proposition.

Other techniques involve transferring assets out of your estate, which also moves the future growth or appreciation on those assets out of your estate. Starting earlier removes more of the future appreciation.

Yet other techniques, keyed to your life expectancy, benefit from your being younger at the time you implement them. In the case of life insurance, premiums are generally lower the younger you are. If you wait until "later" to take out the insurance, future health problems could increase the premiums or you could even become uninsurable.

So it's really in your interest to develop a plan and begin to implement it as soon as you can reasonably do so.

Communicate Your Love and Ethical Values

While actions certainly speak louder than words, many of us take for granted that our children and grandchildren appreciate how much we love them, and know and understand our ethical values.

But verbalizing all of this in what is called an *ethical will* can be a fulfilling experience for you, and will give your family something to cherish and remember. It may also clearly express your feelings on a number of issues which are important to you, and on which you hope they will follow your lead. The not-yet born children of your children's children will thank you and bless you for it.

Ethical Will Resource

Most attorneys – and most clients – are not familiar with ethical wills. However, you will find valuable insights into this concept, and numerous real life examples from the past and from current times, in a classic work on the subject, **So That Our Values Live On: Ethical Wills and How to Prepare Them**, Jack Riemer and Nathaniel Stampfer, eds. (1991).

Be Charitable

In the overall context of time, we are here for but a moment, mere grains of sand on an infinitely large beach. In the words of Hillel, a sage who lived in the first century:

If I am not for myself, who will be for me?
If I am only for myself, what am I?
If not now, when?

There is so much work to be done to better mankind, charitable giving is not really an option but an important obligation of each of us, to whatever extent and in whatever way we can.

We say to our clients, "Give until it feels good." Work closely with the charities you favor so that you can see and feel first hand the good that you are doing and how much it is appreciated.

Consider leaving something for charity in your will or trust, and also look into various ways of benefiting charity during your lifetime.

The numerous tax benefits to be derived from the various forms of charitable giving are merely icing on the cake. Your contributions do so much to uplift the minds, bodies, spirits, and souls of those you help. And you will also be leaving a legacy for your children and grandchildren to follow. ■

APPENDIX A

Michigan Probate Forms

This section contains reproductions of selected Michigan Probate forms for information only. These forms have been reduced in size and are not acceptable for filing. Obtain the current versions from the Probate Court, or fillable pdf files of all Michigan SCAO Probate forms are available at http://courts.mi.gov/Administration/SCAO/Forms/Pages/Probate-Court-Index.aspx

This section contains reproductions of the following selected Michigan probate forms, included in numerical order:

PC 551	Petition and Order to Open Safe Deposit Box to Locate Will or Burial Deed
PC 556	Petition and Order for Assignment
PC 557	Notice of Intent to Request Informal Appointment of Personal Representative
PC 558	Application for Informal Probate and/or Appointment of Personal Representative (Testate/Intestate)
PC 559	Petition for Probate and/or Appointment of Personal Representative (Testate/Intestate)
PC 561	Waiver and Consent
PC 562	Notice of Hearing
PC 565	Testimony to Identify Heirs
PC 566	Supplemental Testimony to Identify Nonheir Devisees (Testate Estate)
PC 567	Renunciation of Right to Appointment, Nomination of Personal Representative and Waiver of Notice
PC 568	Register's Statement
PC 569	Order of Formal Proceedings
PC 570	Bond of Fiduciary
PC 571	Acceptance of Appointment
PC 572	Letters of Authority for Personal Representative
PC 573	Notice of Appointment and Duties of Personal Representative
PC 574	Notice to Creditors, Decedent's Estate
PC 576	Notice Regarding Attorney Fees
PC 577	Inventory
PC 578	Notice to Known Creditors
PC 581	Notice to Spouse of Rights of Election and Allowances, Proof of Service and Election
PC 582	Selection of Homestead Allowance and Exempt Property
PC 583	Account of Fiduciary, Short Form
PC 584	Account of Fiduciary, Long Form
PC 585a	Petition to Allow Account(s)
PC 587	Notice of Continued Administration

PC 589	Notice of Intent to Close Estate Administration and Termination Personal Representative's Authority
PC 590	Sworn Closing Statement, Summary Proceeding, Small Estates
PC 591	Sworn Statement to Close Unsupervised Administration
PC 592	Certificate of Completion
PC 593	Petition for Complete Estate Settlement, Testacy Previously Adjudicated
PC 594	Petition for Adjudication of Testacy and Complete Estate Settlement
PC 595	Order for Complete Estate Settlement
PC 596	Schedule of Distributions and Payment of Claims
PC 598	Affidavit of Decedent's Successor for Delivery of Certain Assets owned by Decedent
PC 618	Personal Representative Notice to Friend of the Court

PC 551 - Petition and Order to Open Safe-Deposit Box to Locate Will or Burial Deed

Approved, SCAO | JIS CODE: DBP, DBO

STATE OF MICHIGAN PROBATE COURT COUNTY OF	PETITION AND ORDER TO OPEN SAFE-DEPOSIT BOX TO LOCATE WILL OR BURIAL DEED	FILE NO.

USE NOTE: File this petition in the county where the safe-deposit box is located.

Estate of ______________________________

PETITION

1. I, ______________________________ (Name), am interested in the decedent's estate and make this petition as ______________________________ (Relationship to decedent, i.e. heir, devisee, etc.).
2. Decedent died ____________ (Date), domiciled in ______________________________ (County and state or other jurisdiction).
3. ______________________________ (Name of bank, trust company, or safe-deposit company), as lessor, leased to decedent, alone or jointly, safe-deposit box number ______, located at ____________ (Branch) in ____________ (City or township) in this county, and the safe-deposit box may contain decedent's will and/or a deed to a burial plot in which the decedent is to be interred.
4. **I REQUEST** that this court issue an order directing the lessor to permit ______________________________ (Name) to examine the contents of the safe-deposit box in the presence of an officer or other authorized employee of lessor for the purpose of locating and removing a will and/or a deed to a burial plot only.

I declare under the penalties of perjury that this petition has been examined by me and that its contents are true to the best of my information, knowledge, and belief.

____________________ Date

Attorney signature	Petitioner signature
Name (type or print) Bar no.	Name (type or print)
Address	Address
City, state, zip Telephone no.	City, state, zip Telephone no.

ORDER

IT IS ORDERED:

5. The above petition is granted and the lessor is ordered to permit ______________________________ to examine the safe-deposit box described above in the presence of an officer or other authorized employee of the lessor. Only a will of the decedent and/or a deed to a burial plot shall be removed from the box and shall be delivered by the person named above to the probate register or deputy register of this court.
6. At the time of the opening of the safe-deposit box, all persons in attendance shall execute a written statement certifying whether a will and/or a deed to a burial plot was found and that no other items were removed from the safe-deposit box. The person named above shall file that written statement with the probate register or deputy register of this court within 7 days of opening the box. If no safe-deposit box is located, the person named above shall file a written statement indicating that no box was found.

Date	Judge Bar no.

Do not write below this line - For court use only

PC 551 (9/11) **PETITION AND ORDER TO OPEN SAFE-DEPOSIT BOX TO LOCATE WILL OR BURIAL DEED** MCL 700.2517

PC 556 - Petition and Order for Assignment (p. 1)

Approved, SCAO | JIS CODE: PER, OAA

STATE OF MICHIGAN PROBATE COURT COUNTY OF	PETITION AND ORDER FOR ASSIGNMENT	FILE NO.

Estate of ____________________, decedent XXX-XX-____
Last four digits of SSN

PETITION

I, ____________________, represent that:
Name and relationship

1. Decedent died on ____________.
   Date
2. ☐ Decedent was a resident of ____________ in this county.
   City/Township

   ☐ Decedent lived outside of Michigan and left an estate within this county to be administered.
3. Funeral and burial expenses are $____________.
   The following persons have paid the following amounts toward the funeral and burial expenses: (Statements and receipts are attached.)

NAME	AMOUNT	NAME	AMOUNT

The amount of funeral and burial expenses remaining unpaid is $____________.
The total value of the decedent's property remaining after payment of funeral and burial expenses does not/will not exceed $15,000 as adjusted for cost of living.

4. The decedent's property is as follows. The lien amount on any real property listed is also included (Attach separate sheet if necessary.)

DESCRIPTION OF PROPERTY	VALUE
Provide the gross value of the decedent's property.	
Provide the total lien amount(s) for any real property with a lien/mortgage.	
Subtract the total lien amount(s) from the gross value of the decedent's property. Total	0.00

(SEE SECOND PAGE)

Do not write below this line - For court use only

PC 556 - Petition and Order for Assignment (p. 2)

5. The name and address of the surviving spouse or, if there is not a spouse, the name, age, relationship, and address of each of the decedent's heirs are as follows:

NAME	AGE	RELATIONSHIP	ADDRESS		
			Street address		
			City	State	Zip
			Street address		
			City	State	Zip

6. **I REQUEST** that the property listed above be assigned as follows:

☐ a. for funeral and burial expenses, $________ to ________ (Name), $ ________ to ________ (Name), and $________ to ________ (Name).

☐ b. to the surviving spouse, ________.

☐ c. to the following heirs in the stated proportions, ________ ________.

I declare under the penalties of perjury that this petition has been examined by me and that its contents are true to the best of my information, knowledge, and belief.

Attorney signature	Date
Name (type or print) Bar no.	Petitioner signature
Address	Address
City, state, zip Telephone no.	City, state, zip Telephone no.

ORDER ASSIGNING ASSETS

7. **IT IS ORDERED** that the property described above is assigned as follows:

☐ a. for funeral and burial expenses, $________ to ________ (Name), $ ________ to ________ (Name), and $________ to ________ (Name).

☐ b. to the surviving spouse, ________.

☐ c. to the following heirs in the stated proportions, ________ ________.

For 63 days from the date of this order, the share of each heir other than a surviving spouse or minor child shall be subject to any unsatisfied debt of the decedent up to the value of property received through this order.

Date	Judge Bar no.

I certify that I have compared this copy with the original on file and that it is a correct copy of the original.

Date	Deputy register

PC 557 - Notice of Intent to Request Informal Appointment of Personal Representative

Approved, SCAO JIS CODE: NRI

STATE OF MICHIGAN PROBATE COURT COUNTY OF	NOTICE OF INTENT TO REQUEST INFORMAL APPOINTMENT OF PERSONAL REPRESENTATIVE	FILE NO.

Estate of ____

I, ____, intend to request my informal appointment
Name

as personal representative of the estate. A copy of the application is attached. This notice is being served upon each person whose right to an appointment is prior or equal to my own. The court will not act upon my application until 14 days after the date this notice was mailed or until 7 days after this notice was personally served.

The actions you may take include:

- Upon paying a filing fee, filing a petition for formal proceedings to appoint a personal representative.
- Upon paying a filing fee, filing an application for informal appointment of yourself as personal representative provided you have a higher priority to be appointed.
- Contacting an attorney for assistance in representing you in any proceeding you wish to file in the court.

The court will not be able to provide you with any legal advice in completing or filing the forms.

	Date
Attorney name Bar no.	Applicant signature
Address	Address
City, state, zip Telephone no.	City, state, zip Telephone no.

NOTICE TO APPLICANT: You must attach this notice and a proof of service to the application for informal appointment when you file it with the court. If you are unable to serve an interested person because the address or whereabouts of that interested person is unknown, you must publish notice by using form PC 563a.

Do not write below this line - For court use only

MCL 700.3310, MCR 5.309(C)

PC 557 (9/06) **NOTICE OF INTENT TO REQUEST INFORMAL APPOINTMENT OF PERSONAL REPRESENTATIVE**

PC 558 - Application for Informal Probate and/or Appointment of Personal Representative (Testate/Intestate) (p. 1)

Approved, SCAO JIS CODE: IPA

STATE OF MICHIGAN PROBATE COURT COUNTY OF	APPLICATION FOR INFORMAL PROBATE AND/OR APPOINTMENT OF PERSONAL REPRESENTATIVE (TESTATE/INTESTATE)	FILE NO.

Estate of ______

1. I, ______ (Name of applicant), am interested in the estate and make this application as ______ (Relationship to decedent, i.e., heir, devisee, child, spouse, creditor, beneficiary, etc.).

2. Decedent information: ______ Date of death ______ Time (if known) ______ Date of birth **XXX-XX-**______ Last four digits of SSN

   Domicile (at date of death): ______ City/Township/Village ______ County ______ State

3. ☐ A death certificate has been issued, and a copy is attached.
   ☐ No death certificate is available. Attached is alternative documentation of the decedent's death.

4. As far as I know or could ascertain with reasonable diligence, the names and addresses of the heirs and devisees of the decedent and other interested persons, the relationship to the decedent, and the ages of any who are minors are:
   (Required testimony forms are attached.)

NAME	ADDRESS			RELATIONSHIP (Heir / Devisee)	AGE/DOB (if minor)
	Street address				
	City	State	Zip		
	Street address				
	City	State	Zip		
	Street address				
	City	State	Zip		

Of the interested persons listed above, the following are under legal disability or otherwise represented and presently have or will require representation:

NAME	LEGAL DISABILITY	REPRESENTED BY Name, address, and capacity

5. ☐ a. Venue is proper in this county because the decedent was domiciled in this county on the date of death.
   ☐ b. The decedent was not domiciled in Michigan, but venue is proper in this county because property of the decedent was located in this county at the date of death.

(SEE SECOND PAGE)

Do not write below this line - For court use only

PC 558 (9/12) **APPLICATION FOR INFORMAL PROBATE AND/OR APPOINTMENT OF PERSONAL REPRESENTATIVE (TESTATE/INTESTATE)** MCL 700.1309, MCL 700.3301, MCL 700.3311, MCL 700.3614, MCR 5.302, MCR 5.309

PC 558 - Application for Informal Probate and/or Appointment of Personal Representative (Testate/Intestate) (p. 2)

6. ☐ a. The decedent died intestate and after exercising reasonable diligence, I am unaware of any unrevoked testamentary instrument relating to property located in this state as defined under MCL 700.1301.
☐ b. I am aware of an unrevoked testamentary instrument relating to property located in this state as defined under MCL 700.1301, but the instrument is not being probated because (if this statement is true, the probate register must deny this application according to MCL 700.3311): ______
The instrument ☐ is attached to this application. ☐ is already in the court's possession.
☐ c. The decedent's will, dated ______, with codicil(s) dated ______, is/are offered for probate and ☐ is/are attached to this application. ☐ is/are already in the court's possession.
☐ d. An authenticated copy of the will and codicil(s), if any, probated in ______ County, ______ (State) is/are offered for probate, and documents establishing its probate are attached to this application.

7. To the best of my knowledge, I believe that the instrument(s) subject to this application, if any, was/were validly executed and is the decedent's last will. After exercising reasonable diligence, I am unaware of an instrument revoking the will or codicil(s).

☐ 8. A personal representative has been previously appointed in ______ County, ______ (State) and the appointment has not been terminated. The personal representative's name and address are:

______ Name ______ Address

______ City ______ State ______ Zip

☐ 9. I nominate ______ (Name) as personal representative, who is qualified and has the following priority for appointment: ______. His/her address is: ______ (Address)

______ City ______ State ______ Zip.

☐ 10. Other persons have prior or equal right to appointment as personal representative. They are:

______ Name ______ Name

______ Name ______ Name

Suitable renunciations, nominations, and/or a Notice of Intent to Seek Informal Appointment and proof of its service have been or will be filed.

☐ 11. The will expressly requests that the personal representative serve with bond.

☐ 12. A special personal representative is necessary because ______.

I REQUEST:

☐ 13. Informal probate of the will.

☐ 14. Informal appointment of the nominated personal representative ☐ with ☐ without bond.

☐ 15. The appointment of a special personal representative pending the appointment of the nominated personal representative.

I declare under the penalties of perjury that this application has been examined by me and that its contents are true to the best of my information, knowledge, and belief.

	Date
Attorney signature	Applicant signature
Attorney name (type or print) Bar no.	Applicant name (type or print)
Address	Address
City, state, zip Telephone no.	City, state, zip Telephone no.

PC 559 - Petition for Probate and/or Appointment of Personal Representative (Testate/Intestate) (p. 1)

Approved, SCAO JIS CODE: PFA

STATE OF MICHIGAN PROBATE COURT COUNTY OF	PETITION FOR PROBATE AND/OR APPOINTMENT OF PERSONAL REPRESENTATIVE ☐ TESTATE ☐ INTESTATE	FILE NO.

Estate of ______________________________

1. I, ______________________________ , am interested in the estate and make this petition as
   Name of petitioner
   ______________________________ , as defined by MCL 700.1105(c).
   Relationship to decedent, i.e., heir, devisee, child, spouse, creditor, beneficiary, etc.
2. Decedent information: ____________ ____________ ____________ XXX-XX-________
   Date of death / Time (if known) / Date of birth / Last four digits of SSN

   Domicile (at date of death): ____________ ____________ ____________
   City/Township/Village / County / State

   Estimated value of estate assets: Real estate: $ ____________ Personal estate: $ ____________
3. ☐ A death certificate has been issued, and a copy is attached.
   ☐ No death certificate is available. Attached is alternative documentation of the decedent's death.
4. As far as I know or could ascertain with reasonable diligence, the names and addresses of the heirs and devisees of the decedent and other interested persons, the relationship to the decedent, and the ages of any who are minors are:
   (Required testimony forms are attached.)

NAME	ADDRESS			RELATIONSHIP (Heir / Devisee)	AGE/DOB (if minor)
	Street address				
	City	State	Zip		
	Street address				
	City	State	Zip		
	Street address				
	City	State	Zip		

Of the interested persons listed above, the following are under legal disability or otherwise represented and presently have or will require representation:

NAME	LEGAL DISABILITY	REPRESENTED BY Name, address, and capacity

5. ☐ a. Venue is proper in this county because the decedent was domiciled in this county on the date of death.
   ☐ b. The decedent was not domiciled in Michigan, but venue is proper in this county because property of the decedent was located in this county at the date of death.

☐ 6. An application was previously filed and a personal representative was appointed informally.

(SEE SECOND PAGE)

Do not write below this line - For court use only

MCL 700.1309, MCL 700.3402, MCL 700.3502, MCR 5.302(A), MCR 5.308, MCR 5.310(B)

PC 559 (9/12) **PETITION FOR PROBATE AND/OR APPOINTMENT OF PERSONAL REPRESENTATIVE (TESTATE/INTESTATE)**

PC 559 - Petition for Probate and/or Appointment of Personal Representative (Testate/Intestate) (p. 2)

☐ 7. A personal representative has been previously appointed in ________________ County, ________ State
and the appointment has not been terminated. The personal representative's name and address are

________________ Name ________________ Address

________________ City ________________ State ________________ Zip .

☐ 8. ☐ a. The decedent's will, dated ____________, with codicil(s) dated ____________
is/are offered for probate and is/are ☐ attached to this petition. ☐ already in the court's possession.
☐ b. An authenticated copy of the will and codicil(s), if any, probated in ____________ County, ________ State
is/are offered for probate, and documents establishing its probate accompany this petition.
☐ c. Neither the original will nor an authenticated copy of a will probated in another jurisdiction accompanies the petition. The will is lost, destroyed, or otherwise unavailable, but its contents are (Attach additional sheets as necessary.)

________________________________ .

☐9. The decedent's will was ☐ formally ☐ informally probated on ________ in ____________ County.

10. To the best of my knowledge, I believe that the instrument(s) subject to this petition, if any, was/were validly executed and is/are the decedent's last will. After exercising reasonable diligence, I am unaware of an instrument revoking the will or codicil(s).
☐ a. After exercising reasonable diligence, I am unaware of any unrevoked testamentary instrument relating to property located in this state as defined under MCL 700.1301.
☐ b. I am aware of an unrevoked testamentary instrument relating to property located in this state as defined under MCL 700.1301, but the instrument is not being probated because

________________________________ .

The instrument ☐ is attached to this petition. ☐ is already in the court's possession.

☐ 11. I nominate ________________ (Name) as personal representative, who is qualified and has the following priority for appointment: ________________. His/her address is ________________ Address

________________ City ________________ State ________________ Zip .

☐ 12. Other persons have prior or equal right to appointment. They are:

________________ Name ________________ Name

________________ Name ________________ Name

☐ 13. The will expressly requests that the personal representative serve with bond.

14. ☐ a. The decedent left a will that directs supervised administration.
☐ b. The decedent left a will that directs unsupervised administration, but supervised administration is necessary for the protection of persons interested in the estate because (Complete on line below.)
☐ c. The decedent died intestate or left a will that does not direct supervised administration, but supervised administration is necessary because (Complete on line below.)

________________________________ .

☐ 15. A special personal representative is necessary because ________________________ .

I REQUEST:

☐ 16. An order determining heirs and that the decedent died ☐ intestate. ☐ testate and the document(s) stated in item 8 is/are valid and admitted to probate.

☐ 17. Formal appointment of the nominated personal representative ☐ with ☐ without bond.

☐ 18. Supervised administration.

☐ 19. Appointment of a special personal representative pending the appointment of the nominated personal representative.

I declare under the penalties of perjury that this petition has been examined by me and that its contents are true to the best of my information, knowledge, and belief.

________________ Date

Attorney signature	Petitioner signature
Attorney name (type or print) Bar no.	Petitioner name (type or print)
Address	Address
City, state, zip Telephone no.	City, state, zip Telephone no.

PC 561 - Waiver and Consent

Approved, SCAO

JIS CODE: WAC

STATE OF MICHIGAN PROBATE COURT COUNTY CIRCUIT COURT - FAMILY DIVISION	WAIVER/CONSENT	FILE NO.

In the matter of ____________________

1. I am interested in the matter as ____________________ .

☐ 2. I waive notice of the hearing and consent to the application/petition for ____________________
Nature of application/petition and name of applicant/petitioner

____

____

____

____

____________________, and I declare that I have received a copy of this application/petition.

☐ 3. I waive notice of the hearing concerning ____________________ .
Nature of hearing

Date

Signature

Attorney name (type or print) Bar no.	Name (type or print)
Address	Address
City, state, zip Telephone no.	City, state, zip Telephone no.

NOTE: Do not use for waivers pursuant to MCL 700.3310.

Do not write below this line - For court use only

PC 562 - Notice of Hearing

Approved, SCAO — JIS CODE: NOH

STATE OF MICHIGAN PROBATE COURT COUNTY OF	NOTICE OF HEARING	FILE NO.

In the matter of ____________________

TAKE NOTICE: A hearing will be held on ____________ (Date) at ________ (Time),

at ____________ (Location) before Judge ____________ (Bar no.)

for the following purpose(s): (state the nature of the hearing)

If you require special accommodations to use the court because of a disability, or if you require a foreign language interpreter to help you fully participate in court proceedings, please contact the court immediately to make arrangements.

	Date
Attorney name — Bar no.	Petitioner name
Address	Address
City, state, zip — Telephone no.	City, state, zip — Telephone no.

USE NOTE TO COURT: If this hearing is for a guardianship matter involving an Indian child as defined in MCR 3.002(5), you must comply with MCR 5.109(2).

USE NOTE: If this form is being filed in the circuit court family division, please enter the court name and county in the upper left-hand corner of the form.

Do not write below this line - For court use only

PC 562 (9/11) **NOTICE OF HEARING** MCL 700.1401, MCL 710.21 *et seq.*, MCR 3.802(A)(3), MCR 5.102, MCR 5.109(2)

PC 565 - Testimony to Identify Heirs (p. 1)

Approved, SCAO | JIS CODE: TES

STATE OF MICHIGAN PROBATE COURT COUNTY OF	TESTIMONY TO IDENTIFY HEIRS	FILE NO.

Estate of ______________________________

1. My name is ______________________________ . My address is ______________________________
______________________________ .

2. I am related to the decedent (or know his/her family) as follows: ______________________________

3. The date and time of the death of the decedent is ______________ (Date) ________ (Time) and at that time the decedent's domicile (residence) was ______________________________ (Address) .

NOTE: IN THE FOLLOWING QUESTIONS, TREAT ALL PERSONS WHO DIED WITHIN 120 HOURS AFTER THE DECEDENT AS IF THEY DID NOT SURVIVE THE DECEDENT. List persons who died within 120 hours after the decedent in item 14 below.

4. The decedent ☐ did not leave a surviving spouse. ☐ left a surviving spouse named ______________________________ .

5. ☐ a. The decedent had the following children, both natural (born in or out of wedlock) and adopted:
____

☐ b. Of the children listed in 5.a, the following are no longer heirs due to their adoption by someone other than a stepparent:
____

☐ c. Of the children listed in 5.a, the following were not children of the surviving spouse: ______________________________
____

Answer question 6 only if question 5.a. was checked.

6. ☐ a. The following children listed in 5.a. died before the decedent: ______________________________
____

☐ b. Children listed in 6.a. left their own children (either natural or adopted) or left grandchildren from one or more of their own predeceased children who survived the decedent. The names of these descendants and the name of the child in 6.a. to whom they are related are as follows:
____
____

☐ c. Of the persons listed in 6.b, the following are no longer heirs due to their adoption by someone other than a stepparent:
____

If decedent left no surviving descendant, complete 7.

7. The decedent ☐ did not leave a surviving father and/or mother. ☐ left a surviving father and/or mother named
______________________________ .

(SEE SECOND PAGE)

Do not write below this line - For court use only

PC 565 (9/10) **TESTIMONY TO IDENTIFY HEIRS**

MCL 700.2104, MCR 5.104(C), MCR 5.302(B), MCR 5.308(B)(2)(a)

PC 565 - Testimony to Identify Heirs (p. 2)

If decedent is not survived by spouse, descendants, or parents, complete 8 (and 9, if applicable).

8. The decedent ☐ did not leave surviving brothers or sisters. ☐ left the the following brothers or sisters, either natural or adopted, whole blood or half blood, who were not adopted by others and who survived the decedent:

____

☐ 9. One or more of the brothers and sisters of the decedent died before him/her leaving descendants, either natural or adopted, who were not adopted by others and who survived the decedent. The names of these descendants, and the name(s) of their deceased ancestor are ____________________.

If decedent was not survived by spouse, descendants, parent, brother, or sister or children of deceased brother or sister, complete 10 (and 11, if applicable).

10. The decedent ☐ did not leave surviving grandparents. ☐ left surviving grandparents (both maternal and paternal) named ____________________.

☐ 11. Both maternal grandparents and/or both paternal grandparents died before decedent. Their surviving descendants and their relationships to the grandparents are

Maternal grandparents: ____________________.

Paternal grandparents: ____________________.

☐ 12. The following heirs listed above are under legal disability. Their name(s), legal disability, and name(s) of their representative(s) are ____________________.

☐ 13. The following deceased heirs survived the decedent by more than 120 hours. Their name(s) and the name(s) of those who represent decedent's interests are ____________________.

☐ 14. The following persons identified above did not survive the decedent by 120 hours. Their names, relationships to decedent, and the date and time of their deaths are:

NAME	RELATION	DATE OF DEATH	TIME OF DEATH

☐ 15. The decedent left a will. ☐ All devisees are heirs. ☐ Some of the devisees named in the will or codicil are not heirs of the testator. (A supplemental testimony form is completed and attached.)

____
Witness signature

Subscribed and sworn to before me on ____________ (Date), ____________ County, Michigan.

My commission expires: ____________ (Date) Signature: ____________ Judge/Deputy register/Notary public Bar no.

Notary public, State of Michigan, County of ____________

Attorney signature	Address
Name (type or print) Bar no.	City, state, zip Telephone no.

PC 566 - Supplemental Testimony to Identify Nonheir Devisees (Testate Estate) (p. 1)

Approved, SCAO

JIS CODE: TSS

STATE OF MICHIGAN PROBATE COURT COUNTY OF	SUPPLEMENTAL TESTIMONY TO IDENTIFY NONHEIR DEVISEES Testate Estate	FILE NO.

Estate of ______________________________

*****USE THIS FORM ONLY IF A DEVISEE NAMED IN THE WILL OR CODICIL IS NOT AN HEIR OF THE TESTATOR*****

NOTE: TREAT ALL PERSONS WHO DIED WITHIN 120 HOURS AFTER THE DECEDENT AS IF THEY DID NOT SURVIVE THE DECEDENT. List persons who died within 120 hours after the decedent in item 18 below.

16. The names of all devisees named in the will and codicils who are not heirs of the decedent (include testamentary trustees and beneficiaries of testamentary trusts) are ______________________________

____

______________________________.

☐ 17. Of the devisees listed in 16, the following died before the decedent. Their names and relationships to the decedent are

____

______________________________.

☐ 18. The following devisees died within 120 hours after the decedent. Their names, relationships to decedent, and the date and time of their deaths are:

NAME	RELATIONSHIP	DATE OF DEATH	TIME OF DEATH

☐ 19. The following are descendants of the predeceased devisees named above, who survived the decedent:

____

____

☐ 20. Class gifts in the will or codicils, where the members are not specifically identified by name, are as follows:

____

____

____

(SEE SECOND PAGE)

Do not write below this line - For court use only

MCL 700.2702,
MCL 700.2707-700.2710

PC 566 - Supplemental Testimony to Identify Nonheir Devisees (Testate Estate) (p. 2)

☐ 21. The following devisees named above are under legal disability. Their names, legal disabilities, and names of their representative(s) are

____

____.

☐ 22. The following deceased devisees survived the decedent by more than 120 hours. Their names and the names of those who represent their interests are

____

____.

☐ 23. The guardian ad litem for each devisee under the will and codicils who is unborn, unknown, or unascertainable is

____.

____
Witness signature

Subscribed and sworn to before me on ____________________ , ____________________ County, Michigan.
Date

My commission expires: ____________________ Signature: ______________________________
Date Judge/Deputy register/Notary public

Notary public, State of Michigan, County of ____________________

____
Attorney signature

____
Name (type or print) Bar no.

____
Address

____
City, state, zip Telephone no.

PC 567 - Renunciation of Right to Appointment, Nomination of Personal Representative and Waiver of Notice

Approved, SCAO | JIS CODE: RRA

STATE OF MICHIGAN PROBATE COURT COUNTY OF	RENUNCIATION OF RIGHT TO APPOINTMENT, NOMINATION OF PERSONAL REPRESENTATIVE AND WAIVER OF NOTICE	FILE NO.

Estate of ______________________________

1. I, ______________________________ , have a prior or equal right to appointment as personal representative.
   Name (type or print)
2. ☐ I renounce that right.
3. ☐ I have the right to nominate and I nominate and request the appointment of ______________________________ as personal representative.
   Name (type or print)

   ☐ I renounce my right to nominate a qualified person to act as personal representative.
4. ☐ I waive notice of the appointment.

Date

Attorney name (type or print) Bar no.	Signature
Address	Address
City, state, zip Telephone no.	City, state, zip Telephone no.

NOTE: A person with priority as determined by a probated will, including a person nominated by a power conferred in the will, does not through this priority have the power to nominate another to be personal representative.

Do not write below this line - For court use only

PC 568 - Register's Statement

Approved, SCAO JIS CODE: RIO

STATE OF MICHIGAN PROBATE COURT COUNTY OF	REGISTER'S STATEMENT	FILE NO.

Estate of ______________________________

1. An application has been filed requesting
   ☐ informal probate of the will of the above named decedent.
   ☐ the appointment of a personal representative.
   ☐ the previously administered estate be reopened.
   ☐ appointment of a successor personal representative.
2. Upon consideration of the application, I determine that all of the following are true:
   a. Venue is proper.
   b. The application is complete and made in accordance with MCL 700.3301 or MCR 5.312.
   c. The applicant appears to be an interested person.
   ☐ d. An original, properly executed, and apparently unrevoked will dated ____________ with codicil(s) dated ____________ is in my possession.
   ☐ An authenticated copy of the will and codicil(s) probated in ____________ County ____________ is offered for informal proceedings and documents establishing probate in another state are in my possession.
   e. The application is not within MCL 700.3304 or MCR 5.144.
   ☐ f. A will to which the requested appointment relates has been formally or informally probated.
   ☐ g. ☐ The person whose appointment is sought has priority to the appointment, with or without appropriate nomination and/or renunciation.
   ☐ The applicant gave notice of his/her intention to seek an informal appointment to each person having a prior or equal right to an appointment not waived in writing and filed with the court.
   ☐ h. There is good cause to reopen the previously administered estate and appoint a personal representative. The estate was not closed under supervised administration.

☐ 3. The will dated____________ with codicils dated ____________ is admitted to informal probate.

☐ 4. ____________ is appointed
   ☐ personal representative ☐ special personal representative ☐ successor personal representative
   of the decedent's estate and upon filing a statement of acceptance, letters shall issue to that personal representative
   ☐ without bond. ☐ upon filing a bond in the amount of $____________ .
   After qualification, the personal representative shall comply with all relevant requirements under the law.

☐ 5. The application is denied because:
   ☐ a personal representative has been appointed in this or another county of this state and continues to serve.
   ☐ this or another will of the decedent has been the subject of a previous probate order.
   ☐ the probate relates to one or more of a known series of testamentary instruments, the latest of which does not expressly revoke the earlier.
   ☐ other:

☐ 6. The estate is reopened. ☐ Letters of authority expire____________ .

______________ Date ______________ Register

______________ Attorney name (type or print) Bar no.

______________ Address ______________ City, state, zip Telephone no.

Do not write below this line - For court use only

PC 568 (9/05) **REGISTER'S STATEMENT**

MCL 700.3302, MCL 700.3303, MCL 700.3304, MCL 700.3305, MCL 700.3308, MCL 700.3601, MCR 5.309, MCR 5.312

PC 569 - Order of Formal Proceedings

Approved, SCAO

JIS CODE: OPF

STATE OF MICHIGAN PROBATE COURT COUNTY OF	ORDER OF FORMAL PROCEEDINGS	FILE NO.

Estate of ______________________________

1. Date of hearing: ____________________ Judge: ____________________
Bar no.

THE COURT FINDS:

2. Notice of hearing was given to or waived by all interested persons.

3. Decedent died ____________________
Date

☐ a resident of the above named county.
☐ a nonresident of Michigan, but left an estate in the above named county.

4. Venue is proper.

☐ 5. Decedent's heirs are determined (specify names and relationships): ____________________

6. Decedent died
☐ intestate.
☐ with a valid, unrevoked will dated ____________________ with codicil(s) dated ____________________.

☐ 7. ____________________ is suitable for appointment pursuant to MCL 700.3203 and 700.3204.
Name

8. ☐ The decedent's will directs supervised administration. Since the execution of the will, the circumstances bearing on the need for supervised administration ☐ have ☐ have not changed.
☐ The decedent's will directs unsupervised administration.
☐ Supervised administration ☐ is ☐ is not necessary for the protection of persons interested in the estate.

IT IS ORDERED:

☐ 9. The petition is ☐ granted. ☐ denied on the merits. ☐ dismissed/withdrawn.
☐ 10. The decedent died intestate.
☐ 11. The will and codicil(s) are valid and admitted to probate.
☐ 12. Estate administration shall be supervised.

☐ 13. ____________________ is appointed ☐ personal representative ☐ special personal representative of the decedent's estate and upon filing a statement of acceptance, letters shall issue to that personal representative ☐ without bond. ☐ upon filing a bond in the amount of $ ____________ .
After qualification, the personal representative shall comply with all relevant requirements under the law.
☐ 14. The petition for supervised administration is denied.
☐ 15. Decedent's heirs are as determined in 5. above.
16. Other:

____
Date

____
Judge

____
Attorney name Bar no.

____
Address

____
City, state, zip Telephone no.

Do not write below this line - For court use only

PC 569 (9/05) **ORDER OF FORMAL PROCEEDINGS**

MCL 700.3204, MCL 700.3409, MCL 700.3410, MCL 700.3414, MCL 700.3502, MCL 700.3601

PC 570 - Bond of Fiduciary

Approved, SCAO | JIS CODE: BND

STATE OF MICHIGAN PROBATE COURT COUNTY CIRCUIT COURT - FAMILY DIVISION	BOND OF FIDUCIARY	FILE NO.

Estate of ______________________________

1. The principal has been appointed ______________________ (Type of fiduciary), accepts the duties of this appointment and, with the surety(ies), agrees to pay $ ______________ to the State of Michigan as obligee for the benefit of the persons interested in the estate if the principal fails to discharge all duties according to law.
2. The surety(ies) agree to be jointly and severally liable on the bond with the principal and with each other.
3. The surety(ies) consent to the jurisdiction of the court that issued letters of authority to the principal in a proceeding pertaining to the principal's fiduciary duties.
4. If this is a bond for a special personal representative who is subsequently appointed personal representative, the obligations and liabilities of this bond remain in effect.

Date

Principal signature

Attorney name (type or print) Bar no.

Address

City, state, zip Telephone no.

Principal name (type or print)

Address

City, state, zip Telephone no.

Surety signature

Surety name (type or print)

Address

City, state, zip Telephone no.

Surety signature

Surety name (type or print)

Address

City, state, zip Telephone no.

Oath of Personal Surety The surety acknowledges personal worth of the amount of the penalty in the bond over and above all debts and legal exemptions.

Subscribed and sworn to before me on ______________ (Date), ______________ County, Michigan.

My commission expires: ______________ (Date) Signature: ______________ (Notary public/Deputy probate register)

Notary public, State of Michigan, County of ______________

Do not write below this line - For court use only

I have examined and approve this bond.

Date

Judge/Probate register Bar no.

☐ No new letters of authority are to be issued.

PC 570 (9/05) **BOND OF FIDUCIARY** MCL 700.3601, MCL 700.3604, MCL 700.5106(3), MCL 700.5410, MCL 700.5411

PC 571 - Acceptance of Appointment

Approved, SCAO | JIS CODE: AOT

STATE OF MICHIGAN PROBATE COURT COUNTY OF	ACCEPTANCE OF APPOINTMENT	FILE NO.

In the matter of ______________________________

1. I have been appointed ______________________________ of the person/estate.
   Type of fiduciary
2. I accept the appointment, submit to personal jurisdiction of the court, and agree to file reports and to perform all required duties.

☐ 3. For a period of ____________ days from the date of my appointment, I exclude from the scope of my responsibility the
not to exceed 91 days

following real estate or ownership interest in a business entity: ______________________________
Describe real property or business interest

____

____

____

____

because I reasonably believe the real estate or other property owned by the business entity is or may be contaminated by a hazardous substance, or is or has been used in an activity directly or indirectly involving a hazardous substance that could result in liability to the estate or otherwise impair the value of property held by the estate.

Date

Signature

Attorney name (type or print) Bar no.	Name (type or print)
Attorney address	Address
City, state, zip Telephone no.	City, state, zip Telephone no.
	Date of birth

USE NOTE: If this form is being filed in the circuit court family division, please enter the court name and county in the upper left-hand corner of the form.

Do not write below this line - For court use only

PC 571 (9/10) **ACCEPTANCE OF APPOINTMENT**

MCL 700.3601, MCL 700.3602, MCL 700.5214, MCL 700.5301, MCL 700.5307, MCL 700.5412, MCL 700.7202, MCR 5.501

PC 572 - Letters of Authority for Personal Representative (p. 1)

Approved, SCAO JIS CODE: LET

STATE OF MICHIGAN PROBATE COURT COUNTY OF	LETTERS OF AUTHORITY FOR PERSONAL REPRESENTATIVE	FILE NO.

Estate of ______________________________

TO: Name and address Telephone no.

You have been appointed and qualified as personal representative of the estate on ______________ (Date). You are authorized to perform all acts authorized by law unless exceptions are specified below.

☐ Your authority is limited in the following way:

☐ You have no authority over the estate's real estate or ownership interests in a business entity that you identified on your acceptance of appointment.

☐ Other restrictions or limitations are:

☐ These letters expire: ______________ (Date).

Date ______________ Judge (formal proceedings)/Register (informal proceedings) Bar no.

SEE NOTICE OF DUTIES ON SECOND PAGE

Attorney name (type or print) Bar no.

Address

City, state, zip Telephone no.

I certify that I have compared this copy with the original on file and that it is a correct copy of the original, and on this date, these letters are in full force and effect.

Date ______________ Deputy register

Do not write below this line - For court use only

MCL 700.3103, MCL 700.3307, MCL 700.3414, MCL 700.3504, MCL 700.3601, MCR 5.202, MCR 5.206, MCR 5.307, MCR 5.310

PC 572 (2/13) LETTERS OF AUTHORITY FOR PERSONAL REPRESENTATIVE

PC 572 - Letters of Authority for Personal Representative (p. 2)

The following provisions are mandatory reporting duties specified in Michigan law and Michigan court rules and are not the only duties required of you. See MCL 700.3701 through MCL 700.3722 for other duties. Your failure to comply may result in the court suspending your powers and appointing a special fiduciary in your place. It may also result in your removal as fiduciary.

CONTINUED ADMINISTRATION: If the estate is not settled within 1 year after the first personal representative's appointment, you must file with the court and send to each interested person a notice that the estate remains under administration, specifying the reasons for the continued administration. You must give this notice within 28 days of the first anniversary of the first personal representative's appointment and all subsequent anniversaries during which the administration remains uncompleted. If such a notice is not received, an interested person may petition the court for a hearing on the necessity for continued administration or for closure of the estate. [MCL 700.3703(4), MCL 700.3951(3), MCR 5.144, MCR 5.307, MCR 5.310]

DUTY TO COMPLETE ADMINISTRATION OF ESTATE: You must complete the administration of the estate and file appropriate closing papers with the court. Failure to do so may result in personal assessment of costs. [MCR 5.310]

CHANGE OF ADDRESS: You are required to inform the court and all interested persons of any change in your address within 7 days of the change.

Additional Duties for Supervised Administration

If this is a supervised administration, in addition to the above reporting duties, you are also required to prepare and file with this court the following written reports or information.

INVENTORY: You are required to file with the probate court an inventory of the assets of the estate within 91 days of the date your letters of authority are issued or as ordered by the court. You must send a copy of the inventory to all presumptive distributees and all other interested persons who request it. The inventory must list in reasonable detail all the property owned by the decedent at the time of death. Each listed item must indicate the fair market value at the time of the decedent's death and the type and amount of any encumbrance. Where the decedent's date of death is on or after March 28, 2013, the lien amount will be deducted from the value of the real property for purposes of calculating the inventory fee under MCL 600.871(2). If the value of any item has been obtained through an appraiser, the inventory should include the appraiser's name and address with the item or items appraised by that appraiser. You must also provide the name and address of each financial institution listed on your inventory at the time the inventory is presented to the court. The address for a financial institution shall be either that of the institution's main headquarters or the branch used most frequently by the personal representative. [MCL 700.3706, MCR 5.307, MCR 5.310(E)]

ACCOUNTS: You are required to file with this court once a year, either on the anniversary date that your letters of authority were issued or on another date you choose (you must notify the court of this date) or more often if the court directs, a complete itemized accounting of your administration of the estate. This itemized accounting must show in detail all income and disbursements and the remaining property, together with the form of the property. Subsequent annual and final accountings must be filed within 56 days following the close of the accounting period. When the estate is ready for closing, you are also required to file a final account with a description of property remaining in the estate. All accounts must be served on the required persons at the same time they are filed with the court, along with proof of service.

ESTATE (OR INHERITANCE) TAX INFORMATION: You are required to submit to the court proof that no estate (or inheritance) taxes are due or that the estate (or inheritance) taxes have been paid. **Note:** The estate may be subject to inheritance tax.

Additional Duties for Unsupervised Administration

If this is an unsupervised administration, in addition to the above reporting duties, you are also required to prepare and provide to all interested persons the following written reports or information.

INVENTORY: You are required to prepare an inventory of the assets of the estate within 91 days from the date your letters of authority are issued and to send a copy of the inventory to all presumptive distributees and all other interested persons who request it. The inventory must list in reasonable detail all the property owned by the decedent at the time of death. Each listed item must indicate the fair market value at the time of the decedent's death and the type and amount of any encumbrance. Where the decedent's date of death is on or after March 28, 2013, the lien amount will be deducted from the value of the real property for purposes of calculating the inventory fee under MCL 600.871(2). You are required within 91 days from the date your letters of authority are issued, to submit to the court the information necessary to calculate the probate inventory fee that you must pay to the probate court. You may use the original inventory for this purpose. [MCL 700.3706, MCR 5.307]

ESTATE (OR INHERITANCE) TAX INFORMATION: You may be required to submit to the court proof that no estate (or inheritance) taxes are due or that the estate (or inheritance) taxes have been paid. **Note:** The estate may be subject to inheritance tax.

PC 573 - Notice of Appointment and Duties of Personal Representative

Approved, SCAO | JIS CODE: NIP

STATE OF MICHIGAN PROBATE COURT COUNTY OF	NOTICE OF APPOINTMENT AND DUTIES OF PERSONAL REPRESENTATIVE	FILE NO.

Estate of ______________________

TO ALL INTERESTED PERSONS:

1. On ____________ (Date) I was appointed personal representative as requested in the application or petition for probate of this estate (copy attached unless previously sent). I am serving ☐ without bond. ☐ with bond in the amount of $ ________ .

   The papers related to the estate are on file with the ____________ County Probate Court located at ____________ (Address). This ☐ is ☐ is not a supervised administration.

☐ 2. Attached is a copy of the will of the decedent which ☐ was ☐ was not admitted to probate and under which I will administer, manage, and distribute the estate.

3. The court does not supervise the personal representative in the administration of an estate except in limited circumstances.
4. If I was appointed informally, you or another interested person may petition the court objecting to my appointment and/or demanding that I post a bond or an additional bond. The petition must be filed with the probate court along with the applicable fee. Unless the court grants the petition, I will continue to serve as appointed.
5. You or another interested person may petition for a hearing by the court on any matter at any time during the administration of the estate, including for distribution of assets and allowance of expenses of administration. The petition must be filed with the probate court along with the applicable fee.
6. If you continue to be an interested person (such as an heir of an intestate estate or devisee or beneficiary under the will of the decedent), I will provide you with: 1) a copy of the inventory within 91 days of my appointment; 2) unless waived by you, a copy of an account including fiduciary fees and attorney fees charged to the estate, within 1 year of my appointment; and 3) a copy of the closing statement or settlement petition when the estate is ready for closing.
7. To avoid penalties, I must have paid any federal estate and Michigan estate taxes within 9 months after the date of the decedent's death or another time period specified by law.
8. The estate may not be closed earlier than 5 months after the date of my appointment except in limited circumstances. If the estate is not settled within 1 year after my appointment, within 28 days after the anniversary of the appointment, I must file with the court and send to each interested person a notice that the estate remains under administration and the reason for the continuation of the estate. If you do not receive such a notice, you may petition the court for a hearing on the necessity for continued administration or for closure of the estate.

	Date of notice
Attorney name Bar no.	Name
Address	Address
City, state, zip Telephone no.	City, state, zip Telephone no.

ATTENTION: **The above duties are not the only duties required of the personal representative**. This notice of appointment must be served on all interested persons within 14 days after the appointment of the personal representative.

Do not write below this line - For court use only

PC 573 (9/06) **NOTICE OF APPOINTMENT AND DUTIES OF PERSONAL REPRESENTATIVE** MCL 700.3705, MCR 5.304

PC 574 - Notice to Creditors, Decedent's Estate

Approved, SCAO JIS CODE: NCT

STATE OF MICHIGAN PROBATE COURT COUNTY OF	NOTICE TO CREDITORS Decedent's Estate	FILE NO.

Estate of ______ Date of birth: ______

TO ALL CREDITORS: *

NOTICE TO CREDITORS: The decedent, ______, died ______ (Date).

Creditors of the decedent are notified that all claims against the estate will be forever barred unless presented to

______, personal representative, or to both the probate court at

______ (Address) ______ (City)

and the personal representative within 4 months after the date of publication of this notice.

______ Date

Attorney name (type or print)	Bar no.	Personal representative name (type or print)	
Address		Address	
City, state, zip	Telephone no.	City, state, zip	Telephone no.

PUBLISH ABOVE INFORMATION ONLY

Publish one time in ______ (Name of publication) in ______ County

Furnish ______ copies to ______

Furnish affidavit of publication to the probate court with copy to ______

Forward statement for publication charges to ______

***NOTE TO PREPARER:** If there is a known creditor whose address is unknown and cannot be ascertained after diligent inquiry, insert "including [name of creditor] whose address and whereabouts are unknown."

Do not write below this line - For court use only

PC 574 (9/12) **NOTICE TO CREDITORS, DECEDENT'S ESTATE** MCL 700.3801, MCR 5.106(A), MCR 5.208(A)

PC 576 - Notice Regarding Attorney Fees

Approved, SCAO OSM CODE: NFA

STATE OF MICHIGAN PROBATE COURT COUNTY OF	NOTICE REGARDING ATTORNEY FEES	FILE NO.

Court address Court telephone no.

This notice must be completed and mailed by the personal representative to all interested persons whose interests will be affected by the payment of attorney fees within 14 days after the appointment of a personal representative or within 14 days after the retention of an attorney by a personal representative, whichever is later.

Estate of ______________________________

TO ALL AFFECTED INTERESTED PERSONS:

1. The attorney named below has been retained to provide services on behalf of the personal representative of this estate. A copy of the agreement for payment of attorney fees is attached for your information.

2. The attorney will send a statement for services to the personal representative before payment is made. The statement shall include time records consisting of the identity of the person performing the services, the date the services were performed, the amount of time spent performing the services, and a brief description of the services. You have the right to copies of all statements and can request them from either the attorney or the personal representative.

3. The attorney fees will be paid ☐ monthly. ☐ quarterly. ☐ other ______________________.

4. You have the right to object to the attorney fees at any time before the probate court allows the fees.

5. If you want to make an objection it must be made in writing or at a hearing. See below for directions on written objections.

   - If this is a supervised administration, a written objection must be filed with the probate court along with a $20.00 filing fee. You may file your objection by mail or in person at the above court address. A copy of the written objection must also be sent to either the personal representative or attorney named below. If you want a hearing on your objection, you must file a motion with the court requesting a time and date for the hearing. You must notify all interested persons of the hearing time and date.

   - If this is an unsupervised administration, a written objection must be filed with the probate court along with a $20.00 filing fee. You may file your objection by mail or in person at the above court address. A copy of the written objection must also be sent to either the personal representative or attorney named below. The court will not hold a hearing on your objection unless you or another person request one. To request a hearing you must file a petition for a formal proceeding with the probate court along with a $20.00 filing fee. A copy of the petition must also be sent to either the personal representative or the attorney named below.

Date

Attorney signature	Fiduciary name (type or print)
Attorney name (type or print) Bar no.	Title
Address	Address
City, state, zip Telephone no.	City, state, zip Telephone no.

PC 577 - Inventory (p. 1)

Approved, SCAO | JIS CODE: INV

STATE OF MICHIGAN PROBATE COURT COUNTY OF	INVENTORY ☐ AMENDED	FILE NO.

NOTE: Do not use this form if you are a conservator. Use form PC 674. You must serve this completed inventory on all interested persons as required by Michigan Court Rule 5.105 and 5.125.

In the matter of ______________________________

I, ______________________________ , ______________________ submit the following
Name (type or print) Title

as a complete and accurate inventory of all the assets of the estate and the fair market valuations as of the

☐ date of death (decedent's estate only).

☐ date of qualification as fiduciary (all other estates).

PERSONAL PROPERTY AND REAL PROPERTY DESCRIPTION (If property has been used to secure a loan [including an equity line of credit], show the nature and amount of the lien. Definitions and instructions for completing the inventory are on the other side of this form.)	**LIEN AMOUNT**	**TOTAL VALUE OF PROPERTY (without reduction for lien)**
	TOTAL ASSETS	0.00

I declare under the penalties of perjury that this inventory has been examined by me and that its contents are true to the best of my information, knowledge, and belief.

	Date
Attorney signature	Signature
Attorney name (type or print) Bar no.	Name (type or print)
Address	Address
City, state, zip Telephone no.	City, state, zip Telephone no.

USE NOTE: If this form is being filed in the circuit court family division, please enter the court name and county in the upper left-hand corner of the form.

Do not write below this line - For court use only

PC 577 (9/12) **INVENTORY** MCL 700.3706, MCL 700.3707, MCR 5.307, MCR 5.310, MCR 5.409(B)

PC 577 - Inventory (p. 2)

DEFINITIONS:

- **Real property** means land, including a building or house that is built on the land.
- **Personal property** means everything that a person owns except real property. Personal property includes bank accounts and checking accounts.

INSTRUCTIONS TO COMPLETE THE INVENTORY:

1. List all real and personal property in the column **"Personal Property and Real Property Description."**
2. When listing real property, provide the legal description of the property and the name of any other owner.
   a. If real property has been used to secure a loan (including an equity line of credit), show the nature and amount of the lien.
   b. If the value of real property is determined by an appraisal, include the appraiser's name and address and a description of the property appraised.
   c. If this form is filed in a guardianship, real property that the ward owns jointly or in common with others must be listed along with the type of ownership. The court may require additional information to support the value of property that is stated in the inventory.
3. When listing personal property, provide enough detail to adequately determine the value. Some items should be listed separately and some items should be combined under one category. Provide the name and address of each financial institution listed. The address of a financial institution shall be either that of the institution's main headquarters or the branch used most frequently by the personal representative.
   a. Examples of items that should be listed and valued separately are:
      - Automobiles
      - Jewelry
      - Bank accounts
      - Antiques
      - Furniture
      - Prepaid burial contracts
      - Life insurance (cash value)
      - Annuities
      - Mutual funds
      - Stocks and bonds
      - Any other individual item of high value (such as a fur coat)

   b. Examples of items that can be listed in categories are:
      - Household items such as dishes, flatware, curtains, linens, utensils, clothing, furnishings, etc. can be grouped into several categories or combined into one category.
      - Multiple copies or pieces of a specific item that have the same value such as stocks and bonds.

   c. If personal property has been used to secure a loan, show the nature and amount of the lien.
   d. If the value of personal property is determined by an appraisal, include the appraiser's name and address and a description of the property appraised.
   e. If this form is filed in a guardianship, personal property that the ward owns jointly or in common with others must be listed along with the type of ownership. The court may require additional information to support the value of property that is stated in the inventory.

PC 578 - Notice to Known Creditors

Approved, SCAO JIS CODE: NKC

STATE OF MICHIGAN PROBATE COURT COUNTY OF	NOTICE TO KNOWN CREDITORS	FILE NO.

Estate of ______________________________

TO: ______________________________
Name

____
Address

____
City, state, zip

The fiduciary believes you may be a creditor of the estate. The attached notice to creditors was published ____________ (Date).

You have four months from the above date of publication or one month from the date this notice is sent to you, whichever is later, to present your written claim or it will be forever barred. You may use the Statement and Proof of Claim (form PC 579) to submit your claim. The written claim must be timely delivered or mailed to the fiduciary listed below. You may also send it to the probate court for filing along with a filing fee of $20.00. You may also commence a suit against the estate in a court.

______________ Date

______________ Name of fiduciary to whom claim should be presented

______________ Attorney name (type or print) Bar no.

______________ Title

______________ Address

______________ Address

______________ City, state, zip Telephone no.

______________ City, state, zip

PROOF OF SERVICE

I certify that on ____________ (Date), I served a copy of this notice on the creditor by

- ☐ personal delivery to the creditor.
- ☐ mailing, with postage prepaid, to the address indicated in this notice.

I declare under the penalties of perjury that this proof of service has been examined by me and that its contents are true to the best of my information, knowledge, and belief.

______________ Date

______________ Signature

Do not write below this line - For court use only

PC 578 (9/10) **NOTICE TO KNOWN CREDITORS** MCL 700.3801, MCL 700.3803, MCL 700.3804, MCR 5.208(B)

PC 581 - Notice to Spouse of Rights of Election and Allowances, Proof of Service, and Election

Approved, SCAO

JIS CODE: NSE

STATE OF MICHIGAN PROBATE COURT COUNTY OF	NOTICE TO SPOUSE OF RIGHTS OF ELECTION AND ALLOWANCES, PROOF OF SERVICE, AND ELECTION	FILE NO.

Estate of ______________________________

NOTICE

TO: ______________________________

As surviving spouse of a decedent domiciled in Michigan, you have the right to elect between certain property interests in this estate.

☐ 1. Your spouse died leaving a will. You may elect one of the following:
  a. To abide by the terms of the will.
  b. To take half of the share that would have passed to you had your spouse died without a will, reduced by half of the value of all property derived from your spouse by any other means other than testate or intestate succession upon his/her death.
  c. If you are a widow, to take your dower right as provided by law.

☐ 2. Your husband died leaving no will. You may elect one of the following:
  a. To take your intestate share.
  b. To take your dower right as provided by law.

3. This election shall be made within 63 days after the date for presentment of claims, or within 63 days after service of inventory upon you, whichever is later. Send a copy of this election to the personal representative. You may also file a copy with the court.
4. You may also have the right of priority to homestead, certain property, and a family allowance.

Attorney name (type or print)	Signature of personal representative
Address	Address
City, state, zip — Telephone no.	City, state, zip

PROOF OF SERVICE OF NOTICE

I served ☐ by mail ☐ personally the above notice on the spouse on ____________ (Date).

I declare under the penalties of perjury that this proof of service has been examined by me and that its contents are true to the best of my information, knowledge, and belief.

Date ____________ Signature ____________

SPOUSE'S ELECTION

Choose only one box.

☐ 1. I will abide by the terms of the will.
☐ 2. I will take half of the share that would have passed to me had the testator died intestate, reduced by half of the value of all property derived from the decedent by any means other than testate or intestate succession upon the decedent's death.
☐ 3. I, as widow, take my dower right as provided by law.
☐ 4. I, as widow, take my intestate share (no will) as prescribed by law.

Date ____________ Signature ____________

PROOF OF SERVICE OF ELECTION

I served ☐ by mail ☐ personally the above spouse's election on the personal representative on ____________ (Date).

I declare under the penalties of perjury that this proof of service has been examined by me and that its contents are true to the best of my information, knowledge, and belief.

Date ____________ Signature ____________

Do not write below this line - For court use only

MCL 558.1-558.2, MCL 700.2202, MCL 700.3705, MCR 5.305

PC 581 (9/04) **NOTICE TO SPOUSE OF RIGHTS OF ELECTION AND ALLOWANCES, PROOF OF SERVICE, AND ELECTION**

PC 582 - Selection of Homestead Allowance and Exempt Property

Approved, SCAO JIS CODE: FAM

STATE OF MICHIGAN PROBATE COURT COUNTY OF	SELECTION OF HOMESTEAD ALLOWANCE AND EXEMPT PROPERTY	FILE NO.

Estate of ______

1. I, ______ (Name (type or print)), am interested in this estate as ______ (Relation) ______ of the decedent.

☐ 2. The following property is selected as homestead allowance as authorized by MCL 700.2402: ______

☐ 3. The following exempt property is selected as authorized by MCL 700.2404:

PERSONAL PROPERTY ITEM	VALUE

☐ 4. A family allowance of $______ per ______ has been determined as authorized by MCL 700.2403 and MCL 700.2405.

5. The interested persons, addresses, and their representatives are identical to those appearing on the initial application/petition, except as follows: (For each person whose address changed, list the name and new address; attach separate sheet if necessary.)

______

Date

Attorney signature	Signature
Attorney name (type or print) Bar no.	Name (type or print)
Address	Address
City, state, zip Telephone no.	City, state, zip Telephone no.

NOTE: See MCL 700.2403 and MCL 700.2405 for provisions regarding family allowances.

Do not write below this line - For court use only

PC 582 (9/08) **SELECTION OF HOMESTEAD ALLOWANCE AND EXEMPT PROPERTY** MCL 700.2401 - MCL 700.2405

PC 583 - Account of Fiduciary - Short Form (p. 1)

Approved, SCAO | JIS CODE: ACC

STATE OF MICHIGAN PROBATE COURT COUNTY OF	**ACCOUNT OF FIDUCIARY, SHORT FORM** ☐ ________ (Number) Annual ☐ Final ☐ Interim ☐ AMENDED	**FILE NO.**

In the matter of ______________________________

In a guardianship or conservatorship, the ward's or protected individual's current address and telephone number are:

____

1. I, ______________________ (Name), am the ______________________ (Title)
   of the estate and submit the following as my account, which covers the period from ______________ (Month, day, year)
   to ______________ (Month, day, year) (may not exceed 12 months).

COLUMN 1. INCOME, GAIN, AND OTHER RECEIPTS		COLUMN 2. EXPENSES, LOSSES, AND OTHER DISBURSEMENTS	
	$		$
Investment gain	0.00	Investment loss	0.00
Total Column 1 (Enter on line 2.b on page 2.)	0.00	**Total Column 2** (Enter on line 2.d on page 2.)	0.00

SEE SECOND PAGE

USE NOTE: If this form is being filed in the circuit court family division, please enter the court name and county in the upper left-hand corner of the form.

Do not write below this line - For court use only

MCL 330.1631, MCL 700.3703(4), MCL 700.5418, MCR 5.308, MCR 5.310(C), MCR 5.313, MCR 5.409

PC 583 - Account of Fiduciary - Short Form (p. 2)

2. a. Balance on hand from last account, or value of inventory, if first account .... $ ________

   b. Enter Total Column 1, Income, Gain, and Other Receipts, from the other side of this form .... $ 0.00

   c. **Subtotal** (Add line 2.a to line 2.b and enter the amount here.) .... $ 0.00

   d. Enter Total Column 2, Expenses, Losses, and Other Disbursements, from the other side of this form $ 0.00

   e. Balance of assets on hand (Subtract line 2.d from line 2.c and enter the amount here.) .... $ 0.00
   This line must equal the last line in item 3. (Itemize assets below.)

3. The balance of assets on hand are as follows:

ITEMIZED ASSETS REMAINING AT END OF ACCOUNTING PERIOD	
	$
Total balance on hand. This line must equal the last line in item 2.	$ 0.00

NOTE: In guardianships and conservatorships, except as provided by MCR 5.409(C)(4), you must present to the court copies of corresponding financial institution statements or you must file with the court a verification of funds on deposit, either of which must reflect the value of all liquid assets held by a financial institution dated within 30 days after the end of the accounting period.

4. The interested persons, addresses, and their representatives are identical to those appearing on the initial application/petition, except as follows: (For each person whose address changed, list the name and new address; attach separate sheet if necessary.)

___

5. This account lists all income and other receipts and expenses and other disbursements that have come to my knowledge.
6. ☐ This account is not being filed with the court.
7. ☐ My fiduciary fees incurred during this accounting period (including fees that have already been approved and/or paid for this accounting period) are $________. Attached is a written description of the services performed.
8. ☐ Attorney fees incurred during this accounting period (including fees that have already been approved and/or paid for this accounting period) are $________. Attached is a written description of the services performed.

I declare under the penalties of perjury that this account has been examined by me and that its contents are true to the best of my information, knowledge, and belief.

	Date
Attorney signature	Fiduciary signature
Attorney name (type or print) Bar no.	Fiduciary name (type or print)
Address	Address
City, state, zip Telephone no.	City, state, zip Telephone no.

(For accounts that must be filed with the court.) **NOTICE TO INTERESTED PERSONS**

1. You must bring to the court's attention any objection you have to this account. Except in guardianships and conservatorships, the court does not normally review the account without an objection.
2. You have the right to review proofs of income and disbursements at a time reasonably convenient to the fiduciary and yourself.
3. You may object to all or part of an accounting by filing a written objection with the court before the court allows the account. You must pay a $20.00 filing fee to the court when you file the objection. (See MCR 5.310[C].)
4. If an objection is filed and is not otherwise resolved, the court will conduct a hearing on the objection.
5. You must serve the objection on the fiduciary or his/her attorney.

PC 584 - Account of Fiduciary - Long Form (p. 1)

Approved, SCAO JIS CODE: ACC

STATE OF MICHIGAN PROBATE COURT COUNTY OF	ACCOUNT OF FIDUCIARY, LONG FORM ☐ ________ Annual ☐ Final ☐ Interim Number ☐ AMENDED	FILE NO.

In the matter of ____________________

In a guardianship or conservatorship, the ward's or protected individual's current address and telephone number are:

____

1. I, ____________________ (Name), am the ____________________ (Title) of the estate and submit the following as my account, which covers the period from ____________________ (Month, day, year) to ____________________ (Month, day, year) (may not exceed 12 months).

2. **SUMMARY**

Balance on hand from last account, or value of inventory if first account	$	
Add income in this accounting period (Total from Schedule A.)	$	0.00
Total assets accounted for	$	0.00
Subtract disbursements in this accounting period (Total from Schedule B.)	$	0.00
Total balance of assets remaining (Itemize and describe in Schedule D.)	$	0.00

If additional sheets are required for Schedule A or B, place all itemization on those sheets and include only category totals on the schedules below.

SCHEDULE A: Income and gain in this accounting period		SCHEDULE B: Expenses, losses, and other disbursements, including distributions to devisees and beneficiaries	
Investment gain	0.00	Investment loss	0.00
Disposition gain, if any, from Schedule C		Disposition loss, if any, from Schedule C	
Total Income and Gain	0.00	**Total Expense, Loss, and Disbursement**	0.00

(SEE SECOND PAGE)

USE NOTE: If this form is being filed in the circuit court family division, please enter the court name and county in the upper left-hand corner of the form.

Do not write below this line - For court use only

PC 584 (9/11) **ACCOUNT OF FIDUCIARY, LONG FORM**

MCL 330.1631, MCL 700.3703(4), MCL 700.5418, MCR 5.308(A), MCR 5.310(C), MCR 5.313, MCR 5.409

PC 584 - Account of Fiduciary - Long Form (p. 2)

SCHEDULE C: Gain and loss on disposition of assets (Use only if needed.)

DESCRIPTION	DATE ACQUIRED	DATE SOLD/DISPOSED	VALUE AT TIME ACQUIRED BY FIDUCIARY	PROCEEDS OF SALE/ DISPOSITION	GAIN (LOSS)
					0.00
					0.00
					0.00
					0.00
TOTAL GAIN (LOSS)			0.00	0.00	0.00

If gain, transfer to Schedule A. If loss, transfer to Schedule B.

SCHEDULE D: Itemized assets remaining at end of accounting period

If additional sheets are required, indicate on Schedule "See attached sheets."

BALANCE OF ASSETS REMAINING (Show this amount on summary.) ....

NOTE: In guardianships and conservatorships, except as provided by MCR 5.409(C)(4), you must present to the court copies of corresponding financial institution statements or you must file with the court a verification of funds on deposit, either of which must reflect the value of all liquid assets held by a financial institution dated within 30 days after the end of the accounting period.

3. The interested persons, addresses, and their representatives are identical to those appearing on the initial application/petition, except as follows: (For each person whose address changed, list the name and new address; attach separate sheet if necessary.)

____

4. This account lists all income and other receipts and expenses and other disbursements that have come to my knowledge.
5. ☐ This account is not being filed with the court.
6. ☐ My fiduciary fees incurred during this accounting period (including fees that have already been approved and/or paid for this accounting period) are $ ______________ . Attached is a written description of the services performed.
7. ☐ Attorney fees incurred during this accounting period (including fees that have already been approved and/or paid for this accounting period) are $ ______________ . Attached is a written description of the services performed.

I declare under the penalties of perjury that this account has been examined by me and that its contents are true to the best of my information, knowledge, and belief.

	Date
Attorney signature	Fiduciary signature
Attorney name (type or print) — Bar no.	Fiduciary name (type or print)
Address	Address
City, state, zip — Telephone no.	City, state, zip — Telephone no.

(For accounts that must be filed with the court.) **NOTICE TO INTERESTED PERSONS**

1. You must bring to the court's attention any objection you have to this account. Except in guardianships and conservatorships, the court does not normally review the account without an objection.
2. You have the right to review proofs of income and disbursements at a time reasonably convenient to the fiduciary and yourself.
3. You may object to all or part of an accounting by filing a written objection with the court before the court allows the account. You must pay a $20.00 filing fee to the court when you file the objection. (See MCR 5.310[C].)
4. If an objection is filed and is not otherwise resolved, the court will conduct a hearing on the objection.
5. You must serve the objection on the fiduciary or his/her attorney.

PC 585a - Petition to Allow Account(s)

Approved, SCAO — JIS CODE: PAA

STATE OF MICHIGAN PROBATE COURT COUNTY CIRCUIT COURT - FAMILY DIVISION	PETITION TO ALLOW ACCOUNT(S)	FILE NO.

In the matter of ____________________

1. One or more accounts listing all income and other receipts and expenses and other disbursements, which have come to my knowledge during the accounting period(s), have been filed with the court.

2. The interested persons, addresses, and their representatives are identical to those appearing on the initial application/petition, except as follows: (for each person whose address changed, list the name and new address; attach separate sheet if necessary)

____

____

____

3. The attached accounts include
   - ☐ a. attorney fees and costs in the amount of $ ____________.
   - ☐ b. fiduciary fees and expenses in the amount of $ ____________.

I REQUEST:

4. The court approve my fees and expenses and attorney fees and costs in the amount(s) stated above as set forth in the itemized statements attached to the account.

5. That the account(s) be allowed as my
   - ☐ interim account.
   - ☐ ____________________ account(s).
     specify whether 1st, 2nd, 3rd, annual, or final

6. ☐ That I be discharged. ☐ That bond be canceled.
   ☐ That the estate be ☐ continued. ☐ closed.

I declare under the penalties of perjury that this petition has been examined by me and that its contents are true to the best of my information, knowledge, and belief.

	Date
Attorney signature	Fiduciary signature
Attorney name (type or print) — Bar no.	Fiduciary name (type or print)
Address	Address
City, state, zip — Telephone no.	City, state, zip — Telephone no.

Do not write below this line - For court use only

PC 585a (9/07) **PETITION TO ALLOW ACCOUNT(S)**

MCL 330.1631, MCL 700.5418, MCR 5.310(C)(2)(c), MCR 5.313, MCR 5.409(C)

PC 587 - Notice of Continued Administration

Approved, SCAO | JIS CODE: NCD

STATE OF MICHIGAN PROBATE COURT COUNTY OF	NOTICE OF CONTINUED ADMINISTRATION	FILE NO.

Estate of ______________________________

1. The original appointment of the first personal representative occurred on ______________ (Date).

   ☐ The administration has been continued annually since the date of the original appointment.

   ☐ The estate was reopened and the first personal representative for the reopened estate was appointed on

   ______________ (Date).

2. The estate remains under administration. The continued administration is necessary because:

   ____

   ____

   ____

3. The interested persons, addresses, and their representatives are identical to those appearing on the initial application/petition except as follows: (for each person whose address changed, list the name and new address; attach separate sheet if necessary)

   ____

   ____

   ____

Date

Attorney signature	Personal representative signature
Attorney name (type or print) Bar no.	Name (type or print)
Address	Address
City, state, zip Telephone no.	City, state, zip Telephone no.

NOTE: Send this notice to all interested persons.

Do not write below this line - For court use only

PC 589 - Notice of Intent to Close Estate Administration and Terminate Personal Representative's Authority

Approved, SCAO

OSM CODE: NCE

STATE OF MICHIGAN PROBATE COURT COUNTY OF	**NOTICE OF INTENT TO CLOSE ESTATE ADMINISTRATION AND TERMINATE PERSONAL REPRESENTATIVE'S AUTHORITY**	FILE NO.

Estate of ______________________________

To the personal representative, interested persons of record, and surety of the personal representative's bond in the above named estate:

TAKE NOTICE:

1. The personal representative has failed to file a notice with the court that the estate remains under administration and the reasons for continuing administration as required by MCL 700.3951.

2. An interested person has not filed a petition regarding the necessity for continued administration, for complete estate settlement, or for a settlement order.

3. The court will close the administration of this estate and terminate the personal representative's authority within 63 days of this notice unless any of the following occur:

   a. The personal representative files any of the following as may be permitted by law:

      - a notice that the estate remains under administration that specifies the reason for continuing administration.
      - a petition for either complete estate settlement under MCL 700.3952 or a settlement order under MCL 700.3953.
      - a sworn statement seeking closing of the estate under MCL 700.3954.

   b. An interested person files either of the following petitions with this court.

      - a petition requesting a hearing on the necessity for continued administration of this estate.
      - a petition for an order of complete estate settlement under MCL 700.3952.

   c. A devisee under an informally probated will files a petition for a settlement order under MCL 700.3953.

______________________ ______________________

Date Deputy probate register

CERTIFICATE OF MAILING

I certify that a copy of this notice was sent to the personal representative and interested persons of record or their attorneys by ordinary mail at their last known address(es).

______________________ ______________________

Date Signature

Do not write below this line - For court use only

PC 589 (9/02) **NOTICE OF INTENT TO CLOSE ESTATE ADMINISTRATION AND TERMINATE PERSONAL REPRESENTATIVE'S AUTHORITY**

MCL 700.3951, MCR 5.203(D)

PC 590 - Sworn Closing Statement, Summary Proceeding, Small Estates

Approved, SCAO JIS CODE: CIS

STATE OF MICHIGAN PROBATE COURT COUNTY OF	SWORN CLOSING STATEMENT, SUMMARY PROCEEDING Small Estates	FILE NO.

Estate of ______________________________

1. I am the personal representative and upon filing this sworn closing statement with the court, this estate will be closed without a hearing.
2. The interested persons, addresses, and their representatives are identical to those appearing on the initial application/petition except as follows: ______________________________.
3. The estate is not under supervised administration and I have not been prohibited by court order from filing this statement.
4. To the best of my knowledge, the value of the entire estate, less liens and encumbrances, did not exceed administration costs and expenses, reasonable funeral and burial expenses, homestead allowance, family allowance, exempt property, and the reasonable and necessary medical and hospital expenses of the decedent's last illness. The value of the estate is shown on the inventory that I sent to all the interested persons.
5. I fully administered the estate by disbursing and distributing it to the persons entitled to it.
6. I delivered a copy of this sworn closing statement to the distributees of the estate and to all creditors or other claimants and demandants, of whom I am aware, whose claims are neither barred nor paid. I furnished a full written account of the estate administration to the distributees whose interests are affected.

Personal representative signature ______________ Address ______________

Personal representative name (type or print) ______________ City, state, zip ______________ Telephone no. ______________

Sworn to before me on ______________ (Date), ______________ County, Michigan.

My commission expires: ______________ (Date) Signature: ______________

Notary public, State of Michigan, County of ______________

Attorney signature ______________ Address ______________

Attorney name (type or print) ______________ Bar no. ______________ City, state, zip ______________ Telephone no. ______________

NOTICE TO INTERESTED PERSON(S): You may object to this sworn closing statement by filing written objections with the probate court mentioned above along with a $20.00 filing fee. If an objection is not filed within 28 days after this sworn closing statement is filed with the court, the probate register will issue a certificate stating that it appears that I have fully administered this estate. The certificate does not preclude any action against me or the surety on a bond that I may have obtained. If an action or proceeding involving me is not pending in this court one year after this sworn closing statement is filed, my appointment ends.

Do not write below this line - For court use only

MCL 700. 3205, MCL 700.3988,
MCR 5.311(A)

PC 590 (9/07) **SWORN CLOSING STATEMENT, SUMMARY PROCEEDING, Small Estates**

PC 591 - Sworn Statement to Close Unsupervised Administration

Approved, SCAO | JIS CODE: SST

STATE OF MICHIGAN PROBATE COURT COUNTY OF	**SWORN STATEMENT TO CLOSE UNSUPERVISED ADMINISTRATION** ☐ **SUPPLEMENTAL**	**FILE NO.**

Estate of ____________________

1. I am the personal representative of this estate. Upon filing this sworn statement with the court, this estate will be closed without a hearing. More than five months have passed since the date of the appointment of the original personal representative.

2. If required by law or court rule, I have published notice to creditors, and the time for presentment of claims has expired.

3. I have fully administered this estate by paying, settling, or disposing of the claims that were presented, the estate and administration expenses, and all other taxes. I have distributed the assets of the estate to the persons entitled to the assets.*

4. The interested persons, addresses, and their representatives are identical to those appearing on the initial application/petition, except as follows:

(Check only one box, as appropriate.)

5. ☐ a. The decedent died before October 1, 1993, and no Michigan inheritance tax is due. A certificate of no inheritance tax liability from the Michigan Department of Treasury is attached or has been filed.
   ☐ b. The decedent died on October 1, 1993, or later and no Michigan estate tax is due.
   ☐ c. Michigan estate or inheritance tax has been paid in full. (Evidence of full payment from Michigan Department of Treasury is attached or has been filed.)

6. I sent a copy of this sworn statement to all distributees and to all claimants whose claims are neither paid nor barred and to all demandants. I furnished a full account in writing to the distributees whose interests are affected by the administration.

☐ 7. I reopened the estate and have completed the administration.

____________________ Personal representative signature | ____________________ Address

____________________ Personal representative name (type or print) | ____________________ City, state, zip | Telephone no.

Sworn to before me on ____________ (Date) ____________ County, Michigan.

My commission expires: ____________ (Date) Signature: ____________

Notary public, State of Michigan, County of ____________

____________________ Attorney signature | ____________________ Address

____________________ Attorney name (type or print) | Bar no. | ____________________ City, state, zip | Telephone no.

NOTICE TO INTERESTED PERSON(S): You may object to this sworn statement by filing written objections with the probate court mentioned above along with a $20 filing fee. If an objection is not filed within 28 days after this sworn statement is filed with the court, the probate register may issue a certificate stating that it appears that you have fully administered this estate. The certificate does not preclude any action against you or the surety on a bond you may have obtained. If an action or proceeding involving you is not pending in this court one year after this sworn statement is filed, your appointment ends.

***Note:** Specify any exceptions. If any claims remain undischarged, state whether the estate was distributed subject to possible liability with the agreement of the distributees, or state in detail other arrangements that were made to accommodate outstanding liabilities.

Do not write below this line - For court use only

PC 591 (9/11) **SWORN STATEMENT TO CLOSE UNSUPERVISED ADMINISTRATION** MCL 700.3954, MCL 700.3958, MCR 5.311(A), (C)

PC 592 - Certificate of Completion

Approved, SCAO | OSM CODE: CIC

STATE OF MICHIGAN PROBATE COURT COUNTY OF	CERTIFICATE OF COMPLETION ☐ SUPPLEMENTAL	FILE NO.

Estate of ______________________________

I certify that:

1. The ☐ sworn closing statement, summary proceeding, small estates
   ☐ sworn statement to close unsupervised administration

   of ______________________________ (Name), the personal representative(s) of the estate, was filed on ______________ (Date), more than 28 days ago.
2. No objection has been filed.
3. The personal representative(s) appear(s) to have fully administered the estate.

______________ Date ______________ Register

Do not write below this line - For court use only

PC 592 (9/02) **CERTIFICATE OF COMPLETION** MCL 700.3954, MCL 700.3958, MCL 700.3988, MCR 5.311

PC 593 - Petition for Complete Estate Settlement, Testacy Previously Adjudicated

Approved, SCAO JIS CODE: PCS

STATE OF MICHIGAN PROBATE COURT COUNTY OF	PETITION FOR COMPLETE ESTATE SETTLEMENT, TESTACY PREVIOUSLY ADJUDICATED	FILE NO.

Estate of __________

1. I am the personal representative appointed on __________ (Date) by ☐ the court. ☐ the register.
2. Testacy has previously been formally adjudicated.
3. The interested persons, addresses, and their representatives are identical to those appearing on the initial application/petition except as follows: (for each person whose address changed, list the name and new address; attach separate sheet if necessary)

____

____

____

4. The time for presenting claims that arose prior to the decedent's death has expired.
5. ☐ All claims properly presented have been paid, settled, or disposed of.
   ☐ A schedule for payment of properly presented claims is filed and served with this petition.
6. A final account
   ☐ has been served on all interested persons.
   ☐ is filed and served with this petition.
7. ☐ All estate assets have been distributed as set forth in the final account.
   ☐ A schedule for the distribution of all remaining assets of the estate is filed and served with this petition.
8. ☐ No Michigan estate or inheritance tax is due.
   ☐ Any Michigan estate tax or inheritance tax has been paid in full (evidence of full payment from Michigan Department of Treasury is attached).

I REQUEST:

9. ☐ The final account be approved and that any fiduciary fees and/or attorneys fees set forth in the final account be approved.
   ☐ The distributions previously made and/or all distributions as set forth in the schedule of distributions and payment of claims be approved.
   ☐ The personal representative be discharged.

I declare under the penalties of perjury that this petition has been examined by me and that its contents are true to the best of my information, knowledge, and belief.

	Date
Attorney signature	Petitioner signature
Attorney name (type or print) Bar no.	Petitioner name (type or print)
Address	Address
City, state, zip Telephone no.	City, state, zip Telephone no.

Do not write below this line - For court use only

MCL 700.3952, MCR 5.311(B)

PC 593 (9/05) **PETITION FOR COMPLETE ESTATE SETTLEMENT, TESTACY PREVIOUSLY ADJUDICATED**

PC 594 - Petition for Adjudication of Testacy and Complete Estate Settlement (p. 1)

Approved, SCAO JIS CODE: PAC

STATE OF MICHIGAN PROBATE COURT COUNTY OF	PETITION FOR ADJUDICATION OF TESTACY AND COMPLETE ESTATE SETTLEMENT	FILE NO.

Estate of ______________________________

1. I am the personal representative appointed on ______________ (Date) by ☐ the court. ☐ the register.

2. Testacy has not been formally adjudicated.

3. The interested persons, addresses, and their representatives are identical to those appearing on the initial application/petition except as follows: (for each person whose address changed, list the name and new address; attach separate sheet if necessary)

____

____

____

4. The time for presenting claims that arose before the decedent's death has expired.

5. ☐ All claims properly presented have been paid, settled, or disposed of.
   ☐ A schedule for payment of properly presented claims is filed and served with this petition.

☐ 6. The decedent did not leave a will.

☐ 7. ☐ The decedent's will, dated______________, with codicil(s) dated ______________ is/are offered for probate and is/are ☐ attached to this petition. ☐ already in the court's possession.

☐ Neither the original will nor an authenticated copy of a will probated in another jurisdiction accompanies the petition. The will is lost, destroyed, or otherwise unavailable, but its contents are: (attach additional sheets as necessary)

____

☐ 8. The decedent's will was informally probated on ______________ in ______________County.

9. To the best of my knowledge, I believe that the instrument(s) subject to this petition, if any, was/were validly executed and is the decedent's last will. After exercising reasonable diligence, I am unaware of an instrument revoking the will or codicil(s).

☐ 10. After exercising reasonable diligence, I am unaware of any unrevoked testamentary instrument relating to property located in this state as defined under MCL 700.1301.

☐ 11. A final account
   ☐ has been served on all interested persons.
   ☐ is filed and served with this petition.

(PLEASE SEE OTHER SIDE)

Do not write below this line - For court use only

MCL 700.3402, MCL 700.3952, MCR 5.311(B)

PC 594 (9/07) **PETITION FOR ADJUDICATION OF TESTACY AND COMPLETE ESTATE SETTLEMENT**

PC 594 - Petition for Adjudication of Testacy and Complete Estate Settlement (p. 2)

12. ☐ All estate assets have been distributed as set forth in the final account.
☐ A schedule for the distribution of all remaining assets of the estate is filed and served with this petition.

13. ☐ No Michigan estate or inheritance tax is due.
☐ Any Michigan estate tax or inheritance tax has been paid in full (evidence of full payment from the Michigan Department of Treasury is attached).

I REQUEST:

☐ 14. An order determining heirs and that the decedent died ☐ intestate. ☐ testate and the document(s) stated in item 7 is/are valid and admitted to probate.

15. ☐ The final account be approved and that any fiduciary fees and/or attorney fees set forth in the final account be approved.

☐ The distributions previously made and/or all distributions as set forth in the schedule of distributions and payment of claims be approved.

☐ The personal representative be discharged.

I declare under the penalties of perjury that this petition has been examined by me and that its contents are true to the best of my information, knowledge, and belief.

	Date
Attorney signature	Petitioner signature
Attorney name (type or print) Bar no.	Petitioner name (type or print)
Address	Address
City, state, zip Telephone no.	City, state, zip Telephone no.

PC 595 - Order for Complete Estate Settlement

Approved, SCAO | JIS CODE: OES

STATE OF MICHIGAN PROBATE COURT COUNTY OF	ORDER FOR COMPLETE ESTATE SETTLEMENT	FILE NO.

Estate of ______

1. Date of hearing: ______ Judge: ______ Bar no.

THE COURT FINDS:

2. Notice of hearing was given to or waived by all interested persons.
3. The time for presenting claims has expired.

☐ 4. The final account is correct and ought to be allowed.

5. ☐ a. The assets of the estate have been distributed, and all claims properly presented have been paid, settled, or disposed of.
   ☐ b. The schedule for distribution and payment of claims correctly identifies the manner in which assets remaining in the estate shall be paid and/or distributed.
6. ☐ a. No Michigan estate or inheritance tax is due.
   ☐ b. Michigan estate tax or inheritance tax has been paid in full. (Evidence of full payment from Michigan Department of Treasury is attached.)

☐ 7. Decedent's heirs are determined as follows: ______

8. Decedent died
   ☐ a. intestate.
   ☐ b. with a valid, unrevoked will dated ______ with codicil(s) dated ______.

IT IS ORDERED:

☐ 9. The decedent died intestate.
☐ 10. The will and codicil(s) are valid and admitted to probate.
☐ 11. The final account is approved.
☐ 12. Fiduciary fees and/or attorney fees are approved except ______.
☐ 13. Distributions already made or as set forth in the schedule for distribution and payment of claims are approved.
☐ 14. Appointment of the personal representative is terminated.
☐ 15. The personal representative is discharged.
☐ 16. The bond is cancelled.
☐ 17. Estate administration is closed.
☐ 18. Upon filing evidence of payment of the claims and distributions as set forth above (if any), the appointment of the personal representative may be terminated and an order of discharge entered.
☐ 19. Decedent's heirs are as determined in item 7 above.

Date ______ Judge ______ Bar no.

Attorney name (type or print) ______ Bar no.

Address ______

City, state, zip ______ Telephone no.

Do not write below this line - For court use only

PC 595 (9/10) **ORDER FOR COMPLETE ESTATE SETTLEMENT** MCL 700.3952, MCR 5.311(B)

PC 596 - Schedule of Distributions and Payment of Claims

Approved, SCAO

JIS CODE: SDP

STATE OF MICHIGAN PROBATE COURT COUNTY OF	SCHEDULE OF DISTRIBUTIONS AND PAYMENT OF CLAIMS	FILE NO.

Estate of ______________________________

1. I, ______________________________, am the personal representative.
   Name

☐ 2. The following properly presented claims have not been paid, settled, or disposed of. If approved by the court, these claims will be paid.

CREDITOR (Name and Address)	AMOUNT OF DEBT	AMOUNT TO BE PAID
	$	$
	$	$
	$	$
	$	$

☐ 3. Distributions to the following devisees/heirs have been made:

ASSET	DOLLAR AMOUNT OR VALUE	DATE OF DISTRIBUTION	NAME OF RECIPIENT
	$		
	$		
	$		
	$		

☐ 4. The following fees and costs will be paid before final distribution:
Attorney $__________ Personal Representative $__________

☐ 5. If approved by the court, the remaining estate will be distributed to the following devisees/heirs in the following amounts:

ASSET	DOLLAR AMOUNT OR VALUE	NAME OF RECIPIENT
	$	
	$	
	$	

____
Date

Attorney signature	Petitioner signature
Attorney name (type or print) Bar no.	Petitioner name (type or print)
Address	Address
City, state, zip Telephone no.	City, state, zip Telephone no.

PC 596 (9/07) **SCHEDULE OF DISTRIBUTIONS AND PAYMENT OF CLAIMS** MCL 700.3952, MCL 700.3953

PC 598 - Affidavit of Decedent's Successor for Delivery of Certain Assets Owned by Decedent

Approved, SCAO

AFFIDAVIT OF DECEDENT'S SUCCESSOR FOR DELIVERY OF CERTAIN ASSETS OWNED BY DECEDENT

Estate of ______________________________

1. I am decedent's successor as surviving ☐ spouse ☐ adult child ☐ other heir ______________ (specify)

   ☐ devisee under the will dated ______________.

   ☐ fiduciary or representative of ______________ (Name) who is an heir or devisee and has a legal incapacity.

2. Decedent died a resident of ______________ (City, township, or village and county and state) on ______________ (Date).

   More than 28 days have passed since decedent's death.

3. No real property is included in the estate.

4. Decedent's estate, less liens and encumbrances, does not exceed $15,000 (as adjusted for cost of living as provided in MCL 700.1210).

5. An application/petition for the appointment of a personal representative is not pending or has not been granted in any jurisdiction. A petition for assignment of an estate not exceeding $15,000 (as adjusted for cost of living) has not been filed with a court.

6. I am entitled to payment or delivery of the following property: ______________.

7. The name and address of each other person entitled to a share of the property and his/her proportion is as follows:

NAME	ADDRESS	RELATIONSHIP	SHARE %

8. A copy of the death certificate is attached.

______________ Signature

______________ Name (type or print)

______________ Address

______________ City, state, zip

Subscribed and sworn to before me on ______________ (Date), ______________ (County and state or other jurisdiction where acting)

My commission expires: ______________ Signature: ______________

Notary public, ______________ (County and state or other jurisdiction where commissioned)

NOTICE: A false statement on this affidavit may subject the person swearing to the statement to prosecution for perjury.

MCL 700.3983

PC 598 (9/11) **AFFIDAVIT OF DECEDENT'S SUCCESSOR FOR DELIVERY OF CERTAIN ASSETS OWNED BY DECEDENT**

PC 618 - Personal Representative Notice to Friend of the Court

Approved, SCAO

PERSONAL REPRESENTATIVE NOTICE TO THE FRIEND OF THE COURT

Estate of ______________________________, decedent

1. The decedent named above died ☐ testate (leaving a will). ☐ intestate (leaving no will). The last known address of the decedent was ______________________________.

2. As required by MCL 700.3705(6), I am providing the friend of the court, in the county where this estate is being administered, with the names and addresses of the decedent's surviving spouse and the devisees (testate estate) or the heirs (intestate estate).

   The estate is being administered in ______________ County. The probate court file number is ______________.

3. | | |
   |---|---|
   | Name of surviving spouse at time of decedent's death | Name of devisee/heir |
   | Address | Address |
   | City, state, zip | City, state, zip |
   | Name of devisee/heir | Name of devisee/heir |
   | Address | Address |
   | City, state, zip | City, state, zip |
   | Name of devisee/heir | Name of devisee/heir |
   | Address | Address |
   | City, state, zip | City, state, zip |

Note: Attach additional pages if necessary. An alternative to completing item 3 is to attach a copy of the completed application (form PC 558) or petition (form PC 559).

	Personal representative signature
Attorney name (type or print) Bar no.	Personal representative name (type or print)
Address	Address
City, state, zip Telephone no.	City, state, zip Telephone no.

CERTIFICATE OF MAILING

I certify that on this date I mailed a copy of this notice to the friend of the court office in this county by first-class mail.

Date ______________ Signature ______________

Instructions to the Personal Representative: This notice should be completed and provided to the friend of the court in the county where the decedent's estate is being administered within 28 days of your appointment.

Do not write below this line - For friend of the court use only

APPENDIX B
Glossary

The following glossary contains some of the more commonly used terms related to estate planning and estate administration.

A-B trust planning - The typical arrangement used in marital deduction estate tax planning by spouses to create at the first death a marital trust, or "A Trust," for the benefit of the surviving spouse for life; and a bypass or "B Trust" containing assets equal to the deceased spouse's remaining estate tax exemption amount. The B Trust is frequently referred to as the "credit shelter trust" or "family trust" and is typically held for the surviving spouse's lifetime for the collective benefit of the spouse and the couple's descendants, and generally passes at the death of the surviving spouse to the beneficiaries, free of estate taxes regardless of the value of the B Trust at that time.

Abatement - A proportional reduction of legacies when the funds or assets of the estate are insufficient to pay them in full.

Account or accounting (annual and final) - A report prepared by a Personal Representative or Trustee and provided to the beneficiaries which reports receipts, disbursements, distributions and any other transactions of the estate or trust. The last accounting will be the final accounting.

Ademption - Situation where a property designated for a person in a will cannot be transferred to that person upon the death of the person who made the will (the testator) because the property is no longer a part of the testator' estate. It may be caused by the destruction, loss, or sale of the property in the intervening period. Some state laws provide that value will be given to the beneficiary instead. Consult your state statute.

Ademption by satisfaction - Ademption by satisfaction takes place when a person making a will (the testator), during the testator's lifetime, gives an heir all or part of the gift the testator had intended to give by will. State statute may provide specific rules as to when this will be considered to take place, and may require independent evidence, such as express statements or writings, that the testator intended this to occur.

Alternate valuation - For federal estate tax purposes the decedent's assets are generally valued as of the date of death. However, the Personal Representative or Trustee may elect to value the estate on a date that is six months after the date of death. This is the alternate valuation dated. For assets sold or distributed during the six month period, the alternate value is as of the date of sale or distribution.

Ancillary probate - Administration of a decedent's estate in another state where the decedent owned real property at death.

Ancestor - Any person from whom one is descended; an immediate or more remote parent, e.g., a grandparent, great-grandparent, etc. *Contrast*: descendant.

Administration - The process during which the Personal Representative or Trustee collects the decedent's assets, pays all debts and claims, and distributes the residue of the probate estate or trust estate according to the will, trust or state law.

Annual exclusion - The amount an individual may give annually to each family member or other beneficiary free of federal gift or other transfer taxes and without any IRS reporting requirements. The annual exclusion is indexed for inflation and is $14,000 per donee for 2013.

Annuity - The right to receive a periodic series of payments, generally either for a term of years or until the recipient's death.

Antenuptial agreement - *See:* "prenuptial agreement."

Anti-lapse statute - A state statute that provides for a bequest that fails because the person to receive it is deceased passes to survivors as provided in the statute.

Ascertainable standard - A standard, usually relating to an individual's health, education, support, or maintenance, that defines the permissible reasons for making a distribution from a trust. Use of an ascertainable standard prevents distributions from being included in a Trustee-beneficiary's gross estate for federal estate tax purposes.

Assessed value - The value placed on real property for real property tax purposes which, under Michigan law, is supposed to be one-half of the fair market value of the property. Also referred to as "state equalized value, "or "SEV." However, the tax is based on the "taxable value," not the assessed value.

Attorney-in-Fact - The person named as agent under a power of attorney to handle the financial affairs of another.

Beneficiary - A person who will receive the benefit of property from an estate or trust. This may be through the right to receive a bequest or to receive income or trust income and/or principal over a period of time.

Beneficiary designation - The document that names a beneficiary of a contract such as life insurance, an annuity, a retirement account, and sometimes a bank account.

Bequest - A testamentary gift of property.

Buy-sell agreement - An agreement between owners of a business providing for the purchase of the owners' interests, either by the other owners, or by the company itself. May state a value or provide a formula to determine the price, and may prohibit certain types of transfers.

By-pass trust - The "B Trust" in A-B trust planning that is sheltered from the federal estate tax by use of the lifetime estate tax exemption and thereby bypassing the estate tax at the deaths of both spouses.

Charitable deduction - The income, gift or estate tax deduction allowed for a transfer of property to a qualified charity.

Claims - Liabilities of the decedent, including funeral expenses.

Codicil - A formally executed addition to or changes in the terms of a will not requiring the complete rewriting of the will. It is an amendment to a will.

Common disaster clause - The clause in a will or trust which provides who will be deemed to have survived if two or more individuals die within a stated period of time. These presumptions may also be included in state statute.

Community property - In certain states, known as community property states, a form of ownership under which property acquired during a marriage is presumed to be owned jointly.

Competent - Legally qualified to execute a document having legal significance.

Conservator - An individual or a corporate fiduciary appointed by a court to care for and manage the property of a minor or an incompetent person.

Consideration - One of the elements of a legally enforceable contract or agreement. The exchange of values by the parties to the contract. Consideration may be money, property, promises, or intangible benefit.

Constructive trust - A trust imposed by a court in the interest of equity and justice. Unlike other types of trusts, constructive trusts are not necessarily based on the expressed or presumed intentions of the parties involved. They are instead employed by courts as a device to prevent injustice where a person has gained unfair advantage or has committed fraud, and where it would be equitable to impose a trust.

Contingent beneficiary - A secondary beneficiary who may receive a gift if its primary beneficiary does not survive. *Contrast*: primary beneficiary.

Contingent interest - An interest in property that depends on a future event that may or may not happen or a present event that may or may not stop happening. *Contrast*: vested interest.

Corporate fiduciary - A bank or trust company that serves as a fiduciary (Personal Representative, Trustee, guardian or conservator).

Corpus of a trust - The assets held by a trust, from which income is derived. Also referred to as the "principal" of the trust.

Costs of administration - The actual costs of administering an estate (as opposed to costs of paying the debts of the decedent), e.g., filing fees, appraiser fees, sales commissions, storage expenses, delivery charges, and the fees of the fiduciary, accountants and attorneys of the fiduciary.

Co-tenant - An owner of jointly owned property.

Co-Trustee - A joint Trustee.

Credit shelter trust - Another name for the by-pass or "B Trust" in A-B trust planning. Sometimes referred to as a "family trust."

Crummey trust - An irrevocable trust that grants a beneficiary the power to withdraw all or a portion of assets that are contributed to the trust. The typical purpose of a Crummey trust is to enable the contributions to the trust to qualify for the annual gift tax exclusion.

Death tax - An estate tax or inheritance tax.

Decanting - A procedure where the Trustee of an irrevocable trust transfers all or a portion of the principal of that trust to another irrevocable trust. This may be allowed by the terms of the first trust, pursuant to the Trustee's power to make discretionary distributions to distribute principal, and/or by a specific state statute. With decanting, instead of exercising a distribution power by making payments directly to a beneficiary, the Trustee pays over the assets to a new trust for the beneficiary. This enables the Trustee to address a variety of potential issues including favorable tax planning, changes to trust management, or state law issues. It permits corrections or changes to be made in an otherwise irrevocable trust setting, and generally without court approval.

Decedent - A person who has died. In this book, the decedent is the person whose estate is being administered.

Descendants - A person's children, grandchildren, and more remote lineal relationships who are related by blood or because of legal adoption. A person's spouse, stepchildren, parents, grandparents, brothers, or sisters are not included. The term "descendants" and "issue" have the same meaning.

Designation of patient advocate - Under Michigan law, a document signed by a principal which authorizes someone (the "patient advocate") to make health care decisions, including life support decisions, if the principal is unable to give directions. May be referred to as a "health care power of attorney" combined with a "living will."

Disclaimer - The renunciation or refusal to accept a gift or bequest, insurance proceeds, retirement benefits, or other assets which is generally done in order to allow the property to pass to alternate takers. To be a qualified disclaimer and thereby not treated as a gift by the person refusing the property (the "disclaimant"), the disclaimer must be generally made within nine months after the decedent's death, before the disclaimant has accepted any interest in the property, and must meet other technical requirements of the Internal Revenue Code.

Discretionary trust - A trust that allows its Trustee to pay as much of the trust income and/or principal to the beneficiary as the Trustee determines. May include standards for distributions.

Disinheritance clause - A clause in a will or trust which specifically excludes certain persons from receiving anything under the will or trust, or under the laws of intestate succession. May or may not be effective, depending on the relationship and state law.

Donee - The recipient of a gift or the person who may exercise a power of appointment.

Durable power of attorney - A power of attorney that does not terminate upon the incapacity of the person making the power of attorney.

Duress - The use of physical force on a testator to make a gift, thus making it invalid. Economic duress may not have the same result.

EIN - See: "taxpayer identification number."

Elective share - *See:* "spousal right of election."

Encumbrance - A lien or claim on property, such as a mortgage.

Equitable interest - The interest held by a beneficiary of a trust, i.e., the right to use or receive property held by the trust. A court may find that a person has an equitable interest in property even if there is no formal trust, as in a "constructive trust."

Escheat - The transfer of property to the state due to a person having abandoned or not claimed the property.

Estate - The aggregate of all property and interests in property owned by an individual. May be in a probate estate, or in a trust, or more broadly the entirety of a person's financial interests, including jointly owned property and property passing by beneficiary designations.

Estate administration - The collection and management of an individual's property, the payment of his or her debts, the determination and settlement of any taxes due, and the distribution of the remaining assets following the individual's death.

Estate planning - A process by which a person designs a strategy and executes a will, trust agreement, or other documents to administer the assets for the beneficiaries. Tax and liquidity planning are part of this process.

Estate tax - A tax imposed on an estate on the right to transfer property at death. This tax may be imposed at the federal level, and at the state level. An estate tax is to be contrasted with an inheritance tax imposed by certain states on the beneficiary's right to receive property. Many states have no separate estate or inheritance tax. Some states have both an estate tax and an inheritance tax. Michigan currently imposes neither an estate tax nor an inheritance tax.

Estate tax exemption - The amount which can be left by a U.S. citizen at death, without incurring federal estate tax. The amount is $5,250,000 for a 2013 decedent, but has varied over the years. There is a corresponding gift tax exemption. Under current law, the exemption amount can either be given away during death, or left on death. Lifetime use by making taxable gifts is applied against the amount of estate tax exemption left for use on death.

Ethical will - A document in which the writer shares personal values and beliefs, life stories, and advice, with the intent of passing them on to future generations.

Executor - A person named in a will and appointed by the court to carry out the terms of the will and to administer the decedent's estate. May also be called a Personal Representative. If a female, may be referred to as the "Executrix." In Michigan, the term is no longer Executor or Executrix, but is "Personal Representative."

Fair market value - The price at which a willing buyer would buy, and a willing seller would sell, an item of property, neither being under any compulsion to buy or to sell and both having reasonable knowledge of relevant facts. Often established by an appraisal by a qualified appraiser.

Family allowance - A decedent's spouse and dependent children are allowed an allowance of a certain amount under statute, with priority over claims of creditors.

Family trust - A trust established to benefit one's spouse, children and/or other family members. Often used in reference to a by-pass trust or credit shelter trust.

Family partnership or family limited liability company - A partnership or limited liability company in which family members own interests, often holding real estate or marketable securities investments.

Fiduciary - In the context of administration of an estate, an individual or a bank or trust company designated to manage money or property for beneficiaries and required to exercise the standard of care set forth in the document under which the fiduciary acts and/or by state law. Includes Executors, Personal Representatives and Trustees.

Fiduciary income tax returns - Income tax returns that must be filed on behalf of an estate or a trust on Form 1041 or the applicable state form (in Michigan, form MI-1041).

Forfeiture clause - *See:* "no contest clause."

Form 706 - The federal estate tax and generation-skipping transfer tax return.

Form 709 - The federal gift tax return

Form 712 - An IRS form by which a life insurance company provides information regarding a life insurance policy, including benefits paid.

Fund - (as a verb) - To transfer assets from one owner or account to another, e.g., from a grantor to a Trustee following the creation of a living trust, or from a living trust to a family trust, marital trust, or children's trusts after the grantor's death.

Generation-skipping transfer tax - Also referred to as "GST." The federal tax imposed on outright gifts and transfers in trust, whether during life or at death, to or for beneficiaries two or more generations younger than the donor, such as grandchildren, that exceed the GST exemption. It is designed to impose a tax on transfers that would otherwise avoid the gift or estate tax at a generational level. Some states impose a separate generation-skipping transfer tax. Michigan does not impose such a tax.

Generation-skipping trust - A trust having a beneficiary which is two or more generations younger than the grantor. The beneficiary need not be related to the grantor if there is a certain number of years difference in age between the two.

Gift - A voluntary transfer of property for which nothing of value is received in return. Bequests under wills and trusts are sometimes referred to as gifts.

Gift splitting - The ability of a married person to use his or her spouse's annual gift tax exclusion or lifetime gift tax exemption in order to effectively double the amount of tax-free gift that may be made to a donee.

Gift tax - The transfer tax on lifetime completed gifts from one person to another. For 2013, a total of up to $5,250,000 may be given, in excess of the annual exclusion, without incurring federal gift tax. Some states impose a separate gift tax. Michigan does not impose a gift tax.

Grantor - A person, including a testator, who creates a trust, or contributes property to a trust. If more than one person creates or contributes property to a trust, each person is a grantor with respect to the portion of the trust property attributable to that person's contribution, except to the extent another person has the power to revoke or withdraw that portion. The grantor of a trust is sometimes referred to as the "settlor," the "trustor," or the "donor."

Grantor trust - When a grantor retains certain control over a trust, the trust is disregarded for federal and frequently state income tax purposes, and the grantor is taxed on the trust's income and pays the income taxes that otherwise would be paid by the trust or its beneficiaries. Such tax payments are not treated as gifts by the grantor. Provided the grantor does not retain certain powers or benefits, such as a life estate or the power to revoke, the trust may be structured so that it will not be included in the grantor's gross estate for federal estate tax purposes.

Gross estate - A federal estate tax concept that includes all property owned at death, or in which the decedent has an interest, and certain property previously transferred by a decedent that is subject to federal estate tax.

GST - *See*: "generation-skipping transfer tax."

GST exemption - The federal tax exclusion that allows a certain amount of generation-skipping transfers to be made without incurring a generation-skipping tax. The GST exemption is $5,250,000 for 2013.

Guardian - An individual or bank or trust company appointed by a court to act for a minor or incapacitated person (the "ward"). A guardian of the person is empowered to make personal decisions for the ward.

Health care power of attorney - A document appointing a person to make health care decisions when the grantor of the power is incapacitated. Often includes the power to make life support decisions, in what is sometimes called a "living will." In Michigan, a health care power of attorney is often referred to as a "designation of patient advocate," and the person who is given authority in that document is a "patient advocate."

Heir -The person entitled to a distribution of an asset or property interest under applicable state law in the absence of a will. "Heir" and "beneficiary" are not synonymous, though they may refer to the same individual in a particular case.

Holographic will - A will that is written in the testator's own handwriting and that need not witnessed, but may nonetheless be admitted to probate as the testator's will if it meets statutory requirements.

ILIT - *See:* "insurance trust."

Incident of ownership - A right regarding a life insurance policy which causes the insurance to be included in the gross estate of the person who has that power, for estate tax purposes. For example, the right to change the beneficiaries under a group-term life insurance policy is an incident of ownership. The policy will be includible in the gross estate of the person with that power, even though the person does not own the policy.

Income - The earnings from the principal, such as interest, rent, and cash dividends. This is a fiduciary trust accounting concept and is not the same as taxable income for income tax purposes.

Income beneficiary - A beneficiary of a trust who is entitled to trust income according to the trust's terms.

Income in respect of a decedent - Income earned but not paid before death. Also referred to as "IRD."

Inherit - To receive something from the estate of someone who died.

Inheritance - Generally, the property that one receives from a decedent's estate or trust.

Inheritance tax - A tax levied on the right to receive property from a decedent. Michigan does not presently impose an inheritance tax.

Insolvent estate - An estate where the debts and other liabilities exceed the assets.

Insurance trust - A trust, generally irrevocable, whose assets consist entirely or in large part of life insurance contracts or proceeds. Also referred to as an "irrevocable life insurance trust," or an "ILIT."

Intangible property - Property lacking physical substance, such as promissory notes, shares of stock in a corporation, membership interests in a limited liability company, partnership interests, contract rights, or rights in a lawsuit.

Interest of a beneficiary - The right to receive income and/or principal provided in the terms of the trust.

Interest in property - A right to property, whether vested or contingent, personal or real, tangible or intangible, present or future, legal or equitable, that will be enforced under the law.

Inter-vivos - Literally, "during life," denoting that the action was taken during lifetime. *See:* "revocable trust."

Inter-vivo trust - *See:* "revocable trust."

In terrorem clause - *See:* "no contest clause."

Intestate - When one dies without a valid will, such that the decedent's estate is distributed in accordance with state law.

Inventory - A list of the assets of a decedent's estate or trust.

IRD - *See*: "income in respect of a decedent."

Irrevocable trust - A trust that can generally not be terminated or otherwise modified or amended by the grantor.

Issue - *See:* "descendants."

Joint and survivor - The right held by two or more individuals to receive property during a time in which any of them is alive.

Joint tenancy - An ownership arrangement where two or more persons own property, usually with rights of survivorship.

Joint trust - A single trust made by two people, with provisions to govern after the first death and after the second death.

Jurisdiction - The power or authority of a court to interpret, apply and declare the law, by rendering a decision.

Last will and testament - *See:* "will."

Letters of authority - In Michigan probate practice, a certificate issued by the Probate Court stating that the person named has been appointed as Personal Representative of a decedent's estate and authorizing that person to administer the estate.

Lien - An interest held by a creditor in property of a debtor as security for a loan. Upon the debtor's default on the loan, the creditor/lien-holder may take the property, sell it, and apply the proceeds against the loan.

Life beneficiary - A person who receives income and/or principal amounts from a trust or similar arrangement for the duration of the person's life.

Life estate - The interest in property owned by a life tenant having the legal right under state law to use the property for life, after which title fully vests in the remainderman (the person named in the deed, trust agreement, or other legal document as being the ultimate owner).

Limited liability company - A business organization in which the owners, called members, do not have personal liability for the contracts or torts of the business. The organization is generally taxed like a partnership, which mean that the entity itself is not taxed, but the income is passed through to the members.

Limited power of appointment - *See:* "power of appointment."

Living trust - A trust created by an individual during lifetime, typically as a revocable trust. Also referred to as an "inter vivos" trust.

Living will - *See:* "designation of patient advocate."

Marital deduction - An unlimited federal estate and gift tax deduction for qualified property passing to a spouse. If the spouse is not a U.S. citizen, the trust must meet the requirements of a qualified domestic trust ("QDOT").

Marital trust - A trust established to hold property in trust for the surviving spouse. Often used in A-B trust planning and designed to qualify for the marital deduction. Sometimes used in second marriages to provide a benefit to the surviving spouse during his or her lifetime, with disposition of the trust property after the death of the spouse being determined by the trust. Sometimes a marital trust is a "qualified terminable interest trust," also referred to as a "QTIP" trust.

Minor - An individual who has not attained a specified age, generally 18 or 21, set by state statute, at which time the individual is accorded full legal rights.

Next of kin - Those persons entitled to take a share of the estate of a person who dies intestate, in a particular order, set by statute.

No contest clause - A provision in a will or trust which provides for the revocation of a gift, or certain other consequences, to any beneficiary who contests the will or trust. Under Michigan law, a no contest clause is unenforceable if the person contesting has probable cause for the contest. Also referred to as a "forfeiture clause" or an "in terrorem clause."

Nonprobate assets - Assets of a decedent which pass outside the probate estate. May include property held as joint tenants with rights of survivorship, payable on death ("POD") accounts, transfer on death ("TOD") accounts, assets which pass by beneficiary designations (e.g., life insurance, retirement accounts and annuities), property held in a revocable trust of the decedent, and property in which the decedent had only a life estate.

Notice to creditors - A notice published in a legal newspaper, and provided by mail to known creditors, advising creditors of the decedent's death and the time by which they must file claims against the estate or trust or their claims will be forever barred.

Outright - Free of any restriction, such as being subject to a trust.

Payable on death - A form of ownership which permits an account to be paid to a named beneficiary on the death of the account owner. Also referred to as "POD."

Personal property - *See:* "tangible personal property."

Personal Representative - An Executor of a decedent's estate. In Michigan, the proper term is Personal Representative.

Per stirpes - A Latin phrase meaning "per branch." A method for distributing property according to the family tree whereby descendants take the share their deceased ancestor would have taken if the ancestor were living. Each branch of the named person's family is to receive an equal share of the estate. If all children are living, each child would receive a share, but if a child is not living, that child's share would be divided equally among the child's children and descendants of deceased children.

POD - *See*: "payable on death."

Post-nuptial agreement - An agreement between a married couple in which they determine the property rights each will have on termination of their marriage by divorce or death.

Pour over will - A will used in conjunction with a revocable trust to pass title at death to property not transferred to the trust during lifetime.

Power of appointment - A provision in a will or trust which gives a person (usually a beneficiary) the ability to choose the recipients of property upon termination of a trust or other specified circumstances. The person given the power is usually referred to as a "holder" or the "donee" of the power. The power of appointment may be "general," allowing the property to be distributed to anyone, including the holder; or "limited" or "special," allowing the property to be distributed only to a specified group. Property subject to a general power of appointment is includible in the gross estate of the holder or donee of the power for federal estate tax purposes.

Power of attorney - A document whereby one individual (the "principal) grants authority to another (the "agent" or "attorney-in-fact") to act in the principal's place in some or all legal and financial matters. The scope of authority granted is specified in the document and may be limited by statute in some states. A power of attorney generally terminates on the death of the person granting the power (unless "coupled with an interest") and may terminate on the person's disability (unless "durable" under the instrument or state law).

Power of withdrawal - A power in the power holder to withdraw assets from a trust. May be limited to certain dollar amounts, percentages, or standards, and may be exercisable only with the consent of another person. To determine the scope of the power of withdrawal, it is necessary to review the terms of the trust.

Precatory language - Words of intent or desire which have no binding legal effect, e.g., "It is my intent," "I hope" or "I wish."

Prenuptial agreement - An agreement entered into between two persons who contemplate marriage in which they determine the property rights each will have on termination of their marriage by divorce or death. Also referred to as a "pre-marital agreement" or "antenuptial agreement."

Present interest - A right to immediate use, possession or enjoyment of property. *Contrast*: future interest.

Pretermitted spouse - A surviving spouse who married the testator after the execution of the testator's will and may therefore be entitled to an intestate share under the statute in certain circumstances.

Primary beneficiary - Under a trust, the beneficiary who has first priority to benefits under the trust. However, under a trust there may be other beneficiaries, and the Trustee may have broad discretion to make distributions among them. Under a contract such as life insurance or a retirement plan, there may be several primary beneficiaries.

Principal - The property (money, stock, real estate, etc.) contributed to or otherwise acquired by a trust to generate income and to be used for the trust beneficiaries according to the trust's terms. Also referred to as trust "corpus."

Probate - The court process of admitting a will and distributing property under the will or distributing property in accordance with the law in the absence of a will.

Probate Court - In Michigan, the court which has jurisdiction over decedents' estates and trusts. In other states it may be referred to by other names, such as the Surrogate's Court or Orphan's Court.

Property - Anything that may be the subject of ownership, whether real or personal, legal or equitable, or any interest therein.

Prudent man rule - A legal principle requiring a Trustee to handle the trust property with the same care that a prudent, honest, intelligent, and diligent person would use to handle the property under the same circumstances.

QDOT - *See*: "qualified domestic trust."

QPRT - *See*: "qualified personal residence trust."

QTIP - *See*: "qualified terminable interest property."

Qualified charity - Generally an organization described in Internal Revenue Code Section 501(c)(3), contributions to which are deductible for federal income tax purposes.

Qualified domestic trust - A marital trust (referred to as a "QDOT") created for the benefit of a non-U.S. citizen spouse containing provisions specified by the Internal Revenue Code to qualify for the marital deduction.

Qualified personal residence trust - An irrevocable trust (referred to as a "QPRT") designed to hold title to one's residence for a term of years subject to the retained right to reside in the home for the term, with title passing to children or other beneficiaries at the end of the term. Used to make a gift of the property while retaining the right to reside in it for a period of time, at a lower gift tax cost than if the property were given outright.

Qualified terminable interest property - Property (referred to as "QTIP") held in a marital trust or life estate arrangement that qualifies for the marital deduction because the surviving spouse is the sole beneficiary for life and must meet other statutory requirements. *See:* "marital trust."

Quit claim deed - A deed which transfers to another any interest the transferor may have in the property, without any warranty that the transferor actually owns any interest in the property transferred.

Real property - Property consisting of land, building, or property contained within the land, such as minerals, crops and trees. *Contrast*: personal property.

Refunding agreement - A document by which a beneficiary who receives a distribution from an estate or trust agrees that if there are any claims or expenses of the estate, he or she will return property to the Personal Representative or Trustee.

Remainder interest - An interest in property owned by the remainderman that does not become possessory until the expiration of an intervening income interest, life estate or term of years.

Residue - The property remaining in a decedent's estate after payment of the estate's debts, taxes, and expenses, and after all specific gifts of property and sums of money have been distributed as directed by the will or trust. Also referred to as the "residuary estate."

Residuary beneficiary - A beneficiary who is entitled to share in the residue of the estate.

Revocable trust - A trust created during lifetime which the grantor reserves the right to terminate, modify, or amend.

Rule against perpetuities - A common law principle invalidating a clause in a will or trust if an interest may vest too long after the death of the testator or grantor. This rule has been repealed in many states. In Michigan, it has been partially repealed.

Right of representation - Under Michigan law, if an applicable statute or a governing instrument calls for the property to be distributed "by representation," the property is divided into as many equal shares as there are surviving descendants in the generation nearest to the designated ancestor that contains one or more surviving descendants and deceased descendants in the same generation who left surviving descendants, if any. Each surviving descendant in the nearest generation is allocated one share. The remaining shares, if any, are combined and then divided in the same manner among the surviving descendants of the deceased descendants as if the surviving descendants who were allocated a share and their surviving descendants had predeceased the distribution date. This rule of construction applies to documents originally created on and after April 1, 2000, and to all instruments amended on and after April 1, 2000.

S corporation - A corporation that has made a Subchapter S election to be taxed as a pass-through entity (much like a partnership). Certain trusts are permitted to be shareholders only if they make the appropriate elections.

Second-to-die insurance - A life insurance policy, generally on two lives (often husband and wife), which pays death benefits only after the death of the second insured. Also referred to as "survivorship insurance."

Section 6166 installment payments - Installments of federal estate tax which may be made over a period of years, at a favorable interest rate, if a specified percentage of the decedent's gross estate consists of an interest in a closely-held business.

Self-dealing - Personally benefiting from a financial transaction carried out on behalf of a trust or other entity, for example, the purchasing of an asset from the trust by the Trustee unless specifically authorized by the trust instrument.

Separate written memorandum - Under Michigan law, a will may refer to a written statement or list to dispose of items of tangible personal property not otherwise specifically disposed of by the will, other than money. To be admissible as evidence of the intended disposition, the writing must be either in the testator's handwriting or signed by the testator at the end, and must describe the items and the devisees with reasonable certainty. The writing may be referred to as one to be in existence at the time of the testator's death; it may be prepared before or after the execution of the will; it may be altered by the testator after its preparation; and it may be a writing that has no significance apart from its effect on the dispositions made by the will. If the property is owned by a trust, this document will have no effect unless the trust refers to the document.

Settlor - Term frequently used for one who establishes or settles a trust. Same as "trustor" or "grantor."

Special needs trust - Trust established for a disabled person and designed to allow the disabled person to be eligible for government financial aid by limiting the use of trust assets for purposes other than the beneficiary's basic care. Also referred to as a "SNT" or "supplemental needs trust.

SEV - *See*: "assessed value."

SNT - *See*: "special needs trust."

Special power of appointment - *See:* "power of appointment."

Spendthrift provision - A trust provision restricting both voluntary and involuntary transfers of a beneficiary's interest, frequently in order to protect trust assets from claims of the beneficiary's creditors.

Spousal right of election - A statutory right provided to a surviving spouse to elect to take a specified share of the decedent's estate instead of what is provided under the decedent's will.

Statute - A law enacted by a legislature.

Statute of limitations - A law which bars all lawsuits, even upon a valid claim, after the expiration of a specified period of time, which varies by state law and depends on the type of claim.

Step-up in basis - The increase in the tax basis, or tax cost, of property which results from property having been received from a decedent.

Successor Trustee - A Trustee who follows the original or prior Trustee in office.

Supplemental Needs Trust - *See*: "special needs trust."

Tangible personal property - Property that is capable of being touched and moved, such as personal effects, furniture, jewelry, and automobiles. Tangible personal property is distinguished from intangible personal property that has no physical substance but represents something of value such as cash, stock certificates, bonds, and insurance policies. It is also distinguished from real property, which is land and items permanently affixed to land such as buildings.

Tax apportionment clause - A clause in a will or trust which specifies the source of funds for the payment of the decedent's estate tax.

Taxable estate - Total gross estate less total allowable deductions. The estate tax is levied on the taxable estate, and after applying the available exemption.

Taxpayer identification number - A number issued by the IRS to identify an estate or trust. Also known as "TIN" or "employer identification number" or "EIN."

Tenancy by the entirety - A joint ownership arrangement between a husband and wife, generally with respect to real property, under which the entire property passes to the survivor and while both are alive, may not be sold without the approval of both.

Tenancy in common - A co-ownership arrangement where each owner possesses rights and owns an undivided interest in the property and under which each owner may sell, give, or leave by will or trust such owner's undivided interest.

Testamentary - Relating to a will or other document effective at death.

Testamentary trust - A trust established in a person's will which comes into operation after the will has been probated and the assets have been distributed in accordance with the will.

Testate - Literally, "having made a will."

Testator - A person who signs a will. If a female, may be referred to as the "testatrix."

TIN - *See*: "taxpayer identification number."

TOD - *See*: "transfer on death designation."

Transfer on death designation - A beneficiary designation on a financial account that automatically passes title to the assets at death to a named person or revocable trust without probate delays and expenses. Frequently referred to as "TOD" or "POD" (payable on death) designations. POD designations are common on U.S. savings bonds.

Trust - An arrangement whereby property is legally owned and managed by an individual or corporate fiduciary as Trustee for the benefit of another, called a "beneficiary."

Trust instrument - A document executed by a grantor that contains terms of the trust, including any amendments thereto. Also referred to as a "trust agreement" or "declaration of trust."

Trustee - The person designated to hold and administer trust property under a trust. The term usually includes original (initial), additional, and successor Trustees. A Trustee has the duty to act in the best interests of the trust and the beneficiaries and in accordance with the terms of the trust instrument. A Trustee must act personally (unless delegation is expressly permitted in the trust instrument and by law), with the exception of certain administrative functions.

Trustee's deed - A form of deed executed by a Trustee which conveys title but warrants only against acts done during the time the Trustee was in office, and therefore does not provide a full warranty of title. Also referred to as a "fiduciary deed," which may be executed by the Personal Representative of an estate or a Trustee.

Undivided interest - The interest in property which is owned by a co-owner, who is referred to as a "tenant in common." Each tenant owns an equal right to use the property. On the death of one owner, the owner's interest will not pass to the surviving owner or owners.

Undue influence - The use of psychological pressure or a close relationship to take advantage of a person and have the person do something, such as make a gift or will or trust, in favor of the person exercising the undue influence. May invalidate the gift.

Uniform Transfers to Minors Act - A law, also referred as "UTMA," enacted by some states providing a convenient means to transfer property to a minor. An adult person, the "custodian," is designated by the donor to receive and manage property for the benefit of a minor. Although the legal age of majority may be 18, the donor may in many states authorize the custodian to hold the property until the beneficiary reaches age 21. Formerly the Uniform Gifts to Minors Act.

UTMA - *See*: "Uniform Transfers to Minors Act."

Ward - The individual who is the subject of a guardianship or conservatorship.

Waiver - The intentional giving up of a right, privilege or claim, or a document evidencing such act.

Will - A writing specifying the beneficiaries who are to inherit the testator's assets and naming a Personal Representative to administer the estate and be responsible for distributing the assets to the beneficiaries.

Wrongful death - A death caused by the wilful or negligent act of another.

APPENDIX C
COLA Adjustments

This section contains a table of cost of living adjustments to specific dollar amounts provided under the Michigan Estates and Protected Individuals Code

Under the Michigan Estates and Protected Individuals Code ("EPIC"), specific dollar amounts are provided for a surviving spouse's intestate share of a decedent's estate, as a base amount. Statutory amounts are also provided for certain allowances, for small estates, for transfers by affidavit (outside of probate), and for termination of small trusts. All of these are subject to future cost of living adjustments.

The intestate share of a surviving spouse is discussed further in Chapter 15 , "Who Shares in the Estate?" When originally enacted the amounts were $150,000 and $100,000, under Michigan Compiled Laws (MCL) 700.2102.

EPIC also provides for a homestead allowance (originally $15,000) under MCL 700.2402; exempt property (originally $10,000) under MCL 700.2404; and a lump sum family allowance which may not exceed a certain amount (originally $15,000) under MCL 700.2405. These are discussed further in Chapter 20, "Putting the Horror Stories in Perspective."

In addition, EPIC provides for a small estate proceeding where the gross estate (after payment of funeral and burial expenses) is valued at or below a certain amount (originally $15,000) under MCL 700.3982; and a procedure where an estate which does not include real property can be transferred without probate, by affidavit, if the probate estate, less liens and encumbrances, does not exceed a certain amount (originally $15,000), under MCL 700.3983. These procedures are discussed further in Chapter 17, "To Probate or Not to Probate." EPIC also provides for termination of small trusts (originally $50,000), in MCL 700.7414.

The discussion of these topics in this book is based the statutory amounts as adjusted for 2013. The table in this section includes historical figures over the years. Check to make sure you are using the correct figure for the year in question. Adjustments are announced by the Michigan Department of Treasury near the end of January in each year.

The complete text of the statutes referenced can be found at www.michiganlegislature.org.

Michigan Estates and Protected Individuals Code
Cost-of-Living Adjustments to Specific Dollar Amounts

	Original Amount	Amount for 2001	Amount for 2002	Amount for 2003	Amount for 2004
MCL 700.2102	$150,000	$161,000	$165,000	$168,000	$172,000
MCL 700.2102	$100,000	$107,000	$110,000	$112,000	$115,000
MCL 700.2402	$15,000	$16,000	$17,000	$17,000	$17,000
MCL 700.2404	$10,000	$11,000	$11,000	$11,000	$11,000
MCL 700.2405	$18,000	$19,000	$20,000	$20,000	$21,000
MCL 700.3982	$15,000	$16,000	$17,000	$17,000	$17,000
MCL 700.3983	$15,000	$16,000	$17,000	$17,000	$17,000

	Amount for 2005	Amount for 2006	Amount for 2007	Amount for 2008	Amount for 2009
MCL 700.2102	$177,000	$183,000	$188,000	$194,000	$201,000
MCL 700.2102	$118,000	$122,000	$126,000	$129,000	$134,000
MCL 700.2402	$18,000	$18,000	$19,000	$19,000	$20,000
MCL 700.2404	$12,000	$12,000	$13,000	$13,000	$13,000
MCL 700.2405	$21,000	$22,000	$23,000	$23,000	$24,000
MCL 700.3982	$18,000	$18,000	$19,000	$19,000	$20,000
MCL 700.3983	$18,000	$18,000	$19,000	$19,000	$20,000

	Amount for 2010	Amount for 2011	Amount for 2012	Amount for 2013
MCL 700.2102	$201,000	$204,000	$210,000	$215,000
MCL 700.2102	$134,000	$136,000	$140,000	$143,000
MCL 700.2402	$20,000	$20,000	$21,000	$21,000
MCL 700.2404	$13,000	$14,000	$14,000	$14,000
MCL 700.2405	$24,000	$24,000	$25,000	$26,000
MCL 700.3982	$20,000	$20,000	$21,000	$21,000
MCL 700.3983	$20,000	$20,000	$21,000	$21,000
MCL 700.7414	$50,000	$68,000	$70,000	$72,000

INDEX

J

L

Q-R

S

T

U-V